The New Maginot Line

By the same author

Fraud (with Douglas Sutherland) 1979
Siege! (with the Sunday Times Insight team) 1980
The Dirty Bits (with Craig Brown and Leslie Cunliffe) 1981
The Falklands War (with Insight) 1982

The New Maginot Line

JON CONNELL

Secker & Warburg
London

First published in England 1986 by
Martin Secker & Warburg Limited
54 Poland Street, London W1V 3DF

British Library Cataloguing in Publication Data

Connell, Jon
  The new Maginot line
  1. Military policy
  I. Title
  335′.0335′1821   UA11

  ISBN 0–436–10586–1

Printed in Great Britain by
Richard Clay (The Chaucer Press) Ltd,
Bungay, Suffolk

To My Parents

Contents

The Divad Gun: a technological marvel that died of embarrassment. It cost the US taxpayer $1.8 billion and it didn't work.

Acknowledgements

I would like to thank Peter Grose, the managing director of Secker and Warburg, whose enthusiasm and patience enabled me to see this book through; the *Sunday Times*, for appointing me as their correspondent in Washington – the best place in the world to report on the defence debate; and all those people who gave up precious time to help with my research. They are too numerous to mention and those who are in government would anyway prefer to remain anonymous. I would also like to thank those who read all or part of this book in draft form and offered much constructive advice, including James Adams, Steven Canby, Paul Eddy, Will Ellsworth Jones, Lawrence Freedman, John Fialka, Tom McNaughes, and David Rivkin. Any errors which remain, of course – whether of fact or of judgement – are entirely my own responsibility. Finally, I must thank my editor, Stephen Cox; Christopher Will, who helped in the early stages of the research; Elizabeth Bode, my assistant in Washington, who found time amongst all her other duties to provide valuable assistance; and my family and friends who helped in all kinds of ways and lent trusty support throughout.

J.C.
July 1986

Introduction

Historians have not had many kind words to say for Charles VIII of France. He was, in most respects, utterly undistinguished: small, pale and ugly, he had an oversized head, blank, staring eyes and a nervous twitch. 'He was not better off for sense than for money,' observed one of his followers. He died young – after bumping his head in a low doorway – and without issue.

Only one episode in his reign captures the imagination. In August 1494, in pursuit of a heroic dream, he set out to make good his family's claim to the Kingdom of Naples, an objective which he achieved with quite extraordinary speed, conquering a considerable part of the rest of Italy in the process. Unfortunately, he lost what he had gained with almost equal speed, when a hostile alliance of Venice, the Pope, Milan and Spain banded together to drive him out, and his adventure did France the dubious favour of entangling it for generations in the tortuous politics of Italy.

But though his conquest was ephemeral, the manner in which Charles achieved it earned him a small but important footnote in history. Up until that time, in the late Middle Ages, the key to a successful defence had lain in fixed fortifications. Sturdy walls guarded towns and castles with towering ramparts sat astride key invasion routes. True, gunpowder had been introduced to Europe more than a century before, but the standard artillery of the Middle Ages was cumbersome and crude, no match for a well-prepared defence.

It is not difficult, therefore, to imagine the discomfiture of the people of Italy when Charles rolled southwards and into Naples with what was then a modern miracle: a weapon as different from the traditional cannon of the Middle Ages as a tank loaded with armour-piercing shells is from horse-drawn artillery. Instead of firing laboriously sculpted balls of stone, and firing them while resting precariously on blocks of wood, the forty or so siege guns which Charles took with him fired balls of iron – much more lethal and accurate over an equivalent range – and, even more to the point, truly mobile (instead of having to be hoisted on to ox carts to be moved, they had their own wheels).

Just how devastating were these new weapons emerges from an account by a contemporary historian. The cannons, he records, were

> planted against the walls of a town with such speed, the space between the shots was so brief, and the balls flew so speedily, and were driven with such force, that as much execution was inflicted in a few hours as used to be done in Italy over the same number of days.

The new mobile cannon changed the way people thought about warfare. The fortresses which had been so central to defence in the Middle Ages began to decline in importance. Charles VIII's Italian campaign was a rare instance in which technology, and technology alone, proved critical in enabling one side to defeat another in land warfare.

It is hard to find another example as clear-cut as this in the next five hundred years. One might cite the first use in Europe of the breech-loading rifle, in 1866, when the Prussians, who possessed it, defeated the Austrians, who did not, or the first use of breech-loading artillery, four years later, when the Prussians beat the French, but even here other factors came into play. In air and sea warfare, of course, examples of the triumph of technology are more plentiful, since air forces and navies, unlike armies, are the creatures of technology and are thus inevitably more dependent on it. (The British government's decision to develop the chain radar in 1938 proved vital in the Battle of Britain; the atom bomb cut months of fighting out of World War Two.)*

But in general it is the human, not the technical, factor which has decided wars. The vast majority of battles, both ancient and modern, have turned not so much on differences in weaponry as on intangible qualities such as training, morale, courage, leadership and, of course, luck. When Napoleon destroyed the Habsburg armies in 1805, his secret weapon was the confidence of his troops and their marshals in his invincibility. When the Japanese invaded Burma in 1942, their reputation as fearsome warriors went before them (especially significant since the American public had been told the Japanese were too feeble and short-sighted to be effective).

---

*Two hypothetical examples from World War Two illustrate the potential of key advances in weapons technology. Had the Germans brought their V1 and V2 rockets into service a few months earlier than they did, they might have been able to pound Britain's Channel ports before D-Day and prevent the landings in Normandy. Similarly, had their most sophisticated U-boat, the Type 21, gone into action in March 1944 as originally planned, instead of in March 1945, it might have made a dramatic difference to the Battle of the Atlantic.

The exploits of the US marines in the Pacific, at the end of World War Two, owed more to courage than to the quality of their equipment. The Germans defeated France in 1940 not because their hardware was better – it was not – but because they organized their troops, tanks and aircraft in a devastating tactical formation; the performance of the British army in the Falklands depended far more on professional skills than on sophisticated hardware.

This lesson now seems in danger of being forgotten. The greatest fallacy in modern military thinking is the notion that somehow hi tech can do it all, that endless refinements in military hardware can be a substitute for the more traditional military arts. We may fondly imagine, in a world of word processors and micro-wave ovens, that scientists can take all the effort out of defence and that microchips and pieces of metal, if only they can be configured in the right way, are all we need. But history suggests it is a delusion. Defence is not a video game. You do not win wars simply by pushing buttons.

It is in America that push-button thinking has become most pronounced. There are various reasons for this. They involve the nature of the country, the ingenuity of American scientists, the lack of a military tradition and, perhaps most important of all, institutional pressures. There are enormous sums of money involved in modern defence. Everyone who is part of the procurement process has a vested interest in pushing technology to its limits, in 'going to the next generation'. The services, which are not, of course, spending their own money, are reluctant to settle for anything less than 'the best'; industry knows that exploiting high technology is a means to stay in business and that, more often than not, the fancier the hardware, the larger are the profits; congressmen tend to worry more about bringing jobs to their constituencies than about preparing to fight the Russians. In his remarkable valedictory speech, Dwight Eisenhower drew attention to the dangers of a 'military industrial complex' which might take on a life of its own and work to its own distortion. His warning has come true.

Those who seek to justify the current obsession with hi tech point across the Iron Curtain. We have no choice, they say. Hopelessly outnumbered by the Warsaw Pact in conventional forces, we must exploit our technological edge. But as the Washington defence analyst Steven Canby has pointed out, 'Trying to offset quantitative force inferiority solely by exploiting new technology is a policy marked by constantly diminishing returns.' It simply doesn't make sense.

It makes no sense because there is not the dramatic gulf between Nato and the Warsaw Pact which existed, for example, between European nations and their opponents in nineteenth-century colonial wars, and because the West, unlike Charles VIII of France, is unable to spring startling new weapons upon an unsuspecting enemy. Among a bunch of porous democracies in an age of mass communications, technological secrets do not remain secret for long. What the Russians cannot find in *Aviation Week* they can buy or steal. And what they know about they can react to, by imitating, by taking countermeasures, or simply by changing their tactics. Tightening up on 'technology transfer' to the Eastern bloc is unlikely to have more than a marginal effect.

There are other reasons why the current over-reliance on hi tech makes no sense.

First, instead of the careful, sensible application of technology, much of what goes on in modern military procurement consists of a mere fixation on gadgetry. The military want the best that scientists can dream up, but they also want to keep their traditional weapons platforms. Thus, unlike many weapons of the past – by today's standards comparatively cheap and easy to develop, and sometimes relying on very simple breakthroughs like the stirrup, which ushered in the age of heavy cavalry – modern hardware tends to be extraordinarily complex and fragile, with a price tag out of all proportion to any conceivable benefit.

Second, new inventions are often swept into service prematurely. They tend not to work as well as anticipated, and they invariably cost more. *Imitating* technology, on the other hand, can prove easier, and cheaper, than making the breakthrough in the first place. Arguably, the Russians often *benefit* from being the slower horse in the technological race.

Third, creating modern weapons is, paradoxically, such a long-drawn-out process – they take, on average, ten to fifteen years to progress from drawing board to battlefield – that any advantage they might have had when conceived has frequently vanished by the time they come into service. (The Russians have traditionally developed their weapons more quickly, and enhanced them more incrementally, than the West.)

Fourth, modern weapons cost so much that other vital elements of defence – ammunition stocks, fuel, training, etc.– are skimped in order to pay for them. (It has been argued, for instance, that only Israeli pilots get enough practice to be effective in America's super-sophisticated front-line fighter, the F15.)

So while they may enrich their manufacturers, many modern weapons do little to make us more secure. The constant sacrifice of *quantity* for *quality* leads to a vicious circle: fewer and fewer weapons are expected to do more and more, which in turn puts a premium on even greater sophistication. Some hi-tech devotees advance the argument that the Russians are now developing super-sophisticated hardware themselves, so we can do no less. There are many claims, and some evidence, as we will see, that the Russians *are* beginning to fall into the same gold-plated trap as the West. But Western defence policy is not made in Moscow: its aim is not to ape what the Russians do.

The hi-tech approach to defence has weakened America, and threatens to weaken it further. Since the successful Inchon landing in South Korea in 1951, America's military record has been a catalogue of disasters: the army's uninspiring performance in Vietnam, where a cornucopia of sophisticated hardware failed to defeat an elusive, poorly armed guerrilla force; the *Mayaguez* incident, when Cambodians captured an American ship and the rescue effort was botched; the attempt to rescue the American hostages in Iran in 1980; and the storming of Grenada, which despite its elevation within the Reagan administration to a victory akin to Agincourt or Trafalgar, was in fact a badly bungled operation. Not all of these failures, it is true, can be traced directly to technological problems. They do, however, reflect the distorted priorities of the modern American military and a general lack of seriousness about warfare, a lack of seriousness manifest, perhaps, above all in its push-button mentality, its passion for hardware and its neglect of strategy, tactics, and the intangibles of conflict.

Meanwhile, the West has suffered further from the inability of America's European allies to cooperate effectively with one another, and from Europe's long-standing reluctance to take on more of the burden of Western defence. 'They could not agree among themselves about objectives, they trusted one another less than they did the United States, and they had no particular inclination to incur the costs and risks of greater independence,' wrote William Kaufman, one of the wisest of America's postwar defence experts, in the 1960s. His charge still has a ring of truth.

What makes all this the more disturbing is that conventional forces are crucially important, and, I will suggest, ought to become more so. It is only because of a pronounced conventional weakness that we are forced to rely on the inherently implausible threat to resort to the use of nuclear weapons if we face defeat.

I have arranged this book in three sections. In the first I look at the West's conventional arsenal and illustrate, with examples, the fallacy of pinning too much faith in technology. Inevitably, I concentrate mainly on American weapons, because America provides the best examples, and because America is by far the most important Western power, its research and development effort setting the pace for the rest.*

In the second section of the book I look at the West's nuclear arsenal. If gold-plating conventional weapons is one way in which the West has

---

*In 1985, according to the *New York Times*, America spent $107 billion on research and development, 'more than the combined research and development spending of Britain, France, West Germany and Japan. More than a third of this total [was] devoted to defence ... Defence claims only 4 per cent of West Germany's research and development budget and less than 1 per cent of Japan's.'

become too hooked on technology, I argue that the overdependence on nuclear weapons is another. Some of the current plans for upgrading nuclear forces, and for developing new systems, are unnecessary, a diversion of energy and resources which would be better applied elsewhere. The fact that there has been no world war since 1945 may owe a great deal to the presence of nuclear weapons – on both sides – but theories of limited nuclear wars make little sense outside laboratories and thinktanks, and attempts to make nuclear weapons more 'controllable' (by constantly developing smaller, more accurate, 'low-yield' warheads) are ultimately futile. We have long passed a point of diminishing returns. *Wars cannot be fought with nuclear weapons.* The notion that the West can save itself from conventional defeat by 'going nuclear' is an illusion.

The third section of this book follows from the second. In it, I concentrate primarily on President Reagan's 'strategic defence initiative', popularly known as Star Wars. This, the attempt to create a space-based defence against Russian nuclear missiles, represents the search for the ultimate technological fix. In its purest form it is the product of millennial dreaming, like the peace movement, and it reflects, like unilateralism, a failure to think through the realities of the arms race. In its less Utopian form – the form in which it is supposed to 'boost deterrence' – I will seek to show that it is equally ill-conceived, and furthermore that while it is unlikely to buy us more security it is certain, if pursued, to drain away vast resources which would be better applied to badly needed usable (and hence 'credible') weapons.

The theme of this book, in essence, is that there is no technological solution to the problem of the Soviet Union, or to the problem of modern security. No amount of magical conventional weapons, or Stealth cruise missiles, or laser battle stations is going to remove the Soviet threat.

There is a school of thought, of course, which holds that if only we can keep the pressure up, by constantly harnessing new developments in technology, we can force the Russians to keep reacting and to keep spending ever larger sums of money simply to 'stay in the game'. In the end the hope is that their economy will fail to take the strain and that their political system will collapse, bankrupt, on the scrap-heap of history.

The rationale is scarcely convincing. For one thing, in a world now spending around $700 billion a year on armaments, it is not only in Russia that high levels of defence spending are causing strain. America's recent military build-up has helped create huge federal deficits which have caused distortions throughout the world economy. By 1990, according to Fred Hiatt and Rick Atkinson in the *Washington Post*, 'nearly enough will have been spent on defence [by America] during the Cold War – $3.7 trillion in constant 1972 dollars – to buy everything in the United States except the land: every house, factory, train, plane and refrigerator.' Besides, even if the existing Soviet system *were* to collapse, the world would not necessarily become a more stable, secure place. At the moment Russia's thousands of nuclear weapons are at least under the centralized control of a regime which, however unpleasant, is notably cautious and chary of the risks of war. A break-up of the Russian empire could make things decidedly worse for the West.

Technology, in short, is no substitute for diplomacy. International politics, as one scientist puts it, cannot be made 'subject to an engineering solution'.

Old habits die hard, and the magic weapon mentality is now deeply ingrained in Western defence. But the situation is not irreversible. With a more realistic approach to 'the threat', with less emphasis on overcomplicated hardware, less worrying about nuclear weapons and a realization that there are no Star Wars-type panaceas, we can make ourselves more secure. That, at least, is the belief on which this book is based.

PART ONE

The Arsenal of Democracy

'Whatever happens, we have got
The Maxim Gun, and they have not.'
                              Hilaire Belloc

I

The Threat – and How Nato Proposes to Deal with It

The nightmare which the West lives with is of a massive Soviet assault across the border of the Federal Republic of Germany, sweeping, with blitzkrieg speed, through its agricultural and industrial heartland into the Low Countries and on across the continent to the English Channel. That is what brought Nato into being, and what sustains it.

Many find the threat hard to take seriously. Why, after all, would Russia go to war? What could it possibly hope to gain by overrunning Western Europe? It already faces enormous difficulties coping with its existing satellites in Eastern Europe, so why would it want to add to them and saddle itself with more, and with having to rule an even more turbulent empire full of troublesome West Europeans?

The answer is that Russia would stand to gain little. And at the moment the prospect of a Soviet tank assault on West Germany seems remote. (Indeed, one of the thorniest problems facing those who devise Nato war games is in coming up with a plausible scenario for actually getting the war going.) But though it is hard, most of the time, to imagine circumstances in which the Russians might choose to invade, it is not impossible. Wars happen. They do not always begin for rational reasons: they can arise out of crises – even, like World War One, out of relatively trivial incidents – and if a war arose out of a crisis between the superpowers then West Germany would almost certainly become the central battlefield. That is where, in one analyst's phrase, the troops are lined up like two football teams, and in the circumstances Russia would be likely to pre-empt, determined, for deep-seated historical reasons, that a war, if it looked inevitable, should not be fought on its territory.

Besides, although the 'steam may have gone out of the ideological balloon', in George Kennan's phrase, Russia remains committed to the Marxist doctrine and to the notion of the ultimate triumph of communism.

Even at the height of détente, the then Soviet premier, Leonid Brezhnev, told the twenty-fifth Congress of the Soviet Communist Party: 'Relaxation of tensions does not to the slightest extent abolish or alter the laws of the class struggle. No one should expect that because tensions have been reduced, Communists will reconcile themselves to the capitalist system or monopolists will become followers of the Revolution.' The state of the Soviet empire, moreover, scarcely reassures many Western observers. With its huge defence establishment, seemingly larger than anything it could conceivably need for pure defence, its rickety economy, its starved consumer market and its unhappy allies, Russia has become an ailing tyranny, and ailing tyrannies, like wounded animals, can be dangerous. Just as the junta in Argentina attacked the Falkland Islands in 1982 largely to divert attention from an internal crisis, so it is not impossible to imagine that the Kremlin might be tempted to believe that the best hope of shoring up its empire might lie in becoming increasingly adventurous abroad.

Thus, however implausible the threat of war in Europe may seem, it nonetheless exists. And anyone who visits the 'Inner German Border' – the dividing line between East and West – becomes instantly aware of it.

West Germany is divided from East Germany by two barbed-wire fences which are separated, for the most part, by about 100 yards of dead ground. Stretches of this are mined, and most of it is patrolled by dogs. The fences themselves are made of razor-sharp wire, and parts of the inner fence are electric. At regular intervals are mounted SM70 machineguns, which automatically open fire on people trying to cross the border from East to West. There are frequent watchtowers and the whole length is regularly patrolled by border guards. The fences are no respecters of history: they cut towns, sometimes even homes, in half.

Thousands of East Germans have attempted to cross this barrier since it was constructed in the 1950s and 1960s. Some have succeeded; others have been caught, yet others have died trying.

Seeing this monstrous barrier, as a CBS television reporter once put it, 'your first thought is that a government that could do this could do anything, even go to war'. Or as a veteran of Nato patrols of the Western side of the line put it to me: 'You have to remember that it's built to keep people in ... and you know that, whatever good there may be in communism, any system which built that must be rotten.'

It is across this barrier that an attack on Western Europe, if it ever happened, would come. So supposing, in some dire crisis, the Russians did decide to breach their fence and invade West Germany, could Nato stop them?

In the early 1980s, the Supreme Allied Commander, Europe, General Bernard Rogers – Nato's top soldier – toured a succession of gatherings of Alliance politicians, officials and defence analysts with a gloomy prognosis about the threat the West faced. The balance of forces was tilting dangerously in favour of the East, he said; if the Warsaw Pact ever invaded, the likelihood would be that he, as the Supreme Allied Commander (SACEUR), would have no alternative but to request the use of nuclear weapons in Europe's defence at a very early stage. Nato, he implied, now had a strategy scarcely distinguishable from the one developed in the early 1950s, under which its conventional forces, spread out along the Central Front in Europe like Kipling's 'thin red line of heroes', were there simply as a 'tripwire' which, if ever broken by the Red Army, would have triggered a massive nuclear retaliation from America. Nowadays, in Rogers' view, Nato simply had a 'delayed tripwire', a frankly incredible position in an age when the two superpowers had rough parity in nuclear weapons and when massive retaliation might all too easily lead to a holocaust.

Rogers was never very specific about how long Nato would last – obviously it would depend on the circumstances of the attack, the margin of warning, and a host of other factors. But many seasoned analysts in the US army, both in Washington and serving under Rogers in his headquarters in Mons, Belgium, believe the Alliance would be hard pressed to last more than two weeks. 'The very best case for Nato I ever heard,' one American officer – a veteran of countless war games – told me, 'in which we assumed that Nato had plenty of ammunition and gas and spare parts, and that we were ready and the Warsaw Pact wasn't – that they were dragged reluctantly into this war, didn't want it and showed up late! – had a catastrophic breakthrough [i.e. one requiring a nuclear response to save the war] occurring on *Day 16*.' Another case, said this source, this time in a war game which began with a confused (and, for Nato, confusing) riot in East Germany (it turned out that the Soviets had deliberately staged the 'riot' as a diversion), had the West going nuclear on *Day 13*. And the worst case, with the Warsaw Pact surprising Nato, and the West quite unprepared, had the West compelled to go nuclear as early as *Day 5*.

The conventional balance, of course, has always looked daunting. From the start, Nato failed to muster the political will to finance and construct a proper conventional defence of the West, and in this lies the source of all its problems. After getting off on the wrong foot, Nato never recovered, and though for a while in the 1960s things looked better, over the last twenty years they have been growing steadily worse. Let us briefly consider the history of Nato's struggle to match the Warsaw Pact.

In early 1949 a group of American and British army officers met secretly in London to discuss the requirements for a fully fledged conventional defence of Europe. The formal foundation of Nato was still eight months away but it was already clear that Western Europe's security would depend, ultimately, on America and probably on the presence of US troops in

Europe. Ranged against an estimated 175 Soviet divisions in Eastern Europe were the forces of occupation left behind in Germany after the war – one American, three British and three French divisions, two Belgian brigades and some Dutch, Norwegian and Austrian troops.

At the London meeting, the army officers discussed US military aid to Europe – how much, and in what form. But in considering this they tried to work out how much the West might have to spend to provide itself with adequate troops and equipment to hold the Soviets if they ever attacked. The figure they eventually came up with, according to one man who attended the meeting, was $45 billion.

It was a staggering sum. In the late 1940s, Europe was still suffering acutely from the ravages of war. Rationing was widespread, raw materials in short supply. America, in an effort to breathe new life into European countries' faltering economic and political institutions, had just launched the Marshall Plan: the economic health of Western Europe was seen in Washington as vital to America's own and, moreover, as vital if the seeds of communism were to be deprived of fertile soil. But the plan put together by the then Secretary of State, George Marshall, envisaged spending only $13 billion, in total. The notion of spending more than three times that on the defence of Europe seemed out of the question. As Paul Nitze, a State Department official who attended some of the later sessions of the London talks, was keenly aware, it was beyond not just the Europeans but America too. And so too, it seemed, was a robust conventional defence.

Yet by early 1949 many in Washington were convinced that the West should construct a conventional defence strong enough to contain a Soviet conventional attack. When the Russians exploded their first atomic bomb in June 1949, Harry Truman's secretary of state, Dean Acheson, talked in his office with Nitze, then Deputy Director of the policy planning staff and already an expert in European security. The two men agreed that the nuclear forces of both sides would eventually become 'self-cancelling': that is, the incentive for a US president to press the button on Europe's behalf would diminish rapidly as it became clear that Russia could retaliate in kind. (A number of senior US army officers were making the same point, none more succinctly than General Omar Bradley: 'When the Russians get a bomb to neutralize our bomb,' he said in 1949, 'we'd better get an army to neutralize their army.')

The Truman administration began an energetic effort to persuade Europe to rearm – an effort kept up by successive US administrations – but the results were scarcely dramatic. Even the outbreak of the Korean war, seen by many in Washington as a possible 'blind' aimed at diverting attention before the Russians launched a second, major attack on Western Europe, did little to change things. It produced a brief flurry of activity and some grandiose promises from the allies, but as the danger of a European war receded and the pessimists were proved wrong, so the promises were forgotten. And the last gasp of the Truman campaign came at a famous Nato meeting in Lisbon in 1952, when the foreign ministers approved an extraordinarily ambitious – and rather arbitrary – list of 'force goals': essentially, these anticipated Nato having 96 divisions and 9,000 aircraft by 1954, with 35 to 40 of the divisions ready for combat at all times and the rest capable of being mobilized within a month.

The force goals agreed in Lisbon were clearly beyond Nato, and many have come to see the Lisbon conference as the last occasion the Alliance seriously contemplated a full-scale conventional defence of the continent. Nevertheless, by the early 1960s the West seemed in a far stronger position than at one time had been thought possible.

In the first place, Nato, by then, had better intelligence. While the Soviet Union might possess 175 divisions, theirs were much smaller divisions than Nato's, many were deployed in the east to guard against the threat from China, and the bulk of them were not at full strength. Nato meanwhile had gradually bolstered its own forces with more troops and equipment, and in the mid-1960s the odds looked more even than Western military planners in the early days of Nato would have dared hope. Against 56–57 small Soviet divisions were arrayed 25–26 larger Western ones: manpower figures were roughly equal; and in weaponry the Pact's advantage had shrunk from an estimated five to one in the late 1940s to 1.5 to 1.

The mid-1960s, however, were the high point for Nato. Since then, it has been downhill all the way: America became involved in debilitating conflict in South-East Asia, France left the military structure of the Alliance, and the Soviets added extra manpower and huge amounts of extra equipment to their front-line forces. Five divisions and 70,000 men joined Soviet forces in East Germany, Czechoslovakia and Poland as a result of the invasion of Czechoslovakia in 1968, bringing the total of forward divisions from 22 to 27 (though the overall figure of 56 to 57 in Eastern Europe and the western USSR has remained constant). More than 100,000 construction and support troops were added to these divisions. Much more significant than the manpower, however, was the equipment. According to Phillip Karber, a prominent American defence consultant who works for the BDM Corporation in Virginia, the Warsaw Pact, between 1960 and the early 1980s, added *four* new weapons for every one added by Nato. The Pact, in mid-1985, had more than twice as many tanks as Nato (16,000 to 7,000), three times as much artillery (6,000 to 2,000 pieces), over six times as many multiple rocket-launchers (1,000 to 150), and twice as many aircraft (3,000 to 1,500).

In addition to this, the Pact had – and has – other advantages over

Nato. First, Nato, like the French in the 1930s, is committed to a strategy of forward defence, understandable enough since almost half West Germany's heavy industry and a third of its population reside within fifty miles of the border. Clearly any strategy which envisages giving up a sizeable chunk of West Germany is quite unacceptable to its people, who are committed to forward defence as an ironclad prerequisite for their continuing support for the Alliance. But forward defence is a risky strategy: it denies the defender the ability to trade 'space for time', in other words he has to devote most of his forces to defending the front line, and thus has difficulty creating large enough 'operational reserves' to act as back-up.

The second major problem the Alliance has is geography. In a European war, the Russians would be able to bring the full weight of their forces to bear on Nato simply by moving them overland, a much easier prospect than the one which faces the West, divided as it is by the Atlantic Ocean and with its major power 3,000 hazardous miles from the battlefield.

Finally, the Warsaw Pact would have the initiative in a European war. In 1977 the Pentagon began a study to measure the significance of this. For purposes of comparison, a team of military experts studied the battles between Germany and the Allies in 1940: by analysing a number of factors – equipment, manpower, etc. – they decided that Germany's 'combat potential' was only four fifths that of France and its allies. By most standards, then, the Germans looked, on paper, the weaker side: the secret of their success lay in their ability to concentrate their forces on key sectors, while the allied forces, for their part, were more spread out. In the actual places where the panzer divisions under General Guderian penetrated the line they usually enjoyed a superiority of two to one, and sometimes three to one. At one stage, the analysts examined 50 separate tank battles (mainly involving French and German forces): their overall conclusion is summed up by Phillip Karber, who took part in the Pentagon study: ' A skilful opponent, even with only equal forces, will, if he seizes the initiative and orchestrates the action for decisive impact, have a substantial edge over a side which is purely defensive.' One of the lessons of 1940 was that even though the war itself had started nine months earlier, the attack on France still caught it, to some extent, by surprise. Similarly, even if Nato got two weeks' warning of a Soviet thrust into Europe the Red Army would almost certainly still catch the Alliance less than fully prepared.

One of the most fraught questions, indeed, is whether, even if it got warning time, Nato would take the kind of action necessary. The signals would almost certainly be ambiguous; the pressures not to act would be strong. Say tension mounted in high summer, for example: with the tourist season at its height, would European governments be prepared to close down airports, commandeer ferries and trucks, and in general take the kinds of action which might simply precipitate the very crisis which everyone was trying to avoid?

So the odds against Nato are long. But they can be exaggerated. Military men tend to deal in worst-case scenarios: to wrest money out of democratic governments who have other priorities to attend to they have to conjure up a vivid picture of the danger we face; they also worry – understandably – about being blamed should there be an attack and Nato forces fail to hold the line. The Warsaw Pact has a deeper front, and it can ultimately bring more force to bear than Nato. But as we shall see the Warsaw Pact has its problems too (the longer a war dragged on, for example, the more the Russians would have to worry about their supply lines and the reliability of their East European allies). And the immediate odds confronting Nato are far from impossible: in manpower, for example, Nato's 27 divisions comprise a total of 740,000 men; whereas the 58 Soviet divisions assigned to the Central Front total 900,000 men. The advantage in equipment, though considerable, is not the five to one it was in the late 1940s (overall, it is now more like 2.2 to 1). It is not beyond Nato's power to mount a much more credible defence than it does now, and so to buy precious time: time for negotiations and second thoughts, and time to let American reinforcements reach the battlefield.

But if Nato is to achieve this it will have to change the way it thinks about defence, and specifically, the way it buys its weapons.

That the West, and in particular America, should pin great faith in technology is not altogether surprising. In the early days of the Alliance, when the prospect of mobilizing a large enough ground force to match the Russians soldier for soldier and tank for tank seemed hopeless, Western inventiveness seemed the best, indeed the only, way to make up for Soviet numbers.

And there was no question that the West was more inventive. The democratic societies in the West provided conditions for science to flourish in a way that totalitarianism did not. The West led the way in most of the key developments in defence technology, from towed array sonar (the listening device used by surface ships and submarines) to the conversion of the torpedo into a guided weapon and the development of the vertical take-off jet. A wide range of new inventions (from thermal imaging techniques to liquid crystals, satellites and nuclear propulsion) were pioneered in the West.

In America nowadays, where defence provides the best opportunities for pushing technology to its limits, approximately 25 per cent of the nation's scientists and engineers work for the defence industry and the Pentagon. The philosophy therefore was quite straightforward, and often repeated. The United States, said General George Brown, chief of staff of the US air force and later chairman of the Joint Chiefs of Staff, 'has never attempted to match the Soviet Union either in ground force personnel or material, relying instead on technology'. In March 1975, Dr Malcolm Currie, then the director of research and engineering at the Pentagon, testified as follows to the Senate Armed Services Committee:

> In this increasingly competitive, often hostile and rapidly changing world Americans seem to have only one real choice. Clearly our national well-being cannot be based on unlimited raw materials or on unlimited manpower and cheap labour. Rather it must be based on our ability to multiply and enhance the limited natural and human resources we do have. Technology thus appears to offer us our place in the sun – the means to insure our security and economic vitality.

Five years later, Harold Brown, President Jimmy Carter's defence secretary, echoed this. America's military strength, he said in autumn 1980, 'rests on a scientific ability and a technology ability'. 'Technology,' agreed Edmund Muskie, the then secretary of state, 'is another American advantage. "Faster", "more accurate", "more advanced" – these generally are terms that apply to American weapons and American systems. Soviet technology has lagged behind.'

America's technological prowess therefore was – and remains – beyond dispute.

In the midst of New Mexico, at Hollaman air force base, is a 'sled track' – a straight 50,788-foot-long railway which runs through the desert. Along this, rocket-propelled sleds have travelled at phenomenal speeds. The fastest a human being has travelled on one, in December 1954, is 632 mph (the test was made by an air force pilot and the G force was so strong that his eyeballs almost popped out). Unmanned vehicles, however, have travelled considerably faster than that: one Pentagon official described to me how he watched a test in which an unmanned sled, propelled by nine rocket motors, shot down the track at 5,000 mph. From a starting point three miles away, the sled took just two and a half seconds to reach the vantage point: by the time those watching had turned their heads it had vanished. Even that was a relatively modest test: the unmanned land speed record, set at Hollaman air force base in October 1983, is a staggering 8,900 ft per second – 6,060 mph.

The sled track at Hollaman has allowed defence engineers to explore the sheer technical challenge of making vehicles travel at enormous speeds. It has also, more practically, enabled the air force to test everything from the aerodynamic properties of a new wing design for a fighter to the stresses and strains which migh bear on an aircraft ejection seat or a missile's re-entry vehicle when released in space. Firing the relevant component along the sled track proves, say the Pentagon, a cheaper and simpler way of doing this than tests in space, or in the air. The sled has also been used for testing human strain – by shooting instrumented dummies wired to computers down the track at extraordinary speeds.

The Pentagon is proud of its sled track in the desert.* It is an example, they say, of a facility the Soviets could not match: for one thing, they have lagged behind America in the development of the computers and micro-electronics which make the tests possible. So why have these advantages which the track reflects not translated into better, cheaper and more efficient military hardware? Why, despite Muskie's claim that American weapons are 'faster', 'more accurate' and 'more advanced', have they not given us a commensurate measure of extra security?

The short answer is that the West has got carried away. There is a story, apocryphal no doubt, about one of the guests of the stricken liner *Titanic*, who happened to be in the bar as the ship began to sink. 'I asked for ice,' he is supposed to have quipped, 'but this is ridiculous.' In its effort to achieve technological supremacy over the Russians, Nato has turned what should be an asset into a liability. It has tried, through sophisticated weaponry, to achieve 'security without risk', and the consequences of this have been almost uniformly bad.

In the early 1930s, the French attempted something very similar. They constructed a line of fortifications along their south-eastern border with Germany. The intention was to render France utterly secure against the threat which, even then, was looming from German rearmament. The French were determined never again to endure the huge losses they had sustained in World War One.

The Maginot Line, when complete in 1935, was hailed far and wide as a technological marvel, the most sophisticated set of fortifications ever constructed. Romantically, it came to be dubbed 'the shield of France', and almost until the eve of war, the French government continued to express confidence in its remarkable creation. 'Be reassured,' said Edouard Daladier, the defence minister, in January 1937, 'our fortified works are sufficiently equipped to halt a sudden attack even on a Sunday ...'

The government's confidence, of course, was stunningly misplaced. In the history of warfare, there have been few campaigns decided as swiftly and dramatically as the German conquest of Western Europe in May and June 1940. And though it was inevitable that Belgium and tiny Luxemburg

---

* America has test facilities even more sophisticated than the one at Hollaman. The air force, for example, has a series of wind tunnels at Tullahoma, Tennessee, for testing high-performance aircraft and rockets; NASA has a similar facility near San Francisco.

should collapse rapidly under the superior weight of the German forces, the fall of France – a country which had ended World War One with the strongest army in Europe – was a catastrophe which could and should have been averted. The evidence suggests that the Germans themselves were staggered by the speed of their victory.

What went wrong? Why did the supposedly invincible Maginot Line prove, in the end, so utterly useless?

What happened is that the Maginot Line ended up not as one component of French strategy but as almost the sole component. This was not intentional: the government's plan had been to use these fortifications to block their vulnerable south-eastern border, thus freeing their troops to deny access to Germany through Belgium. But projects as vast and ambitious as the Maginot Line have a habit of consuming so much attention and energy that little is left over for anything else. Whatever the military planners might have hoped, the Maginot Line led France into a trap: it created, in itself, the illusion of security. It exhausted both the country's funds and its initiative. In the end, it cost close to seven thousand million francs – about fifty million pounds – a staggering sum at that time, and more than twice as much as had originally been anticipated when the chamber of deputies gave the go-ahead in 1930. (This is a classic example of how big defence projects tend to overrun: even had France's planners voted to extend the line after the collapse of the Franco-Belgian accords in 1936, there simply would not have been the money with which to do it.)

As a result of the Maginot Line, other military programmes had been fatally squeezed: the French air force was neglected until it was too late; the army itself was forced to suffer all kinds of handicaps, with some units forced to fall back on horses for transport. There were interminable hagglings over the replacement of the standard automatic rifle the army used, the actual new model not being selected until 1936, and by 1939 only a few hundred thousand had been issued. In addition, on the eve of a war in which rapid communication between armoured units was to prove vital, the French army continued to rely on the telephone – unlike the Germans, who had spotted the potential of radio and were experimenting with it intensively from the early 1930s onwards.

The malaise went deeper. The army which had ended World War One as a fearsome fighting unit had, under the shadow of the old men who led it, declined: training had become inadequate, morale had sagged, and the fighting spirit which had seen France through to victory in 1918 had evaporated. As Alistair Horne wrote in his graphic account, *To Lose a Battle*:

Rapidly the Maginot Line came to be not just a component of

strategy, but a way of life. Feeling secure behind it, like the lotus-eating mandarins of Cathay behind their Great Wall, the French Army allowed itself to atrophy, to lapse into desuetude. A massive combination of factors – complacency, lassitude, deficiencies of manpower and finance – conspired to rust the superb weapon which the world had so admired ...

As we consider modern weapons, and the mentality which creates them, the parallels with what happened in France in the 1930s will become clear. France lost its battle against Germany in 1940 because of a failure of imagination. The problem was not so much the decision to fortify part of a vital border – in itself, quite sensible – as the fact that, to be effective, French strategy required not just fortifications but substantial operational reserves to be available behind them. France, because one great project absorbed so much money and energy, got one but not the other. Modern defence planners have become similarly over-dependent on microchips and data links and all the other attributes of space-age technology, while neglecting other crucial elements necessary for a coherent defence. (One could push the parallels further: just as France left itself open to General Guderian's daring thrust through the Ardennes and the rapid advance to Paris, so modern defence planners have made unrealistic assumptions about how the Russians would actually fight a war in Central Europe. France misused technology; so has the West.) France, through the Maginot Line, tried to substitute equipment for men, to minimize potential loss of life and to achieve an absolute security. In doing so, it ended up with far *less* security than it needed. The West has fallen into a similar trap.

2

Weapons

Geniuses, it has been said, think more simply than ordinary mortals. This clearly sets them apart from the Pentagon, which (collectively, at least) does not think simply about anything. The art of modern US weapons procurement appears to be to find the most complicated and expensive way of performing even the slightest task.

On 30 May 1985, the Pentagon confessed that it had paid out $659 apiece for seven plastic ashtrays installed in the arm rests of the navy's E-2C Early Warning planes. Saying there was 'no excuse' for what he called a 'silly transaction', the defence secretary, Caspar Weinberger, questioned whether the Pentagon might not explore the idea of using 'old mayonnaise jars' in the future – or consider banning smoking on its planes. And responding to the clear need to take some form of punitive action, Weinberger decided to transfer the three senior naval officers who were responsible for the supply depot which had authorized the purchases.

But the three officers, one of them an admiral with 33 years' service behind him, felt, with some justice, that they were being made scapegoats. For as the manufacturers, Grumman Corporation, pointed out, the specifications approved in the Pentagon (which included an extraordinarily elaborate drawing) called for ashtrays made up of eleven separate parts, which would take thirteen man-hours to assemble – the idea apparently being to ensure that they would withstand the jolt which would occur when an E-2C landed on an aircraft carrier. And though the company had clearly overcharged the navy – it agreed to a refund of $610 per ashtray – it was in part these absurdly detailed specifications which made the inflated price possible.

Thus to single out three naval officers for punishment was ridiculous. In a Defence Department which bulges with 36,000 officers and 359,000 civilians (an estimated 54,000 people are directly involved in buying equipment), and in a defence industry with few incentives to keep down costs, overspecifying and overcharging are a way of life. In the billions spent by the Pentagon each year, $4,600 for seven ashtrays is a trivial sum, but it is an example which vividly brings home the way the Pentagon does business. And the grotesquely over-complicated, over-expensive ashtray at least has one virtue: it works. That is more than can be said for some of the equipment supplied to the US arsenal.

The Divad Gun

General Sir Archibald Wavell, who commanded British forces in the Middle East in the early years of World War Two, had an old-fashioned view of military equipment. He believed that, to survive on a battlefield, it ought to be sturdy. 'Whenever in the old days a new design of mountain gun was submitted to the Artillery Committee,' he wrote in his memoirs, 'that august body had it taken to the top of a tower, some hundred feet high, and thence dropped on to the ground below. If it was still capable of functioning it was given further trial; if not, it was rejected as flimsy.'

One wonders what General Wavell would have made of the American army's Divisional Air Defence Gun, or Divad for short. No one, so far as I know, ever dropped it from a 100-ft tower. Available information suggests they would have been ill advised to try. The Divad found it hard enough to cope with considerably lesser trials.

According to evidence which emerged at a Senate subcommittee hearing in early 1985, the Divad did not work in the cold. It was supposed to be an all-weather weapon, able to 'acquire' its target automatically and line up on it by means of its elaborate, computer-directed fire control system. But when a Divad was tested in a cold chamber, with the temperature 25 degrees below zero, it registered readings 180 degrees off, meaning it aimed at targets in precisely the opposite direction to the ones its operator had in mind – 'hardly reassuring to your reserve units', as Senator Mark Andrews of North Dakota pointed out to the assembled army brass. Only when the Divad had been heated for six hours with the field equivalent of a hair dryer did it seem ready to perform.

The news of the Divad's allergy to cold shocked Senator Andrews, who is a farmer (and incidentally a Republican who believes in a strong defence). On his farm, he said, his cattle would starve if machinery failed to work at 40 degrees below zero. 'Unless the Army plans to fight only in the balmy, 70-degree temperature of early summer, this implement is far from satisfactory ...'

This was putting it mildly. In spite of constant attempts by the army to reassure its critics (the cold weather troubles, for example, were put down to a failure to use diesel fuel), the problems afflicting the Divad continued to multiply. It was a classic of its kind: a bafflingly complex and fragile weapon which showed little evidence that it could withstand the rugged and unpredictable conditions of a battlefield (what the great Prussian strategist Clausewitz called 'friction'). So bad did it prove to be that in August 1985, after eight years of development, and the waste of $1.8 billion, it was cancelled – a rare fate for a modern weapon, especially one so far into production. More clearly, perhaps, than any weapon before, the Divad illustrated the excesses of the Pentagon procurement process: the tendency to exaggerate the threat, the incessant 'gold plating', the unrealistic tests, the lack of coherent thought about military missions and roles. And what made it even more depressing as a case history was the fact that it had actually been conceived to avoid these very pitfalls.

By the early 1970s, the US army were thoroughly convinced of the virtues of an air defence gun. The Surface to Air missiles (SAMs) on which they were becoming increasingly reliant were complicated and cumbersome, difficult to use against low-flying aircraft. They were expensive, too: and if a missile was fired, and missed, there was seldom time for a second shot. Fast-firing guns were different. They could pump a stream of shells or tracer into the sky, sometimes to devastating effect. Visually aimed guns shot down more than 4,000 jets in the Korean, Vietnam and Arab-Israeli wars. (The conflict between Britain and the Falklands in 1982 even illustrated the value of the old-fashioned machinegun: on some of the British vessels which sailed to the South Atlantic, machineguns were hastily bolted to the deck to bolster what at times seemed patently inadequate missile systems.)

In any war on the Central Front in Europe, air defence would be vital. America and its allies would be under fierce bombardment not just from fixed-wing aircraft delivering gunfire, napalm or rockets, but from helicopters armed with anti-tank precision munitions. A helicopter is a tempting target: it lacks the speed and small radar profile of a low-flying jet, and in Vietnam the ill-equipped Viet Cong accounted for some 4,643 American helicopters, almost 85 per cent of them shot down not by sophisticated missiles or aircraft but by rifles and machineguns.

In the early 1970s, the only air defence gun the army had at its disposal was one of World War Two vintage called the Vulcan. It was quite cheap, and by all accounts quite effective, but it could fire only 20 millimetre ammunition, and by the 1970s it was clear that the new generation of Soviet aircraft and helicopters would have armour thick enough to withstand such a small round. It was also of limited range and difficult to move around; it had to be replaced. The idea at first was simply to upgrade the Vulcan, but as the army's designers became embroiled in the project, and consultations with industry began, that changed. 'Pretty soon,' one of those involved told Gregg Easterbrook, a journalist who first exposed the shortcomings of the Divad gun in the *Atlantic Monthly* in October 1982, 'we were adding every bell and whistle you could think of.' (In the Pentagon lexicon, bells and whistles are extravagant frills.)

Three factors help explain the transformation of the new gun, which the army named the Sergeant York, after a World War One sharpshooter who single-handedly killed 25 Germans and captured 132 others in a battle in the trenches. First, the army could not make up its mind what it wanted. The procurement bureaucracy were divided about the merits of a new gun: some, primarily civilian analysts, argued that ground-to-air missiles were more effective, and though these people lost, their arguments prompted the Sergeant York's advocates to promise the development of a very special gun. The second problem – closely related to this – was that having settled on a gun the army kept changing the requirements for it. And this, in turn, reflected a wider conceptual failure: a failure to think through with any precision the virtues and limitations of air defence guns as compared to surface-to-air missiles.

Perhaps the key catalyst in the development of the Divad, or Sergeant York, was a Soviet weapon called the Shilka. The American army got its hands on one of these, officially designated ZSU-23-4 by the Russians, at the end of the 1973 Arab-Israeli war. It had been captured by the Israelis, and was shipped back to the American Army's testing range at Fort Bliss, Texas, where it was put through its paces. There are differing accounts of its effectiveness. Some say it performed quite well in the 1973 war, accounting for a number of Israeli Skyhawks and Phantoms over the Golan Heights, but most experts I have talked to describe it as an unimpressive weapon; when tested at Fort Bragg, apparently, it proved slow to pick up a target and inaccurate, and it rapidly exhausted its ammunition when fired. Agile aircraft, according to the sceptics, were beyond its power to hit. But whether or not the Shilka was evidence of wasted Soviet roubles, the US army was fascinated by it, especially by the radars which supposedly enabled it to pick up its targets and the computers which, in theory, permitted the gun to lock on to those targets automatically. As then available the Shilka might not be ideal, but what if the Russians perfected it?

So the army set out to create a gun which, like the Shilka, would operate automatically, so that it could perform at night and in foul weather, too. To save time and money, it was decided to use components from existing weapons – the chassis from the old M-48 tank, the radar from the F16 fighter, with two Swedish Bofors anti-aircraft guns supplying the armament.* But for what the army had in mind, all this had to be put

*Some argue that a chief reason why the Divad failed was that it consisted of a 'cost-cutting hodge-podge' of existing technology. But this is hardly convincing, for reasons which its dismal history will make clear.

together in an immensely complicated way. Initially, the Divad was conceived to knock down fixed-wing aircraft, but in 1978 the 'requirement' was changed to include rotary-wing aircraft (i.e. helicopters) – a *very* different target. Later still, another even more demanding requirement was added: in order to strike Soviet Hind helicopters before they could threaten forces the Divad was supposed to defend, the new weapon would have to be able to achieve 'kills' at a range of four kilometres.

All of this, of course, necessitated a dazzling array of super-sophisticated components, and aspiring contractors were soon putting them together: computers to track enemy aircraft, to 'assess the threat levels' of these aircraft, to predict their movements, to monitor all the other computers and provide instant analysis of failure; computers to resist radar jamming, and to find out whether the aircraft flying overhead were friendly or not – a so-called Identification Friend or Foe, or IFF, system. (In all, the Divad would require some 240 separate software programmes.) Then there was the laser rangefinder, the infrared nightsight to back up the radars, and the air conditioner to keep all this apparatus cool. According to its eventual manufacturers, Ford Aerospace, Divad would require essentially no skill to operate. It would simply be a question of turning it on, waiting for a light on the control panel to flash 'Fire Now' and pulling a trigger. Nothing would be simpler. Even the dumbest GI would be able to do it.

The first time the Sergeant York was put through its paces was in early 1982, when some of the army's top brass assembled for a test display at a firing range at Fort Hood in Texas. It was a sunny day, and a small Huey helicopter hovered in the clear air above the range. This was the designated target. Given the weather, it did not seem an exacting test. In this 'optimized environment' the Divad might be expected to demolish the Huey the instant it was switched on.

The Divad was wheeled out – an ungainly-looking vehicle, closely resembling a tank, though with its radar and two Bofors guns mounted on top instead of the normal projecting barrel. A technician switched it on. Unhappily, instead of aiming at the Huey, its cannons swung round towards the reviewing stand and its audience of army brass. Officers dived for cover. Luckily Ford had thought to put a lock on the gun barrels to prevent them turning far enough to threaten any damage, but it was not an auspicious start. Ford technicians earnestly examined the Divad and it was tried again. This time it did point at the target, but only briefly, then the cannons began blasting at a patch of tumbleweed 300 yards away.

It is customary to dismiss the snags experienced in such a test as teething troubles. All the same, Ford's explanation for the debacle was hardly convincing: they said that the Divad gun used in the test had just been washed, and that its performance might have been degraded because of water affecting the electronics. But on the Central Front, or on any potential battlefield, military equipment is likely to have to survive all kinds of weather, not to mention dust and rough treatment. Besides, the evidence that Divad was no miracle weapon continued to accumulate: it emerged that it could not hit an aircraft which jinked (i.e. dodged) in flight, or a helicopter which 'popped up' (i.e. rose quickly from behind some trees or from the ground to loose off anti-tank missiles before ducking down again swiftly). Indeed, it did not seem able to do any of the things it might be expected to do.

There was a ready explanation for this. The problem with guns which fire automatically is that the computers which make them work deal with the past rather than the future. Computers can track the 'history' of an approaching aircraft and calculate where it will be based on that history, but they cannot allow (or allow *sufficiently*) for unpredictable movement. To shoot down a plane, you must aim ahead of it in the direction you anticipate it will follow, and since pilots flying over a modern battlefield weave and dodge for all they are worth in the endeavour to escape being hit, the Divad was relatively easy to foil. No pilot in his right mind, as one air force veteran put it, is likely to fly straight and level over hostile terrain. There is only one truly effective device for tracking and aiming at an agile combat plane, and that is the human eye. A human gunner, aware of his surroundings, and of the kind of mission an enemy plane might be flying, is in an infinitely better position to predict its course than a computer. (The human eye, for example, can see a plane banking before it turns: a computer can't.) The Divad, moreover, was expected to cope not just with aircraft but with helicopters, too, which travel at very different speeds to aircraft, and which often have no momentum at all. Helicopters baffled the Divad; a human gunner, however, finds it relatively easy to adapt from one kind of target to another.

Even if the Divad had worked, its vaunted ability to shoot down aircraft at night and in fog seemed to some critics an overrated asset. Even modern jets have trouble flying successful missions in bad weather, and for night fighting, a nighsight called a 'flir' (forward-looking infrared) would have been of more value than all the computer wizardry of the Divad. Some US fighter planes have flirs, which allow the pilot to see a narrow stretch of ground in front of them almost as clearly as if it were day. As Gregg Easterbrook notes, aircraft with flirs, however, might be countered by anti-aircraft guns with flirs:

In a flir-to-flir duel, ground gunners would have a distinct advantage. Aircraft flying against the cold, empty background of the sky provide an excellent thermal contrast, sharp and easy to see. Vehicles prowling amid the clutter and retained warmth of the ground, on the other hand, provide only a small thermal contrast; heat 'camouflages' them against infrared detection the same way trees and colours camouflage them against visual detection.

Installing a flir on the Divad might have made sense. Installing an automatic fire control system demonstrably did not. It accounted for an estimated $2 billion of the programme's $6.5 billion price tag, and it didn't work.

Now, admittedly, trying to aim a gun *visually* at four kilometres is a tall order – which is one reason why the army is so keen on automatic fire control. But was the four-kilometre range requirement really a sensible one? In the first place, long-range shells have to be bigger than short-range ones because they have to travel further, and the ammunition chosen for the Divad was 40 mm, twice the size of the Vulcan's. It consisted of 'proximity rounds', triggered to detonate several feet from a target and spray a cloud of shrapnel and tungsten pellets at it. These proximity rounds were very expensive – $200 apiece – and there was considerable doubt as to whether they would be able to penetrate heavily armoured Soviet aircraft. In addition, the shells were so large that they made it that much harder to create the 'wall of lead' effect on which a gun depends: instead of being able to fire 3,000 rounds a minute, like the Vulcan, the Divad could manage only 600. The special nature of the shells, moreover, meant that in a war the guns would require a special logistical support system (although, as *Newsweek* noted, the guns 'jammed so frequently' in testing that this might not have been a serious problem).

So was the emphasis on extra-long range, and therefore extra-special shells, a necessary one? Probably not. As the *New York Times* pointed out: 'Knocking out a tank requires precision, and an attacking plane, armed with homing missiles, must first get close enough for the pilot to see the target and identify it as the enemy.' Yet the obsession with range grew rather than diminished as the Divad was developed. In the early 1980s alarming reports began to reach US intelligence from Afghanistan that the Russian Hind helicopters had become theoretically capable of firing guided missiles at a target from six kilometres away, two kilometres beyond the Divad's maximum range. This sent a tremor through the Pentagon. Some officials began to argue that the Divad's range was *too short*. The army, to be fair, tried to point out that the Hind threat was being exaggerated. After all, 'Soviet pilots would not be able to hit targets from six kilometres in an actual battle, especially in the frequent overcast and rolling hills of Europe'. It appeared to have little effect, even though the *real* trouble with the Divad was not that it could not shoot far enough but that it could shoot too far ...

Meanwhile, the programme struggled on, and the Pentagon preferred to ignore the message and blame the messenger. With stout backing from Ford, it labelled the press and congressional criticism of the Divad inaccurate, unfair and incomplete. 'The programme,' said Major General James. P. Maloney, who was in charge of the Divad, 'is problem plagued in the press only.'

Sometimes, perhaps, the press overdid it. On one occasion the Divad's acquisition radar picked up, instead of the intended target on the test site, a bathroom fan in a building 100 yards away. The gun never actually opened fire, but subsequent jocular headlines in the newspapers (e.g. 'battle of the latrine fan') gave, in the army's view, the false impression that it had. It was something for the army to seize upon as they tried to stem the tide of criticism.

Essentially, though, Maloney's claim was unconvincing. The basic charge against Divad, that it could not 'acquire' let alone hit the right target, was never properly answered, save by continual claims that the gun's problems were only minor ones. 'I would say,' declared General Maloney to a television reporter in mid-1984, 'that practically all of the problems that we have found with this system have been corrected. If the totality of problems were 100 per cent, I would say at this point, 97 per cent of those problems have been corrected.'

'Divad experienced normal start-up problems,' echoed Ford spokesman Susan Frutkin. 'None of them are show-stoppers. Most of them have been fixed.' By this stage, however, some powerful critics were joining the fray. In the summer of 1984, the Divad was put through its paces again. At the army's test site at White Sands, it mistook about half of 180 decoys sent against it for real targets, and hit only about one third of its aerial attackers when they employed electronic countermeasures to fool the gun's radars.

Its inability to hit 'pop-up' helicopters was still plainly evident, and in one particular round of testing, when it seemed quite unable to hit a stationary helicopter placed on an elevated platform some distance from the gun (an electric motor was used to turn the rotor blades), the army added 'radar reflectors' to the target to provide a clearer signal for the Divad's radar. The procedure was described in the *Washington Monthly* as 'like testing a bloodhound's ability to track a man covered with beefsteaks standing alone and upright in the middle of a parking lot'. In this instance, the army argued, they had had to shorten the helicopter's rotor blades so that it didn't simply take off: by adding reflectors all they had been trying to do was to compensate for the consequent reduction in radar signature. Still, the Divad needed a lot of this kind of help (called 'target enhancement' or 'success-oriented testing'): apparently cans of petrol were even loaded into the helicopters to increase the chances of their exploding when hit.

The summer testing proved, if not the last straw, disquieting enough to provoke an unusual step. By now concern about the Divad was widespread in official circles. The army's Operational Test and Evaluation Agency, faced with the Divad's record of failure, acknowledged in private meetings that the testing raised serious questions about the weapon's performance and reliability. And it wasn't just the 'ultra' components which were giving trouble: even the relatively simple ammunition feeder on the Divad did not work properly.

As the recriminations mounted, the army deflected some of the criticism to Divad's manufacturer, Ford Aerospace. In March 1984, they produced a report charging the company with a 'totally unacceptable' performance, though the fact is that the army had created considerable controversy by giving the contract to Ford in the first place.

In the initial competition for the lucrative $4.5 billion contract, two firms emerged as front runners, General Dynamics and Ford. The two, each of which had built a prototype Divad, held a shoot-off, and this was won hands-down by General Dynamics. According to a Pentagon report, Ford hit half as many targets as General Dynamics, and the longest range of a Ford hit was only just over half the longest range of a General Dynamics hit (in all, General Dynamics shot down 15 helicopters, Ford only eight). The army, however, decided to opt for Ford. Ostensibly, this was for two reasons: first, said the army, Ford had technically superior ammunition; second, Ford had more 'near-misses' than General Dynamics, and if near-misses were counted as hits, then Ford emerged the victor.

General Dynamics, naturally enough, were disgruntled by the decision, and there were suggestions that Ford had got the contract because it was in financial trouble, and that the Reagan White House, philosophically opposed to bailing out companies yet anxious to help, had suggested that the Pentagon should look favourably on Ford's attempts to win defence contracts. Whatever happened, General Dynamics, already hugely dependent on Pentagon business and in some difficulties with their submarine programme, were not anxious to cause a public row. But the controversy only added more fuel to a roaring fire.

In the wake of the tests in summer 1984, the inspector general of the Pentagon, Joseph Sherick, produced a report which proved depressing reading for those involved in the Divad project. The inspector general is an important man in the defence department – he acts as an in-house watchdog – and now he charged Ford with unacceptable behaviour. No sooner had the company won the contract, he said in testimony to a congressional committee in late September 1984, than it proceeded to negotiate price reductions with its subcontractors. This clearly indicated, according to Sherick, that it had overcharged the army in the first place. Not only that: he complained that the prices for spare parts for the Divads were far too high. Ford, for example, after originally charging $7,900 for a power control assembly, were now ready to charge $151,500, an increase of 1,840 per cent.

But Sherick was not content simply to blast Ford for the way it had handled the contract, and for its seeming eagerness for huge profits. He also told Congress that the charts indicating the test data produced by the army in 1982, when production was first authorized, left much to be desired. These charts, he said, which attested to a high level of effectiveness in field trials, 'were oversimplified, and therefore misleading and based on a selective analysis of the results'. The Pentagon, in other words, had been so keen on the Divad that they had staged the tests to make it look better than it was.

Finally, in October 1984, after a series of hearings in Congress, and after the army had finally admitted that their Sergeant York had missed the target 75 per cent of the time at a recent firing, Caspar Weinberger, the defence secretary, decided he had had enough. It is unusual for a weapons system to be suspended once in production: there are too many vested interests tied up in it by then, and too many jobs. But Weinberger suspended production of Divad, ordering the army to stop purchasing it: the four billion dollar programme would await the results of new tests scheduled for 1985.

Already, however, fifteen Divads had been delivered to the army and funds for a further 130 had been approved by Congress (each gun then cost $6.3 million). Over a billion and a half dollars had been spent, and this despite the appalling record of the Divad since it was first conceived. 'What is so awful,' one Pentagon sceptic told me at the time, 'is that there is nothing we know now that we didn't know two years ago.' Yet in the meantime a fortune had been wasted.

The army continued to insist that the Divad's problems were only temporary, and would be solved, but even if this were true, the original concept of an air defence gun had long since been lost. 'We've finally found a way of making a gun more expensive than a missile,' commented one army sceptic.

In mid-December 1984, shortly after Divad's suspension, the viewers of the current affairs television programme *20/20*, made by the ABC network, were treated to a remarkable piece of film. Reporter Geraldo Rivera had spent the best part of a year investigating the Divad gun: he had heard the horror stories about it; he had also listened to the army's protestations about its effectiveness and decided to hold back his report until after the tests in summer 1984. These, of course, proved no more successful than any previous tests, but Rivera was anxious to see for himself, and finally the army agreed to invite him to Fort Bliss to attend a demonstration. Flanked by a group of high-ranking military officers from around the

world, Rivera and his camera crew watched as a Divad prepared for firing.
'To demonstrate that the tracking and computer system of this gun is so
sophisticated that absolutely anyone can fire it, General Maloney made a
bold decision,' he told his viewers. 'He allowed the gun to be operated by
a civilian aide to the secretary of the army. The aide had never done
it before. Perhaps the general should have selected someone more
experienced.'

What viewers of *20/20* saw next was the Divad gun opening fire on a
ground target 100 yards away. Given that the Divad would probably have
to fire at ground targets in a war as well as at aircraft and helicopters –
indeed it had been designed with this in mind – it was not unreasonable
that it should be tested in this manner. But judging from the results, enemy
ground forces would have little to fear. The Divad fired a burst, and
missed, the tracer shells exploding in the clear sunlit air a safe distance
away. It fired again a few seconds later and missed. A third time ... and
a fourth. Same result. The target remained unscathed. Seemingly the
world's most sophisticated gun, which had been designed to be able to
strike aircraft flying above it at great speed, was not even able to hit a
stationary target a mere 100 yards away. After this display, however, the
civilian aide at the Divad's controls turned his attention to the 'main event'
of the day – a QH50 helicopter drone hovering gently about 300 ft up.
This is not the kind of height helicopters usually fly during war: they either
hug the ground very tightly (Vietnam helicopter pilots often returned from
missions with grass on their skids), or they climb as high as possible to
escape anti-aircraft fire: fifty to twelve hundred feet, according to one former
Vietnam pilot, 'is dead man's height, no helicopter in war would be
performing as the QH50 was during the test'. Still, the fact that the airborne
target was a sitting duck did not appear to help the Divad much. One
round in the first burst appeared to wing it, though it continued to soar
peacefully three hundred feet up. Another burst missed entirely. Finally, by
which time the target had descended to closer range, a hit.

Following this display, Rivera, the reporter, turned to General Maloney.
'How do you characterize the demonstration we've just seen?' he asked.

Maloney was unruffled. 'Well,' he said, 'it was absolutely a total success.'

Eight months after this, Caspar Weinberger finally cancelled the Divad
gun outright. The army continued to maintain, to the end, that its problems
could be solved. So did the Ford Motor Company. Even in March 1985,
the ever-optimistic General Maloney was telling Congress he believed that
'testing in the future will prove that the Sergeant York is the finest self-
propelled anti-aircraft gun in the world'. (Maloney also impugned the
motives of the gun's leading congressional critic, Representative Denny
Smith, a Republican from Oregon. Smith, he said, was 'not doing this
[attacking Divad] for the good of the country'.) And Weinberger, described

by critics as a man 'who never saw a weapons system he didn't like', knew that the army had nothing else on its stocks to close the air defence gap.

But the Divad's final test, in June 1985, proved as ludicrous as any which had gone before. At first it seemed otherwise. Ford put out a paper saying that the Divad, in a 'live-fire' exercise, had managed to destroy 'six out of seven high-performance aircraft and three of three helicopters presented'. But this, it turned out, was somewhat misleading. First, as Denny Smith quickly learnt, the army had presented their targets many more than ten times; second, these targets appear to have flown in straight lines with little or no manoeuvring, except for a roll in front of the guns to provide a *larger* target. And third, four of the planes to be brought down were not hit by the Divad at all but destroyed by the range safety officer on the ground. The army was worried that they might veer off course and cause damage, it said, even though the test took place in the middle of the New Mexico desert. So the target aircraft, which were filled with explosives, were 'command destructed'. At the same time, however, the army claimed that the Divad's proximity shells would eventually have brought the planes down. The evidence suggested otherwise.

In the end, as Bill Keller of the *New York Times* put it, the Divad could be said to have 'died of embarrassment'. It had managed to combine *all* the drawbacks of a surface-to-air missile system – namely, elaborate fire control, complexity, and cost – with *none* of the advantages of an air defence gun. Guns make sense if they are cheap and simple enough to be produced in large numbers, so that on the battlefield they can throw up a 'wall of lead' in front of enemy aircraft and helicopters. Lead can neither be decoyed nor spoofed, unlike missiles, because it does not depend on 'locking on' to the heat or radar signature of a target. It depends, or should depend, on the eye of the gunner. (Not least of the Divad's drawbacks was the likelihood that, in a war, its powerful active radar would act as a homing device for the Soviets' radar-seeking missiles.) Had the Divad been properly designed – had the army, in other words, pushed for less elaborate requirements, settled for a shorter range and thought more about tactics and less about technology – a formidable weapon could have emerged, available in large numbers. As it was, the army wasted a lot of time and money. For even if all the proposed 618 Divads had been purchased, and had worked, they would still not have been available in anything like the necessary numbers.

The Bradley Fighting Vehicle

The job of an army is the most fundamental in warfare: it is to take or regain land, and traditionally the PBI, 'the poor bloody infantry', have been less susceptible to gadgetry than their sister services. In World War Two the US army relied on abundant quantities of simple, rugged, easy-to-maintain equipment: US procurement, indeed, became synonymous with basic and mass-produced weapons like the tommy-gun and the Sherman tank. The idea was to overwhelm through sheer numbers, and there was logic to it. In war, numbers count.

Now, however, the philosophy in the Pentagon is that a few 'ultra' weapons are better than a lot of less sophisticated ones, and the army has become a true believer in that philosophy.

But 'ultra' weapons, like the Divad, built 'at the leading edge of technology' are extraordinarily expensive. And because they are so expensive, and you can thus build so few of them, they have to be very good indeed because: (a) you are presenting fewer targets for the other side to destroy; (b) you are leaving the other side with more 'weapons platforms' to fire from and more targets to lose. It is commonly assumed, in fact, that if the enemy outnumbers you by two to one then your weapons have to be between two and four times as good as his if you are to be equally strong. The Divad gun hardly lived up to this equation. And nor does another example of the shiny new hardware which, in the early 1980s, began to arrive on the battlefield as part of the army's ambitious, across-the-board, 'weapons modernization' programme.

The Bradley Fighting Vehicle, or M2, is built by the FMC Corporation, a company which until the early years of World War Two specialized almost entirely in building fruit-processing and canning equipment. When America entered the war, FMC adapted its expertise in metal bending, welding and mechanical engineering to the military and secured a contract to produce tracked amphibious vehicles for the army. The model FMC built was simple and sturdy, and FMC, who christened it the Water Buffalo, had churned out 11,000 of them by the time the armistice was signed. FMC followed this up in the 1950s with another armoured personnel carrier, the M113. It was poorly protected and built of aluminium but it served its purpose – depositing soldiers on the edge of a combat zone – and it was cheap ($183,000 apiece when the army bought the last batch in 1984). FMC has sold a total of more than 70,000 M113s throughout the world, and it proved one of the (few) notable successes of the Vietnam war. Christopher Foss, the editor of the authoritative *Jane's Armoured Fighting Vehicles*, describes it as 'one of the most successful vehicles ever in the US Army service'.

To understand why the Bradley will never win such praise one has to go back to 1964, when the US army (after consultation with the West Germany army) changed its doctrine. There was now a need, it decided, for a vehicle which would not simply deposit mechanized infantry at the edge of a battlefield, but would be able to carry them into the thick of any fighting and enable them to fight while they were still aboard. Even at the time, some army experts doubted the wisdom of this. They pointed out that it is very difficult for infantry to shoot at enemy forces while on the move, rolling across (probably rough) countryside. They pointed out, furthermore, that the prime use for mechanized infantry is in terrain where tanks are highly vulnerable – and surely if tanks were highly vulnerable in such terrain, so-called 'mechanized infantry combat vehicles' would be, too?

Nonetheless, the requirement stood, and the army, who were already considering a replacement for the M113, began to investigate ways of meeting it. They dismissed as too large, too heavy and too under-powered three 52,000-pound prototypes built for them by a company called Pacific Car & Foundry (now, Paccar Inc.), but their conception of what they did want grew steadily more and more ambitious and, as with the Divad gun, more and more confusing.

In 1972, FMC, the makers of the M113, put together a detailed and comprehensive package which, in the shape of a foot-high stack of documents and a wooden model of the envisaged end product, they sent to the Pentagon. As FMC knew, the army were now worrying about a new Soviet infantry fighting vehicle which had first been fielded in the late 1960s and which was armed with a cannon, able to carry eleven men into combat, and supposedly capable of being dropped by parachute and crossing rivers. Nevertheless, given that the army were already demanding something vastly more complicated than the M113, the company put forward a relatively simple design. They emphasized ruggedness, reliability and prompt delivery. The army was impressed. FMC got the contract.

It was at this point that the trouble started. By all accounts, FMC found themselves bombarded with specifications from different army departments – the Infantry Center in Georgia wanted to move men around, the US Army Armour Center wanted to kill tanks, the army's light cavalry disliked the whole project because they were keen on a new scout vehicle – and the new carrier began to sink in a morass of bureaucratic indecision, design changes and gold plating. FMC executives were bewildered by their dealings with the Pentagon: the days when the army issued simple specifications and let them get on with the job appeared to be over. Washington had changed. 'What we're dealing with now is a multi-headed monster,' said one executive. 'The Bradley project is rather like a tree,' commented another. 'The army keep pulling it up by the roots to see if it's still growing.'

The project stumbled on and the problems multiplied. It must go as fast as modern tanks, said the army, to keep up with them on the battlefield, a requirement which meant that the vehicle kept 'throwing its tracks' in testing (centrifugal force around the drive gear which built up when the vehicle was travelling fast caused the tracks to slip off); the transmission system installed by GEC broke down frequently; the price began to rise. The anticipated 1976 production date came and went and then a high-level study group in the army rewrote specifications yet again, saying that the vehicle should have two TOW missiles, a night vision system and a stabilized Swiss cannon. The TOW – 'Tube-launched, Optically tracked, Wire-guided missile – is a useful enough weapon for infantry, when operated on the ground, but it had a drastic effect on the design of the new vehicle. It required a large turret to accommodate it, and this in turn meant that the number of soldiers who could be squeezed aboard the new vehicle would have to drop from twelve to nine. And three, instead of one, of the nine – the driver, gunner and commanding officer – would have to remain aboard the vehicle at all times. In effect, the vehicle would be able to carry *half* as many men as had originally been anticipated.

Meanwhile, as FMC slowly drowned in a sea of specifications, the army decided to rechristen its new creation in order to reflect its increased importance. Choosing the name of a distinguished general, Omar Bradley, they called it the Bradley Fighting Vehicle.

The Bradley Fighting Vehicle, when it finally emerged (after much prodding from Congress), was a kind of hybrid between a traditional battlefield taxi and a full-blown tank. Ten feet tall, and weighing 50,000 lb, it was, however, less well armed than a tank (only a 25 mm gun) and naturally more vulnerable (higher and less heavily armoured). 'If it gets blown up there where everybody can see it, it does not make any difference how sophisticated the gun is or anything else,' said Senator Sam Nunn, one of Capitol Hill's most respected defence experts, in June 1983. He might have added that if the Bradley is hit, it will burn, very fast: it is largely made of aluminium. Another Senator, Gary Hart, has described it as a 'powder keg'. Moreover it is so cumbersome that the C141 aircraft intended to carry it will only hold one at a time. And even getting one Bradley into a C141 is hard enough: it took, according to one test, 153 minutes in all: 72 of them spent unbolting the side armour and squashing the vehicle down on its springs to make it shorter, and then another 81 winching it on board because, having been squashed, it could no longer move itself. Despite its bulk, however, the vehicle, because of its elaborate weaponry and fire control systems, is so cramped inside that, as Paul Hoven of the Washington-based Project on Military Procurement put it: 'The Bradley is an infantry fighting vehicle with almost no room for the infantry.' It is also extremely heavy, and an early effort to demonstrate its supposed amphibious capability ended when a Bradley, complete with a rubberized collar round its frame, plunged into the Ohio River at Fort Knox in Kentucky – and sank like a stone.

By the time the Bradley began rolling off the production lines in the early 1980s the army were saying that its troubles were over and that all problems had been solved. 'An infantryman's dream,' said the Pentagon. But in the course of its tortuous route to the battlefield the costs of the dream had soared. Set, in 1968, to cost $108,000 ($363,000 in 1985 dollars), its price tag had risen by 1985 to $1,459,000, which meant that it was four times more expensive (allowing for inflation) than originally anticipated. Not only that: you could have bought at least eight improved versions of the M113 for one Bradley, and each of those eight would have been able to transport eleven instead of six soldiers to the battlefield ...

So what did this huge sum of money buy the army? More weapons, to be sure, and thicker armour thanks to new materials and new techniques (mainly the application of lightweight fibres). But did this really make up for all the additional money and lack of space in the Bradley? The fact is that the M113 was – sensibly – designed not to enter the thick of battle but to deposit soldiers on the edge of a combat zone. And the chances are that for all the army's plans, this is precisely what the Bradley Fighting Vehicle will have to do. Like the Divad, it has been trapped by its own technology. As the distinguished military expert, Edward Luttwak, has observed:

Unfortunately, while the Bradley was slowly being developed, becoming more and more elaborate in the process, the antitank revolution was under way. The modern rockets, less modern guns and recoilless weapons, and the many kinds of antitank missiles that now saturate the battlefield are not really very effective against the latest 50–60 ton battle tanks. But they are devastating against all tank-sized targets that do not have tank-like levels of protection. With its thin armour, the 20-ton Bradley cannot survive on the battlefield – i.e. within the inner zone of close combat – any better than the one-tenth-the-price M-113 could. But if the Bradley is employed as a mere troop carrier, to be left behind by the infantry before it enters a fight, then its million-plus dollars' worth of weapons will be wasted.

The M1 Tank

The keystone of the US army's modernization programme is its new tank, the M1 Abrams. At $2.7 million a copy, the M1, on which the army will pin its faith in the 1980s and 1990s, is very sophisticated: its fans, and there are many, describe it as 'the Cadillac of tanks'. Like the Bradley Fighting Vehicle, the M1 was a long time in the making. The American army started shopping around for a new tank in the early 1960s: first Robert McNamara, the then US defence secretary, forced it to consider jointly developing and building one with the West Germans. The advantages which would accrue from shared ammunition, spare parts, maintenance and operational procedures seemed attractive and desirable. But no one could agree on the design, and by 1969 the MBT70 (MBT for Main Battle Tank) foundered, as so many Nato projects have, on the rocks of diverging national interests. The army then redesigned the MBT70 into another tank, the XM-803, but Congress considered this too complicated and costly and gave it the thumbs down. Not until 1972 did the army finally come up with a plan which Congress found acceptable: this was for the M1.

The initial estimate of the M1's cost was about $500,000 per copy; in the early 1980s it was rolling off the production line at just over $2.7 million, though, to be fair, most of the added cost was accounted for by inflation and the sheer length of time it took to develop. Still, $2.7 million is a lot for a tank. It it worth the price?

The M1's main armament is a 105 mm gun which is capable of striking targets very accurately at great distances. Thanks to its fire control computers, its laser rangefinder and its night vision devices, it is in theory able to hit other tanks when they are almost two miles away. But is this capacity worth the money it costs and the reliability problems it creates? Some army experts doubt it. They believe that long-range tank encounters would be the exception rather than the rule. History suggests, they say, that most tank engagements take place over quite a short range – 1,000 metres or less – and certainly analysis of the tank battles of World War Two, and subsequently in Korea and the Middle East, suggest that most took place when the gunners of both sides were able to see what they were firing at. There is a natural enough reason for this, which is that tank battles rarely take place on completely flat land: trees, hills and often buildings get in the way and make it hard for tank gunners to get a definite fix on their targets. Even in the Middle East wars of 1967 and 1973, which were fought on relatively flat terrain, the average engagement range for tanks was between 300 and 800 metres, and in West Germany, where much of the terrain is hilly and wooded, and where even when it is flat – as on the North German plain – it is heavily built up, with villages and towns very close together, tanks would be greatly hampered in long-range firing. Once a war had begun, and the two sides had become closely entangled, the problems, say the sceptics, would intensify.

The defenders of the M1 argue that its computerized gear may make all the difference to Nato by giving our tanks perhaps three times as long to engage the enemy and allowing them to knock out perhaps three times as many of his tanks in each engagement. Even if true, the problem with this is that the cost of extending the range of the gun means there will be fewer tanks than there otherwise might be, and the unreliability of the hardware – which would undoubtedly become more pronounced amidst the smoke and harsh conditions of the battlefield – would reduce numbers still further. According to George Kuhn, a consultant to the conservative thinktank the Heritage Foundation, who served with the army in Vietnam: 'The overwhelming evidence is that, as in air combat, ground conflict will be won or lost in close encounters. Yet it appears that over 90 per cent of our anti armour force development funds go to achieving kills at extraordinary ranges.'

The emphasis on long-range kill is not the only questionable feature of America's new tank. The M1 can travel at 45 mph on roads (30 mph over flat ground), and accelerate from nought to 30 in 12 seconds. Some argue that this is an unnecessary luxury: no advance, or retreat, they say, is likely to necessitate travelling at 45 mph and nothing on the battlefield is likely to be able to keep up with the M1. Others argue that the capacity to 'sprint' across short distances would bolster the tank's chances of survival. But whatever the truth, the powerful Lycoming AGT 1,500 horsepower gas turbine engine, which gives the tank its power, is scarcely ideal for the battlefield. Though quiet (tank crews in Europe sometimes call it 'whispering death') it gives off tremendous heat, making the M1 especially vulnerable to heat-seeking missiles, and making it hard for infantry to shelter behind it. It caused considerable problems during development, and it burns up much more fuel than diesel engines do. (The British toyed with the idea of installing a jet engine in their own 1980s tank, the Challenger, but rejected the idea, as did the West Germans who, when offered the chance of buying the American engine – in exchange for selling the US their 120 mm tank gun – baulked at the prospect.) The gas turbine has added hugely to the M1's reliability and service problems: it takes no less than seven different types of oil, each of which has to be applied in the correct place, and it has to travel into battle with a wagon train of fuel trucks – the M1 does only one third of a mile to the gallon – technicians and spare-parts vans. This 'rolling traffic jam', as one army commander called it, would, of course, be highly vulnerable in a shooting war.

Meanwhile, doubts persist about some of the M1's gadgetry. At a 'tank Olympics' in West Germany in June 1981, for example, the Americans and the British entered tanks with laser rangefinders. (The M1 was not yet in production, but the M60A3, which the Americans used, was fitted with most of its accoutrements.) Yet the Germans, whose Leopard 1A4s and 1A3s had no thermal imagers and no laser rangefinders, won the contest, and the Belgians, similarly handicapped, came second. 'The competition is a test of marksmanship,' reported *Defense Week*, 'yet the laser rangefinder in the US and British tanks seemed to help them little.' 'The optical rangefinder is better,' a German tank commander told the magazine.

The M1 has fewer detractors than the Divad or the Bradley Fighting Vehicle. It plainly works, and its 'stabilization system', which enables it to fire while on the move, has been highly praised. So has its Chobham armour, a secret mixture of superalloy reinforced with fibreglass, invented by the British. But many wonder whether America would not be better off with greater numbers of simpler, cheaper and lighter tanks. Because of its armour and its weaponry the M1 weighs 67 tons, and that means that there is only one aircraft in the world which can carry it, the C5A Galaxy. And just as the C141 can only squeeze in one Bradley at a time, so the C5A can only carry two M1 tanks. Even fans of the M1 admit this is a major problem.

There are also serious questions about its reliability. How much trouble it will give on the battlefield is hard to predict, but early test results were not reassuring. A study by Dina Rasor of the Project on Military Procurement, the Washington pressure group, found that the M1 experienced a serious breakdown, on average, once every 34 miles. Rasor did her analysis, which was based on an internal army report, in 1980, when the M1 was still a relatively new programme. Two years later, however, things had not improved much. The General Accounting Office, a congressional watchdog, issued a study suggesting that of 39 tanks which covered 178 miles in a test at Fort Hood in Texas, only 21 completed the course without breaking down. These results may not be an accurate guide to the future, but the experience of the air force in the 1960s suggests that maintaining and repairing the army's new generation of equipment on the battlefield is going to prove excruciatingly difficult.

In the late 1960s, when the US air force were in the throes of developing a new range of fighter aircraft, air force technical experts predicted that a new avionics system then being built – the Mark II – would make the F111D a far more reliable aircraft. The Mark II was so good, it was said, that it would *increase* the mean time between system failures (MTBF) to more than 60 hours and *reduce* the 'maintenance manhours per sortie' (MMHS) to only 1.4. In fact, the Mark II turned out to experience an MTBF not of 60 hours but of less than three; and an MMHS not of 1.4 hours but of 33.6.

The example was offered to the Senate Armed Services Committee in 1980 by a Pentagon analyst called Franklin 'Chuck' Spinney. Spinney, a slim blond man who is not greatly liked by his superiors because of his tendency to deal in uncomfortable truths, also told the senators that the air force's star fighter, the F15 (which we will examine in a moment), had turned out to require over 27 maintenance manhours per flight hour compared with the 11.3 which had been predicted, and was experiencing a major systems failure once every 1.25 hours in the air – not, as promised, one every 5.6. The experience of the air force in the 1970s, therefore, scarcely augured well for the experiences of the army in the 1980s and 1990s. Besides, the business of identifying faults and repairing them on the battlefield promises to be nothing short of a nightmare.

Amidst the extraordinarily delicate, computer-driven gadgetry of weapons like the M1 are buried small black boxes called BITEs (for 'built-in test equipment'). When weaponry breaks down, BITEs are supposed to be able promptly to identify the fault, thereby saving hours of painstaking labour by mechanics. But the air force's experience of the 1970s suggests that BITEs frequently create work by suggesting that a specific part has broken down when in fact it is working perfectly, and on other occasions they fail to identify the right part when there is a snag. The Defense Science Board, a panel of scientists under the aegis of the Pentagon, reported in 1981:

> In the early 1970s, the proliferation of complexity within avionics equipments, coupled with the advancing state of digital technology, led to the birth of the 'Built-in Test (BIT)' cult. Concerns relative to the maintenance of equipment with a multiplicity of removable assemblies were quieted with the promise of automatic fault detection and isolation capabilities that stretched into the high ninety percentile range. While these promises looked good on paper and were incorporated into almost all specifications, the actual field performance has been nothing short of a disaster.

The same is likely to prove true for the bigger test sets which army maintenance engineers use to identify faults *not* identified by BITEs. Air force experience suggests that the army's logistics personnel may take up to eight times longer than planned to test the individual electronic components in major new weapons. 'The Army's new test sets may accurately isolate faults only half as often as projections allow,' writes George Kuhn. 'The sets themselves may require major repairs and not be available for testing three times more often than planned.' To take one small example, army maintenance engineers looking after the Hawk missile system in the early 1980s were spending almost a quarter of their time dealing with false alarms generated by the test equipment. Thus the army will not only face problems with its equipment: the sets supposed to identify the problems will break down a lot too, especially on the battlefield, and even when they are working they will identify problems which do not exist. The logistics problem this is likely to create on the battlefield – especially since the army will have to have available hundreds if not thousands of different electronic components for use in repairs – can be readily imagined.

The F15 Fighter

The abiding preoccupation of the Pentagon, says George Kuhn, is with 'fighting wars at a distance'. Like the creators of the Maginot Line, modern defence planners are anxious, above all, to ensure that, if war comes, loss of life is kept to a minimum. In this respect, they are pursuing a noble goal. But as the Maginot Line illustrated, elaborate attempts to reduce the risks, and 'dehumanize' war, can backfire.

The emphasis in the exotic M1 tank is on high speed, computerized fire control, 'long-range kill' and all the other wonders which science has made theoretically possible. With modern aircraft, such as the air force's F15, and its navy equivalent the F14, the pattern, as I have indicated, is much the same. The story, once again, is one of soaring costs, 'marginal' improvements and declining numbers.

The F15 is America's top-of-the-line fighter. It is astonishingly fast, with a top speed of almost three times the speed of sound, and its sophisticated avionics, data display indicators, cathode ray tubes, head up visual display for the pilot, and 45 computers are geared towards giving it the ability to shoot down other aircraft when they are still up to 80 miles away (although the missile supposed to enable it to achieve this, the AMRAAM, which we will examine in a moment, is still not in production!). It is this capacity to strike the enemy before he is even in sight which accounts most for the F15's bulky size and for its cost (almost \$40 million in 1985 prices). The F15 needs a large, powerful active radar to search the sky in front of it; it is built to carry, slung under its undercarriage, missiles which can be guided to their targets 'beyond visual range' by that radar. Not for nothing is the F15 known as the 'Eagle'.

In 1977 and 1978 the F15 Eagle was put through its paces in an unusual and ambitious series of exercises at Nellis air force base in Nevada. For almost two years, some of America's best pilots duelled with one another high above the desert, pushing both themselves and their planes to the limit. And the lessons which were learnt at Nellis base in the course of these mock engagements taught the air force some surprising things.

On one side was the F15, and its naval equivalent, the F14; on the other were the comparatively small and cheap F5 'Tiger Shark' (which the US air force does not consider good enough to be a front-line fighter, though it sells some to its allies) and the Phantom F4 – these aircraft costing a fraction as much as the F15s and F14s.

It wasn't combat, but it was intended to be the next best thing. During the exercises, every possible kind of combination was tried out: one fighter meeting another in solitary encounter; two fighters taking on two others; one fighter ambushed by two, three or four enemy ones; four taking on four, and so on. The controllers of the exercises, who monitored everything from the ground, assessing probable kills, were determined to find out exactly how America's best fighting aircraft measured up. And though you might have expected the F15s to triumph every time, it did not work out that way.

To be sure, in the one-to-one dogfights, the F15 invariably came off best, its superior technology allowing it to vanquish the less mighty F5s and F4s. But when the combat became more confused, the F15's advantages faded. When it met two or three F4s and F5s it was not nearly so successful: it might get one of the smaller planes but invariably it would be shot down by another; and when four F15s met four F5s the results were usually fairly even: in the confusion of the battle, both sides would sustain losses and the F15's technology simply did not appear to help it.

The results of the exercises at Nellis air force base have been fiercely debated since, but they amount to a sobering reminder of the limits of hi-tech defence. The organizers afterwards confessed to some shock at the outcome. Writing in the air force's *Tactical Analysis Bulletin*, one of them, Lieutenant Colonel George Dvorchak, commented that one of the findings of the tests was 'there isn't any way to out-technology the other guy. If he has some good basic capabilities, numbers are a basic driver. The reason that incremental weapons improvements wash out in the long run is that people learn to adjust to them.'

Now it must be acknowledged that the F15 pilots were denied one crucial luxury – the ability to shoot at their opposition before they could see them with the naked eye. And much of the technology which goes into the F15, as we have observed, is designed to permit it to use just such a 'beyond visual range' capability. Much of the emphasis in the F15 is on high speed, powerful radar and long-range, deadly accurate homing missiles.

But the men who staged the exercises argued that in this respect they were a fair representation of what a war would actually be like on the Central Front. Just as tank experts argue that most tank battles in history have taken place at ranges of 1,000 metres or less, so history suggests that aircraft kills are achieved when the pilots are able to see their enemy. And in a war in central Europe this would almost certainly be the case. For – and this is a crucial point – Nato does not have a common IFF – Identification Friend or Foe – system, which means that American fighter pilots, seeking to establish whether aircraft heading towards them were friendly or not, would have no foolproof way of doing so: they would be able to exchange signals with fellow American pilots but not with British, Dutch, Belgian or German ones. The dangers therefore of shooting at enemy aircraft before they become visible are readily imaginable.

There is a further problem. The long-range missiles – like the Sparrow – introduced into the inventories of the US air force and navy in the 1960s and 1970s have proved less than satisfactory in combat. Unlike shorter-range, heat-seeking missiles such as the Sidewinder (essentially a very simple invention), they are full of complex, delicate mechanisms and inherently less reliable; they are also easier to foil through countermeasures or evasive action. Enemy pilots can see long-range missiles approaching and have more time to try and avoid them. By flying in pairs, it would seem, they also have a good chance of foxing the Sparrow. Tests showed that the Sparrow, if faced with two targets, would sometimes split the difference – confused, according to air force sources, by the contradictory messages emanating from the two targets, it would be unable to work out which it ought to hit and end up flying harmlessly in between. In Vietnam the US air force had to fire 100 Sparrows for every eight planes they actually brought down, whereas heat-seeking missiles brought down 16 per 100 firings, twice as good a strike rate.

Besides, to fire the Sparrow, or other radar-guided missiles, pilots have to switch on their own 'active radar', which searches the sky for enemy aircraft but also risks giving away their position. Switching on an active radar, in the view of one air force expert, is like switching on a torch in a darkened room when you know there's a killer inside: you may well get shot at before you can fire a shot, and pilots will be chary of using active radar in battles over the Central Front. Modern radar-guided missiles are also wildly expensive: the Phoenix, for example, which has a range of 80 miles and is carried by the F14, cost $1.85 million apiece in 1985, making it a difficult missile for pilots to practise with.

An even more sophisticated missile in the works for both air force and navy is the AMRAAM, or 'advanced medium-range air-to-air missile'. This is what the F15 was developed to carry. It is intended to have a 'fire and forget capability', meaning that pilots will not have to keep their active radar locked on to a target until the missile has actually struck, as they are forced to do with both Sparrow and Phoenix. In theory, AMRAAM will also enable pilots to fire several missiles simultaneously at different enemy targets. But the AMRAAM has had a troubled history: there have been disputes about testing, about whether pilots will be able to manage the complicated 'multi-shot' sequence, about whether the new missile will be able to perform in the face of enemy electronic jamming, and of course about whether it is necessary at all. Meanwhile, the price has steadily climbed. Once intended to be a cheaper alternative to Sparrow, it now looks like being far more expensive. In 1979, the then assistant defence secretary for programme analysis and evaluation, Russell Murray II, pointed out that it was set to cost 50 per cent more than Sparrow which, he said, 'is already so expensive that we are not able to afford more than two missile loads per F15'. The AMRAAM, Murray predicted in 1982, will turn out to be 'an expensive bird with limited utility'. Nothing has happened since then to invalidate that judgement, and even if

AMRAAM can eventually be made to work – even if it proves affordable – why does it have to be fired from *a fighter*? Why can't it be slung underneath huge transport or reconnaissance aircraft like C130s, or AWACs, or even (though this would dismay the air force) from *ground* launchers?

As a result of the exercises in the Nevada desert, other attributes of the F15 also began to look more questionable: its enormous speed for example. The F15 can travel at almost three times the speed of sound, but how often would that kind of speed be required? As far as I can tell, there is simply no need for fighters to be able to fly faster than Mach 1.5. The faster you go, the more fuel you burn up, and pilots have a saying: you only reach top speed in order to run out of fuel. Many, indeed, believe that agility counts for more than a high top speed in aerial combat – a successful plane, they say, should be agile and small.

Small the F15 is not. Geared for speed, it has a large profile. It can carry bulky engines and in particular a substantial radar – in order to be able to pick up an aircraft 40 miles away, it has to have a 36-inch diameter radar disc in the nose, which automatically means that the nose must be considerably broader than it otherwise might be. As Bob Fay, an air force officer who monitored the Nevada exercises, put it: 'When you're up in the sky searching for something in that grey mass or blue mass, your eyes tend to gravitate to the first object you see. And you can see large planes quicker than you can see small airplanes. Well, that's not too bad if you're a small airplane driver, because the large airplanes are – the enemy. But if you're a large airplane driver and all you're seeing is large airplanes, who are your wingmen or your colleagues, then you're in trouble.'

In the melee of a war above the European battlefield, small, agile planes, with the surprise their size would help them bestow, would have certain advantages. In a war against the Russians, single long-range dogfights would almost certainly be the exception rather than the rule. As Lt. Col. Dvorchak puts it: 'In massed fighting, similar to the swarm warfare everyone says would be likely in European battle, confusion plays a much larger role and exotic weaponry a much smaller one – most of the kills came [in the Nevada exercise] from visual sightings, as they had in the dogfights in World War Two (and Vietnam), rather than from the elegant, computerized systems. High performance capabilities, so impressive on paper, are blunted by the disorderly circumstances of war.'

Critics make another point. Even if the F15's 'high performance capabilities' might, in certain circumstances, make a difference, these very capabilities require considerable practice to use properly, especially as the F15, unlike the previous-generation F4 Phantom, only has one pilot (meaning that there is one less pair of eyes, and even more dependence on complex cockpit controls). I have quoted the view that only Israeli pilots train intensely enough to get the maximum benefit out of the F15: American pilots find it hard to get enough time in the air to do so. When the budget is squeezed, it is usually training – hours spent in the air, or at sea, or in the field – which suffers. During the 1970s, the number of flying hours allotted to each pilot in the US air force was cut dramatically, from 20 or 25 per month to 16 or 17 per month (partly as a result of the steep rise in the price of oil). And though flying hours rose sharply in the early 1980s, when the Reagan build-up began, they look certain, at the time of writing, to plunge again as the defence budget comes under increasing strain in the second half of the 1980s.

The real sacrifice forced on the air force by the stress on hi tech is numbers: fewer and fewer aircraft are available year by year for taking on the Russians. The F15 needs twice as much time at the depot as the Phantom F4; it needs almost 50 hours of servicing for every hour in the air.* The F15 is an unusually complex aircraft, and its complexity is evident in almost every aspect, from its avionics, which cost 1,000 times as much as World War Two avionics, to its engines, which cost 50 times as much. Its fuel control alone consists of 4,500 parts, four and a half times more than the fuel control of the 1950s vintage F4 Phantom which proved so successful against it at Nellis air force base. The radios and radars used by commercial airliners average about 800 hours between breakdowns, according to a report by the systems analyst Pierre Sprey: their military counterparts, which cost between ten and 100 times as much, average five to ten hours. So the total number of F15s possessed by the air force should not be mistaken for the total number which, on any given day, will be available to fight in a war.

That total number, however, is not very high to start with – about 750 in 1985. The navy have the same problems with their equivalent and equally expensive plane, the F14. Given the staggering costs of both aircraft, this is not surprising. In World War Two the US navy's main fighter was the Hellcat. It cost $65,000 apiece; the country could afford to buy 12,000 of them. The modern navy can afford to buy just 900 F14s. More generally, $7 billion in 1952 bought 6,300 jet fighters; nowadays, the Pentagon is paying $8 billion for just 270. In 1983, the navy and air force together bought just 399 planes, less than the number it lost through accidents and old age.

Norman Augustine, the boss of Martin Marietta, a major defence contractor, has a famous 'law' for the direction in which complex technology is taking the US air force. If the costs of military hardware continue to rise at the rate at which they have been rising for the last 50

---

* When a squadron of 24 F15s moves to a new base, it requires a total of 29 C141 transport planes to follow behind, bringing support equipment and mechanics.

years or so, he says, 'in the year 2054 the entire defence budget will
purchase just one tactical aircraft. This aircraft will have to be shared by
the Air Force and the Navy three and a half days per week, except for
leap years, when it will be made available to the Marines for the extra
day.'

By the mid-1970s, the rocketing costs and complexity, coupled in their
view with declining performance, led a small band of air force insiders to
write a proposal for an alternative fighter. The dissidents, among them a
former fighter pilot called John Boyd, and a group of Pentagon officials
and consultants believed that fighter development since the early 1960s
had been going in precisely the opposite of the right direction. In the
'lightweight fighter' they proposed the emphasis would be purely on agility:
doubtful that all the beyond-visual-range technology of the F15 would be
much use in a real war, and aware that a plane carrying fewer 'black
boxes' and long-range missiles would be much more agile, they envisaged
a plane which would be able to do only Mach 1.6 but could out-accelerate
and out-turn any existing aircraft at all speeds below that.

The lightweight fighter ended up as the F16, now undoubtedly the best
fighter in the US inventory, and costing just over half the price of the F15,
at $16 million a copy. It might have been cheaper than that, except that
the air force crammed back into it many of the gadgets the so-called
'fighter mafia' had scrupulously removed, such as active radar and long-
range missiles. But the US is now buying a 'mix' of F15s and F16s,
otherwise the financial picture would look even worse than it does.

The Tornado

America is not the only country to pin its faith on super-sophisticated
fighter aircraft: Europe has followed its example.

In the late 1960s, three European countries, Britain, Germany and Italy,
developed plans for a fighter bomber which came to be called Tornado.
Once described by the former German chancellor, Helmut Schmidt, as
'the greatest technological project since the birth of Christ', the idea behind
Tornado was that by working together all three countries would save
money: production lines could be longer and thus the unit costs of each
plane would be smaller. In an alliance full of unnecessary duplication in
weapons procurement, the Tornado, it was hoped, would demonstrate the
benefits of collaboration.

Like so many American weapons systems, however, the Tornado was
plagued by spiralling costs and inefficiency. The problems once again arose
from competing and complicated specifications: each country wanted a
plane with different attributes. The British RAF wanted Tornado for two

roles: long-range strike and defence of the homeland; the Italians wanted an 'air superiority' fighter like the F15 or F16; and the Germans wanted a plane for close air support on the battlefield. So the plane had to be light and agile enough to achieve 'air superiority' in combat, while at the same time able to carry enough fuel and payload for long-range strike, and, in order to operate on the battlefield, be capable of short take-off and landing. Thus Tornado became a truly multi-role aircraft (though the British developed a separate 'interceptor' version for strategic air defence).

Meanwhile, the costs have shot up. In 1970 for example, the German Luftwaffe estimated that Tornados would cost them DM15 million (£3.5 million) each. Ten years later that 'fly away' price (extras not included) had risen to at least DM35.2 million each (£8.2 million), and the overall system price (including spares, cost of pilot training, etc.) to DM67.36 million (£15.8 million). In Britain it was the same story, and in all three countries the plane produced enormous pressures on defence budgets. During the 1980s the price continued to rise, and the cost of Tornado is now roughly equivalent to the cost of the F15. It has become the biggest single European defence project of the last fifteen years.

Of all the roles for which it was intended, Tornado is clearly best suited for 'deep strike'. Expensive and full of modern technology, it is ill-equipped for the role the Germans initially had in mind: close air support. Its technology is primarily intended, as one British Air Marshal points out, to enable it to reach and hit 'critical military targets behind the front line such as concentrations of armour, headquarters and airfields in all weathers, day or night'.

Thus Tornado, like the F15, reflects the trend in Nato's attitude to air power. The emphasis is on long-range striking power – hitting the enemy before he can even reach the battlefield. In the air force view of World War Three, according to defence analyst William Kaufman, the idea is to create such havoc for the enemy behind his lines that his front-line forces 'will simply wither on the vine' and the various Nato armies will, if not quite reduced to passive spectators, be left with a relatively small role to play. Indeed, Kaufman estimates that a mere 640 aircraft on the Central Front would have as their primary role 'close air support' of ground forces: the remaining 2,400 which would be initially available for war would be dedicated to long-range missions.

This arrangement strikes analysts like Kaufman as absurd. They argue, with good reason, that Nato ground forces would benefit from many more aircraft dedicated to their support – and to killing enemy tanks. Yet the American army, for example, is forbidden to purchase aircraft for its own protection. At a series of high-level meetings which began at Key West in Florida in 1948, the individual American services were allocated their postwar roles and missions. Eventually, as a result of these meetings,

Congress created the US air force as a separate entity (previously it had been part of the army), and gave it control of all land-based aircraft, with the exception of training planes – and helicopters.

The army has therefore been forced to rely very heavily on helicopters for close air support (and now has some 9,000 of them), though many experts argue that they are much less effective in this role than planes. But the air force has the planes, and it has consistently shown itself unenthusiastic about helping the army.

The A10

The air force, however, does have one tank-busting aircraft: the A10. Regarded by many defence experts as one of the most effective weapons in the US arsenal – and a weapon which illustrates sensible, economical use of new technology – it was built in the early 1970s, in part, it seems, in response to the rapid growth of the army's helicopter fleet. The air force, evidently concerned that the army's demands for increasingly exotic helicopters might affect their own budget, believed they could design a plane which would perform the 'close air support' role more cheaply and more effectively. They were right.

The plane they came up with is indubitably ugly: barrel-shaped, with short stubby wings, and protruding from under those wings, two cannons and eight missiles; it is a single-seater and the cockpit is surprisingly free of any kind of gadgetry. Set against sleek, elegant monsters like the F15, it looks like a relic of World War Two. It cannot fly very fast – less than the speed of sound (pilots joke that when flying it they are in danger of being hit in the rear by birds), but it can stay in the air a long time and fly very low. It is agile, and it is heavily armoured. It is also, in the view of some experts, the most lethal tank-killing aircraft in the world. The reason is that its primary weapon is not a missile but a simple cannon.

This cannon – called the GAU8/A – has seven barrels, and the 30 mm armour-piercing shells it uses, made of 'depleted' uranium of low radioactivity, are an example of high technology which works. The shells are heavy, twice as heavy as lead, and move at enormous speed – 3,240 feet per second – enabling them to cut through the side and rear armour of tanks with relative ease. They can be fired at a rate of 4,200 rounds per minute. And because they are extraordinarily cheap, they are affordable in large quantities: each shell costs $20, which means that a 30-round burst – judged adequate, in most circumstances, to cripple a tank – costs only $600, less than the cost of one of the navy's ashtrays, and the same as just three of the Divad's 'proximity rounds'.

In a series of tests at Nellis air force base in Nevada in 1975 and 1976,

A10s destroyed six out of ten Soviet T62 battle tanks, by striking them in the rear or in the sides, and put the other four out of action. As Morton Mintz noted in the *Washington Post*: 'The 60 per cent kill rate was four times higher than had been predicted by computer studies during development of the gun . . .'

The only problem with the A10, which itself costs only just over $3 million, about a fifteenth the cost of the F15, is that the gun cannot be used for 'long-range kills'. The attraction of missiles is that they enable the pilot to fire long before he reaches his target, thus theoretically giving him a better chance of being brought down by anti-aircraft fire. This argument might make sense if pilots were confident that air-delivered anti-tank missiles would work properly, but as we will see in a moment they have little reason to be confident. 'If the question is, which would you rather take in against the target of interest, I would unhesitatingly say guns,' says Colonel John Verdi, a retired marine corps weapons expert, who led one of the first marine fighter squadrons in the Vietnam war and who holds the Legion of Merit and 30 other medals. 'You have to have a gun on a plane that's going to fight somebody. Anything else is absurd.' And although Verdi acknowledges that guns mean you have to risk going in very close, the problem with 'standoff' missiles is that if they miss *you will probably still end up getting close for your second shot*. The chances of their missing are substantial. So the argument for having cheap, simple, reliable, effective aircraft which can do the job and which are affordable in huge numbers is strong.

This kind of logic, however, counts for little in the modern American military, or in Congress. The A10 was never regarded with much enthusiasm by air force leaders, who had kept the project simple and cheap – in large part, critics charge, because they did not want to waste money on the unglamorous mission of protecting the 'grunts' on the battlefield. In 1981, for example, the air force tried to drop 60 A10s it was due to purchase (to his credit, Caspar Weinberger, the defence secretary, promptly reinstated them). And in 1982, by which time the air force had acquired some 800 (though it had managed to hive off 72 to the Air National Guard, the air force reserve), the programme finally died.

Just as the A10 never excited Pentagon imaginations, nor did its gun. Air force leaders 'don't like the gun', says Thomas Hahn, a one-time member of the House Armed Services Committee staff. 'Missilery is what people are all enthused about.' For politicians fascinated by glamorous hi-tech weaponry, guns, as another analyst put it, 'are far too simple'. Much more stirring was the A10's alternative armament, the Maverick.

The Maverick

The Maverick is everything the GAU8/A is not. It is expensive, complicated and it doesn't work – precisely (as will now be evident) the characteristics likely to ensure it a long and successful life in the Pentagon procurement system. It costs 100 times as much as the 30-round burst from the GAU8/A required to fulfil a similar mission. Its testing record is a joke. It has attacked telephone poles, fence posts and rocks. And in its second, even more sophisticated version it promises to be even worse than in its first.

The Maverick has its origins in the mid-1960s. As the West sought to place greater reliance on conventional weapons, so the air force decided it needed a stand-off 'air to ground' weapon which would enable its planes to attack ground targets while staying away from the thickest air defences. The army had the 20 mm Vulcan, the predecessor to the Divad Gun, but though this worked quite respectably against aircraft, it 'pelted a tank as ineffectually as raindrops pelt a window'. Clearly what was needed was a lethal missile which could pelt tanks very effectively from a safe distance.

The missile which came to be called the Maverick was designed to be slung under the wings of tactical aircraft. It was to be 'television guided'; that is to say, it was to have a tiny video camera in its nose which would enable it to spot and then home in on an enemy tank. It was a beguiling idea, very much in tune with Congress's love affair with hi tech, and the air force got the go-ahead. Eventually the air force had spent $500 million on some 20,000 of the eight-foot-long, first generation Mavericks and sent them to Europe and – most importantly – to South-East Asia.

There was, of course, a war going on in South-East Asia, giving the Maverick early and ample opportunity to demonstrate its capacity to kill tanks. Instead of doing that, according to General John W. Vogt, who commanded US air operations in Vietnam, it proved almost totally useless. 'Clearly it didn't do the job out there,' he said in early 1982. And in bad weather, he added (fog or heavy rain), 'this kind of weapon craps out completely'. One problem with the Maverick was its tiny field of view: the sensor in its nose can see only about a three-degree-wide segment in front of it. 'It's like looking at the world through the end of a drinking straw,' according to one weapons analyst; thus, unless the missile was lined up very accurately in the first place it would almost certainly miss.

A second problem was described by General Vogt, who tried to use the Maverick to stop the enemy on the Ho Chi Minh Trail. To use a Maverick, a pilot had to climb to a higher altitude in order to have a straight clear view of his target. The TV sensor in the Maverick's nose needed a clear contrast between target and background if it was to find its target. But according to Vogt the 'pop-up' manoeuvre used by Maverick-carrying aircraft was usually sufficient to alert the Viet Cong to move exposed tanks in amidst foliage or into the shade, thus degrading the visual contrast between target and background and making it hard for the Maverick to strike home. (According to a later set of tests, indeed, the Maverick's sensor only locked on to a tank which was camouflaged, or close to a tree line, less than five per cent of the time. Against moving tanks, the outcome was even worse: the Maverick never locked on to its target long enough to hit it.)

Yet the fact that it did not work in tests or, according to a top general, in combat was not enough to deter the air force. By the early 1970s, they were developing a new version of the Maverick, this one a 'heat-seeking' infrared model which would be able to work in the darkness and have a much longer range – up to eight miles. Congressional testimony and other analyses on the new missile already run to thousands of pages, and by all accounts it has been one long history of trouble, delay and failure. To fire the new Maverick, the pilot has to study a small five-inch video screen in his cockpit. On this he is supposed to be able to detect his targets – enemy tanks – but what tests showed was that the images appearing on the pilot's tiny scope made it very difficult to distinguish between all kinds of 'hot objects' (sun-warmed rocks, bonfires, burning armour hulks, even flare grenades) and actual tanks. According to Thomas Hahn, the former staff member of the House Armed Services Committee and a physicist: 'What you get on your display is a bunch of bright spots ... You don't know what you're looking at ... If you can't determine there's a gun barrel, all you can determine is that there's a blob and it's hot.'

Even on a test range at Fort Polk, Louisiana (in February 1977), when the pilots knew exactly where the tanks would be, and where there were no competing 'hot targets' to confuse the Maverick, the success rate was hardly encouraging. Of 123 passes made by pilots, less than 60 per cent produced 'lock-ons' (i.e. occasions when the missile 'recognized' and homed in on its target without losing sight of it). A year later, at a series of tests in West Germany, the Maverick fared even worse: again, pilots knew exactly where the 'enemy' tanks would be: the record shows that 317 practice runs simply were not counted by the air force, and of the 215 which were, only 113, or 53 per cent, achieved 'lock-ons'. Despite urgings from the congressional watchdog, the General Accounting Office, to stage a test in 'a realistic battlefield environment', and unease among many congressional staffs, the air force pressed on. Eventually, between October 1981 and January 1982 they scheduled five operational live firings: one aborted, two failed and the other two were finally postponed. After this, it seemed, the air force decided to think again: the decision to produce the 61,000 new Mavericks the air force wanted was put off indefinitely. In

1984, however, it was decided that the Maverick Mark Two would overcome its problems, and Congress gave it the go-ahead once again.

The Viper

The preoccupation with complex tank-killing weapons extends far beyond the Maverick. I will end this dismal catalogue by glancing at three other examples, all of which have been developed by the US army. The first, the Viper, is a weapon which was intended to be a lightweight, shoulder-fired, bazooka-type rocket for use by the infantry. It was priced at $76 apiece when first proposed in 1976, though over the next six years its price rose tenfold, partly because of pernickety Pentagon specifications (relating to maximum weight and noise) and partly because its manufacturers, General Dynamics (with the army's blessing), tinkered endlessly with a quite ingenious original design.

But although the Viper's cost had soared by 1982 to $787 a round, its chances of knocking out Soviet tanks dropped equally rapidly. It had become clear that the rocket's small charge had no hope of penetrating the frontal armour of the T64s, T72s and T80s which were rapidly coming to constitute the sharp end of the Red Army tank force. The army's response to this discovery, in 1980, was not to scrap the project but to 'clarify' the Viper's mission. That meant reduce it. From now on the Viper would only have to perform against the older T55 and T62 tanks, or strike modern tanks in more vulnerable places than the front. And while it is true that the US army has had persistent trouble attempting to devise an anti-tank missile which can penetrate the frontal armour of modern Soviet tanks, and while it is also true that the attempt to devise 'risk-free' weapons is often, as we have seen, a self-defeating one, Viper does seem to have had little to recommend it (compared, for example, with the more cumbersome but much more effective TOW). Many former army men believe that its newly 'clarified' mission scarcely justified the investment, especially since the Viper's effective range was only about 250 yards. Their view was summed up by Hyman Baras, the director of Land Warfare Audits at the General Accounting Office, who wrote a critical report on the Viper in 1981:

> I'd have grave doubts about hanging around with my Viper until the enemy tank is only 250 yards away. For one thing, if I miss, they're going to blast away with machine guns, and I've had it. And if I have to attack the tank from the side or rear, what they're saying is that I have to ambush a tank. Now that strikes me as a very risky

thing, particularly if I have a low probability of killing it. I think I'd want to be out of there. I'd want to be as far away as I could be.

Another critic went further, calling the Viper a 'Medal of Honor' weapon, meaning you would only use it if you were prepared to die. Congress became concerned about the tendency of its launch tube to explode during testing. When the White House budget director, David Stockman, talked of the 'swamp of $10–$20–$30 billion of waste' in the Pentagon budget in a magazine interview in 1981, it seems likely that the Viper was one of the projects he was referring to. The marines, unlike the army, turned the Viper down. 'You want something that hurts the enemy,' said Senator Warren Rudman, 'not just pisses him off.' Nevertheless the army committed itself to buying almost 650,000 Vipers. It was only after Senate and congressional critics of the weapon had forced the army to test it against cheaper, European-made anti-tank weapons, that the army cancelled the project. That was in 1983, by which time the initially $76 'fire and discard' Viper had risen to a staggering $1,200 a copy.

The Copperhead

A weapon the army have stolidly refused to cancel, however, is the Copperhead, a 'smart' artillery projectile of dubious merit. An army brochure about Copperhead boasts that 'its accuracy is so good that it can literally drop down the open hatch of a moving tank' – though there was little evidence of this in its testing programme – and the concept behind Copperhead has given critics a field day.

Essentially, it involves a complicated and exacting sequence. A soldier crouching on the forward edge of the battlefield selects his target, an enemy tank, and aims a so-called 'laser designator' at it. He then focuses a laser beam on the tank, which is reflected skyward, enabling the Copperhead missile, fired from several miles away, to sense the beam as it descends and 'ride' it down to the tank. That, at least, is the theory. The critics are troubled by three things.

In the first place, the whole operation depends on a lonely soldier on the battlefield who will be perilously exposed. Unlike the target spotter of old who called in artillery – and who was equipped simply with a pair of field glasses and a radio – his successor in today's US army would have to keep a laser beam on his target until the Copperhead struck home – a dangerous exercise, since the laser would quickly give his position away. The actual 'designator', besides, has been criticized in an official army report as being 'too bulky and heavy' and presenting 'too high a silhouette', requiring 'the operator to assume a sitting or kneeling position'. The

second problem (also identified in the internal report) is that Copperhead
will only function in perfect weather: laser beams have trouble guiding it
through mist, rainfall or even smoke. Critics point out that mist and
rainfall are not unknown in Europe, and smoke not unusual on a battlefield.
Third, even the army has admitted that the coordination between the
artillery battery in the rear and the soldier up front would have to be
'excessive', especially for 'a fast-moving battlefield or in high-stress
situations'.

Finally, some critics – notably the Project on Military Procurement –
complain that the Copperhead has a minimum range of one kilometre and
cannot be used if a tank is closer. 'Thus,' says the project, 'it will be
unusable for approximately 85 per cent of real tank engagements.'

While on the subject of Copperhead it is worth noting another US army
device which may be used in conjunction with it. This is a new 'remotely
piloted vehicle' (RPV), currently being developed and now, after years of
gold-plating and soaring costs, expected to enter service in 1989.

Like many of the army's weapons, the new RPV arose from a simple –
and sensible – idea. RPVs, essentially radio-controlled model aircraft, can
be extraordinarily effective on a modern battlefield. They can play a variety
of roles – eavesdropping on enemy radio traffic, jamming enemy radio
transmissions, delivering missiles, and, most important of all, taking
pictures of enemy emplacements. They survive by being small enough to
escape being tracked by radar or hit by missiles, and by operating beyond
the range of anti-aircraft guns; their virtue is (or should be) that they are
cheap, available in large numbers and expendable.

The US made limited use of fairly basic RPVs in Vietnam, but it is the
Israelis who have best understood their value, and sought to exploit it.
The Israeli air force bought a cheap and simple RPV in the 1970s. It was
armed with a zoom-lens video camera which could relay back live pictures;
it cost about $40,000 per plane; and it proved highly effective. In 1982,
the Israelis used their RPVs to achieve detailed reconnaissance of the
Syrian anti-aircraft batteries in the Bekaa Valley and to jam Syrian radar;
largely because of this they destroyed the 18 batteries they identified within
an hour. When the US attempted to destroy new Syrian batteries the
following year they did so without the help of RPVs and lost two planes
in the process. As a result, according to an investigation by the ABC
television programme, *20/20*, the US military borrowed several Israeli
RPVs and used them to good effect in the Lebanon. (The RPVs tracked
the salvos of the battleship *New Jersey* and enabled the ship's gunners to
correct their aim.)

So why did the US army not simply buy its RPVs from the Israelis, or
at the very least imitate their design? The answer is that the army was
already in the throes of developing its own model: an RPV with a

difference, called Aquila, the Latin for eagle. Initially, when the army began serious work on this in the mid-1970s, it was hoped that the Aquila might cost only $100,000, which, though expensive compared with the Israeli RPV, was not excessive by US army standards. Since the mid-1970s, however, the Aquila has been transformed.

First it has become extraordinarily complex. Instead of following the trail blazed by Israel (making a basic RPV and developing different models for more specialized roles), the US army has created an 'all-purpose' RPV designed to perform all kinds of different roles, one of which is designating targets by laser for attack by Copperhead or other military shells. According to *International Defense Review*, it is crammed full of electronics and carries a sophisticated data link 'including two steerable EHF antennae in dorsal and ventral thimble radomes. It has its own strapdown intertial-navigation system and it is nuclear hardened.' And that is not all.

> The airframe for Aquila is highly blended and has an ultra-low radar cross-section, which imposes restrictions on payload weight and volume, so that any payload has to be specially designed and developed. Aquila has also been designed for fully automatic recovery, requiring the development of a special electro-optical precision guidance system to steer the vehicle into the landing net.
>
> Finally, Aquila was designed from the outset to meet all US army specifications for compatibility with other systems, operability in all climates, and quality of construction.

Despite – or more probably because of – all this gear the Aquila has had a sorry track record. Ever since the mid-1970s, test models have kept crashing. A champion flier of model aeroplanes, Garry Korpi, who was a test 'pilot' for the Aquila programme in 1975–6, described some of the early crashes to ABC's *20/20*, suggesting that several could have been avoided had the army taken more precautions and that the army might have wasted rather less money had they not insisted on installing expensive video cameras in the test models. But the crashes did not end in the mid-1970s. Under the Freedom of Information Act, *20/20* obtained actual test footage of much more recent test flights which showed that, though some worked well – with the Aquila taking off, completing its mission and then landing safely in a net – others did not. In 1984, for example, according to the film, at least three went badly wrong, two of these ending in crashes.

This might not matter much, had the army stuck to its original budget. But by 1984, the Aquila was no longer costing $100,000 a plane. That price had now risen to $1,000,000 – a staggering increase, even allowing for inflation. Moreover the army, by now, had spent some $700 million on the programme, and after eleven years of development, was still scarcely ready to deliver. Indeed, according to a special army investigation, so many Aquilas had crashed in tests by the end of 1985 that there was some doubt as to whether there were enough left to complete the test programme. Whether the US army will get the funds to make that possible is, at the time of writing, unclear. But even if they do, the point of the device has long ago been lost. RPVs make sense if they are cheap and simple, and Aquila now represents a quite valueless investment. Indeed, Aquila and Copperhead together, one a simple device wrecked by gold-plating, the other a complicated missile dependent on an over-elaborate firing sequence, seem destined to do more damage to the army's budget than they do to any enemy.

Hellfire and the Apache

Working on the same principles as the Copperhead, but on a much grander scale, is the army's new missile-firing helicopter programme.

Since the late 1970s both superpowers' sides have been putting tank-killing missiles on helicopters, but the project the US army is planning to have operational by the late 1980s is threatening to become the most exotic – and expensive – in its entire modernization programme.

The missile-firing helicopter has been code-named the AH64 Apache, and as helicopters go it is bulky, heavily armoured and bristling with weapons. The original idea was that it should fire TOW missiles, but in 1976 this changed: the TOW concept fell by the wayside to be replaced by a much more glamorous weapons system called Hellfire. Hellfire meant that a designator in the helicopter would have to fasten a laser beam on an enemy tank; then the missile would be fired down the beam. But Hellfire required a helicopter with a special turret filled with exotic gadgetry and since, by the early 1980s the Apache helicopter was set to cost $11 million apiece, the army felt that they had better think again. The result was yet another change: instead of there being one helicopter involved there would now be two: the Apache, which would actually fire the missile, and a smaller, cheaper, 'scout' helicopter which would fulfil a similar function to the Copperhead's laser designator.

More precisely, the system would work like this: the scout helicopter would hide behind trees and use a novel electronic periscope perched just above its rotors to spot tanks and to fasten a laser beam on one of them. The Apache would pop up from behind a tree or hill, fire a missile locked on to the scout's beam, then drop down again out of danger.

Whether this system will prove successful is anyone's guess. But it would appear to suffer from many of the same defects as the Copperhead, and the small, 'cheap' scout helicopter – originally designed to cost $700,000 –

was by 1983 set to cost $4.3 million a copy, partly because of the complex engineering involved in its pop-up periscope with its TV sight, infrared sight for night operations, laser designator and laser rangefinder. That means that the whole package – Apache, scout plus Hellfire – will come to about $16 million.

Helicopters, bravely piloted, provide a vital means of transporting soldiers to the front end of a battlefield, and armed with sensible weapons, especially in hilly or tree-covered country, they are potentially useful tank-killers. But how frequently will helicopters need – or be able – to strike enemy forces while they are six kilometres away (the principal justification for Hellfire: TOW missiles can only manage four kilometres)? Not often, I suggest. Yet in order to be cost-effective the Apache AH64 will have to kill a very large number of tanks before being knocked out, since at the current $16 million estimate it will cost more than eight times as much as the M1 – and the M1, of course, is the world's most expensive tank. At that price, how many Apaches will the army end up being able to buy?

The weapons I have described in this chapter are, for the most part, egregious examples of gold-plating, baffling complexity, spiralling costs and dubious effectiveness. Some, as we have seen, scarcely work at all, let alone yielding advantages commensurate with their cost. I do not mean to suggest that every American weapon – or every European one – is as over-technologized as those we have examined. Clearly they are not, or we would be in dire straits indeed. But these weapons are indicative of a trend, and it is not a healthy one. A prominent military analyst once observed that too much faith in hi-tech wizardry might one day mean that we in the West would be reduced to depending on an army of men clad in skins and wielding clubs. 'Indeed,' he added, 'those who come to rely too much on technology may find one morning that just such an army has captured them, lock stock and laser.'

3

People

'We can spend billions on the most modern and sophisticated weaponry,' commented a Republican senator in 1981, 'but in the final analysis it is the infantryman, sailor, pilot and medic that will determine our nation's strength.'

History suggests that the senator is right. Yet the prevailing philosophy seems quite different. The US defence establishment appears vastly more concerned about weapons than it is about the human aspects of war. Indeed, the obsession with hi-tech gadgetry suggests a belief that somehow war can be 'dehumanized', and that through an array of 'smart' hardware, the chances of victory can be enhanced and the risks to human life minimized.

Consequently, a gulf has opened up between the sophistication of modern equipment and the skills of the modern servicemen who are called upon to operate and maintain it. And while the aim in creating much modern equipment, it is true, has been to install gadgets which require little or no skill in operation, the gadgets have scarcely compensated for the problems which have beset the American military during the 1960s, 1970s and early 1980s. These problems have been many and varied: low morale, inadequate training, low pay, poor leadership. The problems intensified when the draft was wound up after Vietnam, and the American middle class virtually opted out of the military. At the beginning of the 1980s, the service chiefs were unanimous in telling Congress that they faced grave problems with personnel: the army was declared 'hollow', the navy was said to be suffering a 'haemorrhage of talent' and the air force was in 'critical' condition.

Under President Reagan, things began to improve (indeed some believe that boosting the sense of purpose and morale in America's armed services has been one of his most significant achievements). But the improvements were inevitably limited. The prevailing philosophy did not change. And the problems run very deep.

The classic case, of course, is the US army. After the Vietnam war, the army's morale and confidence plummeted, and the drive for sophisticated hardware scarcely compensated for this. As a former Pentagon official, Thomas Etzold, noted in 1981: 'America's much-vaunted computer edge loses some of its keenness in the face of ... reports that 77 per cent of the people who operate computer and automated systems in the field failed their skill qualification test in 1978.' Almost four fifths of the soldiers who had to operate and maintain sophisticated equipment, in other words, were unable to do so properly. And as Etzold added, the 1978 test occurred a year before the American army took in one of the poorest intakes – in terms of intellectual calibre – in its history. Another survey in the late 1970s found that 40 per cent of new recruits to the army were unable to read above seventh grade (12-year-old) level – that is, inadequately: not for nothing was the US army dubbed the world's largest remedial reading programme. Worse, units stationed in Europe were plagued with alcoholism, even drug use. In Nato exercises they rarely distinguished themselves. Often they finished last.

The top brass have struggled to put things right. In 1982, for example, the army unveiled a new doctrine: after a history of fighting 'attrition' wars – heavy firepower allied to mass production back home – the plan, from now on, would be to rely on more subtle tactics. In a 90-page green and yellow booklet the army outlined its thinking: highly mobile units would operate independently, and be prepared to yield ground temporarily if need be before mounting swift counter-attacks. 'Airland Battle', as the new doctrine was called, represented the outcome of the army's soul-searching since the Vietnam war and had much to recommend it. But there was one fundamental snag, as critics were quick to point out. Manoeuvre warfare is a high-risk strategy. It envisages fighting battles without flanks and risking being cut off from supply lines in the rear. As defence consultant Steven Canby has observed, it requires high standards of training and very different equipment to the kind the army is buying.

The army has tried to improve its training. At Fort Irwin in California, for example, it has established what is intended to be the most realistic training area in the world: in a thousand square miles of desert, American army units come to practise against a division which imitates Soviet tactics and whose armoured vehicles, though American, are 'visually modified' to look like Soviet ones. The men who make up the division even wear red stars on the front of their black berets. With the help of video cameras and radio relay stations, which monitor all the activity, the visiting units are put through their paces and get a chance both to try to defend themselves against the 'Opfor' (opposing force) and to attack it. To make the effect even more realistic, the tanks and guns at Fort Irwin are equipped with 'Miles' (Multiple Integrated Laser Engagement System), which means that when they fire they project a laser beam towards their targets. These targets – all infantrymen and vehicles on the battlefield – are in turn equipped with laser receivers which register direct hits and even near-misses. If a tank is 'hit', struck by a laser beam, a strobe light on its casing begins to flash, indicating that it has been 'killed'. Similarly, if a soldier is 'hit', the laser activates a continuous high-pitched sound next to his ear.

Yet though Fort Irwin is a step in the right direction, many army experts insist that training overall is not nearly rigorous enough. The US army's priorities, they say, become evident if you compare its basic infantry training manual with the Israeli army equivalent. In the course of a 12-week training course, American recruits are obliged to spend a mere 28 hours on forced marches and camping out ('marching and bivouacking'). The Israeli programme, by contrast, subjects its recruits to a 19-week basic training course, in which the stress is almost entirely on forced marches and bivouacking (first week, 10-kilometre forced march; second week, 15-km and three-km jog with loaded stretcher to each four men; third week, 15-km forced march and then 10 km with stretchers, and so on, steadily increasing, until the 19th week when the recruits undergo an 85-km forced march). Through bitter experience, the Israelis have learnt that you cannot depend on hi tech alone; to win wars you need highly trained soldiers.

But if a doctrine of manoeuvre calls for highly trained soldiers, it also requires equipment which is flexible, reliable, and easy to maintain. (If you are engaged in a counter-attack, perhaps behind enemy lines, and cut off from your main force, the last thing you want is tanks – or anti-aircraft guns – which are prone to breakdown.) Yet instead of acquiring this, the army, by 1982, as we have seen, was busy buying some of the most elaborate, fragile and hard-to-maintain equipment ever con-ceived.

An exception to the tendency towards obsessive elaboration was the Ninth Infantry Division (Motorized), based at Fort Lewis in Washington State. This – the army's experimental hi tech division – *is* seeking to develop itself into a leaner fighting force. It has created a 'Fast Attack Vehicle', which is small, agile and armed with an anti-tank missile. But I have found few army experts who believe that this 'dune buggy for the Pepsi generation', as the *Wall Street Journal* called the FAV, would be very useful against Soviet tanks on the Central Front or anywhere else. And while the Ninth has undoubted virtues – 'its tactics – in-and-out attacks, surprise, night fighting – put it squarely in the mainstream of the Army's new doctrine of mobility and surprise' – it appears to suffer from the standard disease: a fixation with technological rather than operational solutions to problems.*

So though the army got itself a new strategy in 1982 it was (and is) still a long way from being able to implement it.

In some respects, all four American services have pulled back from the nadir of 1980. President Reagan's attitude to the military helped; so did the 11.4 per cent across-the-board pay rise which he instituted in 1981. Through offering better pay, and helped by growing unemployment from the recession of 1981–2 and intensive recruiting campaigns, the services managed to stem the 'haemorrhage of talent' which had been occurring and to attract more high school graduates into their ranks. But even if recruiting standards continue to rise, the problems of the US military are too deeply entrenched to be solved without some fundamental rethinking.

Just before Reagan took office, the Pentagon made its ill-fated attempt to rescue the American hostages being held in Iran. It was a disaster, a classic failure, and as Jeffrey Record, a defence consultant at Georgetown University in Washington, and critic of the hi-tech mentality, describes it, 'one of the few military miscarriages the responsibility for which – the entire responsibility for which – can be laid at the doorstep of the military'. The problems extended well beyond any single shortcoming; they stemmed from inter-service rivalries, lack of leadership, ridiculously bureaucratic procedures and an apparent inability among the Pentagon's military planners to think things through. Because all the services wanted in on the act, no one was really in charge: while an army captain ran the assault force, the helicopters (which were not checked properly and broke down) were run by the marines, the C130 aircraft by the air force, while the overall operation was directed by a naval admiral 2,000 miles away in the Persian Gulf. The actual plan was never properly rehearsed, and never checked for possible shortcomings. The communications gear did not work properly and the different services involved could not communicate with each other. And when the operation went wrong, the assault force was unable to withdraw without a humiliating and fatal accident in which eight men died. Reading the report on that disaster, as one observer put it: 'You are left to wonder if our military leaders are capable of successfully staging even a small joint operation.'

Any notion that the arrival of the Reagan administration had affected

---

* The 'division of the future', as the Ninth calls itself, has certainly come up with its share of zany ideas. One which didn't last long was a helicopter which could be 'folded' to fit into a suitcase (someone came up with a design, apparently, but its fuel tank was so small that it would only have been able to stay aloft for 30 minutes). Another project which fizzled, according to the *Wall Street Journal*, was '"the flying trash can" – a machine straight out of James Bond, that enabled individual soldiers to levitate: too noisy and too expensive.'

the underlying problem was rudely dispelled three years after the Iranian hostage rescue attempt – by another uninspiring military performance. This was the storming of the small Caribbean island of Grenada.

Grenada, of course, was not a disaster. Quite the opposite. After all, America won. The Pentagon managed to lay on an operation to defeat a mighty force of 679 Cubans, which included 43 professional soldiers (the rest were construction workers). And this was a matter for celebration. But in Grenada many of the problems which had surfaced in Iran recurred. All four services wanted to be involved (the army was especially eager because it wanted to justify its request to Congress for a new 'Ranger' battalion) and the navy's original plan was overruled by the Joint Chiefs. Instead, an enormous armada sailed off into the Caribbean – the aircraft carrier *Independence* with its associated battle group, complete with naval fighter bombers; helicopter gunships; a 1,250-man heavily armed marine amphibious unit; and eventually (reinforcements had to be sent for) a total of eight army battalions: six of infantry, and two of elite Rangers.

Yet in spite of this breathtaking display of force it took the US forces no less than three days to conquer Grenada, in the course of which they lost nine out of the 85 helicopters deployed in combat (more than the British lost during the Falklands war) and the lives of 18 servicemen, less than half of whom were killed by the enemy (the rest died in accidents). Twenty-one Grenadans also died, due to a misaimed American bomb.

Though the marines and the army Rangers performed adequately, the regular army units (of the famous 82nd Airborne Division) advanced across the island with such caution that General John Vessey, the Chairman of the Joint Chiefs, is said to have complained at one point: 'We have two companies of Marines running all over the island, and thousands of army troops doing nothing. What the hell is going on?'

Altogether, Operation Urgent Fury, as it was called, gave plenty of cause for concern. The root of the trouble, as in Iran, was the inability of the four services to work together. There were difficulties in coordinating naval fire support. There was no unified land commander (as Britain had had in the Falklands), with both marine units in the north of the island and army units in the south reporting direct to Admiral Joseph Metcalf aboard the USS *Guam*. There were a host of logistics problems, despite the fact that a new 'Joint Deployment Agency' had been set up in the Pentagon in 1979 specifically to coordinate the rapid deployment of forces. Unfortunately, it was excluded from the planning of Urgent Fury 'because it did not have adequate communications gear to process highly classified messages'. Commenting afterwards, retired general Volney Warner, a former commander in chief of the Readiness Command, said: 'The JDA's major purpose in life is planning that kind of situation. To rule them out is unconscionable.'

But according to a congressional report, the biggest single problem was the inability of certain units to communicate with each other. The reason for this was the fact that each of the services 'continues to purchase its own communications equipment which all too frequently isn't compatible with the equipment of the other services'. Sometimes, as a result of this, the situation was quite farcical.

For example, the army elements initially on the ground were unable to speak to the navy ships offshore to request and coordinate naval gunfire. It has been reported that one army officer was so frustrated in his efforts to communicate with the navy ships that he used his AT & T calling card to place a call on an ordinary civilian pay telephone to his office at Fort Bragg in an attempt to coordinate fire support. It has also been reported that some of the early communications were conducted via a ham radio operator.

At the end of 'Urgent Fury', Admiral Metcalf, who was in overall command, declared proudly: 'We blew them away.' Clearly the army agreed. Unlike the marines, who played down their role in securing victory, the army congratulated itself, handing out a total of 8,612 decorations, including 170 medals for valour.

The fundamental problem with the US military is that, consciously or unconsciously, it sees its prime task in peacetime as buying hardware rather than using it: the main aim is to wrest money out of Congress for weapons platforms it wants – tanks, armoured personnel carriers, ships, aircraft (complete with elaborate gadgetry) – and the main enemy in this process is not the Russians, or the Iranians, or the Cubans, but each other. 'The main game in town,' says one veteran Washington defence analyst, 'is not the US versus Russia but the navy versus the air force versus the army.'

Thus, as Edward Luttwak points out in his caustic study, *The Pentagon and the Art of War*, all three services are now grotesquely top-heavy with officers – most of whom spend most of their career thinking and acting like bureaucrats. The US has eight times as many admirals per ship as it did in World War Two, seven times as many air force generals per aircraft and two to three times as many army generals per soldier. Or to put it another way, the American military now has nearly as many officers at the rank of colonel, navy captain and above as it did at the end of World War Two. (On 30 June 1945, the figure was 17,057; on 31 May 1983, it was 15,455, though in 1945 the US armed forces totalled over 12 million men. Now they total just over two million on active duty.) Thus in 1945 there was one officer for every 703 enlisted men. Now the figure is one officer for every 129 enlisted men.

As Luttwak observes:

> Very few of these officers can find normal command or staff duties in the small peacetime forces. So the vast majority are placed in layers of higher headquarters and a multitude of administrative, logistic and equipment-acquisition commands, all of which have been expanded over the years to keep officers busy in peacetime, in readiness for the day when all might be fully employed in the war-mobilized forces.

Thus the emphasis in the peacetime American military has shifted away from fighting skills towards procurement and technological management: the over-elaborate bureaucracy in the Pentagon, as Luttwak notes, reproduces itself on the battlefield (in over-elaborate weapons), and this, in a kind of synergistic effect, has a corrupting effect on attitudes throughout the military. The best way to promotion, these days, is through running a successful procurement programme in the Pentagon: leading troops in the field is a secondary occupation. The emphasis on procurement and management has even permeated officer selection boards, which tend to be dominated by what Luttwak calls 'maintenance and support types'.

But if the services are chock-full of ribbons and rank, and thousands of officers are engaged in over-specifying for equipment and supervising its progress from laboratory to battlefield, the services are still chronically short of skilled leadership at vital levels. Good non-commissioned officers, or NCOs, are crucial to any army; they form the link between the elite, specially trained senior officers and the men; on them hinges the discipline, training, attitude and morale of an individual unit. (The regimental sergeant-major has long been the key to the success of the British army, to take the best example.) But the all-volunteer army has consistently found it hard to attract enough good recruits to enable good soldiers to rise through the ranks and perform this crucial task. At the time of writing, the US army is short by almost 25,000 skilled NCOs.

There are deep-seated national reasons for the state of the armed services in America – reasons which make it unlikely that the situation will dramatically change. In Europe, where war has been a central part of life for centuries, military men are still highly regarded; belonging to the armed services is a matter of pride. There is a tradition of martial exploits, of heroism and of sacrifice which is largely absent in America. And to some extent the technological bias, the desire to create weapons which can kill at a distance and save lives, and the failure to create well motivated, well trained military forces reflects a national revulsion against war – a failure to come to grips with the realities of it. It has been said, brutally but with a grain of truth, that the USA, as a nation, is essentially frivolous about defence. No one, for example, is ever punished for failure.

In 1757 the British executed Admiral Byng for gross incompetence after he had lost a battle with French men-o'-war. They did it, observed Voltaire, 'pour encourager les autres'. Byng behaved no worse than many who have led American military operations over the last twenty years. I am not suggesting that Congress begin executing senior officers, but the nearest the Reagan administration has come to punishment was transferring three senior naval officers from their posts for allowing too much money to be spent on ashtrays. And these officers were, I suspect, doing no more than countless senior officers do every day of the week. They were part of a cumbersome and inefficient procurement system. Their removal had nothing to do with their fighting skills.

Defence, then, has become a matter of buying weapons. There has been no overall guiding sense of strategy, no real attempt to decide priorities. The links between hardware and strategy have grown more and more tenuous. Each service has simply pursued its own chosen weapons systems, designed more to satisfy internal needs and long-standing traditions than to meet a plausible threat.

Nothing makes this clearer than a glance at the present state – and plans – of the US navy.

4

The Navy: a Special Case

When President Reagan came into office in January 1981 he launched the biggest peacetime military build-up in American history. He proposed to spend a trillion and a half dollars in four years – a sum whose vast proportions he had difficulty in conveying. 'I've been trying to think of the best way of illustrating how big a trillion is,' said the president in his first major economic address after arriving in the White House. (He was talking about the evils of large federal deficits!) 'If you had a stack of 100 dollar bills four inches high you would be a millionaire. A trillion dollars would be a stack of 100 dollar bills 67 miles high.'

The administration had a long list of things it wanted to spend the money on: the modernizing of America's nuclear forces, command and control facilities, more pay for the military, and a variety of modern weapons (including most of those examined in chapter 2). But it was soon clear that the most distinctive feature of the Reagan build-up was to be its emphasis on the navy. The president did not mince words: what he was after, he repeatedly made clear, was naval superiority. If America was to be secure in the world, nothing less would do.

The man chosen to be the architect of the navy build-up was a one-time naval aviator called John Lehman. At the age of 38, Lehman was brought into the Pentagon as navy secretary. His plan was to expand a navy which stood at 480 surface vessels at the start of 1981 into a navy of 600 ships by the late 1980s, and within a year or two his tough, single-minded approach and bureaucratic skills were drawing gasps of admiration from Washington. As Robert Komer, an under secretary of defence under Jimmy Carter, put it, Lehman soon proved himself 'without doubt the most energetic service secretary we've had for twenty years'.

Komer's praise, however, stopped short of the programme Lehman was so successfully promoting. This, he said, 'would lead to strategic disaster in the event of a major conflict with the Soviet Union'. It was a verdict shared by many strategists in the American defence community. They could see no sound military rationale for a 600-ship navy. It was 'wildly wasteful' said one; 'a classic example of spending without regard to strategy' said another.

The programme was certainly ambitious. The 600-ship navy, in the view of its proponents, held the key to being able to wage a global conventional war with the Russians. There were, of course, other more traditional 'rationales' for surface ships: 'showing the flag' or 'projecting force' in the Middle East, the Third World and elsewhere when the occasion demanded it (such as Lebanon, 1982, or Grenada, 1983), and, in the event of a major war, controlling vital sea lanes so that, for example, weapons, soldiers and supplies could be brought across the Atlantic to reinforce the defence of Western Europe. But none of these purposes demanded a 600-ship navy (indeed they scarcely required a navy of 480 ships). The only possible justification for such a huge surface fleet was taking on the Russians – worldwide – and the question was: was this either *possible* (in the way Lehman imagined it) or *necessary*?

At the heart of the Lehman plan was a new and daring concept of naval strategy. Lehman wanted to increase by three the number of America's aircraft carriers – from 12 to 15 – in turn requiring a radical expansion of the number of surface escorts (frigates and destroyers), for each carrier operates as part of a large 'battle group'. Lehman's plan was to deal much more aggressively with the Soviet Union's northern fleet, the one which, in the event of war, would pose the greatest threat to Nato. The traditional idea is to deploy naval forces along a defensive line connecting Greenland, Iceland and Britain – the so-called GI-UK gap. That way, the Soviet fleet would be intercepted as it tried to head out into the Atlantic. Lehman wanted instead to attack the enemy in their home waters, and the strategy he envisaged would probably include a direct assault on the northern fleet's home port of Murmansk. 'I take an oath to defend Norway as if it was an attack on Long Island,' he told me in 1983. 'It makes no sense to turn the Norwegian Sea and the Baltic over to the Soviets in time of conflict if we can win in the northern flank with aggressive policies and aggressive defence.'

Common sense alone would suggest that this is a tall order. Lehman may have taken an oath to defend Norway, but the American battle groups would be operating within easy range of Russian land-based aircraft, and history suggests that the dangers would be enormous.

In 1940, the British made an ill-fated attempt to recapture Norway from the Germans, but the expeditionary force they sent, lacking air support and fatally exposed to the Luftwaffe, was cut to pieces, losing four ships sunk and 18 badly damaged, including a carrier and a battleship. Later in the war the Japanese 'kamikaze' pilots (forerunners of guided missiles) again showed how devastating aircraft can be to surface ships. And though many of today's guided missiles, as we have already seen, are not as effective as the glossy defence manuals suggest, technology has undoubtedly rendered surface ships more vulnerable than they were during World War Two. Even against a decidedly second-rate, though bravely and skilfully manned air force, the British navy had a harrowing time during the Falklands war: it lost six ships, mainly due to aircraft of 1950s vintage operating at the extreme edge of their range and armed with old-fashioned iron bombs (though the Argentinians also possessed the hi-tech – if relatively simple and effective – Exocet missile).* A US naval force attempting to take Murmansk would have to brave the full might of the Soviet air force operating within easy striking range of their bases and including Backfire bombers armed with long-range cruise missiles.

The American aircraft carriers, of course, would provide their own air support. The huge Nimitz class, nuclear-powered vessels, for example, carry some 90 apiece, ranging from the super-sophisticated F14s, to airborne radar aircraft, anti-submarine planes like the S-3 and helicopters. The snag is that most of these aircraft are intended for defending the carrier herself, and her accompanying flotilla of destroyers and frigates. Only a small number – 34 at most – would be free to attack land targets. Thus the combined offensive punch of a formidable carrier group operating in hostile waters is relatively puny – 34 aircraft, at most, with which to attack land targets. 'The mighty whale,' as Ed Luttwak observes, 'gives birth to a sprat.'

So the chances of America being able to mount a successful assault on Murmansk look tiny. Even John Lehman's own chief of naval operations, Admiral James Watkins, no slouch when it comes to extolling the capabilities of the US navy, privately confessed to doubts about it (though he later maintained that he and Lehman were 'very much in harmony on strategy'). And retired admiral Stansfield Turner, who was head of the CIA under Jimmy Carter, declared: 'I have yet to find an admiral who will attempt it.' Many strategists believe that Murmansk is so well defended that it would be impossible to destroy without nuclear weapons.

But if taking Murmansk from the sea lacks credibility, so do the assumptions underlying Lehman's strategy. Basically, they are two. The first is that if war breaks out in central Europe, Nato, badly outnumbered, could quickly be faced with the unacceptable choice of losing or going nuclear, and that the best hope of prolonging the conflict would lie in the US navy moving quickly to assert control of the seas. The second assumption is a broader one. It is that a 'big war' in central Europe is not very likely – not nearly so likely, at least, as a brushfire war somewhere

---

*The total of ships lost might have climbed as high as 14 if a number of Argentinian bombs which scored hits had actually gone off.

else (say, in the Third World) – and that America is therefore best served by a strategy which places considerable emphasis on a large, flexible and powerful navy.

These propositions are less logical than they may seem. The problem with naval superiority is that it doesn't get you anywhere. As Bob Komer points out: 'Even if Lehman knocked out all the Soviet naval bases and swept the Soviet navy from the seven seas, he could not prevent them from taking over Western Europe and the Persian Gulf and cowing Japan. The exercise would be like sticking pins in the hide of an elephant.'*

Nothing makes this clearer than the fallacy of 'horizontal escalation'. Horizontal escalation was a notion which surfaced in the Pentagon in 1981, its exponents maintaining that if America was attacked in a place where it faced heavy odds it should attack the Russians somewhere else, in a kind of global tit for tat. But supposing the Russians attacked Western Europe, or the Middle East (a favourite scenario when horizontal escalation was conceived)? Would this mean that the US would then attack, say, Cuba ('they get the oil, we get the cigars,' as a Nato friend put it), or Angola, or Nicaragua? It scarcely seemed a 'fair exchange'. 'The problem with horizontal escalation,' as one former Pentagon official says, 'is who the hell do you horizontally escalate against?'

As for the argument that America should plan not so much for the most dire contingency imaginable as for the likeliest – what Bob Komer calls 'the likelihood fallacy' – this might make sense if America, and the West in general, had unlimited resources. But since it does not, it must surely concentrate on protecting its most vital interests, even if this means not being able to protect everything. Indeed, the danger foreseen by Komer and others is that the more America shifts its emphasis towards the navy and away from ground forces, the harder will those vital interests become to defend. 'What is really happening,' says Komer, 'is that *the United States is drifting by default toward a primarily maritime strategy*' (italics in original).

Neither Komer nor other critics of the Lehman plan, of course, were advocating abandoning the surface navy. But in a full-scale war against the Russians it would play a limited role and the kind of ships being built – bristling with advanced radar and missile systems and hugely expensive – made some critics of the navy even more uneasy.

At $3.4 billion apiece, 90,000-ton, nuclear-powered aircraft carriers are the most expensive single items in the US defence budget, and including the price of the escorts and the aircraft, the total for a carrier battle group

---

* 'Breaking windows with guineas' was the criticism levelled at the similar strategy espoused by the British prime minister, William Pitt, in the 1790s.

comes to about $17 billion – a staggering sum to pay for a unit which has to devote most of its efforts to defending *itself*. Carriers are easily tracked by modern surveillance systems and provide a tempting target for attack by submarines and land-based aircraft. The admirals are reluctant to acknowledge their vulnerability: according to former defence official Thomas Etzold (he now works for the Arms Control and Disarmament Agency), carriers are never 'sunk' in war games, even though a missile or a well-aimed bomb can put them out of commission; even so, the admirals were reluctant to send a carrier into the Persian Gulf during the Iranian hostage crisis: like the professional armies in Europe in the seventeenth and eighteenth centuries, the aircraft carriers of today sometimes seem to constitute too valuable an instrument of force to risk using.

Yet the whole US navy is built round these carriers, and the navy is currently investing in some extraordinary new technology in efforts to defend them. In particular, it is busy deploying an ultra-sophisticated system called Aegis.

The Aegis was the magical shield used by Zeus and Athene for protection against their enemies. Just looking at it was enough to make you tremble. Critics, however, doubt whether it will be the same with the modern version. 'The modern Aegis, alas,' commented the *New York Times* in April 1984, 'has a way to go before it makes anyone tremble, except maybe the taxpayer.'

The US navy plans to spend $80 billion in all on ships equipped with Aegis – 26 cruisers and 60 destroyers – by the early 1990s. It is a computerized battle management system, an elaborate network of computers intended to enable an array of radars to track up to 200 targets at a time and shoot down 18 missiles or planes in one salvo. Lehman has called it 'the key to the survival of the battle group', and Weinberger, the defence secretary, called it 'the centrepiece' of the navy's effort to defend the fleet against air attacks.

At the time of writing there is only one Aegis-equipped ship afloat, the $1 billion cruiser, USS *Ticonderoga*. The *Ticonderoga* has a very high superstructure, projecting from which are antennae containing the thousands of small radars, each of which seeks out potential targets; once the targets – attacking planes or missiles – have been picked up, the system sends out signals to determine whether these are 'friend or foe', then another radar bounces signals off the targets identified as hostile so that the cruiser's missiles can home in on the reflected radar energy.

There are signs that Aegis may not prove the magic shield of the fleet it is intended to be. In two sets of tests in April 1983, the *Ticonderoga* hit only four out of 16 missiles aimed at the ship, and in another test, five months later, it hit only two out of six targets. Moreover, four of the missiles fired at the ship in the earlier test were low-flying: the *Ticonderoga* hit none of them. In September three of the targets flew in low: the ship hit only one. And the low-flying missiles 'were not as low-flying or as fast as the kind the Argentinians used against the British in the Falklands war', according to one man who saw the test results.

Yet the Soviets would be bound to attack Aegis-class ships with low-flying and other anti-ship missiles. To be sure, in a fresh set of tests, in May 1984, the *Ticonderoga* fared better. According to the navy, it hit 10 out of 11 drone missiles in a simulated attack on a carrier battle group. But critics of the 1984 test maintain that it was unrealistic: a navy aircraft, they say, flew above the *Ticonderoga* during the test, and on a course parallel to that followed by the missiles, thus enabling the Aegis to get a 'fix' on the plane before it had to follow the missiles.

John Lehman has maintained that the Aegis is the most carefully tested combat system ever built, and that 'operational requirements have been met or exceeded' in the *Ticonderoga*. Critics dispute this, saying that there is no evidence that the system will be able to cope properly with the swarm of targets it might be expected to face – especially in hostile waters against low-flying, long-distance missiles. In 1984 Representative Denny Smith, an Oregon Republican and a leading critic of Aegis, charged that there was 'a serious mismatch between the navy's publicly stated performance of the USS *Ticonderoga* and the navy's own test results'.

But the Aegis has another drawback, one it shares with the navy's other principal air defence system, the F14 interceptor aircraft. Both rely on active radar to find and destroy their targets. But active radar, as we have seen, acts like a powerful beacon, making it much easier for the enemy to find its target – a problem which would be especially apparent at sea. Thus the Aegis and the F14, called upon to defend huge, vulnerable battle groups, possibly close to the Soviet mainland, would have to cope with very intense, concentrated attacks.

Besides, as defence analysts have shown, the need for extra escorts to back up the new carriers is going to place a huge, and probably impossible, strain on the navy budget. According to one study by the Congressional Budget Office (CBO), the navy will need 60 new escorts in the water by 1992 to protect its new carriers, yet even under Lehman's plan there will only be 25 at sea by 1991. 'The consequent imbalance between ships needing protection and the number of escorts will put tremendous pressure on the available escorts,' George Kuhn has observed. Another study by the CBO suggested that navy budgets would have to keep rising five per cent faster than inflation just to pay for the fleet which Lehman has planned. He dismisses this as an exaggeration, and it cannot be denied that he has had some success in improving the navy's contracting procedures, keeping prices down and clamping down on waste and fraud. But a principal reason the navy is expanding is not so much the fact that new ships are being built as that old ones are being retired more slowly, which means that the navy's bill for maintenance and repairs is going to get bigger and bigger, and that in turn means that the overall pressure on the navy budget will grow, especially when it becomes clear that the planned new ships are going to cost more – far more – than had been anticipated.

The strain, indeed, is already apparent. In October 1985, in one effort to save money, the navy ordered a cutback in the amount of time its ships are to spend at sea. There is already a drastic shortage of skilled seamen with many ships lacking a full complement. On a visit to the aircraft carrier *Coral Sea*, the *New York Times* Pentagon correspondent, Bill Keller, found that the engineering crew which kept the ship's twelve boilers going had 'dwindled from 820 to 650 as the Navy stretches to man its expanding fleet'.

No one questions that America needs a navy, and in operating the ballistic missile submarines which form the least vulnerable part of the nuclear deterrent, it fulfils one of the most critical missions of Western defence. Clearly, too, there is a need to protect sea lanes in the Atlantic and Pacific. But Lehman's plans, which envisage spending vast sums of money on carriers, might make 'sea control' *more difficult*. Submarines and long-range aircraft operating from land bases increasingly look the best means of performing many of the functions which once fell to surface ships. The navy, naturally, would baulk at this: it would fear losing one of its missions to the air force. Bob Komer's solution: 'Give the navy responsibility ... and let it have its own AWACS and F15s.' It would certainly make more sense than the baffling decision to build such a vast, carrier-heavy surface fleet.

However, the admirals wield considerable influence amongst the politicians on Capitol Hill, partly because a lot of jobs hinge on the nation's shipyards, and partly because support for the navy, in America as in Britain, is deep-rooted, based as much on sentimental attachment as on practical realities. America, unlike Russia, is a sea power; it has long depended on the oceans for trade and access, and a mystique has clung to the navy since the days when US admirals were received in foreign ports like government plenipotentiaries. Until 1947, the navy had its own representative in Cabinet: there was no secretary of defence, but a secretary of war, responsible for the army, and a secretary of the navy.

There is a further reason for the navy's continuing success. The procurement system in the Pentagon works to promote narrow service interests rather than a broader strategic interest. In the committee of the joint chiefs of staff, each chief tenaciously fights for his share of the budget and his own cherished programmes: the chairman, under the present arrangement, is able to exert little influence. He can express his own views but his job is merely to achieve a consensus within the committee. Most retiring chairmen have complained about the impotence of the post, but the navy – more than any other service – has a vested interest in its continuance: it knows that a reform of the system could lead to its share of the procurement budget, which has stayed more or less constant at about 40 per cent since the war, being substantially reduced.

Nothing illustrates the US navy's sense of priorities more clearly than the fact that while the surface fleet expanded rapidly under Reagan, the submarine force did not. Submarines are much less vulnerable than surface ships, and, as was evident in World War Two, can prove a menace to shipping during a war. They are also hard to detect: technology has been used to much greater advantage in submarines than in surface ships, making them much quieter than their predecessors and able to travel much further under water. Yet the navy has never been as keen on attack submarines as it has been on surface ships, and those it does have reflect the usual bias in favour of sophistication. They are large, fast, nuclear-powered craft, undoubtedly effective but also expensive. The navy has 90 to 100 of them and admits that it needs at least 130. Yet it will neither sacrifice surface ships to build them nor purchase any *smaller*, nuclear-powered submarines – which would be cheaper – nor any conventional diesel-powered submarines, which would cost one quarter as much. As George Kuhn points out:

> In rejecting the smaller nuclear boat the Navy baulks at the loss of five knots top speed. Though such a speed difference can be useful in ocean transit and in escaping immediate attacks, it also makes the sub much noisier and more easily detected. The navy rejects the conventional sub, arguing that it is more vulnerable to airborne detection (since it must snorkel occasionally) and that it cannot perform the same range of missions as a nuclear boat.

These objections, while they may be valid, miss the point. In a world where costs did not matter, the navy could have as many large nuclear submarines as it wanted, just as the army could have an unlimited supply of M1 tanks. But since money does count, and the navy anyway prefers to spend most of what it has on gadget-ridden surface ships, the need for a larger submarine fleet suggests that smaller boats would make sense.* Moreover, the critical areas in which American submarines would operate – choke points such as the GI-UK gap – would probably be *dominated* by

---

*The same argument applies to Britain, where the Royal Navy, though obsessed with gold-plated 'through deck cruisers', Type 22 frigates and nuclear submarines, has shown itself decidedly reluctant to buy *conventional* attack submarines.

friendly aircraft, so the risks conventional subs would have in rising to the surface for air occasionally would be relatively small (certainly tiny compared with the risks faced by surface vessels), and as Kuhn observes, 'because conventional boats are much quieter and smaller and could carry the same sensors and weapons load, they might actually better perform many stealth missions and the hunter-killer mission in barriers and shallow areas against Soviet attack submarines. Moreover, they can operate on long-range missions – they could be based abroad more readily than nuclear vessels.' The navy, however, pays no heed to this kind of logic.

5
'Shooting Fish in a Barrel'

No one who believes that defence should be taken seriously can fail to be appalled by what goes on in American military procurement. It comprises an obsession with hi tech and an endless chase after super-expensive, super-sophisticated weapons many of which do not work and/or are irrelevant to any real 'threat'. This may satisfy the institutional and traditional needs of the individual services, but it can satisfy no one who believes that the task is to prepare for a possible war with the Russians, or with anyone else.

It would be foolish of course to suggest that most of those involved in military procurement are anything other than decent, patriotic, well-intentioned people. There is no overarching conspiracy to defraud the taxpayer ('nothing so inefficient could ever be a conspiracy,' as one Pentagon joke has it). Nevertheless the taxpayers do get defrauded: they do *not* get what they pay for; they pour money into a system which is wide open to abuse and where most of the checks and balances do not work properly.

What makes the situation all the more depressing is that there is little incentive for change. Too many vested interests are involved; too much money is at stake; too much of what happens has become accepted as common practice. In his farewell address as president, Dwight D. Eisenhower warned of the danger. 'We have been compelled to create a permanent arms industry of vast proportions ...' he said. 'The potential for the disastrous rise of misplaced power exists and will persist.' Gradually the forces of what Eisenhower called 'the military industrial complex' have come to dominate procurement: a system has grown up which works against the national interest – and which is hard to escape.

The state of defence procurement emerged with unusual clarity in a case which hit the headlines in 1984 and 1985. It involved General Dynamics, one of the Pentagon's top contractors, and the supplier of an array of crucial hardware to army, navy and air force, ranging from F16 fighters to M1 tanks to the Trident submarines which form the vital, sea-based leg of America's nuclear deterrent. The 'defection' of one of General Dynamics' top executives, C. Takis Veliotis, a Greek businessman who absconded to Greece after retiring from the company, allowed investigators to gain a unique glimpse of the relationship between one major defence contractor and the US government. Veliotis, seeking to defend himself against charges that he had defrauded the company, made a whole series of charges against top General Dynamics executives, including the chairman, David Lewis. And the picture which he and others painted was one of quite scandalous behaviour by the company.

By May 1985, it had been clearly established (among other things) that General Dynamics had given gifts worth $67,628 to retired Admiral Hyman Rickover, 'the father of the nuclear navy', and that it had 'ripped off' the US taxpayer by charging millions of dollars for expenses, ranging from $491,840 for Lewis's personal flights on corporate jets to a $155 kennel fee for an executive's dog. For this, General Dynamics – which at the time was doing $23 million of defence business *a day* – was fined $676,283, two of its major divisions were (temporarily) suspended from doing business with the Pentagon, and two of its existing contracts were cancelled. John Lehman, the navy secretary, stopped short of accepting a recommendation from the Pentagon inspector general that Lewis and two of his fellow executives should be barred from doing business with the military again. But even then General Dynamics was not out of the wood. A federal grand jury set about investigating charges that the company had defrauded the government by putting in a bid for a submarine contract, knowing it to be too low, and then blamed the Pentagon for the consequent additional huge costs; that it attempted to blackmail the government into paying costs that resulted from its own shoddy workmanship; and that it tried to stop its stock price from sliding by lying about delivery time-tables.

At the time of writing, it is true, none of these charges has been proved, but the allegations themselves were enough to send shockwaves through Congress. And it was becoming clear that the General Dynamics case was not unique. 'I think the company's excuse is exactly correct,' says A. Ernest Fitzgerald, a veteran Pentagon whistle-blower, who exposed huge cost overruns in the 1970s. 'Everyone's doing it.' By then, nine out of America's top ten defence contractors were under criminal investigation for some abuse or other.

Allegations swirled around General Electric of improper billing for nuclear warhead contracts, around McDonnell Douglas of 'accounting irregularities', around Sperry of falsifying bills for the MX missile, around National Semiconductor Industries of cutting corners in the testing of electronic chips, around Boeing of billing the Pentagon for contributions to political campaigns.

A spate of 'small', 'spare parts' horror stories in the press (the $659 ashtray, the $640 lavatory seat, the $7,600 coffee pot, the $1,000 plastic cap for an air force seat, etc) added to the impression that the defence industry was not yielding value for money. Indeed, these trivial items almost certainly did the most to arrest public attention. 'People have no idea what a fighter or a spare part for a fighter should cost,' said one defence official, 'but everyone knows that coffee pots shouldn't cost $7,600.'

Indeed, according to Ernest Fitzgerald, the overpriced coffee pot reflects a general trend of overcharging for small items. 'What you're seeing when a military aircraft flies overhead,' he says, 'is an overpriced collection of spare parts.'

The way the Pentagon procurement system operates, of course, does provide the perfect climate for 'rip-off'. There is the enormous and unwieldy bureaucracy – compared by Thomas V. Jones, the president of the Northrop Corporation, to 'a log floating down a river with 10,000 ants aboard, each one thinking he's steering'. Within this structure, where control from the centre is lax, and where the services compete fiercely for their share of the budget, officers win their spurs by running big weapons programmes and, in their efforts to obtain the 'best' possible weapons, constantly bombard manufacturers with elaborate and ever-changing specifications.

Thus the air force, when drawing up specifications for the B1 nuclear bomber, included a demand that the pilot be able to eject while the plane was flying at 200 ft – upside-down. Having the capacity to eject at 200 ft right side up might just make sense, and it is possible, but adding the technology necessary to permit upside-down ejection would have added $1 billion to the programme. In this instance, the air force were eventually persuaded to drop the requirement, though not until money had been spent on research and development, but the defence industry can argue legitimately that the services are forever making similarly absurd demands.

Norman Augustine, the shrewd and witty former Pentagon official who in the early 1960s became chairman of the Martin Marietta Corporation, likes to compare the contract the Wright Brothers signed with the army in 1908 to build the first military aircraft, which was two pages long, with the proposal for the building of the C5A transport plane – a hugely complex piece of equipment – which ran to one and a half million pages and weighed 25,000 pounds. The most critical aerospace material nowadays, says Augustine, is not cobalt or titanium but the wood pulp which goes into a contractor's proposal. Hence his 'law': 'If all the contract proposals were piled one on top of the other at the bottom of the Grand Canyon, it would probably be a good idea.'

Hugely complicated specifications are the rule not just for large weapons systems. Even ashtrays, as we have seen, have to be made to a precise and elaborate plan. And the specifications for the plastic whistle used by drill instructors run to 16 pages of single-spaced detail, dictating everything from the size of the tiny cork ball inside the whistle to the type of tissue wrapping paper it should be dispatched in.

In fulfilling these ridiculous demands, industry can justifiably protest that it is hardly being encouraged to save money. But the truth is that elaborate specifications, by and large, suit the defence industry as well as they suit the services, precisely because they afford an opportunity to push up costs. What makes the cooperation between services and industry especially close is the phenomenon known as 'the revolving door'. Every year hundreds of top military men leave the Pentagon to take lucrative jobs in industry, often with the firms whose business they have been handling. A study by the New York-based Council on Economic Priorities found that 1,672 former military and civilian employees of the Pentagon and NASA had been recruited by eight major contractors between 1970 and 1979 (270 executives from these firms had joined the Pentagon and NASA over the same period of time).

Thus it is often difficult to tell who is responsible for changes in specifications, though it is, of course, the Pentagon's responsibility to approve them. And because of the Pentagon's fixation on high technology, and its determination to make tiny adjustments in the light of new information about the 'threat', there are constant excuses for change.

For example, the High-Speed Anti-Radiation Missile known as HARM, designed to be fired from aircraft and to home in on enemy radiation systems, was expected to cost $48,000 apiece in 1976. But in an effort to keep up with what was thought to be increasingly sophisticated Soviet radar technology, HARM steadily acquired extra 'capabilities' and its price raced up to $600,000 apiece by 1978. By 1981, when the first 80 HARMs were ordered by the navy, the missile was being built from 10,000 design drawings, and the price was $1.3 million.

Whether or not the HARM missile now being fitted to military aircraft will work properly is unclear. At the time of writing, its test record is undistinguished. But what is evident is that a missile initially designed for use by fighter pilots in large quantities against Soviet radar defences had become instead a missile which would have to be used very sparingly for 'the surgical removal of high-priority, extremely sophisticated enemy air defence systems', as an air force general put it. Once again, the Pentagon has put all its eggs in the hi-tech basket: it had purchased a missile so expensive that it was quite unsuited to the role for which it had been originally planned. And in doing so it had ensured that the cost soared.

Clearly, the Pentagon deserved much of the blame for this: as the customer, it encouraged the kind of tinkering which transformed HARM.

But the manufacturers – in this case Texas Instruments – have much to gain and little to lose from increasingly elaborate specifications. Talking of the defence industry generally, John Lehman, the navy secretary, told the *Washington Post*:

> They've got their order book out. 'The latest study shows you ought to have 20 miles more range? Sure, we can give you that, piece of cake. We'll hire more engineers.' ... When you get paid for overrunning, and get profits on top of that for overrunning, you're disserving your stockholders if you don't overrun.

As Lehman suggests, the defence industry often seems to work in a precisely opposite way to the rest of the private sector. In standard business practice, you make money by keeping overheads as low as you can and selling your product as cheaply as you can: in that way you outdo your rivals and maximize your profits. In what Ronald Reagan likes to call 'the arsenal of democracy', however, the secret is to jack up your overheads as much as you can and sell your product at the steepest price you can get: you don't, on the whole, have to worry about competitors. According to an estimate by Charles Grassley, the conservative senator from Iowa, and a leading Pentagon critic, only a tiny fraction of Pentagon dollars are spent after genuine competition between two or more firms. Many firms are monopoly suppliers of particular pieces of equipment and get paid what they charge. And often what passes for competition turns out to be meaningless because the firm which 'wins' has submitted a deliberately low 'bid' (and may even have spent some of its own money on research and development). It does this knowing that once it has secured the contract, the Pentagon, with or without its encouragement, will probably proceed to dream up, or agree to, new bells and whistles it wants included, providing ample excuse to inflate the original contract price. And the more fancy the technological frills, the more difficult it becomes for the Pentagon to estimate what a realistic price should be.

But there is an even more fundamental problem. In many instances, the trouble starts before a 'fixed-price' contract has been agreed between Pentagon and contractor, and before cost overruns and the adding of *new* bells and whistles have entered the picture. For until the Pentagon has 'frozen' the specifications for a particular weapon – and decided precisely what it is it wants to buy – the contractor is being paid for research/ technology demonstration/ initial development/ development and initial production/ the building of a prototype – all this, usually, on a 'cost plus' basis. (The Pentagon, in other words, pays the company's costs plus an agreed profit formula.) It is clearly, therefore, *in the contractor's interest* to stretch out this process, playing along with and encouraging gold-plating ideas, and delaying as long as possible the fixing of a unit price. Defence contractors, after all, exist to make profits, not to make equipment.

Thus the initial bidding for contracts is often a charade, one that is played out by both the contractors and the services' procurement people. Anxious to win approval from Congress for their pet schemes, they indulge in what has been aptly called 'a conspiracy of optimism'. In an unusually frank moment, one Pentagon official put it like this:

> If we told the truth we would never get our programmes approved. So we have to understate the cost and overstate the performance. Our military bias is to get as much as we can – after all, we don't know who the future enemy is or what he will have in the way of weapons. We are the ones who have to fight the war, not the people in Congress or the average taxpayer.

Thus the services justify their yearning for hi-tech equipment with the argument that only the best will do (even though it is often not the best at all), and the defence industry exploits their unwillingness to think economically by grossly overcharging them. There is little, if any, incentive to think about offering value for money. 'Everyone's missed the point of what we're buying,' says Ernest Fitzgerald. 'We're not buying products, we're buying costs.'

In the rare instances when competition is threatened, results can be dramatic. When the price of the HARM missile soared over $1 million, for example, the navy suggested to Texas Instruments that it might seek another bidder. Once before, during the manufacture of an earlier anti-radiation missile, it had threatened the same thing, and Texas Instruments had found itself able to drop its price by 77 per cent. This time the firm tried to resist the competition, arguing that they were the only qualified anti-radiation missile builder in the country and that the Pentagon would have to invest millions enabling a second bidder to become familiar with the technology. Texas Instruments won their case, but even the threat of competition had an effect: three times in three months, according to the *Washington Post*, they dropped their price, eventually coming down from $1.3 million per missile to $400,000 per missile. (Texas Instruments maintain they would have dropped their price anyway, as they grew more efficient and production techniques improved. Even if true, however, there is little doubt that the spectre of competition was a potent catalyst.)

Similarly, in June 1980 General Dynamics suddenly cut the unit price of its F16 fighter by $6.2 million, or 30 per cent. It did so because Northrop Corporation had spent $800 million of its own money developing an alternative fighter, the F20, and frustrated by air force reluctance to hold a fly-off between the two planes, had made the Pentagon an attractive offer. General Dynamics, threatened with this competition, then felt compelled to make a new bid of its own: a stripped-down version of the F16 (minus some of the more exotic gadgetry) for $13 million apiece, and spare parts guaranteed at $554 per flying hour. As the *New York Times* put it: 'The lesson is clear. Even if one plane should prove to have the overall edge in quality, the Air Force needs to buy at least some of each so as to keep both contractors competing.'

More often than not, however, the services, instead of fostering competition, hand their manufacturers a licence to spend. In chapter 2 we examined the less than distinguished record of the Viper anti-tank missile. In 1979, however, the army were so desperate for an anti-tank missile that they ordered Viper's manufacturer 'to get something that worked in the field, regardless of cost'. The cost quadrupled, as such costs will, and eventually went so out of control that the army ended up paying $77 apiece just for simple slings – made out of cloth and worth 52 cents – which are necessary for carrying the weapon. When Hughes ran into trouble producing another missile of dubious value, the Maverick, in 1982, they persuaded the Pentagon to modify their contract: instead of paying $111 million for 490 missiles, the air force would pay $100 million for only 200 missiles. In addition, apparently, Hughes charged the Pentagon $20 million for contract changes.

'What you're seeing,' says one British defence expert, 'is socialism in action. Anyone who has studied a nationalized industry will recognize exactly what is going on. The difference is that in the case of the defence contractors things are much worse. They have shareholders who are anxious to see big profits.'

Or, as another long-time observer of the US defence industry put it: 'If I were in the KGB, I would make enormous efforts to encourage this system. You could scarcely make it more inefficient if you tried.'

In the first four years after Reagan took office, the American procurement budget doubled and, overall, the Pentagon spent over a trillion dollars – a pile of 100 dollar bills over 67 miles high, the equivalent of $28 million an hour, night and day, seven days a week. As a result, the defence industry enjoyed its greatest spending spree ever. Contractors reported record profits, and many of them, thanks to loopholes in the tax laws, managed to pay little or no tax. Indeed, seven top defence contractors either paid no taxes at all or claimed money back from the Treasury between 1981 and 1983. (Take General Electric, for example: profits, 1981–3, $6.5 billion; taxes, none; refund, $283 million.) Thus as Robert McIntyre, an unusual kind of tax lawyer who runs an outfit called Citizens For Tax Justice, pointed out, these defence contractors managed to exempt themselves from paying so much as a dime towards the huge build-up from which they profited so handsomely.

The defence industry, then, boomed under Reagan. Lee Iacocca, chairman of the Chrysler Corporation, likes to ask fellow industrialists who sell to the Pentagon whether they think there's easy money in defence contracting. According to Iacocca, they usually start chuckling, look around to ensure they are not being overheard and reply: 'It's like shooting fish in a barrel.'

To be fair, Reagan's defence secretary, Caspar Weinberger, and his deputies, especially John Lehman, the secretary of the navy, tried to crack down on the pervasive waste and fraud. They themselves exposed a litany of horror stories and attempted to encourage competition. But many believe they did little more than scratch the surface. Even a CIA survey, completed well into the Reagan build-up, reportedly concluded: 'Anything that succeeds in US weapons acquisition seems to do so in spite of the system, rather than because of it.' The evidence is that the huge influx of cash did vastly more for contractors' shareholders and employees than it did for American defence. Much of it went into high costs and overheads rather than into weapons, and the evidence of inefficiency mounted. F18 aircraft came rolling off the McDonnell Douglas production lines with cracks in their tails. (They tried to get the navy to pay to fix them, but John Lehman, to his credit, refused.) Semiconductor chips produced by Texas Instruments turned out to be defective, hence endangering the reliability and performance of a whole range of sophisticated weapons. According to documents supplied to Congress, one major defence company working on the MX nuclear missile was paid for 5,050 hours of labour when its own 'factory efficiency' data suggested the same work should take only 370 hours. That meant the firm was seven per cent as efficient as it should have been. And the Hughes Corporation in Tucson, Arizona, was found to be taking up to 17 times longer than it should have been – by its own estimate – to produce each Maverick missile.

These were not unusual cases: in some instances, of course, the problems stretched back to the 1970s, but everywhere investigators looked, they found that the defence industry was proving hugely more inefficient than most firms in the private sector. Meanwhile, however, they were paying their executives proportionately much larger salaries (not insignificant, since 70 per cent of contract dollars underwrite wages), and reaping proportionately much larger profits. To take one example: the Boeing Corporation, in 1983, made three times as much profit on its military as it did on its civilian work. One navy study, according to the *Washington Post*, found that defence work in the early 1980s was in some cases proving ten times as lucrative as other business.

The huge Reagan build-up, therefore, scarcely translated into a dramatic increase in security. America, thanks to an inefficient defence industry, operating to a bureaucratically top-heavy and technology-obsessed Pentagon, got precious little bang for its bucks. In the four years between 1981 and 1985, the Pentagon

- bought only 6.4 per cent more missiles despite a 91.2 per cent increase in the missile budget;
- bought only 8.8 per cent more aircraft despite a 75 per cent increase in the aircraft budget;
- bought only 30 per cent more tanks and combat vehicles despite a 147.4 per cent increase in the budget for tanks and combat vehicles.

The build-up, too, promised trouble for the future. From early on, a number of seasoned defence analysts, such as the former defence secretary, James Schlesinger, and the MIT professor, William Kaufman, had warned of this. They saw a clear pattern, based on the experience of the past. The services, assured of large amounts of money, would order large quantities of new equipment; they would therefore pave the way for a bigger defence establishment – more ships, planes and tanks to maintain, etc. They would then find, when the bills fell due, that they had wildly underestimated how large these would be. So they would have to 'squeeze'. How do the services 'squeeze'? They cut down on vital things like flying and sailing hours, training, spare parts and ammunition, all essential if you wish to be ready for war. So, though short-term readiness (thanks to the size of the budget) improved under Reagan, the eventual effect of the Reagan build-up promised to be a defence establishment less ready for war than ever.

Some critics, like Senator Grassley, argued that pumping ever-increasing sums into the Pentagon simply encouraged abuses. A conservative from Iowa, Grassley found himself appalled by the behaviour of the defence contractors. Isolated from competition and from the consequences of their mistakes, with a government always prepared to bail them out if necessary, they appeared to him an anathema in a country based on competitive private enterprise. The envy of their 'civilian' opposite numbers, they had become what Grassley called 'the new welfare queens', sponging on the taxpayers and squandering public trust as speedily as they enriched their shareholders.

Grassley was not alone in his disillusion with the Pentagon. As congressmen and senators grew sick of having to answer questions about $7,000 coffee pots and $658 ashtrays from their constituents, the consensus for a steeply rising defence budget began to evaporate. In 1980, a Harris poll found that 71 per cent of those who replied supported increased defence spending; a similar poll, taken in 1985, found that figure shrunk to a mere nine per cent. Just as Congress had discovered that throwing money at social programmes was not a long-term answer to the problem of poverty, so a similar feeling now set in about defence. For the first time, many politicians in Washington came to appreciate the significance of Eisenhower's dark warnings about the military industrial complex.

But Congress, though grown collectively weary of the defence industry, is in fact part of the problem. Too many individual congressmen are prepared to acknowledge abuses in the abstract, but reluctant to punish firms which operate in their districts, and though ready enough to 'micro-manage' defence, through a swarm of different committees, Congress rarely shows itself able to see broad strategic perspectives.

It is not just that defence contractors make handsome contributions to campaign funds (though they do, and the amount of defence money poured into 'political action committees' doubled during the Reagan build-up). Nor is it just that the 'conspiracy of optimism' – i.e. the constant lying about costs and performance – makes it hard for congressmen to judge individual programmes: though both the baffling complexity of modern hardware and the length of time it takes to progress from drawing board to battlefield (ten to fifteen years on average) militate against Congress's ability to make rational judgements. The real problem is that Congress has a stake in the system as it currently operates. For one thing, the economic recovery which began in late 1982 owed a huge amount to the upsurge in defence spending (financed, of course, in classic Keynesian fashion, by growing federal deficits). And the defence industry in the US employs millions of people: indeed, the jobs of one in ten Americans depend directly or indirectly on defence spending; there are twice as many defence workers as farmers; in some states, notably California, defence-related employment is the largest single source of personal income. So defence, as Senator William Proxmire once put it, has become 'a public works programme'. Politicians may be genuinely outraged by the behaviour of the defence industry and the Pentagon but they are reluctant to take steps which will increase unemployment in their districts. The Soviet threat to the West may seem shadowy at best, but the prospect of a major defence plant closing, or of a whole spate of new jobs for a struggling district, is a matter of more immediate concern in a country where the breathing space between elections is short.

Thus Representative Joseph Addabbo, who led the campaign to kill the B1 nuclear bomber, realized the immensity of his task when he visited the headquarters of the manufacturer, Rockwell International Corporation. He saw on the wall a map of America with strings radiating from Rockwell's main plant to dozens of subcontractors involved in building individual parts of the plane. The strings spread over the whole map. As Addabbo knew, many of his fellow congressmen were unhappy about the B1, a bomber designed to penetrate Soviet air defences in the 1980s and 1990s which had been cancelled by Jimmy Carter but revived by Ronald

Reagan (estimated cost: $26.5 billion for 100 planes). In the end, however, parochial considerations won out. Potential supporters told Addabbo: 'Joe, they've built a plant in my district. I need the jobs.'

Actually, the B1, though an extraordinarily complicated aircraft – it is so full of tubes and wires that it has been described as resembling a heart transplant patient – represents a sounder investment than many other Pentagon projects. (It is, for example, a better addition to America's arsenal than the MX missile, because it can perform a dual nuclear/conventional role and is not as vulnerable to pre-emptive strike.) But the fact is that support for the B1 seemed to depend more on its job-creating capacity than its military value. Among its supporters was Senator Alan Cranston from California. He made the establishment of a 'freeze' on the nuclear arsenals of both superpowers the prime plank of his challenge for the Democratic presidential nomination in 1984. Despite this, and despite arguing that 'one of the worst ways to provide jobs is through defence spending', Cranston has continued to be a fan of the B1. And no one except perhaps his closest aides doubts for a moment that the main reason he supports it is because Rockwell's main plant is in his state. No congressman or senator is free from the kind of pressures which were operating on Cranston. Even Addabbo, though a long-standing and vehement critic of the Pentagon, tenaciously looked after the interests of the Grumman Corporation, manufacturers of the navy's F14 fighter. Grumman has a base on Long Island; many of its employees live in the Queens district of New York which Addabbo represents.

When, in 1983, senators began to talk of cuts in defence spending, John Tower, the chairman of the Senate Armed Services Committee, wrote a letter to all his 99 colleagues asking them to list which defence projects they would be willing to give up *in their home states*. He got just six replies.

Consider the F18, which is the navy's answer to the air force's relatively cheap lightweight fighter, the F16. It has turned into another cuckoo in the nest. Conceived in the early 1970s as a simple, cheap navy fighter to supplement the horrendously expensive F14 (which it was clear the navy could not afford in adequate numbers), it grew rapidly into an all-purpose, all-capable plane as the navy and its manufacturers, McDonnell Douglas, crammed into it the familiar technological wizardry: new engines, new radar, fancy computers. From a plane which, when planned, might have cost $5 million apiece, it was set by 1982 to cost $30 million – almost as much as the F14.

By then, of course, cancellation was almost out of the question. Weapons programmes acquire a momentum of their own, and by the late 1970s thousands of jobs all over the country were tied up in the F18. Some 20,000 companies scattered among 44 states were building parts of the plane, a powerful incentive for Congress and the Senate to press ahead with it. Among those backing it were two stalwart liberals, Tip O'Neill, the House Speaker, and Senator Edward Kennedy: both were from Massachusetts where, as it happened, General Electric were making the engines for the F18.

The F18 has many backers. It also has many critics, among them hawkish defence analysts like Jeffrey Record, a former Capitol Hill staffer, who charges that the F18 is an aeroplane without a role, and will not help the navy at all but simply preserve their requirement for large carriers. But whatever its merits, the point is that the F18 is not now what it was conceived to be, that Congress, having once given it the go-ahead, was powerless to insist that costs be kept down. Though strong on principle, its members are too bound up in the system they have helped create to exercise any real powers of supervision. And the services and industry, needless to say, do all they possibly can to ensure that their pet projects survive unscathed. As well as contributing heavily to political campaigns, defence contractors also spend large sums on sophisticated lobbying operations. The mere anticipation of Reagan's five-year defence build-up, according to the *Los Angeles Times*, was enough to persuade several top defence contractors to double the size of their 'government affairs offices' in Washington.

Just how thorough lobbying efforts can be emerged in June 1982, with the leaking of a computer printout from the Lockheed Corporation, manufacturers of the C5 transport plane. When it was built in the early 1970s, the C5A 'Galaxy' was the world's largest aircraft (at the time of writing it still is). But the programme was consistently plagued by engineering and design problems: first the undercarriage proved unsatisfactory, then the wings began to crack, and though Lockheed, the major contractor, suggested this wasn't serious ('We know that a new wing is not necessary. We know that a report will not come out that a new wing is necessary,' declared a company executive to Congress in 1979), new wings did have to be built, and the tab, of course (an extra $1.6 billion), was picked up by the taxpayer. The process dismayed many congressmen, such as Allard Lowenstein, who felt that the project was such a dismal one that it should have been terminated:

I speak with some sadness ... I love this place [Congress]. To be elected to it is easily the greatest honour I shall expect to attain. Yet much that happens here leaves me feeling that we are not conducting ourselves as we should ... We have greater obligations to the country than we have shown in our behaviour today.

When the air force decided to buy a new, modified version of the C5A – to be called the C5B – they anticipated a good deal of opposition. So did

Lockheed. (This fear was reinforced because Boeing came up with a competing proposal: they suggested adapting 747s for military purposes, which would have been cheaper and, in the view of some powerful legislators, more suitable.) But the computer printouts which leaked in June 1982 suggested what the Boeing forces had to contend with. Technically, the services are forbidden *by law* to lobby, though the law is largely ignored. The printout made it clear that a specially convened C5 Group, comprising air force officers and Lockheed executives, prepared a careful campaign to win congressional support for their project.

The Group's activities provide an object-lesson in American political tactics. They drafted a letter for Caspar Weinberger to send to the heads of key committees on Capitol Hill, for example; developed a 'target list' of members to approach directly; prepared a 'soft sell' Dear Colleague letter in the hope that backers of the project would send it other potential supporters; persuaded Andrew Young (ambassador to the United Nations under Jimmy Carter) to 'work' the black caucus in Congress (knowing that he might have the clout to influence a group which is traditionally anti-defence); compiled a list of members who were 'PAC-wired' (i.e. had political action committees behind them into which financial contributions could be pumped) and persuaded congressmen from Georgia, where Lockheed had its main plant, to play an active role in the campaign. Their efforts paid off: in the end the requisite funds for the huge $5.35 billion C5B project were safely appropriated and the Boeing rival fell by the wayside.

And afterwards, when the printouts revealed the extent of the lobbying, an air force general responsible for the C5 programme, Lt. Gen. Kelly Burke, justified the approach as common practice: 'You're just wrong if you think this is a highly unusual happening. Any time you get competing views, it's customary for government to work with those contractors whose views are congruent with the president's ... I do not want to sound platitudinous, but all you're seeing is democracy in action. This is the way the system is supposed to work.'

Among America's Nato allies procurement problems do not loom as large as they do in America. This is largely a function of size: the Europeans have much smaller defence establishments; they are not nearly as rich. (It is also, in part, a function of secrecy: the debate about procurement is much more open in America than it is anywhere in Europe.) To be sure, on a smaller scale, a fascination with high technology is apparent. The latest generation of British and German tanks, the Challenger and the Leopard II, contain much of the computerized gadgetry which adorns the M1 (though the Leopard took only five years to produce, a quarter of the time it took for the M1, and many consider it a better tank). The British armoured personnel carrier, the MCV 80, has some disturbing similarities to the ill-fated Bradley fighting vehicle; it, too, is a hybrid between the traditional battlefield taxi and a tank, and many critics say it is overpriced and over-burdened with 'bells and whistles'.

A new telephone switching system called Ptarmigan, built for the British army, follows the familiar pattern of unnecessary complication. The handset alone costs £3,000 apiece, and though it is capable of performing all kinds of marvels – encrypting human speech into code so that the enemy cannot listen in; transmitting pictures; feeding data directly into a computer – the army were offered a handset only marginally less capable at a much cheaper price. But Plessey, the manufacturer, was obliged to build a telephone 'hardened to withstand nuclear weapons effects' – meaning there had to be an extremely expensive steel cover rather than the plastic one originally suggested – and this, along with other elaborate finishing touches, sent the price of the telephone soaring up (and also, incidentally, helped dash Britain's chances of selling the Ptarmigan system to the US army, which preferred a cheaper alternative made in France).

But, on the whole, European defence establishments are less obsessed with 'state of the art' technology than the Pentagon. Disposing of less money, they tend to be prepared to settle for less. Thus Britain's Harrier jump-jet, which performed well in the Falklands, stemmed from a breakthrough in vertical take-off technology in the 1950s. Since then it has steadily been improved: but the improvements have been 'incremental'. There has been no attempt to add on a whole range of untried new gadgets.

Nevertheless the history of European defence since the war has, like America's, been one of exploding costs and declining value for money. European inventories of tanks, planes and ships are shrinking too. Europe, like America, is on what has been called the 'road to absurdity': if costs keep rising as they are no one, in the end, will be able to afford any equipment at all.

A major problem is the lack of any real cooperation between the allies. There have, of course, been certain collaborative projects, most notably the joint effort by Germany, Italy and Britain to build the Tornado. But such projects do not always save money: with all the difficulties of competing specifications and liaison between different countries, Tornado turned out to be formidably expensive, probably more so than it would have been had it been produced by any of the partners acting alone. And the fate of the European Fighter Aircraft, a new mutilateral venture, may be precisely the same.

What militates against effective cooperation – against what Nato jargon calls 'rat, spec and stan' (rationalization, specialization and standardization) – is each country's commitment to preserving balanced forces and its own 'defence industrial base'. At heart the issue is one of national sovereignty. Effective cooperation would require each ally to accept a significant diminution in its own national sovereignty, and that is not a likely prospect. Hence Western Europe, as a whole, duplicates the inefficiencies of the Pentagon. Just as congressmen want their states to have a fair share of defence work, so European governments, especially in a time of rising unemployment, are reluctant to close down defence industries and buy from abroad.

Thus Nato nations, according to one survey, are now busy developing some 21 different ground-to-air, air-to-ground and anti-tank missiles, 14 combat aircraft, four tanks and six new tactical communications systems – none of which are compatible with one another. There is duplication in all kinds of other weapons, too, from recoilless rifles to fire control radars and naval guns.

Instead of buying the American Apache attack helicopter the West Germans decided to build their own, expecting to be able to do it for half the cost. By 1985 the new West German helicopter looked as if it would cost perhaps twice as much as its American equivalent. Similarly, the British decided to build the Nimrod early warning aircraft instead of buying Boeing's Airborne Warning and Control System (AWACS) planes. This was an especially silly decision. By 1985 Nimrod was millions of pounds over budget and still not airborne. The role it is intended to play is a vital one: to fly out over the North Sea during a war and, using its radar and highly sophisticated computers, track up to 1,000 Soviet Mig fighters and cruise missiles coming in from the north-east. But by 1985, two years after it was due to be in service, the Nimrod's radar still did not work properly (performing, according to one August 1985 account, at 40 per cent of required efficiency), and its airframe, based on an ancient 1948 Comet aircraft, could not accommodate all the necessary gadgetry (including cooling equipment designed to prevent the whole system from overheating). 'Without Nimrod, there is a bloody great hole in the UK's air defences,' one source told the *Sunday Times*. 'The Tornado is toothless and the Shackletons [Britain's 1950s vintage early warning aircraft] are being held together with bits of glue.'

But cases like this, to be fair, arise in part because of US procurement policy. The Europeans complain that because pressures from the US Congress mean that America rarely buys equipment from Europe, so they themselves have considerably less incentive to buy their hardware from America.

The lack of cooperation between the allies would cause all kinds of problems in a war – not least for the huge influx of reinforcements which would be expected to arrive after an attack on the Central Front. As defence expert Robert Kleiman has observed, Nato forces would often be unable 'to refuel each other's planes, repair each other's tanks and shoot each other's ammunition'. Worse, pilots would have great difficulty avoiding shooting down their allies. In an exercise in 1974, because of the lack of a common 'identification friend or foe' communications system, Nato forces themselves 'shot down' 30 of about 60 of their own aircraft. Ground forces would have a similar problem.

Pilots returning from bombing runs over enemy territory would be all right if they returned to their own sector, but in the confusion of battle this would not always be easy or possible. One Pentagon veteran of Vietnam and an expert on Nato's problems offers this assessment of the pilots' predicament: 'They all know there are privates on our side on the ground, armed with Stinger [anti-aircraft] missiles, capable of taking them out. It you're coming back from a mission you're supposed to fly low, with your flaps down. The idea is, if you do that – which is like walking around with your drawers down, i.e. not very reasonable – the private down on the ground will know you're not a Russian because no one expects a Russian to come in slow. So if someone comes in slow with his flaps down he has to be a Nato pilot. But the pilots know if they're in the position of having to trust a private on the ground with a Stinger, Murphy's law will apply. So these pilots are telling me: screw these goddam procedures. I'm coming back at full bore 50 ft off the ground. I'll be past that goddam guy before he knows I'm there ... Oh, and another reason you don't want to fly low and slow is that you have to start being low and slow over Soviet air defences. And that's the box we're in simply because the Germans, the British and the US cannot decide which goddam black box to buy and they're all buying different black boxes that are not interoperable. You're OK if you fly back in your own sector. But if you get knocked off course or for whatever reason get out of sector, all bets are off.'

Like America, the Europeans have also tended to concentrate on 'big ticket' items (planes, ships, tanks) rather than on 'readiness'. There are drastic shortages all over the Central Front.

Ammunition. In some sectors, the 155 mm ammunition used by most Nato artillery pieces would run out after a week or ten days. So, in about the same amount of time, would anti-tank missiles and even much mortar and rifle ammunition. Air-to-air missiles are also in short supply.

Transport. Nato is very short of transport, especially of five-ton trucks to take ammunition and supplies to the front line during a war.

Communications equipment. 'If the cee cubed eye [C3I, for command, control communications and intelligence] doesn't work, it doesn't matter what we have,' says one Pentagon expert. 'It's every man for himself, and that's no way to fight a war.' Yet much of the equipment designed to facilitate this crucial role is very fragile. For example, there are a handful of microwave towers on the Central Front which would be critical in enabling commanders to communicate with each other in time of war. They are currently guarded by barbed wire and lightly manned guard posts. In a war, say US army experts, these would present few problems for a skilled saboteur ('or even for a good marksman with a rifle,' said one specialist). Sometimes, inadequate communications – and differences in systems used among the allies – lead to farcical moments. In one exercise, under pressure, an American general requested permission from his HQ to 'go nuclear'. There was no reply. An inquiry later revealed that his message had been rerouted to the Italian public telephone system and vanished.

Protected air bases. America's European allies agreed, in the mid-1970s, to provide a whole series of so-called 'collocated operating bases' for the Americans. These would consist of maintenance facilities and hardened shelters on exposed runways near the front line, so that American aircraft flying across the Atlantic in time of war – and some 1,500 fighter planes would be expected in the first ten days – would have adequate protection when they arrived. So far none of these 'COBS' have been built (they were supposed to be paid for out of Nato's common, or 'infrastructure', budget, but this has been kept short of the requisite funds). Thus the American air force, naturally enough, worry that their highly prized modern fighters will arrive in Europe only to become sitting targets – as likely to get destroyed on the runway as in the air.

The American hi-tech bias, combined with a lack of effective cooperation among Nato allies, has done much to weaken Western defence. Fortunately for the West, however, the Russian fighting machine is not as formidable as it is often cracked up to be. The Russians have their problems, too, and though their attitude to conventional weapons remains, by and large, more sensible than the West's, they have fallen into some similar traps.

The basis of Russian strength is numbers. They have consistently managed to outproduce the West in everything from tanks and aircraft to anti-aircraft guns and personnel carriers. They have done this by making simpler, cruder, cheaper weapons. In the early 1960s, General Creighton Abrams, who was once described by his World War Two superior, General George Patton, as 'my champion tank commander', inspected a Soviet tank captured during the Korean war. Abrams, who was posthumously to lend his name to the most complex tank ever built, the M1 Abrams, said afterwards: 'I got in the goddam tank, and it didn't do all the fancy things the colonels want in our tanks. You couldn't push the joystick and make the thing turn around, but it could do every damn thing you want a tank to do.'

In the late 1970s, a team of American engineers compiled a report for the Pentagon on the different approaches taken by the superpowers to weapons design. The engineers concluded that the difference lay not so much in the amount of money spent as in the Russians' ability to churn out greater quantities of equipment because they 'think poor': on the whole, Russian weapons systems have been less the victims of technological complexity and cripplingly high costs than American ones.

Among the examples the engineers used to illustrate their case were tank tracks. The tracks of a tank, which enable it to move smoothly over rough ground and to keep stable, clearly need to be solid and durable. Those of the T55 and T62 (throughout the 1950s and 1960s the mainstay of the Red Army) were just this, simply a 'rough casting which did not even need machining', according to the design report. This meant there were fewer parts to assemble, and less danger of the tracks 'slipping off' in combat – a problem which has afflicted many modern tanks and which has been compared to a boxer losing his shorts in the middle of a round.

Similarly, the standard Soviet jet engine, designed by the Tumansky Design Bureau (near Moscow), was much simpler than its US counterpart. 'The total number of parts,' say the US engineers, 'including fasteners, washers, and so forth, of Tumansky engines is estimated to be only thirty or forty per cent of the number found in American engines with comparable performance characteristics. One Tumansky engine, which was used in a Mig fighter, had less than one sixth as many parts as the comparable J79 engine used in American aircraft.' The Soviet engine, according to the US report, proved altogether more reliable than its American counterpart – and cost one third as much (indeed, it has been estimated that the Tumansky engine, even if built in the US – with American materials and with the labour force paid American wages – would still be less than half the cost of the US one).

The watchword in the Soviet design bureaux, then, was caution, and the US study team suggested that the make-up of the bureaux themselves helped promote this. In contrast to the Pentagon, where programme managers tended to change disconcertingly often, Soviet design bureaux tended to work together for long periods, sometimes 25 years or more. One key difference between the two sides was that whereas the average 'lead time' for a weapon in the West (i.e. the amount of time it takes to progress from drawing board to battlefield) was 10 to 14 years, much of this made up of endless wrangling over specifications and constant design

changes, the average lead time in the Soviet Union was much less –
between eight and ten years. The advantages, as the engineers pointed out,
were obvious: the West was always making 'quantum leaps' from one
generation of equipment to the next, with many more untried bells and
whistles than the Soviet Union. The Soviet Union, on the other hand,
could proceed more incrementally because there was less of a gap between
one generation of equipment and the next, and less gambling on half-
understood gadgetry. As a former Pentagon official, Leo Sullivan, once
put it, they appeared to have 'made a conscious decision to stay below
the leading edge of technology'. To put it another way, they clearly took
note of the precept of the Soviet helicopter designer, Mikhail Mil:
'Comrades, make it simple, make it rugged, make it reliable, make it
work.'

Not that it did always work. But Soviet shortcomings tended to be more
the result of sloppy engineering and poor construction on the factory floor
than over-ambitious design. The gear change on the old T55 tank, for
example, was so stiff that its drivers had to keep a sledgehammer by their
side to hit the gear lever with when they wanted to change gear. And the
T55s were scarcely reliable: various accounts suggest they broke down
frequently. Still, the Soviet approach emphasized numbers and has
continued to do so: because the Russians modernized more often, but less
dramatically, they managed to keep their numbers up more easily than
the West. The Russians have also tended to build more different types of
system than the Americans – they have a whole range of anti-aircraft guns,
for example – rather than relatively few 'all-capable' systems.

There are signs that this approach is changing, and that the Russians
are 'catching up' with the West's hi-tech obsessions. Instead of being
relieved by this, however, Caspar Weinberger, President Reagan's defence
secretary, believes that it justifies the current Pentagon shopping list:

> There's a sort of myth around that what we should do is buy a great
> deal more of very much less sophisticated kinds of weapons and
> planes very much less expensively, and that this quantitative advantage
> is all we need. This myth is based on the assumption that the Soviets
> don't have very good equipment, and that is – a myth. They have
> very good equipment, and they have an ability to produce very large
> numbers of very sophisticated, complicated, expensive and high-
> quality equipment. So we cannot do less.

This begs a number of questions. For one thing, Weinberger makes the
clearly false assumption that 'sophisticated' is interchangeable with 'good'.
For another, he disparages his critics by suggesting that they believe

'quantitative advantage is all we need', which is not true at all. They simply believe that quantity should not be sacrificed lightly.

The fact is that the Soviet Union, in its attempt to close the 'technology gap', is falling into many of the same traps as the West. The concern which has driven them to do this has been well expressed by Michael Binyon, a former Moscow correspondent of *The Times*. 'The worry that they have, not only in the military sector but in almost every aspect of life,' he says, 'is that they're not as good as the West, and whatever they do it's not going to be as good; and that, therefore, they don't actually believe that they're superior, even when objective analysis of what they've got on the ground would say they are. They don't believe that they're better off, that they're stronger, until they hear the West saying it.' Even then, they worry. Somehow, the West, they fear, with devilish cunning, is going to pull a technological rabbit from its hat and thus defeat all their efforts. So, as Andrew Cockburn charts in a study of the Soviet military, the tendency has been to try and catch up with the West. 'The Soviet Air Force is now busily imitating [Western] "advanced technology" systems, including "all-weather" radar, and complex "look-down-shoot-down" systems – the same features that have made American fighters so expensive and unreliable.'

Not only the air force: the Soviet T64 and T72 tanks have had plenty of problems too. Though ostensibly at least in the class of the American M60, they are in fact much slower and break down twice as often; they are highly flammable and are cursed rather than blessed with an 'autoloader' which is intended to spare the tank gunner the task of ramming shells and charges into the breech. This works by means of a special pair of 'grippers'. It is said, however, that the autoloader has a tendency to try and load not shells but the gunner himself into the breech. Says one US army officer: 'We believe this is how the Red Army chorus gets its soprano section.'

The Russians have other problems, too. The Red Army may be large but it is uneven in quality: it is plagued by all kinds of problems from nationalism (only 50 per cent of conscripts are Russian) to alcoholism to lack of initiative. (Until recently, at least, no one under the rank of company commander in the Soviet Union was taught map-reading, so in the event of a Soviet invasion of Western Europe some Soviet units may simply get lost.) Too much can be made of this ('even the Black Watch get drunk,' as a British official put it), just as too much can be made of the potential unreliability of Russia's allies. Were the Russians to invade Europe, the Warsaw Pact would undoubtedly fight – 'better a Nato bullet in the chest than a KGB one in the back,' as Victor Suvorov, a Soviet defector, has observed – but the longer a war lasted the more concern Moscow would have to feel about Eastern Europe, and about its long, vulnerable exposed lines of supply.

The Soviet threat therefore is often exaggerated. The Red Army is not ten feet tall, and its equipment is not as wonderful as Caspar Weinberger suggests. Yet the tendency of Pentagon analysts to overestimate Soviet weapons has long been used to justify the American hi-tech bias. The Shilka air defence weapon, which provided the inspiration for the Divad gun, turned out far less magical than had been suspected: it was inaccurate and unreliable. And the Soviet Foxbat Mig 25 fighter – supposedly capable of travelling at three times the speed of sound and made of titanium – turned out to be far less awesome when the Americans managed to take one apart and evaluate its technology. A defecting Russian pilot, Viktor Belenko, landed one on a Japanese airstrip in 1976, and the US was soon aware that it was not built of titanium but of steel and that whereas it might just be capable of reaching Mach 3 it would only do so in time to run out of fuel.

By overestimating the threat, and over-technologizing weapons, American defence procurement is caught in a vicious circle: outnumbered by the enemy, the Pentagon tries to overcome this through technology; the result is spiralling costs and fewer systems. So the Pentagon is even more outnumbered, and tries even harder to compensate, and so on. As Chuck Spinney, a Pentagon analyst who has braved the wrath of his superiors time after time to argue against the trend, puts it:

> By ignoring the real world, we have evolved a self-reinforcing yet scientifically unsupportable faith in the military usefulness of ever-increasing technological complexity. The costs ... can be generalized into low readiness, slower modernization, and declining forces ... our strategy of pursuing ever-increasing technological complexity and sophistication has made high-technology solutions and combat readiness mutually exclusive.

A Belgian general once suggested in a meeting with allied and American top brass that the Alliance might be able to mount a more effective defence against Russia if it replaced all its existing equipment with men on bicycles armed with bazookas. It was a joke, of course, but maybe not that much worse an approach than the existing one.

The obsession with technology is threatening to bust budgets and sapping the West's ability to fight. As Jeffrey Record puts it: 'Technology proved indecisive in Korea, ultimately irrelevant in Vietnam, and unreliable in Iran. But this seems not to have shaken that faith [in] technical advance as the solution to most problems on the battlefield ...'

Every so often, a good and effective weapon *does* make it through the Pentagon's procurement system, though, as a CIA report noted during the

Reagan build-up, this is usually in spite of the system rather than because of it.

One example is the A10 anti-tank aircraft we looked at in chapter 2. Another is a navy bomb called 'Skipper'. Skipper was born after the Soviet invasion of Afghanistan in 1979, when the US navy worried that it might have to go into action in the Persian Gulf carrying nothing except 1960s-vintage bombs to attack Soviet surface ships. So the remote naval weapons centre in China Lake, California, produced a very simple design. Working against the clock, its inventors had a bomb ready to be dropped in just ten months. And they did it, as the *Washington Post* noted, by sticking to 'off-the-shelf' technology – a 1,000-pound bomb, a rocket motor, a 'seeker' in the nose capable of homing in on a target illuminated by a laser beam.

They used hacksaws and a sand blaster to shave superfluous parts from the motor. The ignition system was salvaged from the pilot ejection system in an F104 warplane. Finally, the engineers tacked on a couple of matchbook-size pieces of metal worth 50 cents apiece to make the bomb spin during flight for stability.

After an early failure or two, the Skipper began to work well. It could be dropped six miles from its target and guided to it by a laser beam (easier to do from a naval aircraft than on the battlefield). But though the naval officers and engineers were impressed by Skipper, they had to fight hard to enable the unsexy, indubitably ugly $20,000 bomb to survive. Competing against it, under an air force contract to Texas Instruments, was another bomb, called Triple L (Low Level Laser Guided), an altogether more sophisticated and more expensive weapon. Triple L, however, had some powerful backers in Congress and the Pentagon, and though Skipper fared well in tests, it almost fell by the wayside for lack of a patron. Only when the navy secretary John Lehman got to hear about it and personally intervened, and the Triple L was cancelled because of cost overruns, did the Skipper finally earn itself a definite place in the US procurement system. But the Skipper, as the *Washington Post* pointed out, started life as an 'orphan'. With no strong backing from industry or from a bureaucracy in love with 'the expensive, complex and sleek', it seemed to survive more by good luck than good management.

6

ET

It is known, like Stephen Spielberg's famous character from outer space, as ET. To its advocates, and there are many, it could be Nato's salvation, a breakthrough which could finally enable the West to even up the balance of forces. To its detractors it is a delusion, another example of Nato clutching at a technological solution to its problems, as unreal as the hero of the Spielberg film.

In the Pentagon script, ET stands for Emerging Technology. Many of the weapons involved, in other words, are still a gleam in developers' eyes. But the theory behind them is already complete. It goes like this.

Nato, though badly outgunned by the Warsaw Pact, might just be able to hold the line in the first phase of a war on the Central Front. The greatest danger would come later, for the Soviet attack would unfold in waves, or echelons. The first echelon would be followed within 48 hours by a second, and moving up from deeper in Eastern Europe and, ultimately, from Russia itself would come a third and possibly fourth echelon. 'It would be like a bloody battering ram coming at you,' as one Nato general once put it to me.

In 1973, as the US army began to turn its attention back to Europe at the end of the Vietnam war, a team of defence analysts began a secret and detailed assessment of Soviet operational plans. The analysts worked for the BDM Corporation, a major US army thinktank sited in a large office building on the south back of the Potomac in Washington, and they concluded that the Russians had worked out very carefully how they might take Europe, with the armies in East Germany (the first echelon) taking West Germany up to the Rhine, the armies in Poland and the Slovak part of Czechoslovakia moving up to take the Low Countries, and the armies in the western Soviet Union, the third echelon, completing the conquest.

It was out of BDM's work in 1973 that there grew the whole concept of 'deep strike' or 'follow on forces attack' – and ET. The idea was that if Nato could mount accurate strikes deep behind enemy lines at the outset of war, it might prevent the second, third and fourth echelons from ever reaching the battlefield. That way, Nato ground forces would have to deal only with the first echelon, and perhaps not even with all of that, since the rear elements of the first echelon would be vulnerable to deep strikes too. Thus would Nato be able to exploit the principal weakness in the Soviet attack, disrupt its timetable and crush its reinforcements before they could even be brought to bear.

That was what BDM thought the Pentagon should seek to do. The question was, how to do it? When the initial analytic work was done there seemed only one possible way, and that was by using nuclear weapons: only they could provide the combination of accuracy and blast needed to destroy the kind of targets BDM had in mind. The notion of going nuclear at the outset of a war, however, was unthinkable. Bernard Rogers, when he became SACEUR, knew that he would never get the political authority to do it. Neither a US president nor any of his allied heads of government would consider going nuclear so early.

A second option might be to use aircraft, and indeed some of the ET bombs and rockets being developed have been designed for aircraft. But modern aircraft, for all their computerized gadgetry, remain vulnerable to anti-aircraft fire and scarcely constitute a foolproof way of implementing the kind of precisely coordinated strike against small, well-defended targets which was envisaged. The best option, it seemed to the most dedicated advocates of ET, was the use of long-range, conventionally armed cruise and ballistic missiles.

As it happened, the use of such missiles, by the late 1970s, was becoming conceivable. Thanks to new propulsion fuels and better guidance systems, missiles were in theory at least becoming much more accurate; similarly, it was becoming easier to spot and identify targets quickly, thanks to the development of the new high-resolution 'doppler' radar which could track not only stationary targets but moving vehicles as well (this was being incorporated in the huge AWACS early warning aircraft which would fly high over the battlefield, and also in crucial surveillance satellites). Most striking of all were the advances in computer technology which theoretically made possible the mammoth task first of 'acquiring targets' – having the information from the satellites or radar systems relayed back to a central point and correctly assessed – and second of 'battle management' – coordinating a whole series of strikes against a huge number of very precise targets.

According to Dr Malcolm Currie, one-time director of research and development at the Pentagon, these developments had, by 1975, 'brought us to the threshold of what will become a true revolution in conventional warfare.' Many scientists agreed. So did the US army, which saw ET as the perfect complement to its new stress on more flexible 'manoeuvre' tactics. But would ET really transform the military balance and give Nato the edge? Were the hopes of its backers really justified?

There were two kinds of targets which the advocates of ET had in mind. The first of these were critical fixed targets and 'choke points' – these ranged from communications facilities and major airfields (80 per cent of the Warsaw Pact air force is based at only 24 airfields) to railway lines (specifically the power stations which feed them and the rail yards where troops brought from Russia would disembark), and, most important, the 60 or so bridges which span the main rivers in Eastern Europe (the Oder, the Elbe and the Vistula). But to strike these targets, and sever the Russian advance, would be a tall order. Putting airfields out of action, for example, is notoriously difficult: despite successive British attempts to put the airfield at Port Stanley out of action during the Falklands war, the Argentinians managed to keep it operational until the very end: no sooner had it been bombed by Vulcans in a night raid than it was swiftly repaired. And though the bridges spanning the Elbe, the Vistula and the Oder seem attractive targets, bridges can be rapidly replaced. Whatever the Red Army's shortcomings, it is clearly well aware of the hazards it might have to face in crossing three rivers, since its inventory contains a formidable array of mobile bridges and bridge-building gear, including huge rafts which would carry tanks across in an emergency. Some experts believe that the Warsaw Pact would be able to replace most of its bridges, if struck, within two hours.

There is a further complication. Like so much of modern technology, ET assumes that the Russians will behave in a setpiece, predictable fashion. But before we examine this we must glance at the second set of targets which Nato was contemplating.

The second set of targets were not 'fixed' but 'moving': enemy tanks, to be precise, as they surged forward towards the battle area. The problems here, needless to say, are horrendous – much worse than in killing fixed targets. (Not the least of these problems would be actually distinguishing the targets to be hit. According to one man who spent a year studying radar screens in South-East Asia, all you see are white blips: you can't tell whether they are tanks, or trucks, or cars, or even houses.)

By the early 1980s, a number of different systems were under study in the Pentagon, all of them involving extraordinarily complex technology. Typical of these was 'Assault Breaker'. Assault Breaker is not a weapon. It is really a series of different technologies harnessed together to form a weapon. In an interview in 1981, James Tegnelia, the Pentagon official in charge of the Assault Breaker project, explained how it would work. 'I have an airborne radar (mounted on a TR-1 plane, say, or a Boeing 707) which surveys a geographical area of 200 square kilometres,' he said. 'The airborne radar is at 30,000 ft and is normally 50 kilometres behind the battle line' to stay out of range of enemy surface-to-air missiles. This radar would find and track targets, and the targeting data it gathered would be transmitted to a special 'tactical fusion' processing station. The station, 30 kilometres or more behind the battle line, would also receive intelligence from satellites, sensors and other intelligence sources. Once information had been assessed, and a target identified (an enemy tank formation), an army or air force commander on the spot would make the decision to attack it. Then, according to Tegnelia, a missile would be fired and the radar plane would track both missile and targets, whether stationary or moving. The plane would issue mid-course guidance commands to the missile, which would have a range of 100 kilometres or more. Then, once the missile was in the vicinity of its targets, it would dispense a payload of 'smart' submunitions or bomblets (perhaps 24 in all), each of which would have its own infrared guidance system and each of which, in theory, would home in with devastating accuracy on an individual tank.

Will these missiles, with their tiny submunitions, actually work? The history of 'smart' anti-tank missiles (such as Maverick: see chapter 2) suggests that it is wise to be sceptical. The technology required for success is exotic, to say the least. One proposal, for example, involves a system called Skeet, the brainchild of the Avco Corporation. A total of 228 heat-seeking bomblets would be encased in special delivery vehicles. These vehicles would be released by the Assault Breaker missile and descend by parachute. At a predetermined height the vehicle would then release its Skeets in pairs and each Skeet, with its infrared guidance system, would seek out an individual tank (drawn by the heat from the engine) and fire a molten lump of metal into its relatively unprotected top. (A similarly exotic system, being developed for the air force, is called Wasp; in this instance, the submunitions would work thanks to millimetre wave guidance systems rather than infrared.)

No one has any idea whether Skeet, Wasp or any of the other potential components of Assault Breaker can be made to work effectively. The tests which have taken place, as at the time of writing, have only succeeded in the most benign environment. In 1982, for example, an Assault Breaker missile did manage to drop infrared submunitions on to five tanks in the White Sands desert in New Mexico. But according to the magazine *National Journal*, the target tanks were old and stationary and their engines more exposed than those of modern tanks, making it much easier for heat-seeking missiles to home in. These were not the only steps taken to make the test work. The land round the target tanks had been bulldozed and graded and the vegetation removed so that the tanks stood out clearly amidst the 'ground clutter'; and since the test occurred early in the morning the 'thermal contrast' between the desert surroundings and the tanks was strong.

With such carefully organized 'success-oriented' testing the Pentagon may yet convince itself that even in the Skeet project (an unmitigated failure in early tests) it has a winner on its hands. The real snag is that the Russians have been more or less left out of the picture. This is unfortunate, since even if Assault Breaker can be made to work in peaceful New Mexico, that is no guarantee that it will work on a battlefield in central Europe.

Assault Breaker is what is known as a 'sequential' system, and the best analogy for such a system is the 'accumulator' bet which inveterate gamblers sometimes place at race meetings. To win an accumulator you have to pick not just one winner but a series; if all the horses you select come in first you stand to make a considerable return on your investment; if just one fails, you lose your stake. The odds against success, therefore, are long. Prudent gamblers do not bet on accumulators.

Assault Breaker is the military equivalent of an accumulator. To work successfully, it requires a whole string of extraordinarily complicated things to work perfectly. To make it fail, the enemy, in this case the Russians, would simply have to disrupt one link in the chain. The likelihood that they would be able to do this would seem to be strong. First the airborne radar which would be used to track the enemy's tanks could be jammed, or shot down. It would clearly be a high-value target, according to one official who has worked closely on the research for ET, which the Soviets 'will try to suppress just as we will try to suppress [any Soviet equivalent]'. The process of relaying the information from the radar back to the 'fusion' centre on the ground would be equally vulnerable to disruption; so would the next link in the sequence, communicating with the relevant ground commander. The next step which would have to work perfectly would be the launch of the expensive munitions-carrying missile or missiles; then would come the separation of the delivery vehicle from the main rocket and the release of the individual warheads ... The tanks would still have to be roughly in the same area they were when the intelligence was first gathered, and the submunitions would have to home in on their separate targets and, since they would be very small, strike them with pinpoint accuracy in order to destroy them. As one analyst put it: 'If you attach a 90 per cent probability to each of the links in the chain, which is high, you still may end up with a 50-50 proposition.' Not for nothing has the Assault Breaker been called 'a thirteen-miracle weapon'. The Soviets, to disrupt any of these miracles, could devise appropriate countermeasures, and probably at a fraction of the cost. If, for example, their tanks maintained an irregular speed on the way to the battlefield it would become that much harder – given the time between spotting them and delivering the warheads – to be sure of success.

In a detailed paper on Assault Breaker and its brethren, Steven Canby has given some examples of what could be done just to stop the submunitions from achieving their end. They could deploy a World War Two invention called 'chaff', thin metal or plastic rods which can be dispensed into the air and appear on radar screens as false targets. They could force civilian vehicles to mingle with tanks and thus 'draw the fire' of the submunitions as they descended (the high-resolution radar which Nato plans to use would supposedly be able to distinguish between tanks and other vehicles, but as yet there is no real evidence that it will be able to). The Soviets could even cover the trees along their attack route with 'emitters' giving off heat or radar images (strung parallel to roads like Christmas tree lights) – a further distraction for the submunitions. And finally, since the new weapons would be unable to pack much of a punch because of their small size, the Soviets would probably find it cheaper to harden the tops of their tanks than the West would to increase the explosive power of the submunitions. (Canby even suggests that the judicious placing of bags of children's marbles along the top of tanks might be sufficient to defeat the bomblets.)

There is another, more basic step the Russians might take to avoid the worst effects of ET, however. They could change their strategy.

In October 1981, the Russians staged a major military exercise on the Baltic Coast. It was called Zapad 81, and Western intelligence, which took a close interest, noted that, for the first time, the Red Army were experimenting with a different concept of operations: one which depended not on applying force right across the front but instead on making fast, concentrated attacks through the weakest sections of enemy lines.

Nato strategists were not taken unawares by what they saw. For several years, in the arcane pages of Warsaw Pact military journals, a debate had raged on the value of what have been called 'Operational Manoeuvre Groups' (OMGs). October 1981, however, provided the first glimpse of theory being turned into practice.

OMGs work by exploiting the weakness of the defence. Rather than trying to force breakthroughs right along the front line, the Red Army would instead launch a series of probing thrusts to try and find the most vulnerable points – like a pitchfork probing the soil or water trying to find gaps in a gutter. As soon as the crack had been found, a fast, heavily armed, heavily mechanized force which had been kept in reserve would close in and follow up the initial probe, attempting to force rapid passage deep behind enemy lines. It was a tactic the Russians used with some success against Germany in World War Two, but abandoned in the late 1940s because the danger of a war on the Central Front going nuclear argued against too much concentration of force (offering a more attractive target for nuclear attack). Besides, OMGs, as military strategists point out, are difficult to coordinate, especially in an army as bureaucratic as the Red Army, and pose considerable command and control problems. It is a risky strategy, too: 'nobody to get you out of trouble when you're deep in enemy territory', as one analyst of the Soviet military put it.

But the Russians are clearly working on it. They are perhaps less worried now than they used to be about Nato using nuclear weapons early in a conflict (we' will see why in the next chapter) and they could reap considerable advantages in terms of surprise and catching Nato off balance by deploying OMGs. Some analysts believe that they might be able to take West Germany, if not the whole of continental Europe, without ever having to draw on the divisions stationed back behind the critical rivers in Eastern Europe and Russia.

Thus ET, like the Maginot Line, could turn out to be irrelevant, and in attempting to achieve it, Nato, like the French, might come to neglect more immediate concerns: before dealing with the second, third and fourth echelons of the Warsaw Pact forces, after all, they would have to deal with the first.

If Zapad 81 is anything to go by, the Russians, as Professor John Erickson, one of Britain's leading Soviet experts, puts it, 'are not going to line up so that they can be bombed by Nato one sunny Friday afternoon'.

There is no doubt that ET would also be very expensive: the missiles envisaged are veritable 'silver bullets'. Once the technology is properly developed, 'smart' missiles may play a larger and more useful role in Western defence than they do now. And some of the systems contemplated may make it easier for aircraft to find and strike fixed targets, and even moving ones. (Pilots, at least, can see what they are shooting at. They can also call in reinforcements.)

But the Pentagon's hopes that ET will radically transform the military equation have little basis in reality. First, as in so many previous cases, they depend on inflated expectations of how well the new technology will work. Second, much of this technology is not even available yet. 'It's pure Buck Rogers just now,' as one army sceptic put it. 'This stuff doesn't exist, much as we might wish it did. It's just a gleam in some developer's eye.' Third, there are a whole range of countermeasures the Russians could deploy to defeat it, and which seem likely to work out cheaper than the technology. Fourth, the Russians could attack in such a way as to render ET irrelevant. And fifth, history suggests that if the Americans deploy ET the Russians will soon follow suit. ET fans suggest that this wouldn't matter. The virtue of ET, they say, is that it would benefit the defence more than the offence. But would it?

In 1977, Richard Burt, a young American analyst working in London who was subsequently to become assistant secretary for European affairs in the State Department under Reagan – and later US Ambassador to West Germany – wrote an incisive paper pointing out that whereas ET might make land harder for an enemy to take, it might also make land – once taken – harder to regain. (He was assuming, of course, that the systems could be made to work effectively.) Burt also noted that if we move into an age of 'one shot one kill', where conventional rockets unerringly find their targets, then this could actually make things worse for Nato, since it has fewer weapons platforms to lose than the Warsaw Pact.

ET, therefore, is as unlikely as the Divad Gun or any other of the Pentagon's magical creations to transform the conventional balance in Europe or anywhere else. (It would also, by the bye, create political problems for the Europeans, uncomfortable with the notion of beginning a war by launching 'deep strike' into enemy territory.) The implications are stark. Attempts to solve the problem of conventional weakness through technology alone seem doomed to failure. What is more, they condemn the Nato Alliance in Europe to what is becoming a more and more implausible strategy – the threat to use nuclear weapons first to stave off conventional defeat.

PART TWO

The Dilemma of Nato's Nuclear Doctrine

'Everything about the atomic bomb is overshadowed by the twins facts that it exists and that its destructive power is fantastically great.'

Bernard Brodie

7

Battlefield Nuclear Weapons

If there is one episode which should have been seminal in the history of US policy making on nuclear weapons, it came in autumn 1961. That, to borrow a phrase used at the time by the then national security adviser, McGeorge Bundy, was America's 'moment of thermonuclear truth'.

Throughout 1961 a crisis had been building over West Berlin, the tiny allied enclave in East Germany, which had long been a source of contention between the superpowers. On 6 January 1961, Nikita Khrushchev, the Soviet premier, raised the stakes. In a sabre-rattling speech, he declared that 'wars of liberation' would be supported by the communists 'wholeheartedly and without reservation', and warned that the occupation of West Berlin by America, Britain and France could not continue. 'These powers,' he said, 'cannot fail to realize that sooner or later the occupation regime in that city must be ended ... And should they balk, then we will take resolute measures ...'

Six months later, Khrushchev repeated his determination to end the division of Berlin in a summit with President Kennedy in Vienna – and effectively threatened war if America resisted. Throughout the summer, tension mounted. Kennedy gave a dramatic televised speech about the dangers menacing Western freedom in Berlin; Khrushchev, who had apparently concluded from the Vienna summit that Kennedy was weak and lacked the will to resist, continued to increase the pressure. In the early hours of 13 August, Soviet troops occupied the border line between East and West Berlin and began, with brick and barbed wire, what was to become the Berlin Wall.

In Washington, the Kennedy administration prepared for war. Everyone knew that if the Russians decided to occupy West Berlin, and cut it off from the West, it would be immensely hard to prevent the seizure solely through the use of conventional weapons. West Berlin, after all, was in

Soviet territory. So though Kennedy made plans to increase dramatically the size of the US army, navy and air force, the chances were that a war over Berlin would go nuclear.

In the light of this, Kennedy's defence secretary, Robert McNamara, examined existing plans for nuclear use. The official contingency plan for dealing with Berlin, the Joint Chiefs of Staff told him, called for sending a few brigades down the autobahn from West Germany to Berlin and then, if the Warsaw Pact resisted them, launching a huge all-out nuclear strike. But during the summer of 1961, as Fred Kaplan has documented in *The Wizards of Armageddon*, the crude thinking enshrined in the JCS plan was refined into something much more precise by one of McNamara's aides, a man called Carl Kaysen. Working on the latest information about the Soviet nuclear arsenal (which had revealed that the Russians, at the time, only had four operational intercontinental missiles, far fewer than anyone thought, some bombers capable of reaching United States and a small number of submarines carrying nuclear weapons), Kaysen and a small task force did a detailed study on the possibility of a disarming 'counterforce' strike. They decided that such a strike could be pulled off 'with high confidence'.

America, at the time, was still vastly superior to Russia in nuclear strength. And according to Kaysen it would be able to pre-empt in a war and knock out most of the Soviet nuclear forces before they could be used. There was, however, a snag. Even under the Kaysen plan, some Russian nuclear weapons would survive: indeed, it was calculated that Soviet retaliation could kill between two and three million Americans (best case) or perhaps as many as ten to fifteen million (worst case). What's more, Europe would be left desperately vulnerable to a strike from Soviet short-range missiles – there were hundreds of these, and knocking out most, let alone all of them, would be impossible. So the number of European fatalities could be in 'the low tens of millions'.

In the abstract, the Kaysen plan might have made sense: Russia would lose, in that it would end up much worse off than America; its nuclear arsenal would be wiped out once and for all; and Western losses, as worked out in the cold statistical world of nuclear planners, might be considered 'acceptable'. But in the real world of political decision making, and in a real crisis, the plan seemed horrifying. Kennedy and his Cabinet baulked. To students of Western nuclear strategy, it was a revealing moment. As Fred Kaplan has observed:

If ever in the history of the nuclear arms race, before or since, one side had unquestionable superiority over the other, one side truly had the ability to devastate the other's strategic forces ... the autumn of 1961 was that time. Yet approaching the height of the gravest crisis that had faced the West since the onset of the Cold War, everyone said: 'No'.

Among those aghast at the notion of a nuclear strike was Robert McNamara who remembers a meeting, as the crisis reached its climax, with Admiral of the Fleet Lord Louis Mountbatten, the British chief of staff. Mountbatten, during a trip to Washington, was invited by McNamara to visit him in his third floor office in the Pentagon. Asked for his advice over Berlin, Mountbatten ran through a number of possible military options. When he had finished, McNamara said: 'But you haven't mentioned nuclear weapons.'

Mountbatten looked at him in disbelief. 'Are you insane?' he asked.

The conversation left a deep impression on McNamara. The scare over Berlin proved mercifully short-lived. The administration stood its ground (as it was to do over Cuba in July of the following year). Khrushchev backed down. But the problem he and other top Kennedy advisers had been forced to address seemed to have profound implications for Western policy. If you couldn't use nuclear weapons to defend Berlin – and their use, as Mountbatten suggested, seemed to defy sanity – then when could you use them? And if you couldn't use them *at all* (except in response to a nuclear attack), then where did that leave Western military strategy, which was then, and still is, predicated on the first use of nuclear weapons?

McNamara now says that after this experience he became convinced that the first use of nuclear weapons could never be an option for the West, no matter how grave the situation. He goes further. 'In long conversations with successive presidents – Kennedy and Johnson,' he has written, 'I recommended, without qualification, that they never initiate, under any circumstances, the use of nuclear weapons. I believe they accepted my recommendation.'

Some of McNamara's former colleagues dispute this. They maintain that even if he gave such advice, which they doubt, it was not accepted. But whether or not McNamara's recollection is accurate in this respect, there is no doubt that he became rapidly concerned about the implications of nuclear 'first use'. There is no doubt, too, that if there was reason for concern then, there is much greater reason now. Nuclear use looked far more plausible in the early 1960s than it does in the mid-1980s.

Yet Nato still clings to a strategy which envisages the West being prepared, in certain circumstances, to be the first to press the nuclear button. Because of its conventional weakness on the Central Front, the argument goes, it has no alternative but to threaten to unleash the unimaginable carnage of nuclear warfare to stave off defeat on the battlefield. It has continued to stick with this strategy despite the evidence that if war broke out no one, not the Americans and not the Europeans, would want to see the threat implemented.

In 1961, when Kennedy's cabinet faced its 'moment of thermonuclear truth', Nato's official nuclear doctrine was one of 'massive retaliation'. In theory, any Soviet conventional attack (in Europe or elsewhere) would be met by automatic and massive retaliation by the United States. Indeed, Nato's conventional forces on the Central Front were seen only as a 'tripwire' which, once broken, would unleash a tremendous nuclear assault on Soviet territory.

By 1961, however, massive retaliation was beginning to seem highly implausible. (Indeed, it had begun to seem implausible even before the crises faced under the Kennedy administration concentrated official minds.) The doctrine might have made sense in the very earliest days of the arms race, when Russia had first none and then very few weapons of its own. But during the late 1950s and early 1960s that changed. If we could massively retaliate against the Soviets, it became clear, they could massively retaliate back. (Indeed, it was only a couple of months after Berlin that the Russians detonated a 50-megaton hydrogen bomb, the biggest man-made explosion in history.) What had been a plan to 'blow up Russia' was rapidly assuming the outlines of a plan to blow up the world.

So throughout the early and mid-1960s, and pushed hard by McNamara, Nato struggled to find a replacement for 'massive retaliation', and eventually, in 1967, after a bitter row within the Alliance and the departure of France from the military structure, Nato settled for its current doctrine of 'flexible response'.*

Flexible response took it as read that the West could no longer hope to launch a massive nuclear blow against the Warsaw Pact and remove its capacity to retaliate. Basically, it was a doctrine of minimal force: the Alliance would resist the use of force conventionally, only resorting to nuclear weapons if the alternative was defeat. But though a less obviously suicidal doctrine than massive retaliation, flexible response still failed to solve the essential dilemma: it anticipated using nuclear weapons in some *limited* way but it continued to assume that the West would use them *first*. How could this be done? How did you use nuclear weapons in such a way as to prevent a war from escalating into an all-out nuclear exchange?

Even the three men who drafted the official document, entitled MC14/3 (MC for Military Committee), Tim Stanley, a Pentagon official, General Gert Schmuckler of West Germany and Sir Arthur Hockaday of the British Ministry of Defence, did not see it as more than a stopgap, a

---

* In fact, Nato's adoption of the new doctrine lagged behind US adoption of the same strategy by some six years.

political compromise which everyone could endorse until something more coherent was devised. They certainly felt that flexible response provided a less than perfect blueprint for fighting a war, and after completing MC14/3 they repaired to a Brussels restaurant for dinner wondering whether they would be sacked for their pains. They weren't. Almost 20 years later, flexible response remains official Alliance doctrine.

The best way to understand the dilemma of flexible response is to look first at the short-range, or 'battlefield', nuclear weapons stockpiled on the Central Front in Europe. These, because of their size and their proximity to the front line, would almost certainly be the first to be used if a conventional conflict in Europe went nuclear.

With names like Long Tom (a 280 millimetre cannon), Honest John (artillery) and Matador and Regulus (early, short-range, cruise missiles), the first battlefield weapons began flowing into the continent in the mid-1950s. They were made possible by developments in the accuracy of delivery systems and the creation, at nuclear weapons labs like Los Alamos in New Mexico, of small, low-yield warheads. According to John Foster Dulles, the secretary of state under President Eisenhower:

[The] resourcefulness of those who serve our nation in the field of science and weapon engineering now shows that it is possible to alter the character of nuclear weapons. It seems now that their use need not involve vast destruction and widespread harm to humanity. Recent tests point to the possibility of possessing nuclear weapons the destructiveness and radiation effects of which can be confined substantially to predetermined targets.

The hope was that battlefield nuclear weapons could be used to make up for Nato's conventional weakness. 'If seventy divisions, for example, are needed to establish a conventional line of defence between the Alps and the Baltic,' said General Alfred Gruenther, Nato's Supreme Allied Commander, in a speech in Paris in January 1954, 'then seventy minus x divisions equipped with atomic weapons are needed.' The assumption, of course, was that x was a substantial number: battlefield weapons were seen, quite simply, as bigger and better artillery.

Among those who believed strongly in battlefield weapons was the scientist Robert Oppenheimer. Tormented by conscience after his work during the war on the Manhattan Project, which developed the first atomic bomb, Oppenheimer had been struck by the crudity of America's early plans for delivering nuclear weapons on Russia. The notion of dropping multi-megaton weapons on cities, and obliterating millions of civilians, appalled him, and tactical weapons at least appeared to offer a way of restoring war to the place it belonged: the battlefield. To many, since,

Oppenheimer's faith in battlefield weapons has come to seem a classic example of the way in which the road to hell is paved with good intentions.

The Central Front in Europe is the most built-up area in the world. There are 4,000 towns and villages in West Germany alone, and much of the country has become a continuous urban sprawl – hence the old Nato saying that the towns and villages of West Germany are less than two kilotons apart. Yet this is the area in which Nato, if it ever pushed the nuclear trigger, was contemplating fighting its nuclear battle.

The implications of using nuclear weapons in this environment became clear even in the 1950s. In 1955, Nato staged a war game in West Germany, the Low Countries and north-eastern France. For reasons of space the game, codenamed 'Carte Blanche', was played on a north-south rather than on an east-west axis, but the casualty figures gave some indication of the fate which might be in store for Europe. The weapons employed were bombs, dropped by aircraft, and in total the aircraft of the 'blue' (Nato) and 'orange' (Warsaw Pact) forces dropped 335 bombs on more than 100 military targets. German civilian casualties were estimated at 1.7 million killed and 3.5 million wounded, and that did not include the victims of radioactivity. Incredibly, the Nato hierarchy decided to publish the results of 'Carte Blanche' in an endeavour to 'reassure' people of Nato's determination to defend Europe. The reaction was widespread horror: in Britain and elsewhere the peace movement latched on to 'Carte Blanche' as evidence of what they saw as the suicidal nature of Nato strategy; in Germany, particularly, politicians and public alike wondered anew whether Nato did not intend to blow up their country to save it. No one, in short, was reassured by the war game. And a year later, General Maxwell Taylor noted in an article which the State Department considered too sensitive for publication:

In Europe, we have some 250,000 soldiers accompanied by thousands of dependents living in close proximity to superior communist forces deployed in the satellite countries. If the latter suddenly advanced west without warning, they would soon be locked in close combat with the Nato armies in such a way as to restrict the employment of atomic weapons against them.

Another American general, James Gavin, concluded after a series of war games carried out with his Seventh Army Corps that because nuclear war fighting would be so destructive, 'more rather than less manpower would be required to fight a nuclear war successfully' – battlefield weapons, in other words, were no compensation for conventional weakness.

Under the doctrine of 'massive retaliation', however, in the 1950s and early 1960s, this kind of logic scarcely seemed to matter. Little serious thought was given to the precise usage of battlefield weapons: they would simply be fired, along with everything else, as part of the all-out strike which Nato contemplated in the event of war in Europe.*

It was only after the introduction of flexible response, in 1967, that battlefield weapons suddenly fell under the spotlight. Now Nato had to contemplate precise, flexible nuclear strikes in the event of conventional defeat. What was envisaged was a 'ladder of escalation' under which Nato, if it faced an overwhelming breakthrough on the battlefield, would first mount a relatively small nuclear strike; if that failed to halt the enemy, it would then raise the stakes by authorizing a larger strike; finally, if all else failed, the awesome power of America's strategic arsenal – the intercontinental rockets and bombers based on the American mainland and the nuclear firing submarines in the seas round about – would be invoked.

The crucial rung of the ladder, however, was the first one. And this comprised battlefield weapons, of which Nato had almost 7,000 in place when flexible response was unveiled in 1967. These weapons – artillery shells, rockets and bombs – were actually stationed on the Central Front. They would be used first because they are relatively 'small' and 'low-yield', because they would offer the best hope of keeping a war 'limited', and because, being near the front line, they might have to be used before the troops possessing them were overrun.

When Nato began to look in detail at the potential uses of battlefield weapons in the late 1960s and early 1970s, the concerns of generals like Maxwell Taylor and James Gavin came to seem very prescient. However Nato contemplated going nuclear, at whatever stage in the battle, it was hard to see how it would benefit – and how it could avoid risking the destruction of the very prize it sought to save, namely Western Europe.

In a series of secret studies produced between 1968 and 1974, the Alliance grappled with the difficulties of possible nuclear use. The studies were conducted by the Nuclear Planning Group, a special committee set up by McNamara in response to European demands for a greater say in nuclear policy making. An early attempt by Washington to achieve this end by creating a so-called 'multilateral nuclear force' (MLF) had failed

---

*Purists might point out that in 1957 the US *did* introduce a small degree of flexibility into its strike plan by dividing massive retaliation into two phases: in the first, Nato would fire its battlefield weapons; if that failed, there would be an all-out strategic attack on the Soviet Union.

dismally, and the Nuclear Planning Group emerged, essentially, out of the ashes of the MLF.* To an extent the Nuclear Planning Group was, and is, a PR exercise – a means of keeping the non-nuclear allies, especially the West Germans, happy, by making them feel involved in the shaping of nuclear policy. Nevertheless the Nato studies represent an exhaustive attempt to think through precisely how nuclear weapons might be used. The intention was to provide a clear set of political guidelines for Western leaders should they ever be faced with the awesome decision to cross the nuclear threshold.

Not surprisingly, such guidelines proved difficult to write. European ministers and officials, led by the British defence secretary, Denis Healey, were from the outset firm in their belief that it was pointless to plan to *win* a 'theatre' nuclear war in Europe. And what worried them was that the Pentagon and the strike planners at SHAPE (Supreme Headquarters, Allied Powers, Europe), now based at Mons, Belgium, appeared to be planning exactly that: they envisaged that the use of battlefield weapons, if it came about, would be on a truly massive scale.

The Nuclear Planning Group undertook two sets of studies – one on 'initial use', and another, even more detailed, on 'follow-on use' (i.e. what Nato might do after one side or the other had 'gone nuclear' and the Warsaw Pact kept coming). Both studies made it abundantly clear that the idea of Nato benefiting from massive use – and of 'winning' nuclear wars in Europe – was fantasy. In almost no circumstances, indeed, would the Alliance stand to reap *military* gains from using nuclear weapons.

The reason for this was simple enough. No nuclear strike, however massive, would be able to remove the Soviet capacity for an equally massive counterstrike. And even a small, selective strike, aimed at a handful of military targets – and intended to stop Nato losing any further ground – raised all kinds of problems. There was, in the first place, no guarantee that the Russians would play by the same rules. What if they simply responded, even then, with a massive counterstrike – precisely what Western intelligence anticipated they *would* do (at least during the 1960s and 1970s)? But that did not illustrate the full extent of the problem, for suppose the Russians merely responded *in kind* – the minimum assumption

---

*The multilateral force was an elaborate scheme dreamt up by the State Department by which, in essence, Nato would have a force of 25 surface ships equipped with 200 Polaris missiles and manned by crews from several member countries whose governments would have to reach a joint decision before use. It sounded grand, but there were too many snags: the cost; the vulnerability of the ships; the exact composition of the fleet; command and control – how would the release procedure work? who would give the orders? how could it be done fast enough? The Multilateral Nuclear Force, as it became known, soon ran well and truly aground. Eventually, in December 1964, President Lyndon Johnson decided enough was enough and the idea died.

Nato could make? In other words, say Nato exploded two or three warheads over a Soviet armoured division, and the Russians did the same over a Western division, would Nato then be better off?

The answer, it soon became clear, was that it would not. Even after an *equal* exchange of nuclear fire Nato would end up suffering not equally as badly as the Warsaw Pact, but *worse*. Nato, after all, is conventionally the weaker side. In a war it would start with fewer soldiers, and fewer tanks. If, in a nuclear exchange, both sides lost the same amount of men and equipment, then the odds against Nato would have worsened. (If you start with ten men, and your opponent with twenty, and each of you loses five, then your odds have lengthened from two to one to three to one.) There were other handicaps. Nato would probably be firing at well dispersed Soviet troops while the Soviets would be firing at Western troops retreating into an ever more crowded area. The Soviets would have an easier task getting reinforcements to the battlefield than Nato – theirs are able to approach by land, while the bulk of Nato's – those from America – have to cross 3,000 miles of ocean. Finally, Nato's key 'assets' – ports, airfields, military storage and communications facilities and the like – are much closer together and more vulnerable than the Warsaw Pact's. Thus in military terms going nuclear would not help the Alliance; it would hinder it. The use of nuclear weapons would actually *accelerate defeat*. That is the dilemma of flexible response.

There were, it must be acknowledged, a few isolated scenarios where nuclear use looked rather more feasible. If the Warsaw Pact, for example, attempted to take (say) Norway or Denmark from the sea, then Nato might be able to detonate a nuclear weapon or two over the beachhead. In such an instance, the theory went, the act of aggression would be so distinct and the use (perhaps of only one weapon) so clear in its purpose that the risk of escalation might be worth running. Unless Nato were staging an amphibious landing elsewhere – an unlikely eventuality – then the Soviets would be hard-pressed to respond in kind. Attacking a beachhead was a rare exception, however. In almost every other scenario the Nuclear Planning Group found that the military gains to be derived from going nuclear first – assuming an equivalent Soviet response – would be temporary and illusory, and the dangers of the strike leading to rapid and possibly uncontrolled escalation would be severe.*

The conclusion which Nato drew from its studies was that the only purpose of going nuclear first could be to send a 'political signal' to the Soviets; by going nuclear, Nato would not be trying for a military *win*; it would merely be trying to show that it was determined not to *lose*. It

---

*Another exception was the use of nuclear weapons at sea, but since Nato was likely to outclass the Warsaw Pact at sea in any case, this did not seem likely to be very helpful.

would thus deliberately, and in the face of terrible dangers of escalation, raise the stakes to demonstrate to the Kremlin that its actions had become unacceptable and to signal that Nato was not prepared to surrender.

In this context, one of the options the officials examined was the 'demonstration shot', the nuclear age equivalent of firing a shot across the enemy's bow. This would be accomplished by exploding one or more warheads over an uninhabited area (the Black Sea, the Baltic, the Polar icecap – a strong contender – or some deserted area such as the Ukrainian mountains). That way, some argued, you could demonstrate unity and resolve without taking the awful step of killing thousands, perhaps millions of people. (The idea of such a warning shot first emerged in 1945, when some of President Truman's advisers had suggested that this might be all that was required to force the Japanese to surrender; in the event, because the US only possessed two bombs, and because a warning shot might fail to have the desired effect, the idea was rejected.)

Firing a pure demonstration shot was heavily debated as a possible option for Nato. But it was hard to see how it would help. After all, if the US exploded a weapon over the Baltic, what was to stop the Soviets doing the same? If they did, would not Nato be left exactly where it had been before pressing the button? And might not a pure demonstration shot show *weakness* rather than strength, *cowardice* rather than courage? By blowing up nothing you might give the impression that you lacked the nerve to go through with a real attack, and instead of deterring further aggression from the Russians you might actually *encourage* swift and terrible retaliation. The Americans argued strongly, and successfully, against purely demonstrative use in the Nuclear Planning Group, and indeed one of the few positive conclusions from the series of Nato studies was that 'purely demonstrative use would demonstrate only inadequate resolve'.

The compromise which Nato came up with was a demonstration shot (or shots), which nonetheless inflicted damage on the enemy. A strike against a military target – or targets – in other words, executed not in the hope of securing military advantage so much as to convince the enemy to back off. Through this 'militarily meaningful demonstration of resolve' Nato would try to walk the tightrope between the danger of rapid escalation and the need to avoid defeat. It was not a very happy compromise, but if flexible response were to be credible at all then the Alliance, as one Nato official has put it, would simply have to attempt 'the balancing act between the need to convey an adequate signal while limiting the risks of escalation'.

The studies of the late 1960s and early 1970s (they were concluded in 1974) remain the basis of Nato's battlefield nuclear doctrine. They represent an exhaustive but ultimately unsatisfactory attempt by the Alliance to come to grips with the problem of nuclear use.

It is worth, at this point, making clear my own position. I do not advocate that all battlefield nuclear weapons be withdrawn from Europe. It is at least arguable that, during peacetime, they boost deterrence; that if they were all to be removed the Russians would probably become more rather than less confident that they could get away with an attack on Western Europe. Equally, a limited number of battlefield systems helps tie America into the defence of Europe and increases the 'hostage effect' of the 300,000 US troops stationed on the Central Front. But, in the light of the Nato studies, it seems quite unnecessary to have the potential battlefield so chock-full of nuclear weapons, and though there are now less than there were when the arsenal reached its peak in the late 1960s – some 5,000 compared with 7,000 – there are still more than can conceivably be justified for the purposes of deterrence or very limited use. The Nato studies showed all too clearly that nuclear warfighting would be both futile and suicidal. (Indeed, when, in the mid-1970s, the Pentagon began to suggest that developments in technology – smaller, 'cleaner' warheads, precision-guided munitions, etc. – might change the picture, the Europeans argued, forcefully, that these developments did nothing of the kind.)

The vital point to be made, however, concerns nuclear first use. I see little purpose in Nato declaring, outright, that it would *not* go nuclear first (a policy now advocated by some eminent former high-ranking officials, among them the Americans McNamara, McGeorge Bundy, George Kennan and Gerard Smith, and Britain's Lord Carver). The Russians would be unlikely to believe such a pledge, and though it might reassure Western publics it would also undermine deterrence. I accept, too, that if you do have nuclear weapons on the battlefield you have to have some sort of idea as to how and when you might use them – deterrence, after all, implies a concept of possible use – and to that extent the Nato studies in the early 1970s were clearly useful.

The fact is, however, that trying to compensate for conventional weakness with battlefield weapons – and planning to go nuclear *first* – is steadily coming to seem more and more incredible.

Consider, for a moment, the idea of 'demonstrating resolve'. Defenders of flexible response argue that this remains plausible. An automatic escalation to all-out war is by no means certain, they say, and the initial use of nuclear weapons, breaching a barrier which has held since 1945, might so horrify both sides that they would recognize an overwhelming common interest in composing their differences. According to the private assessment of one official who has played a key role in developing Nato strategy, the human reaction would be to do everything to avoid escalation. Neither side, he says, would want it; both would be appalled at what was going on, both would be desperately looking for signs that the other was ready to call a halt. Besides, it is argued, Russia would have attacked

Western Europe on the assumption that Nato would *not* go nuclear. If Nato did, then that judgement would of course be shown to be flawed. The Soviet Union would know that if it responded to Western first use it, too, would have to worry about escalation. It might decide that, after all, it was running too great a risk and that retreat might make more sense than risking the consequences of further advance. The stake the two sides had in the conflict, after all, would not be equal. The West would be defending itś homeland, its very existence, and everything vital to it; the Russians would not. They might thus have less resolve than the West to carry on upping the stakes.

I may not do full justice to those who make this case, but that is the gist of it: you can't fight wars with nuclear weapons but you can stop yourself losing, and if Europe is threatened with takeover it must be prepared to do that, or to accept defeat.

The argument, however, makes some heroic assumptions. A conscious decision to initiate nuclear use would take extraordinarily strong nerves; it would also require a brave guess about what the Soviets would do in return. For if they did decide to decimate Europe, where would that leave Nato? If, amidst the confusion of war, with its stresses, anger and desire for revenge, the Soviets decided to respond *in a limited way*, then, as we have seen, Nato would be worse off than it had been before going nuclear. And having taken the awful gamble of invading Europe in the first place, the chances would seem at least even that they would so respond. In the light of this, it would seem a risk which European governments would not wish to run – for fear of losing their continent.* Indeed, Lord Carver, Britain's former chief of staff, argues that 'it would be criminally irresponsible for any Western leader to initiate a nuclear strike on the assumption that the Soviet Union either would not answer back in kind or would do so to such a limited degree that we could regard it as acceptable within whatever were our war aims.'

With some justice, therefore, Nato's strategy has been likened to contemplating burning down your house to get rid of a burglar.

The struggle to make flexible response credible has continued, however. Analysts like Colin Gray, an expatriate Englishman who advises the Pentagon, argue that Nato needs to develop a more serious 'war fighting' posture. They believe that with better civil defence, and much stronger, larger and better protected nuclear forces, the Alliance could hope to call the shots in a nuclear battle with the Warsaw Pact. But the West was able to 'call the shots' in the early 1960s when it was clearly superior to the

---

* It might be argued, of course, that Nato would be losing it anyway. Conventional defeat, however, might not be irrevocable; nuclear defeat almost certainly would be.

Pact, and even then it could not have saved Europe from destruction in a nuclear war; in addition, any beefing up of the Western battlefield arsenal which still comprises 5,000 warheads would instantly be matched by the Russians. And plans for waging a nuclear battle in Europe are unlikely ever to command much favour among those who live there.

Yet the Pentagon has attempted to make battlefield weapons more accurate and more 'controllable' in the hope of making battlefield nuclear use seem more plausible. A classic example is the neutron bomb.

The neutron bomb is tailored for use on the Central Front. It is designed to cause less 'collateral' damage than a traditional nuclear explosion and to be more effective in the built-up environment of the Central Front.* In a traditional nuclear device, the neutrons released by the original explosion are 'checked' by a layer of uranium and it is the interaction between neutrons and uranium which generates the enormous destructive power. In the neutron bomb, the neutrons, instead of being checked by the uranium, are simply allowed to escape. The resulting blast and heat, though fearsome, are reduced by a factor of the order of two and a half. Within a limited radius, however, the neutron radiation effect is ten times as strong, making it just as deadly to life. Thus a one-kiloton neutron bomb would kill people over as wide a radius as a ten-kiloton 'fusion' weapon, though there would be far less blast, heat and radioactive fallout. In a nutshell, the effect on human life (per kiloton) would be more lethal; the effect on buildings and other hardened structures less so.

The neutron bomb has had a controversial history. It was given the go-ahead under President Ford; then, after its existence became known and widely publicized in 1977, President Jimmy Carter suspended production (four years later, this decision was overturned by President Reagan). It is unlikely, however, to make nuclear war fighting in Europe seem any more plausible than it is now. The Pentagon argues that in case Nato ever reaches the point where nuclear weapons have to be used it is better to be armed with modern effective ones rather than with products of the 1950s. Critics, however, question the potential effectiveness of the neutron bomb. Given that it would not destroy tanks themselves, how could you be sure that their crews – when apparently victims – had been killed rather than just temporarily stunned or blinded? And wouldn't the neutron bomb make it easier to cross the nuclear threshold, thus paving the way for the very 'dirty' weapons which everyone fears using?

But whether or not these arguments are convincing, the real problem with the neutron bomb is the problem facing anyone contemplating nuclear use in Europe. As fast as scientists develop supposedly more 'usable'

---

* In particular, it is designed to kill military personnel in armoured vehicles. Against armour, radiation is a much more effective killer, except at close range, than heat and blast.

weapons, so the battlefield on which they would be used becomes more crowded. Every year the area suitable for armoured combat in Germany gets smaller. The area between Bonn and the Hook of Holland, indeed, has almost become one gigantic urban region, 250 miles long, and if a war broke out, much of the combat in open spaces would take place in West Germany's national parks. Even the Fulda Gap, scene of hundreds of simulated Warsaw Pact invasions, is no longer a gap at all; it has been all but filled by the sprawling city of Fulda.

Undoubtedly, in a war, the Soviets would seek to exploit this. Simply by advancing along main roads, and keeping close to cities, they would make it specially hard for Nato to use nuclear weapons against them. The main routes of advance would inevitably run through the main suburban sprawl of West Germany and past its major cities. Thus the least provocative kind of nuclear use Nato could imagine – i.e. striking Warsaw Pact targets on the actual battlefield, that is on West German soil – would be next to impossible. Even a neutron bomb used close to a city might save the buildings, but it would not spare the inhabitants.

Not for nothing, then, has it been said that using nuclear weapons first on the battlefield would be potentially suicidal. Yet military planners continue to devise scenarios for it. Indeed, in trying to assess the results of a nuclear conflict in Europe, the Pentagon has come to depend more and more on computer simulations: the results of these, according to one former Pentagon adviser, suggest that the level of casualties could be contained to a far lower level than the millions who 'died' during the 'Carte Blanche' exercise in 1955. But as this source also points out, the computer simulations are utterly unrealistic.

'Were Nato to engage a conventional attack with nuclear fire,' he says, 'it would have to drop the warheads so as not to destroy its own armies, and "in between" moving refugee columns and cities in West Germany, amidst an environment of false target location reports, mistakes, human fatigue and command authorization breakdowns on both sides.' The computer simulations, however, 'treat Soviet forces as automata who cross into West Germany and advance directly into Nato nuclear killing zones. Here they are detected and destroyed by the lowest-yield nuclear weapon capable of doing the job. Command and control difficulties, confusion, false targeting, and other problems are simply assumed away.' The Red Army, in other words, becomes a strategic dummy which allows military planners to justify an implausible strategy.

So much for the theory. What would happen in practice? Supposing the Russians attacked Western Europe, and Nato began to lose, would an American president 'press the button'? Or would he decide that the risks were simply too great?

General Bernard Rogers, in his role as Nato's supreme commander, has said that he might need to seek 'release authority' for nuclear weapons on the Central Front within 48 hours of a Russian attack. Within that short space of time, he believes, Nato might have 'its back to the nuclear wall'.

What he means is this. Within two days, the Red Army might be poised for a critical breakthrough on at least one point in the Nato front line (precisely where would depend on where the Russians chose to concentrate their forces). From that point on, Rogers would wish to have at least the *option* of using nuclear weapons to stop them.

The mechanism for 'going nuclear' is complicated. In theory, all Nato states must be consulted – not easy, given the problems of communicating with 15 or so governments in their capitals or bunkers in the high confusion of battle. (The communication would be through the Nato council, composed of permanent representatives, or ambassadors, meeting in permanent session in a secret site, probably in Belgium.) But in practice the decision would come down to the nation supplying the nuclear weapons (almost certainly the United States), and the nation where they would be exploded (almost certainly West Germany).

The recommendation to 'go nuclear' might come first from a divisional headquarters unable to hold a strategically vital gap in the hills. It would then pass up the Nato military chain to the Supreme Allied Commander. If he endorsed it, the final authorization – and precise target or targets – would probably be agreed jointly by three men: SACEUR, the American president and the German chancellor. But in reality, even if the German chancellor objected, the American president would still be able to go ahead if he so decided.

So what would an American president decide? Almost certainly, he would receive conflicting advice from his aides. On the one hand, he would be under enormous pressure to use nuclear weapons because thousands, probably tens of thousands, of American soldiers would be dying in Europe, and because the loss of Western Europe would constitute, to put it mildly, the most staggering foreign policy defeat ever inflicted on America (losing Europe, as one official put it, would scarcely help him get re-elected). On the other hand, any president would be acutely conscious of the dangers of escalation – and that going nuclear in Europe might lead inevitably to the destruction not just of Europe but of America and the rest of Western civilization too. As the Australian nuclear expert, Desmond Ball, and others have shown, no one knows how a nuclear war might be stopped once started. So the pressures acting on a president to be cautious – and avoid nuclear use – would be considerable, perhaps overwhelming. (In the view of one Pentagon official, well versed in these matters, he might seek to compromise. He might contact the Soviet leader by means of the 'hot line' and warn him that unless the Warsaw Pact ceased its aggression – and ceased killing American soldiers – he would be forced to use nuclear weapons. He would stress, however, that he would use these only in Europe – providing the Russians did not strike America, he would authorize no strikes on Russia ... But even an option like this would leave open the danger of escalation and would hardly be a comforting one for the West Europeans.)

Yet there is a chance that a nuclear war in Europe might start whether the US president wanted it to or not. The argument, it must be stressed, is a very controversial one, and fiercely disputed by many in the Pentagon. But some nuclear experts, in and out of government, believe that the current organizational arrangements which underpin flexible response make it fairly likely in themselves that nuclear weapons would be used if a conflict began in Europe.

The warheads for battlefield nuclear weapons are stored at special sites in Western Europe, known as 'igloos'. There are about 100 in all, scattered across the continent, though mainly in West Germany. Before any nuclear device can be fired it has to be 'married up' with its warhead, so before the West could use battlefield weapons the warheads would have to be distributed from their igloos to field commanders. Some of these would go to American commanders, others to European ones, under a 'dual key' arrangement (the Americans possessing the warheads, the European allies possessing the means of delivery).

The question of when this act of distribution should take place would be bitterly debated within the Alliance. The act would undoubtedly be spotted by the Russians, and an early decision to undertake it might provoke the very crisis everyone was desperately seeking to avoid. Nevertheless, it would probably happen. During the Polish crisis in 1980, when it seemed as if the Russians were poised to invade Poland, Bernard Rogers sought and got the predelegated authority to distribute the warheads if he believed the situation serious enough to warrant it. That authority, apparently, has never been rescinded. And Rogers would want to distribute the warheads early: the storage igloos would be prime targets during a war and the Soviets would clearly wish to destroy them (conventionally) before the warheads were moved. SACEUR would be intent on ensuring that did not happen.

The possession of warheads is not in itself enough, however, to permit a nuclear strike. Modern battlefield weapons are controlled by an electrical device known as a Permissive Action Link (PAL). Essentially, this is a means of activating an individual warhead by punching into it a special code. The codes are different for each system, and are naturally kept closely guarded. But though tight control of the codes is clearly a sensible precaution in peacetime – it lessens the chances of terrorists being able to use nuclear weapons and of commanders being able to launch World War Three on their own – it would pose horrendous problems in war. As Paul Bracken, a former adviser to the Pentagon, has shown in a detailed study, the difficulties of relaying the right code to the right field commander in war might prove insuperable. Bracken believes, therefore (though the Pentagon denies it), that the codes would probably be distributed along with the warheads – thus making it theoretically possible for commanders in the field to launch their weapons once a war had started. The field commanders, of course, would not have the predelegation to fire; only the means of doing so. They would be told that their weapons were not to be used until they were given specific verbal instructions.

These launch instructions might never come, but the danger of nuclear war would be intensified. With their communications network disrupted, and Nato forces split into 'islands of force' – separated from each other and unaware of the broader picture around them – Nato commanders might assume that their colleagues were dead (not to mention their families) and simply decide to press the button. Once one weapon was fired, the situation could quickly escalate and get irretrievably out of hand. As Bracken puts it: 'If there is an ambiguous or even a rumoured delegation of authority the likelihood of a frenzied orgy of pulling every trigger possible should not be discounted.'

The dangers of Nato's current strategy are thus clear. Even if politicians decide, in a crisis, that the risks of 'first use' are too great to run, the arrangements regarding distribution and release of nuclear weapons are deeply unsatisfactory, and could provoke decisions which would make first use extremely likely. And while there may be little point in Nato declaring, outright, that it would *not* go nuclear first in a war, basing an entire strategy around such a concept – planning for it, and filling the battlefield with weapons which might make it hard to avoid – is foolhardy. It is, however, the price which Nato has elected to pay for failing to provide itself with an effective conventional defence. Indeed, conventional weakness has led the West to some extraordinary contortions in the effort to make the nuclear threat continue to seem credible, as we shall see in the next three chapters.

8

Strategic Weapons

America's strategic nuclear weapons are the foundation stones of Alliance security. They now constitute an arsenal of colossal power, able to blow up Russia and its satellites not once, or even twice, but several times. They come in a variety of guises: bombs carried on some 300 intercontinental bombers, land- and sea-based missiles, which carry between them over 7,000 warheads, and since the early 1980s a rapidly growing arsenal of air- and sea-launched cruise missiles.

It is not easy for the lay observer to understand why so many are needed, still less to follow the twists and turns of modern nuclear strategy, with its baffling 'worst case' scenarios and impenetrable jargon. At times, the logic of modern nuclear planners would do credit to the theologians of the Middle Ages, with their proverbial tortuous debates about how many angels could fit on the head of a pin.

I believe that much of this logic is based on a false premise, that the nuclear debate is in danger of losing touch with reality, and that much of the pressure producing the West's swollen strategic nuclear arsenal in fact stems from the basic flaw in Nato's strategy: its conventional weakness. With robust forces on the Central Front, it would be much harder to justify the degree of overkill currently present in the US nuclear arsenal.

Broadly, what has happened is that American nuclear strategy has moved away from the notion of 'pure' deterrence – in which the presumption was that a strike on the American mainland would result in the destruction of Russian civilization – towards infinitely more sophisticated notions of nuclear 'warfighting'. The movement began under Robert NcNamara in the 1960s. He wondered whether it was either sensible or moral to target Russian cities: doing that, he reasoned, would simply invite a strike against *American* cities. But though he was the first to publicize the idea of a limited nuclear war, McNamara, as I´ have noted, shrank from its implications. He eventually settled for the concept of 'Assured Destruction': if a war broke out, neither side would be able to gain an advantage and each would be able to destroy the other. (We had become, as Robert Oppenheimer had anticipated we would become, like 'two scorpions in a bottle, each able to destroy the other, but only at the risk of losing his own life'.) For America, in McNamara's judgement, this would mean the ability to destroy, in retaliation to a Soviet strike, 20 to 25 per cent of the Soviet population and 50 per cent of its industrial capacity. If that could be achieved, Russia would simply cease to exist as a state. It would therefore have little incentive to start a nuclear war.

Since McNamara's day, plans for fighting a nuclear war have been steadily refined. The idea of 'counterforce' – striking hardened targets (nuclear forces, leadership bunkers and the like) rather than relatively 'soft' ones (cities/industry) – has gradually come to dominate American nuclear doctrine. It was boosted by two technological developments. The first was increased accuracy. With the development of inertial guidance systems for rockets in the 1960s and early 1970s it became theoretically possible to deposit nuclear weapons very close to the spot at which they were aimed, and thus use them to destroy hardened targets such as the concrete silos in which missiles themselves were based.

The second crucial development was 'mirving'. Mirvs ('multiple independently targetable re-entry vehicles') constituted a way of enormously multiplying the potency of strategic rocket forces. Instead of being able to land only one warhead with an individual rocket, mirving, begun in the early 1970s, made it possible to land several; the bus (or front end) of the rocket would release at precisely calculated intervals a series of 'mirvs' each containing a bomb, and each theoretically capable of falling on a predesignated target with an accuracy measured to a few hundred feet.

Thanks to heightened accuracy and mirving, strategic planners could develop targeting options which – in the days of the old intercontinental bombers and crude, first-generation rockets – would have been unimaginable. Thus James Schlesinger, the defence secretary in the early 1970s, developed a set of 'limited nuclear options' for waging nuclear war – ways that the US might attack Russia, or respond to a limited Russian strike, while stopping short of the kind of all-out strike which would invite all-out retaliation.

President Jimmy Carter took this a step further, with his heavily leaked PD (presidential directive) 59, which required 'American forces to be able to undertake the precise, limited nuclear strikes against military facilities in the Soviet Union, including missile bases and troop concentrations ... [and] to develop the capacity to threaten Soviet political leaders in their underground shelters in time of war'. Finally, it emerged in 1982 that the Pentagon was planning for a 'protracted' nuclear war, and that the purpose of the nuclear arms build-up was to put America into a position where it could 'prevail and be able to force the Soviet Union to seek the earliest termination of hostilities on terms favourable to the United States'.

The notion of 'counterforce' has been taken to ludicrous lengths, and the idea of 'prevailing' in a protracted nuclear war is nonsensical. But to understand the thinking behind it we must glance first at the Russians. For the theories developed in the Pentagon have been developed in the name of deterrence, and the argument is often made that whatever Western planners may feel about nuclear war, the Russians take the idea of fighting one very seriously indeed – and believe they can reach a position where they would be able to win.

It is true that Soviet military thinkers have indulged in some strange fantasies about nuclear war. Russia is a more militaristic society than the United States; some of its strategists appear to see nuclear war as no more than an extension of conventional war. Thus it would appear that the Russians intend to go on fighting even after they have turned America into a radioactive desert. 'Combat operations will continue for the purpose of the final defeat of the enemy on his own territory,' reads one military manual, because 'that side which manages during the first days of the war to penetrate more deeply into enemy territory naturally acquires the capability for more effectively using the results of its nuclear attacks and disrupting the mobilization of the enemy.'

Soviet military manuals abound with nonsense like this, and military analysts have a point when they say that the Soviet Union does not think about deterrence in the way the West does. 'There is profound error and harm,' wrote Soviet General A. S. Milovidov in 1974, 'in the disorienting claims of bourgeois ideologues that there will be no victor in a nuclear war.'

But how seriously should we take this? And how seriously should we take the huge Soviet missile build-up, the emphasis on civil defence and the concomitant emphasis on air defence, which seem to suggest – to some – that the Soviet Union is making plans to wage a protracted nuclear war and that it is therefore only prudent for us to do the same? Was President Reagan right when he asserted that the Soviet Union believes it can fight and win a nuclear war?

Common sense is enough to suggest that the answer is no. If some senior Soviet military figures are as silly as Milovidov, there is no evidence that its politicians are. As Leonid Brezhnev put it, rather self-righteously, in October 1981: 'It is a dangerous madness to try and defeat each other in the arms race and to count on victory in nuclear war. I shall add that only he who has decided to commit suicide can start a nuclear war in the hope of emerging a victor from it. No matter what the attacker might possess, no matter what method of unleashing nuclear war he chooses, he will not attain his aims. Retribution will ensue ineluctably.' There is of course no sound reason for believing Brezhnev, any more than there is for believing General Milovidov. Except this: Brezhnev is speaking the truth. Milovidov is not.

Besides, even if Soviet leaders once believed they could get into a position to fight and win a nuclear war, high-level Kremlin statements, at least since the late 1970s, suggest that they now see things differently. This could, of course, be propaganda. Without doubt there are still Soviet generals who believe in winning, just as there are American generals at the Strategic Air Command in Omaha, Nebraska, who believe in winning, too. But many Soviet scholars are convinced that there is more to the change than propaganda. The Soviet leaders accept 'a strategic nuclear balance between the Soviet Union and the United States as a fact,' says Raymond Gartoff of the Brookings Institution, 'and as the probable and desirable prospect for the foreseeable future.'

It is not hard to see why. For as Leon Wieseltier has pointed out in an excellent study called *Nuclear War, Nuclear Peace*, the Soviet Union may not like the notion of deterrence, but it acts on it. And it acts on it because it has no choice:

> Some of the Soviet Union's nuclear notions are evil, yes; but they are also absurd. What does it matter if they are making plans for after the apocalypse? The fantasies of seizing smouldering radio stations are fearful, but they are of no consequence. Nor is the fantasy of civilian defence. Shelters will not work wherever they are. They will save no one from a direct hit, or from the fallout of a direct hit, in Moscow or in Manhattan.

Russia's political leaders live in the real world. They know – whatever their generals tell them – that any kind of nuclear strike against America would almost certainly not just result in their own deaths but dispatch their whole state back to the Stone Age. And against that prospect, precise plans for limited counterforce strikes and protracted wars are meaningless. Besides, the plans are based on quite implausible assumptions about the accuracy and reliability of missiles.

To understand the kind of thinking which drives current nuclear strategy, and the extent to which it has drifted away from reality, we must look at one classic example of it, the idea of the 'window of vulnerability', and the missile which that idea spawned: the MX.

In autumn 1977, the Russians began a series of test firings of their intercontinental missiles from Tyuratam, a remote spot in the desert, west of the Aral Sea. The missiles were aimed at the lonely Kamchatka Peninsula, 4,000 miles away to the east, in the Pacific.

The Americans were able to follow these tests quite closely: an overhead satellite equipped with infrared telescope and a light sensor attuned to rocket firings monitored the take-off; a network of radar stations, including two in Iran, followed the missiles in flight, and an air force Key Hole satellite, supposedly capable of detecting objects eight inches long, picked up the dummy warheads as they landed. US intelligence analysts, studying the data from the tests, concluded that the Soviets had made great strides in improving the accuracy of their missiles. In the light of this, the CIA decided, in mid-1978, that the US land-based missile force could become vulnerable to a Soviet pre-emptive strike as early as 1982. The development, said William J. Perry, a San Francisco businessman who was then serving as the research and development chief in the Pentagon under President Carter, 'gave us a new sense of urgency, told us we were caught short.'

At its baldest, the vision which had come to haunt Perry, and the CIA, was this. The Soviet Union was approaching a point where it might be able, using a proportion of its own land-based missiles, to destroy (say) 90 per cent of America's. This, it was thought, might put a US president in an invidious position. The Americans, to be sure, would probably still have many if not all of their bombers (though bomber bases, too, might be struck in a crippling pre-emptive blow), and they would certainly have their submarines – the largest and most powerful part of the US deterrent. But bombs and submarine-launched missiles (the theory went) would not be accurate enough to strike hardened military targets. Moreover the Soviets would still have enough missiles left in reserve to discourage the US from retaliating. Thus, according to the nightmare scenario, a US president might face an awful choice: either retaliate – against Soviet cities – and thus invite a second devastating attack against his own, or surrender. That, in the fearful calculus of the nuclear planner, was the 'window of vulnerability' which the new Soviet weaponry had opened.

It is important to grasp just what was being contemplated here. America's land-based missile force, in the early 1980s, comprised 52 aging liquid-fuelled Titan rockets and 1,000 of the more modern, solid-fuelled 'Minutemen'. Planners assumed that the Russians would have to target two warheads on each silo to be confident of success, meaning that the strike would involve hundreds of multi-warheaded missiles, each of which would have to work perfectly, depositing its warheads with pinpoint accuracy. Moreover they would have to do this knowing that the price of failure, and probably, as I will show, of success, would be the destruction of tens of millions of Russian lives. One only has to look at each step in the sequence to realize how unrealistic it is.

In the first place, Western intelligence has at best an imperfect idea of

how accurate Soviet missiles are. Despite the sophisticated devices with
which the CIA monitored the tests in 1977 and 1978, for example, they
were unable to establish precisely what the missiles were being aimed at.
Besides, Soviet missiles, in a war, would follow a very different trajectory
to the one they follow during tests – if aimed at American missile silos
their course would take them not east towards the Pacific but west over
the North Pole, exposing them to quite different geodetic, gravitational
and meteorological forces. Some Pentagon analysts deny that this would
make a difference: the Russians, they say, put satellites in orbit over the
pole, measure the geodetic forces, and then programme their missiles
accordingly, precisely what the US does to complement its own east-to-
west test shots from Vandenberg air force base in California to Kwajalein
Atoll in the Marshall Islands. Moreover, say these analysts, the sheer size
of the Russian warheads makes them 'less sensitive' to this phenomenon –
known as 'bias'. (The Russians go in for bigger warheads than the
Americans and would therefore, in the CIA's view, be able to make up in
destructive power what they lacked in accuracy.) Finally, it is said that
both sides have carried out enough space flights to understand the magnetic
bias of the poles.

This analysis, however, takes a decidedly optimistic view of Soviet
capabilities. Even Soviet ICBM warheads would have to come within 400
to 600 ft of missile silos to destroy them, and scientists who study the
upper layers of the atmosphere think 'bias' could throw their warheads
off by two or three times that distance. 'It's our universal feeling round
here that it's nearly impossible to have a passive object land a few hundred
metres from the target,' says Professor James Walker of the Atmospheric
and Oceanic Studies Department at the University of Michigan. 'The
Pentagon may not know how little we know about the upper atmosphere.
The densities vary so radically and change so frequently that there is no
way of knowing with any confidence how it will affect the trajectory of a
re-entry vehicle.' The Soviet warheads, in other words, would approach
totally new targets on a totally untested flightpath, be buffeted about in
the multiple layers of the upper atmosphere, each layer having radically
different densities and wind velocities – and yet still be expected to land
within 400 ft of their target.

What is more, there seems little substance in the American claim that
the 'bias problem' has been solved. According to one weapons analyst
who has seen the secret data of the American missile tests, 'we just can't
make it for counterforce. I've plotted the fall of the warheads and few fall
within the required radius.' Like the Russians, the Americans would have
to fire their missiles on a totally different trajectory in a war to the one
they use in peacetime. And even if during a war, as one joke has it, they
could blast the living daylights out of Kwajalein Atoll (their test

target), that would be very different from striking precise targets in Russia.

But the great pre-emptive strike the Russians are thought capable of presumes something even more basic: it presumes that all, or at least most, of the actual rockets being used will *work*. That means (in each case) not just the fuses in the warheads, the computers and gyroscopes on the 'MIRVs', the release mechanism of the 'bus' and the delicate machinery in each stage of the rocket, but all the complicated electronic gear in the silo which monitors the status of the rocket, keeps it aligned on its target and ensures that it cannot be fired accidentally or illegally. All this must function – perfectly – hundreds of times over, in perfect sequence. The unreliability of modern computer-ridden conventional weapons suggests this to be unlikely.

In the 1970s, the US air force tried four times to launch a Minuteman missile from an operational silo. On three occasions the missile did not even manage to get above ground; on the fourth, it blew up shortly after take-off. After these debacles, which the Pentagon says can be explained by modifications made to the missiles for test purposes, the air force decided to cut their losses and chose to carry out all their tests from a launch pad at Vandenberg – a very different proposition, and a good deal easier than launching from an underground silo. Even then, success was hardly guaranteed. 'We had one Minuteman we tried to launch every night for a year,' Major Ron Peck of the air force told the *Los Angeles Times* in 1984. And it is not just warhead-carrying rockets which have problems. Weather and technical difficulties force frequent postponements in all kinds of rocket launches, from the Atlases which take satellites into space, to the Shuttle. 'I'm always amazed when we launch anything at all,' says Major Peck. He noted that 100 people monitored a rocket launch, any one of whom could cancel it. When controllers were less fussy about their rockets, 'a lot of them blew up'. (The consequences of failing to take adequate precautions appear to have been startlingly demonstrated in the disaster which befell the Shuttle, Challenger, in January 1986.)

It is impossible to predict what would happen if America tried to launch all its Minutemen in one carefully coordinated sequence. But it is a fair bet that some would not get out of their silos, some would blow up, and some would be plagued by mechanical problems en route to their targets which would cause their warheads to fall in quite different patterns to the ones intended. In the 1970s, for example, missile launches depended heavily on electronic chips bonded to circuits, but these chips, it was discovered, tended to 'burn out' after a few years of sitting in silos. According to a technician in Silicon Valley, it took years for the military to cotton on to this phenomenon, known as 'purple plague'. But though purple plague has apparently since been cured, other circuitry problems remain: one involves radiation particles which are given off by electronic packages inside the missile and which can 'zap' the memory of the guidance or communications systems. Others involve the computer software (or algorithms), which is so complex that the only reliable way of 'getting the bugs out' is to test each individual package. For missiles sitting in their silos, waiting for war, this is of course impossible. And in a massive launch of ICBMs, new problems would almost certainly show up which no one knew about or could possibly have anticipated.

In the light of this, the chances of the US being able to execute a perfectly synchronized pre-emptive strike – supposing it ever wished to do so – are very remote.

And if that is true for the US, it is even more so for the Russians. Most Russian rockets are still powered by liquid fuel, which is both unreliable and dangerous. The old American Titan rockets, now virtually antiques, use liquid fuel, and they keep leaking or blowing up in their silos. As the *New York Times* put it in December 1984: 'Guaranteeing to launch even one of those on time, let alone a salvo, must give an engineer heartburn.' In the 1960s, the Americans mastered the technology of solid fuel, whereby the fuel is inserted into the rockets in tightly compressed 'blocks', and now the Russians are catching up. Moreover, the liquid fuel used in their huge SS18 and SS19 missiles is said to be less dangerous and more reliable than the type used in many of their older rockets. But the Russians still lag behind the Americans in computer software, and will face the same problems as the US in ironing out the bugs. US defence consultants who have studied intelligence reports on Soviet missile tests confirm that their rockets are as unreliable as one might expect. Their confidence of being able to execute a pre-emptive strike, therefore, would be infinitesimal.

The more one examines the plausibility of a Soviet pre-emptive strike on US missile silos – a kind of nuclear Pearl Harbor – the more fantastic it seems. Not only would the Soviets have to be sure they had solved the problem of 'bias' (which they would not – and could not – be), and not only would they have to be sure that all their missiles would work (again, utterly impossible), but they would have to execute their strike with split-second timing so that incoming warheads did not blow each other up (a hazard known as fratricide). Moreover, they would have to do this without any kind of practice first. But let us, for the sake of argument, assume that a Soviet premier did consider the operation feasible. He would still be taking a greater gamble than any statesman in history had ever taken if he were to order it carried out.

In the first place, how could he be confident that the US would not 'launch on warning', i.e. retaliate as soon as American spy satellites relayed to NORAD – the North American Air Defense Command at Colorado Springs – that Soviet missiles were on the way? After all, a Soviet pre-emptive strike would be a massively complex operation, and an American president would almost certainly get some notice of it (Soviet submarines putting to sea, intensified radio traffic, hectic activity at Soviet missile fields, movement of civilians, etc.). And if an American president suspected that his country was about to be struck, he *could*, after all, launch his own missiles immediately after the Russians had launched theirs. This would mean that the Russians would actually be disarming themselves by firing first, since their warheads would be on their way to hit (or miss) what by then would merely be empty holes in the ground. The Russian first strike would thus constitute a waste of warheads, while the American counterstrike could be directed so as to do damage to a whole range of more vulnerable Soviet military targets.

Admittedly the president might only have about 20 minutes in which to make a terrifying decision, and US policy, sensibly, is designed so as not to make the president dependent on having to 'launch on warning' – a dangerous notion because it means going to war on the advice of a computer. But faced with such a dire contingency, 'launch on warning' would be feasible – and perhaps likely. And the president would not even have to launch on warning. Almost 75 per cent of American nuclear warheads, some 6,500 altogether, are not based on land at all but in submarines: these submarines, at least half of which are constantly on patrol, are invulnerable to a Soviet pre-emptive strike and would themselves be able to wipe out the Soviet Union several times over. (One modern Trident submarine for example, carries 24 missiles with a total of 192 warheads, each one bigger than the bombs dropped on Hiroshima and Nagasaki.) The theorists of the window of vulnerability say that submarine-launched missiles are relatively inaccurate (though this is also becoming less true), and that a president might be deterred from launching them by the prospect of a second Soviet strike. But even in a so-called surgical pre-emptive strike the Soviets would have killed millions of Americans. Some of America's missile fields are close to centres of population, like Kansas, and an attack on missile silos would cause considerable 'fallout'. Fallout occurs when the dust and debris thrown up by the blast is swept high into the air and carried by the prevailing winds until it descends as highly radioactive particles. Since an attack on missile silos would have to involve ground bursts – in order to cause maximum destruction – there would be considerable fallout.

Yet though 20 million or more Americans, in at least six states, might die from an attack on America's missile silos, the 'window of vulnerability' scenario holds that a Soviet premier is expected to consider this insufficient provocation to persuade an American president to strike back. Only in the rarefied world of nuclear strategy, a world unencumbered by faulty valves, imperfect software, changeable weather or human reaction, could such a scenario survive for long. For such a strike to become plausible, the Soviet Union would have to have fallen into the hands of desperate fanatics, who would be beyond deterrence. And were that situation to arise there is nothing the West could do which would be likely to make much difference.

There is one further though more controversial reason why the window of vulnerability is absurd. No one knows what the effect on the planet would be of thousands of nuclear explosions occurring almost simultaneously, though recently some scientists have begun to speculate that it could be more dire than previously imagined. The reason is not so much the spread of nuclear fallout across the globe – as imagined by Nevil Shute in his 1960s essay in pessimism, the novel *On the Beach* – as one of the simplest though often forgotten byproducts of nuclear weapons: smoke.

Nuclear weapons would create firestorms ten, twenty, a hundred times worse than those which consumed Dresden and Hamburg in World War Two, and these firestorms would create huge funeral pyres of smoke billowing upwards into the atmosphere. According to some scientists, the absorption into the atmosphere of billions of smoke particles could lead to the onset, after a nuclear holocaust, of a 'nuclear winter' in which the sunlight would be largely blotted out: mankind, or what remained of it, would be condemned to live in permanent darkness, and temperatures worldwide would drop dramatically. So if the nuclear winter theory is correct – and no one knows whether it is or not – then the Soviet leaders who authorized a pre-emptive strike on the United States would at the same time probably be signing their own death warrants.

To be fair, plenty of US politicians have pointed out the implausibility of the window of vulnerability. 'It has never seemed realistic to me,' testified Harold Brown, Jimmy Carter's defence secretary. The Soviets, he suggested, would have to be mad to risk their fate on such 'a cosmic throw of the dice'. Even the Joint Chiefs of Staff, in 1980, acknowledged that 'it does not seem likely that attainment of strategic parity or even an overall advantage by the Soviet Union foretells a realistic possibility of a Soviet "bolt out of the blue" strategic attack.'

But the Joint Chiefs of Staff continued to worry about the window of vulnerability. And the reason was not so much military as political: even if US missiles were not vulnerable, the Soviets might *believe* they were. 'A far more likely consequence [of the window of vulnerability],' wrote the Chiefs in 1980, 'is that it will affect the Soviet perception of the military balance in such a way that it will embolden them to act with less restraint in international affairs ... and to exploit instability in the Third World when it occurs.' The view was to be echoed by Richard DeLauer, the research and development chief in the Pentagon under Reagan, who told

Science magazine in April 1982: 'The Soviets don't have to have a pre-emptive first strike. They just present the situation and say, Look. They marched into Afghanistan and what the hell was the best thing we could do? We withdrew from their goddam Olympics. The last time they tried to march in and put their missiles into Cuba, we got their butt out of there. The Soviets don't have to pull the trigger. They have superiority. They've got a deterrent and we don't, and that's the window of vulnerability.'

This, then, is the reason why the fears over vulnerability have persisted so long and run so deep. The Soviets could not actually pull off a first strike, but they could threaten to – and that's enough. The argument, however, makes little sense. Either the Soviets *are* able to mount a pre-emptive strike or they are *not*. If they *are* then we are clearly in dire straits. If they are *not* then there would seem little point in fretting about the consequences. It would seem clear from the evidence that they are not. And if we can recognize the evidence then it is fair to assume that the Soviets are not so stupid as to be unable to do the same.

Underneath the tough talk from Richard DeLauer lies an apprehension which seems to stem from an ideological fixation with anti-communism rather than a sober assessment of the real world. And how can DeLauer seriously compare Afghanistan to Cuba? The Soviet attempt to put missiles in Cuba directly threatened US national interests: in the circumstances, Kennedy was prepared to risk war to stop them (though even then the consequences would have been devastating for both sides). In the case of Afghanistan, there was no direct threat to US security – as the Soviets knew; besides, the Soviets could at least claim that Afghanistan fell into their 'sphere of interest', and that their security was affected by the turbulence beyond their borders. This is not to justify the invasion. It is merely to point out that the Soviets would probably have taken the same action in Afghanistan in the 1960s, if they had felt the situation demanded it – just as they defied the Yalta agreement to crush resistance in Eastern Europe in the 1940s and 1950s at a time when the US had nuclear weapons and they did not.

The essential point is this. Strategic nuclear weapons do not constitute usable units of force. They can have little value except to deter the use of other nuclear weapons, and the notion that at current levels of numbers, relatively small adjustments in the nuclear balance actually affect this is absurd. According to Stanley Hoffman, professor of history at Harvard University: 'It is impossible to prove that the outcome of political conflict in the last thirty years has been determined by the exact ratio of strategic military forces. It is the relative importance of the stake to each side in every crisis which has been decisive.'

Yet worries about the 'political' effects of vulnerability, based on unreal calculations by strategic planners, have led the United States, in the early 1980s, into a series of bizarre and ultimately futile attempts to 'close' the window of vulnerability.

This search amounted to a classic example of the Western habit of trying to find a technological 'fix' which can't – and doesn't.

The hunt began in earnest – ironically enough – not under a hawkish administration but during the presidency of Jimmy Carter, when the air force, alerted to the 'window of vulnerability', decided that the answer lay in a new missile and a 'basing mode' which would insure against Soviet pre-emptive attack. The missile was the MX (for Missile Experimental), a 71-foot rocket, as tall as a six-storey building, which would incorporate the latest in guidance systems and 'mirv' technology and which would theoretically be able to fly from the Midwest of America to, say, Vladivostok on the easternmost extremity of the Soviet Union in a little under 30 minutes and deliver, with an accuracy theoretically pinpointed to a few hundred feet, ten nuclear warheads.

The missile initially got the go-ahead under President Ford, but the problem was: how should it be based? Clearly putting it in fixed silos would make no sense, since in the Pentagon's view these were now lined up like coconuts on a shy. The idea was to find some form of basing mode which would remove the spectre of vulnerability. This was easier said than done. But after examining over 30 schemes, the air force finally settled on one which they believed would work.

The scheme resembled a kind of space-age version of hide and seek. It was a spectacularly ambitious enterprise. Had it come off, it would have been the greatest construction project ever, bigger than the Panama Canal, the Alaska pipeline or the Pyramids, bigger even than the Great Wall of China. It would have cost perhaps as much as $100 billion, and it would have transformed a sizeable chunk of the landscape of two Midwest states – Utah and Nevada. Now in order to understand why Carter, a peaceful, essentially anti-nuclear president, came to bless a scheme he had once called the dumbest thing he had ever heard, it is necessary to embark on a brief digression.

In the early 1960s, after the crises over Cuba and Berlin had fuelled concerns about nuclear war, the superpowers concluded a series of modest arms control agreements: these sought, among other things, to limit the spread of nuclear know-how to countries which did not already possess it, to prevent the placement of nuclear weapons in the Arctic or on the seabed, and to ban nuclear testing in the atmosphere. In the late 1960s, the superpowers began negotiations aimed at a more ambitious end – restricting the size and shape of each other's arsenals.

In 1972 these negotiations yielded two treaties, one of which restricted both sides in the deployment of so-called 'anti-ballistic missile systems' (ABMs) – systems which would be able to shoot down offensive missiles – on the grounds that a defensive race would be costly, futile and encourage an even faster offensive race. The second (the Salt One arms limitation treaty) set limits on the number of missiles each side could deploy. They were very high limits, and they did little to slow down the arms race, since both sides were by then busy mirving their missiles and the treaty did not restrict warhead numbers. But Salt One was intended simply as an interim measure, and after its successful completion both sides began another set of negotiations – aimed at producing a second agreement.

It was the successful completion of this second agreement – Salt Two – which Jimmy Carter devoted considerable efforts to obtaining. And by early 1980 it was complete, and the president went to Vienna to sign it with Leonid Brezhnev. Unlike Salt One, Salt Two *did* set limits on warhead numbers. Carter, however, was not popular in the Senate; his treaty came under fire from powerful politicians; and there was considerable pressure on him to respond to the 'window of vulnerability' – which many thought the treaty did nothing to correct, allowing the Russians to build more than enough warheads plausibly to threaten a 'first strike'.

Carter had given added ammunition to his critics by cancelling the B1 nuclear bomber. He knew that he would have a much better chance of getting Salt Two ratified by the Senate if he agreed to the air force plan for MX. (In the end, it was to no avail; after the Russians invaded Afghanistan on 24 December 1979, Carter withdrew the treaty from the Senate knowing there was now no hope of getting it passed.) In the meantime, however, he had agreed to a basing mode for MX specifically tailored to fit in with the requirements of the treaty.

The plan involved stationing two hundred MX missiles, at a cost officially estimated at $34 billion (sceptics put it at closer to $100 billion), among 4,600 reinforced shelters in some starkly beautiful terrain in the western United States. The shelters, to be dug in a vast area of sagebrush-covered valleys in Utah and Nevada, an area bounded by the neon lights of Las Vegas to the south and Salt Lake City, dusty capital of the Mormon Church, to the north, were to be linked by 8,500 miles of road (almost a quarter of the length of the entire US federal interstate highway system). Gargantuan 28-wheeled trucks would shuffle between those shelters the 200 MX missiles but also, to confuse the Soviets, 4,400 dummies, good enough to be indistinguishable from the real thing to Russia's spy satellites (which can pick up details of weight, heat and magnetic impulse, even if the rockets themselves are kept invisible). Nothing would be left to chance. In order to ascertain the reliability of this 'basing mode', the Pentagon would employ its own 'spies', who would be given a free hand to try and crack the system and identify which shelters housed the real missiles.

In theory, therefore, Russia would only be able to eliminate America's land-based ICBMs by hitting all 4,600 shelters. Since it was reckoned, as we have noted, that you would need to target two warheads at a missile silo to be 'confident' of destroying it, this would mean Russia having to expend a total of 9,200 warheads to execute a first strike. And the beauty of the scheme – from the administration's point of view – was that Salt Two would have limited both sides to a total of 9,200 warheads. So the Kremlin would have to exhaust its entire supply just to destroy MX, leaving itself none left over to deter an attack from American submarines. (Not only that: at prearranged intervals, the hatches over individual missile silos would be opened and Russia's spy satellites would be able to ensure that America was sticking within the limits of the Salt treaty by deploying no more than two hundred real missiles.)

There was something Strangelovian about the whole scheme. Here was the air force proposing to spend tens of billions of dollars on the biggest construction project in history, and to use two million tons of cement plus about 40 billion gallons of water, the most precious of commodities in a land where, as one local miner put it, 'the trees chase the dogs because it is so dry'. Yet they were proposing to do all this to solve a problem which did not exist.

By the time Carter left office, however, things had been set firmly in motion. Congress had approved initial funding for the scheme; contractors had been lined up to do the work; a special office had been set up in Washington to handle public relations for the scheme; glossy booklets showing what it would look like had been printed; and air force delegations had trooped out to Utah and Nevada to give lectures in rickety school halls and talk to local Rotary Clubs, bringing with them slide shows depicting the Soviet threat and diagrams purporting to show that MX would not interfere with the cattle and reassuring words about the opportunities which would open up for local businessmen. Utah and Nevada remained unconvinced, but there was an air of resignation about the air force's power, as reflected in one letter to the *Salt Lake Tribune*: 'Where does a nine hundred pound gorilla sit?' The answer: 'Any damn place he pleases.'

In the end, however, common sense prevailed and the so-called 'racetrack mode' of basing MX was cancelled by President Reagan. But it was not cancelled because it was felt to be unnecessary – quite the contrary. President Reagan arrived in the White House infinitely more worried about the window of vulnerability than Carter. If Carter had been the reluctant bridegroom, Reagan couldn't wait to get to the altar. A major plank in his election campaign had been the notion that America had become 'number two' in the strategic arms race, and a number of influential figures – many of whom were to become key advisers – had formed a pressure group called the Committee of the Present Danger which told anyone who would listen that America had become weaker than Russia, that Salt Two was a fatally flawed, indeed dangerous treaty, and that 'the window of vulnerability' was a real and urgent problem.

But Reagan could not go ahead with the racetrack scheme. To have done so would have made him deeply unpopular in Nevada and Utah (the heartland of Reagan country) and, not insignificantly, it would have aroused fierce opposition from one of his oldest friends, the senator from Nevada, Paul Laxalt. So Reagan's own defence secretary, Caspar Weinberger, had to reopen Pandora's Box. How – leaving aside the 'racetrack mode' – could the window be closed?

The administration reviewed the options: launching missiles from trains, hovercraft, small submarines stationed just off the coast (called submersibles), airships, even giant trucks which could cruise the interstate highways and, in the event of war, pull off the road and launch their missiles (not the least of the objections to this particular scheme was the thought that the missile carrier might get caught up in traffic jams). Meanwhile, less reverent commentators offered a variety of more imaginative sites, ranging from golf courses and obsolete steel plants to dormant volcanoes and the backs of migrating whales.

One scheme closely examined by Weinberger was to launch MXs from aircraft, dropping them on a parachute and having the rockets ignite in mid-air. The air force had demonstrated that it was feasible: in October 1974 a Minuteman missile was dropped from a Lockheed C5A, drifted down on its parachute until its nose was vertical; then the engines fired. The air force in three separate studies had already rejected the so-called 'air mobile' concept as seriously flawed; so too had three presidents: Nixon, Ford and Carter. Yet in summer 1981 the hints which emerged from the White House suggested that 'air mobile' was the scheme Reagan favoured. Lockheed began trying to work out how long it would take to build 100 new C5As, specially modified to carry the giant MXs. And on the air force drawing board was a plane codenamed Big Bird that would, hopefully, stay in the air, ready to release a missile, for a week at a time.

Air mobile, however, was never likely to get off the ground. John Tower, then the diminutive chairman of the Senate's powerful Armed Services Committee, pointed out that the concept had already been rejected as 'too unreliable, too costly and of questionable survivability' and that it would be 'difficult to get through Congress'. For one thing, the air mobile scheme, supposing there *were* a pre-emptive strike, might prove twice as lethal as one designed to take out the hide-and-seek shelters. (Thousands of missiles raining down on Utah and Nevada would kill an estimated 5.9 million

Americans. But if they attempted to eliminate the threat posed by air-based MXs the Russians would be obliged to hit air bases scattered throughout the United States. The estimated toll in that event was 11.3 million.)

Weinberger was forced to think again, and in December 1982 he came up with another scheme, called 'dense pack'. Dense pack had the virtue of working in precisely the opposite way to Carter's 'racetrack mode'. Instead of scattering the missiles over a wide area, the new idea was to deploy them very close together, in clusters. This closeness would make them very difficult targets for a pre-emptive strike because though the first Soviet warheads to arrive would assuredly hit their targets, the blast, radiation and debris from these first incoming warheads would deflect or destroy those which followed (the event known as fratricide). Thus, since the specially hardened MX silos would require virtually a direct hit to destroy them, a portion of the missile force would survive and be able to mount a retaliatory strike.

This scheme was in truth a great deal less outlandish than Jimmy Carter's, and it envisaged wasting considerably less space, but Congress was now becoming collectively weary of MX, and gave it the thumbs down. The eventual result of this was that the administration, thwarted in its efforts to close the 'window of vulnerability' whose dangers it had trumpeted to the world, and after having the whole matter reviewed by a bipartisan commission, elected simply to place the MX in fixed, land-based silos. Understandably, Congress did not think much of this either. The whole justification for the MX in the first place had been the fear that land-based missiles in fixed silos were becoming vulnerable. Now the administration was proposing to spend money on missiles which were not going to solve that problem but *add* to it. If the Soviets really were disposed to launch a pre-emptive strike then the presence of the MXs would presumably make the option even more tempting. Steadily, therefore, Congress cut funds for MX and by early 1985 the Reagan administration was in an ironic position: having inherited from Carter a plan to place 200 missiles in a supposedly 'invulnerable' basing mode, it now looked as if it would only be able to deploy no more than 50 in fixed 'vulnerable' silos.

There was one consolation, however. The bipartisan commission to which the administration turned for advice recommended the development of a new smaller missile, mobile and with a single warhead. The logic behind Midgetman, as it was christened, was more sensible than that behind MX. The fear of first strikes, after all, had arisen because of developments in missile guidance systems and because of 'mirving': it was mirving which made it theoretically possible for a relatively small number of rockets to take out a much larger number – a danger which would be less likely if both sides moved to single-warhead missiles. (Among those who recognized the virtues of this was Henry Kissinger. As secretary of state in the early 1970s, he had played a key role in the United States' decision to develop mirvs but he later admitted: 'If only I had thought through the implications of a mirved world.')

Even more important was the fact that Midgetman would be mobile, meaning that it would be much harder to shoot at than fixed missiles in 'vulnerable' silos. There were, however, a number of snags. The danger raised by Midgetman was of a Soviet 'barrage' attack: the explosion of nuclear weapons, in the air, over potential Midgetman bases, knocking over their launch trucks, killing their crews and fracturing communications so as to make contact impossible between the air force and any crews who survived. Obviously, the aim would have to be to force the Soviets to 'barrage' as large an area as possible – the larger the area, the less confidence they could have in disabling the entire force – and, ideally, for the US, this would mean keeping Midgetman in what is termed a 'state of continuous dispersal'. But since this would mean that the missiles would have to be trundling regularly around America's highways – not a prospect likely to appeal to most US citizens (what would happen if one turned over in an accident? or, worse, got hijacked by terrorists?) – it was quickly clear that the military would have to keep Midgetman on their own patch. This is sizeable – using the ten largest military reservations, the air force have 12,500 miles to work with – and, in a crisis, the area would become even larger because the missiles, stationed, perhaps, not just on air force bases but also at certain fixed missile sites (replacing the existing missiles), would be able to 'dash' in all directions to their firing positions.

Such a requirement, however, called for an ambitious new system: a launch truck not just able to move swiftly but stable enough to withstand the blast from all but a very close nuclear explosion. One vehicle on the drawing board, nicknamed Armadillo, is a squat truck, weighing about 45 tons, which, while not elegant, is intended to be sturdy. At its firing position its crew would make it 'safe' by several methods. First, heavy metal skirts would descend round the wheels to strike the ground on all sides, increasing stability. Second, metal bolts would be fired by explosive charges from underneath the vehicle into the ground, to act like a ship's anchors. Finally, the Armadillo might have hydraulic 'legs' or 'suckers' intended to give it yet more stability.

Thus ensconced, say those contemplating the Armadillo design, it would be able to withstand phenomenal pressure – perhaps as much as 30 lb per square inch, six times what it would take to knock down the average house. In theory, then, a good number of Armadillos would be able to 'ride out' a Soviet attack, and still be ready to launch a retaliatory strike.

The arguments about Midgetman, as I write, are still in their infancy.

But supposing all the technical problems can be overcome to the satisfaction of Congress, there is another problem. Midgetman will be very expensive. One early estimate put a thousand missiles mounted on Armadillos at $70 billion. And the Midgetman is part of an air force modernization programme which includes not only MX, but the B1, the 'Advanced Technology Bomber', nicknamed Stealth – which is already under development, and is intended to be virtually undetectable by Soviet radar – and a new generation of Stealth cruise missiles.* What this means is that Midgetman will face stiff competition for funds. Even so, it makes more sense than MX ever has, or does, or could.

I have reviewed in detail the notion of the window of vulnerability – and the efforts to 'close' it – because it goes to the heart of US strategic thinking.

What happened in the late 1970s and early 1980s is that America's strategic planners identified a problem which did not exist, tried to find a 'solution' to it, and couldn't. In the meantime, however, the pressure to find a solution had become intense because it was claimed that the Soviets might otherwise 'perceive' their advantage and feel freer to exercise political and military muscle when they chose. As George Rathjens of the Massachusetts Institute of Technology said in testimony to Congress:

> ... to the degree there is a problem, it is largely of our own making. We exaggerate the growth of Soviet nuclear capabilities in order to gain support for our own prospective nuclear programmes. Having done so, it is hardly surprising that others expect us to remedy what we have identified as critical deficiencies. Failure to do so would indeed make us appear irresolute by our own standards.

Even William Perry, who as Carter's research and development chief in the Pentagon was one of the first to publicize the vulnerability problem, admitted in an interview in 1982 that 'to a certain extent, we have shot ourselves in the foot. We have inflicted these problems on ourselves by the way we have advertised them.'

The alternative to advertising the 'problems' would have been to discount them: to make clear to the Soviets that any benefits they might think they could gain from theoretical notions of vulnerability would be purely illusory and that any belief that America's resolve had weakened would be both extraordinarily rash and horribly mistaken. No conceivable first strike would remove America's capacity to mount a devastating counter-

---

* The Stealth technology involves the use of non-metallic, composite materials and special techniques for masking the heat signature given off by aircraft or missile engines.

attack, and nothing in the foreseeable future would change that. Instead successive administrations claimed – in effect – that America had become weaker than Russia, which is rather like telling someone you suspect is about to burgle your house that you don't think much of your alarm system. Luckily, most burglars make their own assessment before attempting break-ins, and the Soviets have almost certainly remained more impressed by American nuclear forces than have American strategic planners.

Why then has there developed so intense an obsession with arcane theories about vulnerability? What causes the endless worrying about discrepancy in numbers, and the ceaseless search for better, more accurate nuclear systems? (Why, for example, do the US navy need 760 nuclear-armed cruise missiles?) Does it really make any difference? Henry Kissinger raised a similar question in 1974. 'What in the name of God is strategic superiority?' he asked in a famous speech in Brussels. 'What is the significance of it, politically, militarily, operationally, at these levels of numbers? What do you do with it?'

Kissinger has since appeared to change his mind (a not infrequent occurrence) but the questions remain valid, and the answers to them are (in order) that strategic superiority is meaningless, that it has no significance and that you can do nothing with it. As McGeorge Bundy, once President Kennedy's national security adviser, and one of the most thoughtful critics of nuclear weapons policy, put it in 1969:

> There is an enormous gulf between what political leaders really think about nuclear weapons and what is assumed in the complex calculations of relative 'advantage' in simulated strategic war. Thinktank analysts can set levels of 'acceptable' damage well up in the hundreds of millions of lives ... They are in an unreal world. In the real world of real political leaders – whether here or in the Soviet Union – a decision that would bring even one hydrogen bomb on one city of one's own country would be recognized in advance as a catastrophic blunder; ten bombs on ten cities would be a disaster beyond history; and a hundred bombs on one hundred cities are unthinkable.

Many officials and military men, however, continue to live in the unreal world that Bundy has described. There are various reasons for this. One is institutional pressures: there are many careers, and a lot of money, tied up in the development and production of nuclear weapons. Another is the dry academic reasoning which Bundy identifies as the hallmark of US nuclear thinking. A third is inter-service rivalry – both navy and air force prize their respective deterrents, and whatever the strategic arguments in favour of America moving more and more of its deterrent to sea, the air force are reluctant to give up the 'land-based leg' of the nuclear force, which they own and control. A fourth reason is political pressures. In the late 1950s Jack Kennedy campaigned for president on the notion that President Eisenhower had allowed 'a missile gap' to develop in Russia's favour. It wasn't true, but it spurred a bigger, more ambitious US programme; Jimmy Carter agreed to MX because of pressure from the Senate; and Reagan, having condemned Carter as a strategic weakling, could scarcely be expected to settle for a less ambitious plan.

But there is another source of pressure on the US arsenal, and one which is often ignored. This is the pressure which stems from the West's conventional weakness and the Nato strategy of 'flexible response'. Flexible response anticipates Nato being prepared to go nuclear first if it begins to lose a conventional battle on the Central Front. It also anticipates being able to raise the stakes – if limited use of nuclear weapons in Europe does not persuade the Russians to cease their aggression, it anticipates the US being prepared ultimately to use its intercontinental weapons.

It is this contingency which has driven much of the thinking about 'counterforce' and small, 'selective' nuclear strikes. In an age of such huge and potentially destructive arsenals, no American president would wish to order an indiscriminate assault on Russia – this would certainly lead to Armageddon, and the mere *threat* to behave like this (in defence of *Europe*) would not be credible, either to the Europeans or to the Russians. Instead the American president, so the theory goes, would need to be able to make a more selective strike, using, say, a handful of intercontinental missiles, in an attempt to force the Russians to back down.

To be able to do this, however – it is argued – America needs to feel utterly secure. It needs to know that having launched a small, selective strike it might not then lose the rest of its missile force through a massive counter-assault from Russia. And though the idea of the Russians launching a bolt from the blue might make no sense, the idea of a pre-emptive strike following an American decision to start nuclear war is more understandable.

Thus the most plausible justification for the excessively large US arsenal is the unrealistic demands of Nato strategy. It therefore follows that were Nato to beef up its conventional forces the justification for American 'war fighting' scenarios – with all the dangers they contain – would disappear. These scenarios, as we have seen, have never made much sense. The warheads would not fall where they were supposed to; millions of people would die; and as various Nato experts have pointed out, communications between US leaders and nuclear forces would probably be totally disrupted after a relatively small strike. A 'limited' strategic war would be unlikely to stay limited for long; having once started, it would be likely to prove impossible to stop.

Indeed, the 'war termination problem', as William Kaufman calls it, is 'almost unexplored territory' in US nuclear strategy. Ending a nuclear war would be vastly different from ending a conventional war, where things tend to move comparatively slowly, and both sides are likely to have a pretty good idea of the situation they face – how many forces they have left, how they are disposed, what damage has been done to the enemy, etc. Even so, in World War Two, when the Germans and the Japanese kept fighting long after the 'balance of forces' had swung against them, and when it was clear to any detached observer that their predicament was hopeless, it took traumatic events to bring the fighting to an end. What would it take in a 'protracted' nuclear war, when the horrors of Hiroshima and Nagasaki had become routine, and when, because of shattered communications, neither side would quite know what damage it had inflicted, or even how much it had suffered itself? How would the president, in his emergency 'Kneecap' plane – supposing he was alive and it had not been shot down or crashed because of worn ball bearings – bring the conflict to an orderly end? It is a question which defies the imagination.

If America only had to worry about using its strategic weapons if attacked by Russia – rather than using them first in response to the dictates of Nato strategy – then it could live with a much smaller arsenal. It would also need to worry less about the supposed vulnerability of its land-based missiles and come to depend more on its missile-carrying submarines – the one element of its deterrent which seems likely to remain utterly 'invulnerable' for generations to come.

Nato, however, continues to try and make nuclear forces seem 'usable' in the defence of Europe – not just in response to a Soviet nuclear attack but in response to a Soviet conventional attack, too. And though European leaders, on the whole, have found the arguments about vulnerability overblown, they have helped encourage them. Not only that, while America was worrying about the window of vulnerability and its land-based missile force, the Europeans were worrying about another aspect of the nuclear deterrent – medium-range missiles in Europe.

The decision which their worries led to, and its aftermath, constitutes one of the more revealing episodes in the history of the Alliance, and one worth looking at in some detail.

9

The Ladder of Escalation

On 12 December 1979, Nato made a historic decision. It agreed, at a meeting in Brussels, to deploy 572 new 'intermediate range' nuclear missiles in five European countries unless the Soviet Union agreed – through arms control negotiations – to dramatic reductions in its own theatre nuclear arsenal. Almost exactly four years later, in December 1983, a US transport plane lumbered into Greenham Common, England, bringing in its hold the first of those new missiles. During the intervening four years, the Alliance had had to weather a storm of criticism. There had been moments when it seemed that the decision might not hold and when the prospects for deployment looked, at best, uncertain. One prominent defence expert, writing after lengthy conversations with allied politicians and officials, concluded in August 1981, for example, that the odds were 'no better than evens' that the Nato decision would be put into effect. It was a by no means untypical reaction.

In the end, such fears proved ill-founded. The arrival of the C130s bringing the first American missiles to Europe in late 1983 was greeted by an almost audible sigh of relief in Nato circles. Some suggested that the successful implementing of the decision was a cause for pride: the fact that the decision had been seen through showed Nato to be more robust and healthy than its critics believed. 'The trouble with the West,' remarked one senior US official to a colleague, 'is that we never know when we've won.'

Maybe. Having made the decision to deploy new missiles Nato clearly had to stick with it: to have done otherwise would have been to appear to cave in to Russian pressure and to show itself irresolute and weak. But the decision itself was a gamble. It constituted yet another attempt to prop up flexible response, but it did not really do that. It brought little extra 'deterrence' or 'defence' but exacted a heavy political cost. It gave Soviet propagandists a field day. It played a significant role in reawakening the so-called 'peace' movement. Moreover, it was not – as some on the left fondly imagined – an American plot to cram new nuclear weapons down reluctant European throats. It was almost entirely a 'European' initiative.

The origins of the 1979 decision are complicated and controversial. In September 1974, the first test occurred of a new missile which came to be known as the SS20. It was closely monitored by America's surveillance network, and intelligence analysts soon had a clear picture of the missile. Unlike older Soviet missiles, it was propelled by solid fuel; its compact size and shape suggested it could be easily moved around on a trailer; it had three warheads, each with a 200 kiloton yield (though for the time being they would be filled with sand, or some such substitute for fissile material); and observation of how the warheads separated from the nose deep in space, and then re-entered the atmosphere to land in different places, confirmed that it was 'mirved', meaning, as we have seen, that each warhead could be released independently and directed to a separate target.

The analysts had some indications, too, about its range. It had been fired from Kapustin Yar, two hundred miles south-east of Moscow on the banks of the Volga River where, on a fertile lowland plain, amidst woodland and fields of melons and vegetables, stands a bewildering complex of launch pads, hangars, communications centres and other buildings – rather like Cape Canaveral in Florida. The Americans knew that Kapustin Yar was traditionally used for testing intermediate rather than strategic range missiles (ICBMs). And the new missile, in its test, flew only about 4,000 miles east, unlike the intercontinental missiles whose job is to carry the Atlantic and wreak havoc on the US, and which have a range closer to 6,000 miles. It was soon clear, therefore, that the SSX20 (X for experimental) was an 'intermediate range' weapon.*

News of the SSX20 began to filter through to America's allies at a meeting of the Nuclear Planning Group in November 1974. In June the following year at another NPG meeting in Monterey, overlooking the ocean in northern California, Jim Schlesinger, then America's defence secretary, distributed satellite photographs, one of which showed extensive preparations at an old missile base near Drovenayo in Siberia. This, apparently, was where the first SSX20s were to be sited.

In January 1976 Nato was again briefed on the SSX20, this time more fully, at a Nuclear Planning Group meeting in an old war college in the suburbs of Hamburg in West Germany. The Russians were now well down the testing road with the SS20, the Americans explained, and after some

---

*Early on there was some concern that it might be another ICBM, and that the Russians were only testing the first two stages or 'sections' of the rocket so as to deceive America about their intentions, but this fear soon faded. The proof came, eventually, not from the missile itself but from observation of the supporting equipment: the capsule in which the missile would be stored and the 'transporter erector launchers' in which they would be carried were neither big enough nor bulky enough for ICBMs.

early mishaps it was proving remarkably successful. Out of its 25 flights, the last 20 had gone well, an uncommonly good record in a process often plagued by failure. The missile was supposedly accurate (it was reported to have a CEP – for 'circular error of probability' – of 1,320 feet, which meant that Western intelligence estimated it should be able to fall, at least half the time, within a circle whose radius was 1,320 feet). It also supposedly 'wobbled' little in flight. And from the activity at the missile factories it seemed the Soviets meant business: it was expected that they would produce around 300 of the new missiles.

The news was beginning to alarm European officials. But the first major public speech about the SS20 was made not in Europe but in America, by Dr Fred Ikle, then the head of the US Arms Control and Disarmament Agency. Ikle, a Swiss, and the author of several provocative articles, including one entitled 'Can deterrence last out the century?', subscribes to the view that the Soviet Union is bent on strategic superiority. And in September 1976 he addressed the grandly entitled World Affairs Council in Los Angeles on the subject of the SS20, describing the 'spectre of such weapons' growing 'like a towering cloud over Europe and Asia'. The development, he pointed out, appeared to be unprovoked; its aim appeared to be to deny Nato 'escalation dominance', i.e. the ability to threaten plausibly to raise the stakes because of superior strength, or at least equality, at a particular level. Faced with an array of powerful, new, three-warheaded, mobile missiles in the Soviet Union, aimed at Europe, Nato would stand to gain less than ever by going nuclear first.

Ikle's bleak analysis rattled some dovecotes in Washington. He had not actually charged the Soviets with violating Salt, but he had strongly implied that they were breaking the *spirit*. And with détente and arms control squarely on the agenda, it was important not to spoil the 'atmosphere'. A systems analyst in the Pentagon, James Thomson, was instructed to write an internal paper putting the other side of the case.

This Thomson did. His argument, in essence, was that the SS20 represented a straightforward piece of modernization. The Russians were replacing some older missiles with brand-new ones. What could be more natural than that? It was a case with much to recommend it.

The Russians, after all, had targeted Western Europe with SS4 and SS5 missiles since the late 1950s, to which, at first, America had responded by stationing Thor and Jupiter missiles in Britain, Italy and Turkey, eventually withdrawing them, however, on the grounds that their targets could easily be covered by US strategic weapons. The SS4s and SS5s remained, and by the mid-1970s they were old and – powered by the volatile liquid fuel – in some cases unreliable and dangerous to handle. The SS4, the older of the two, had to be towed to its launching stage by twelve tractors and trailers, and once in flight it had to rely on external fins to guide its flight path. The SS5 was a bit more sophisticated, and had double the range. But both were overdue for replacement. Indeed it has been argued that only the Soviet obsession with building up a substantial ICBM force to counter the US during the 1960s prevented modernization earlier.

That the Soviets had now decided to replace the SS4s and SS5s, Thomson argued in his paper, need not therefore be construed with alarm. And though, to be sure, the SS20 was *qualitatively* superior to the SS4 and SS5 – it was mobile, more accurate, more difficult to target and certain to bring more warheads to bear on Western Europe – it did not mark a radical new departure. In terms of overall warheads, the West was still comfortably ahead. Besides, it had long been assumed that a significant number of Soviet ICBMs, though capable of crossing the Atlantic, had in fact been targeted on Europe. The evidence for this was, to be sure, circumstantial. In three major missile fields in the western USSR the intermediate range SS5s stood shoulder to shoulder with intercontinental SS11s. The backup equipment in these fields, particularly command and control gear, suggested that these particular SS11s – in all, some 150 to 200 of them – might be targeted on Europe.

The point was that the Soviets had so comprehensively targeted the cities and military installations of Europe with nuclear weapons of every kind – short- and long-range – that the addition of extra SS20 warheads was going to have precious little real effect on the overall balance. But the Europeans were becoming jittery about the SS20. Ripples of concern were beginning to spread through defence and foreign ministries, especially in Bonn and London. And the concern was heightened by two other, linked developments. The first was the direction of the Salt process. The second was the emergence of the cruise missile.

The 'European' worry about Salt was a simple one. The aim of the Salt process was, in effect, to create a situation where both sides would have a strategic arsenal of equal power – the idea being that if this could be agreed then neither side would be able to forge ahead, developing weapons in a destabilizing quest for 'superiority'. The old notion of 'mutually assured destruction', by which both sides would know that if they started a war they simultaneously risked destroying the planet, would be reinforced – in effect, codified.

To some European officials, however, there was a danger in this. It served to underline the existence of a nuclear stalemate. With the superpowers actually agreeing (implicitly) in arms talks that neither could strike the other, where did that leave Western Europe? Didn't it puncture a gaping hole in the nuclear umbrella? What possible incentive would the US have to put its cities at risk and come to Europe's rescue in the event that deterrence broke down and war broke out? The fear was especially potent in the West German defence establishment since, at heart, Nato is a code for American involvement in the defence of West Germany. With an accepted strategic balance, and the Soviets allowed an unimpeded build-up of missiles targeted on Europe, might not the code be broken?

However illogical, this fear came to absorb Helmut Schmidt and his defence advisers in Bonn. Schmidt, himself a former defence minister, had long worried about the effects of nuclear 'parity' between the superpowers. Now, it seemed to him, things were getting worse. And one particular facet of the Salt negotiations caused him particular concern. This was the attitude the American administration took to a new *Western* wonder weapon called cruise.

As nuclear weapons go, the cruise missile is a modest affair. In an age when missiles the height of skyscrapers can theoretically deliver ten or more warheads each capable of destroying a medium-sized city with pinpoint accuracy over 6,000 miles or so, the cruise, a mere 21 inches in diameter, and carrying only one warhead, seems almost anticlimactic. It is slow, too. While modern ICBMs can cross half the world in half an hour, the cruise is subsonic, travelling at around 500 mph. But it has two advantages: it is cheap, and, because it travels only at hedge-hopping height, it is difficult to track by radar. It is in fact a small pilotless aircraft, a direct descendant of the V1 buzz bombs which the Germans used to deadly effect against London in the early 1940s. But it was not until the late 1960s, spurred by new developments in micro-electronics and jet engines, that the American armaments industry began to develop the new missile.

At first, it was envisaged for a very specific and limited role. The backbone of America's nuclear bomber force (300 B52s) were aging – many were older than the pilots who flew them – and there was concern that against increasingly sophisticated air defence in Europe, an area in which the Soviets had invested heavily, the B52s would have trouble carrying out their wartime mission. Cruise missiles seemed the ideal answer. They could be fired from an aircraft while still some 1,500 miles from its target, thus drastically reducing the need to penetrate hostile air space and risk getting shot down. Cruise missiles, the Pentagon reasoned, could at least considerably extend the life of the B52.

But once the genie was out of the bottle it was hard to contain. For it began to dawn on defence planners that it was a remarkably versatile genie. It seemed to some that – given its cheapness – it could perform a number of functions, nuclear and conventional, based on land and at sea as well as in the air, to ease the burdens of European defence. It could complicate Moscow's task of defending Mother Russia – and that, the argument went, would enhance deterrence. 'Perhaps the most significant weapon development of the decade,' a Pentagon director of research and engineering later enthused. The Defense Science Board estimated that it would take the Soviets ten years to 'catch up' and achieve a similar cruise missile programme; in the meantime, it would cost them billions of roubles attempting to upgrade their air defences against the threat.

But the cruise missile, though popular among civilian planners in the Pentagon, had few fans in the White House. A number of officials and defence experts believed that it might turn into an arms controller's nightmare – small, mobile and horribly difficult to check up on, or verify. This would become even more true if the Pentagon developed, as many felt it should, *conventional* cruise missiles as well as nuclear ones: short of using a Geiger counter, it would be impossible to tell the two types apart.

The argument, however, was still in its infancy. In late 1976 the Soviets deployed the first SS20 – at Drovenayo in Siberia – and though the issue got lost during the 1976 election campaign, it was squarely on the agenda when Jimmy Carter, the former peanut farmer and one-time nuclear submariner from Georgia, entered the White House in January 1977.

From the beginning, Carter's stance on nuclear weapons was viewed with suspicion in Europe. This increased when word reached European defence ministries that he had asked the Chiefs of Staff if they could live with a drastic cut in the American missile force. Then came the ill-fated trip to Moscow by Carter's secretary of state, Cyrus Vance, who proposed that both superpowers cut in half their arsenals, a proposal which prompted the Soviet foreign minister, Andrei Gromyko, to take the unusual step of calling a press conference to denounce it. And when, in spring 1977, a senior State Department official named Leslie Gelb travelled to Europe to brief the allies on the American cruise missile programme, the West Germans, in particular, found further cause for concern. Gelb's report simply outlined the advantages and disadvantages of cruise, but Schmidt's defence advisers worried that the administration was preparing to sacrifice what they believed might be a potentially useful weapon on the altar of Salt.*

The arrival of the Carter administration added to European worries for another reason. Carter's defence secretary, Harold Brown, and his deputy, Robert Komer, pursued an energetic campaign aimed at persuading America's allies to bolster their conventional forces. European governments have always been ambivalent about doing this, and their concern is not just financial. They fear that if Europe ever became strong enough to resist

---

* Indeed, in April 1977 the Carter administration did decide to offer to the Soviets, as part of Salt Two, a protocol restricting the development and deployment of cruise missiles to last until 1981.

a Soviet attack *on its own*, the Americans might seize on it as the excuse to leave Europe. They might take the opportunity to withdraw their 300,000 troops, for years the glue which has held the Alliance together, and adopt a more isolationist policy. Thus the Carter administration's zeal on the conventional issue (Bob Komer earned himself the nickname 'Nato's Billy Graham') reinforced the dreaded spectre of 'decoupling' – the severance of Europe from America – which the emergence of the SS20 and the progress of Salt had already raised amongst European officials.

At the London summit in May 1977, the Carter administration presented a long-range development plan for Nato. This called for the setting up of nine so-called 'task-forces' to examine different aspects of conventional defence (reinforcements, reserves, electronic warfare, readiness, etc.). But in deference to European concerns about the SS20 and a possible nuclear imbalance, a tenth task force was added to look at the nuclear problem. And European concerns were growing. A month after the London summit, Nato's Nuclear Planning Group met in Ottawa. During the meeting, Harold Brown held a private discussion with his British counterpart, Fred Mulley, about Europe's intermediate-range nuclear force. At the time, this consisted principally of aircraft: nuclear-capable Phantoms and Lightnings (the latter due to be replaced by nuclear-capable Tornados), and, more importantly, the longer range Vulcans and the 220 American F111s based at airfields in Britain. The Vulcans, however, were old and might prove no match for modern Soviet air defences. And though the F111 was relatively modern – a fast, low-flying, supersonic small precursor of the bomber called the B1 – aircraft as a whole were becoming vulnerable, and more importantly, it was argued, so were the airfields on which they were stationed. In addition, the US wanted to free more 'dual capable' aircraft like the F111 for an exclusively conventional role.

But as well as strike aircraft, a total of over 400 warheads from American Poseidon submarines had been specifically allocated to Nato (falling, in other words, under the operational control of the Supreme Allied Commander, Europe, rather than the Joint Chiefs of Staff in the Pentagon). This force had been boosted after the first discovery of the SS20, and it also filled the role of an 'intermediate' nuclear force. What Brown wanted to know was: would this be sufficient? Did Fred Mulley think that Nato could rely simply on America's Poseidon submarines for its 'intermediate'-range deterrent? Mulley did not reply immediately. He returned to London and consulted the recently appointed director of policy and programmes at the Ministry of Defence, Michael Quinlan.

At 47, Michael Quinlan was a rising star in Whitehall. A brilliant though controversial figure, his attitude did much to influence Mulley's eventual reply to Harold Brown. Basically, Quinlan believed that the Poseidon submarines would not, in themselves, constitute a sufficient deterrent. In the light of the added threat posed by the SS20, something else would be needed too. Put simply, Quinlan's belief was this: a potential aggressor must be able to spot no chinks in Nato's armour; deterrence must be a 'seamless robe'; at the moment there was a gap in this robe, and it needed to be filled.

Thus, under the standard scenario, a Warsaw Pact invasion of Western Europe would be met by conventional forces. But if these failed Nato would have to be able (or at least be seen to be able) to go nuclear – probably with battlefield weapons. But supposing the Pact merely replied in kind? Then Nato would have to be able (or be seen to be able) to raise the stakes again. But without a proper intermediate-range arsenal Nato would have to move all the way from battlefield weapons to strategic weapons in one giant step. There would be nothing in between. And such a step might not seem credible to Soviet leaders. Faced with defeat in Central Europe, the Americans might decide that the risks of escalation all the way up to strategic weapons were too grave – and Nato might have to surrender. Or, to put it another way, the Soviets might *believe* that Nato would simply not take the risk.

More specifically, Quinlan felt that the Poseidon missiles, though officially assigned to Nato (and to play the role of 'intermediate-range' weapons), were in fact *strategic* weapons. And submarines, Quinlan argued, pose technical problems: command and control are more difficult than with land-based systems; the missiles are less accurate; they are less easy to use in a 'selective' strike because once a submarine fires a salvo it risks revealing its position. It is therefore more suited to an 'all-or-nothing' strike, which makes it an indiscriminate weapon and gives it, in the calculation of war planners, a different role to the one Quinlan believed necessary for nuclear weapons in Europe.

Quinlan argued from a broader political perspective, too. It was vital, he said, that Russia see Europe as *involved* – sharing the Alliance's nuclear burden, if only by providing its soil for the purpose. To position nuclear weapons in European countries would demonstrate precisely this. It would be a display of collective Alliance resolve.

Mulley was persuaded. He sent a letter to Harold Brown in late summer, 1977. No, he said, he did not think that Nato's nuclear deterrent should be moved offshore. Furthermore, since the SS20s were now plainly putting airfields at risk – and Europe might have to take missiles rather than aircraft – he urged the administration to be careful not to 'give away' cruise missiles in Salt.

The letter came as unwelcome news in Washington. But barely had it arrived than the Americans were given another, more significant, warning. This time it came in public – in the form of a famous but gnomic speech from the West German leader, Helmut Schmidt. Schmidt's speech to the

International Institute of Strategic Studies in London is often taken as the first crucial step on the road which led to the December 1979 decision to deploy cruise and Pershing missiles in Europe. Given as the second Alastair Buchan memorial lecture (Buchan was a prominent British strategist who died in 1975), it was a profound, though veiled, expression of the unrest he felt at the trend events were taking in the US. Schmidt's feelings were compounded by his personal dislike of Carter, whom he felt to be an innocent in the turbulent sea of East-West relations. (The dislike was mutual.) It must be added that many of those unhappy with Carter in Washington had lost no opportunity to bend Schmidt's ear on the subject. They warned him to watch Carter: the president, they said, was trying to sell European interests down the river.

At the IISS, Schmidt talked at length about the economic aspects of defence, and touched on the problems of terrorism. But the key section of his speech (though almost entirely ignored by the press) was nuclear. 'Salt,' he said, 'codifies the nuclear strategic balance between the Soviet Union and the US. To put it another way, Salt neutralizes their strategic nuclear capabilities. In Europe, this magnifies the significance of the disparities between East and West in nuclear tactical and conventional weapons.'

The White House, of course, already knew what Schmidt felt. But by going public the chancellor was dramatically increasing the pressure to find a solution. That autumn, a succession of high-powered American officials from the National Security Council and the State Department trailed across the Atlantic seeking to defuse the issue. The SS20, they argued, as Jim Thomson had a year before, constituted no dramatic change in the strategic balance, and the restraints on cruise deployment would only last until 1981 – by which time Salt Three should take care of the SS20. The American nuclear umbrella, they in effect declared, was as watertight as ever.

But like Cassandra, the White House was now doomed not to be heard. The whole fuss, it seemed to some officials, was unnecessary and irrelevant. Europe had lived for years with a nuclear imbalance on the continent, and what is more with aircraft in Britain as its only land-based, intermediate-range nuclear weapons. As everyone knew, these could if necessary be quietly upgraded when the time came and *not* converted to a purely conventional role, thus fulfilling Quinlan and Mulley's demand that the *whole* intermediate-range missile force dedicated to Europe should not be at sea. (As to the argument that airfields were vulnerable: well, said the sceptics, so were missile bases.) In the meantime, the White House believed, the priorities were to try both to create a stronger conventional defence and to keep a handle on the Russian strategic threat through arms control. What Europe seemed to be moving towards – pressure for the deployment of a set of hard-to-verify new weapons – was going to work against both those goals, making one more difficult, and distracting attention away from the other. Moreover, there were those in the White House who even then were wondering whether the Europeans like Schmidt who were applying the pressure were not in danger of causing a political storm in their own countries that they would be quite unable to deal with.

But things were now moving quickly. On 26 October at a Nato Nuclear Planning Group meeting in Bari in Italy, the Americans had taken a step intended to ease European worries. They had set up, as the tenth task force provided for under the long-term defence plan, a new committee, called the High Level Group, and almost before they knew it the Europeans had seized the initiative.

10

Cruise and Pershing

The group of 50-odd Nato officials who arrived at Los Alamos' one and only motel on 22 February 1978 had little chance or time to admire what is a stunning view across the Rockies. It snowed constantly during their two-day visit, blotting out the surrounding mountains. More significantly, their meeting – the second of the newly formed High Level Group – was one of the most crucial in Nato's history.

The men (and one woman – a member of the US delegation) who made the trip to Los Alamos, flying from Washington to Albuquerque before being brought up to the hourglass-shaped plateau on which Los Alamos is perched in two sturdy green school buses, were high-level defence officials (assistant secretaries in American terms), with backup from other defence and foreign ministry staff. Their allotted brief as members of the tenth task force set up under President Carter's long-term defence plan was to take a broad look at Nato's nuclear arsenal. At their first meeting, in Brussels the previous December, the officials had decided that they should concentrate first on 'intermediate-range' or 'theatre' nuclear weapons.

But whereas the Brussels meeting had produced little of substance, Los Alamos quickly yielded a breakthrough. In the new and suitably spacious conference centre, close by the still highly productive nuclear weapons laboratories and the remnants of the chalet-style boys' school which, 36 years before, had been used by Robert Oppenheimer and his fellow scientists for the Manhattan Project, the various delegations assembled round the outside of a U-shaped table. Down either side sat the Europeans, two from each country, with others sitting round the room, against the walls. Between them, at the end of the U, flanked by his fellow Americans, sat the chairman, David McGiffert, assistant under-secretary for international security policy at the Pentagon. McGiffert's instructions were clear. He was to find out what the Europeans felt but commit himself to nothing. A soft-spoken lawyer who specialized in arbitration cases, McGiffert listened to each delegation in turn. The British (through Michael

Quinlan) and the Germans through Wolfgang Altenburg, then a major general and now inspector-general of the Bundeswehr, took the lead: many of the arguments made in the Quinlan/Mulley letter to Harold Brown were repeated and both delegations, it was clear, believed that there was now a need to station new missiles in Europe capable of striking the USSR.

The key question, however, was how the other European countries would react. To an extent, Nato has always been a two-tier alliance, with the Americans, the Germans and the British in division one and the other European countries playing a less prominent role. No vital decision, though, could be taken without the consent of all members, and therefore McGiffert listened with a keen interest when the Belgian representative, Pierre Champenois, began to give his view.

Afterwards, Champenois' contribution was seen by at least one member of the American delegation as the turning point of the meeting. While careful to emphasize that he did not speak for his government, the Belgian stressed the need for what he called a more 'visible coupling' between the US and Europe. This, he made clear, meant new missiles capable of striking Russia but not, he was careful to add, Moscow. That would be too provocative. Later, in a coffee break, Champenois was to underline his view. 'We must remember,' he said, 'that the Poles are victims too.' That was the point: Nato had a host of short-range systems which could devastate Eastern Europe but none which (except, of course, for bombers) could reach Russia itself. And this despite what was seen as the intolerable provocation of the SS20. With the SS20 the Soviets might feel they could launch devastating strikes against Western Europe from Eastern Europe, and yet preserve Russia itself as a sanctuary. They might, therefore, feel they could confine a nuclear war to Europe.

Champenois' view was supported by the Dutch and, though the Greeks kept silent, by almost everyone else at the table. It dawned on McGiffert that there was a consensus – and the US was on the point of being pressed to make a decision. The High Level Group, admittedly, was composed of officials not ministers. But the officials it comprised were all people close to ministers, having broad responsibility for policy matters – people, as one observer put it, with 'short lines of communication' to their respective governments. So McGiffert was being pushed into a corner. Faithful to his role as chairman, he summed up the meeting by concluding that the HLG believed there should be some 'upward evolutionary adjustment' in Nato's nuclear posture.

The phrase was loaded with bureaucratic vagueness, but the White House, when McGiffert reported back, had not the slightest doubt what was meant. 'They want cruise missiles, don't they?' said one official. Senior policy makers were furious. David Aaron, Carter's deputy national security adviser, who remembered the agonized attempt to launch the 'multilateral force' in the early 1960s (see footnote, p. 116) – and believed the consensus a recipe for trouble and European backsliding – thought the initiative would have to be stopped.

Jim Thomson, the former Pentagon official who was now on the National Security Council, was appointed to the High Level Group for its next meeting to try and stop the idea of an 'upward evolutionary adjustment' becoming a second multilateral force. Like a policeman sent in to restore order after a breach of the peace, he dutifully travelled to Brussels for the brief meeting of the HLG summoned to translate the Los Alamos consensus into a statement for ministers. Thomson did his best. Both he and McGiffert fought to overturn the original consensus. But they failed. Things had gone too far to be stopped. Albeit 'hung with qualifiers', as one source put it, the consensus went to ministers at their full Nuclear Planning Group meeting in Frederikshavn in Denmark in April 1978, and the HLG was authorized to take the process a step further: What kind of weapons should be deployed? How many? And where? Simultaneously, the National Security Council in Washington decided to organize a study group under the leadership of Jim Thomson to look at the implications of the whole business. By this stage Thomson and other US officials had become persuaded by the force of the political and strategic concerns raised in Europe that something would have to be done, and in late summer the study group yielded a document, called PRM (presidential review memorandum) 38, which concluded that new weapons might be necessary.

Still, Jimmy Carter might never have backed the idea – and the decision to deploy cruise and Pershing missiles in Europe might never have been taken – had it not been for an occurrence quite separate from all the technical and doctrinal arguments which were absorbing the HLG. This was the fallout from one of the most damaging episodes in the history of the Alliance.

Walter Pincus is an assiduous reporter. Unlike most of his kind in Washington, he troubles to spend long, painstaking hours reading congressional testimony. And it was because of this habit that, in early June 1977, Pincus was reading the testimony of a hearing held by the Subcommittee on Energy and Water Power of the House Appropriations Committee. It did not sound promising but Carter was engaged in chopping the water budget and Pincus was looking for evidence of new cuts. What he found was something very different. By one of the quirks of Washington bureaucracy, the energy subcommittee also handles the budget for nuclear weapons building, and amidst the testimony was one line stating that funds had been approved for an 'Enhanced Radiation' warhead for the Lance missile (a short-range battlefield system in Europe). Pincus began calling his contacts in the army and on Capitol Hill, and they openly confirmed that, yes, the US was to build an Enhanced Radiation warhead. On 6 June 1977 Pincus published his story. It appeared under the headline: 'Neutron Killer Warhead Buried in ERDA Budget'. The reaction was swift and dramatic.

In all honesty, there was nothing especially sinister about the neutron bomb. Its ability to kill people without destroying buildings was simply the result of one more rather pointless attempt to shore up Nato's 'battlefield' nuclear arsenal. When in January 1976 the then US defence secretary, Donald Rumsfeld, had briefed the allies on US thinking about intermediate nuclear forces, the neutron bomb had been but one item on the list. None of the ministers present had seen any cause for concern; nor had Nato's 'permanent representatives' in Brussels; nor had a special team then studying new technologies for Nato. A total of $43 million had been included in President Ford's last defence budget in 1976 for production of the warhead. And at the time of Pincus's article, Jimmy Carter had probably never heard of the weapon. Since, at any one time, the Pentagon has a considerable array of exotic weaponry in one form or another – as raw ideas, at the research stage, or in full-scale development – there was no particular reason why he should.

But if Carter's grasp on the subject, on 6 June 1977, was sketchy, he soon got a crash course in the theories of enhanced radiation. Pincus's article was the springboard for an immediate and massive Soviet campaign against the 'killer warhead' and 'the weapon which kills people but spares property'. It was just the kind of issue to strike a chord with the European left. In Holland, traditionally the most pacifist of Nato's members, new life was breathed, almost overnight, into a long dormant peace movement, with the Communist party and the Catholic Church, which was notably leftwing and looking for an issue with which to revive its apathetic flock, leading the way. The Soviet phrase 'the capitalist bomb' proved a useful slogan, and a petition against deployment of the neutron bomb quickly collected a million signatures. There were protests in West Germany, where Egon Bahr, executive secretary of the ruling SPD party, and Schmidt's most troublesome leftwinger, pronounced the neutron bomb to be 'the symbol of mental perversion'. And in Britain, too, the anti-nuclear movement, fuelled by the propaganda barrage from the Soviet Union, began to grow.

It was all a little absurd. Jimmy Carter, the 'peace-loving' president, was being seen as betraying many of his supporters, 'secretly' developing a 'capitalist' weapon, and giving another sinister twist to the arms race. Yet there was nothing new in 'burying' the neutron bomb in the energy committee's budget. It was standard practice, a quirk of Washington bureaucracy, for such new nuclear projects to be listed in this manner.

Besides, the neutron bomb had not been dreamt up by the Carter administration. Far from it. The technology, in fact, had existed since the 1950s; all that had held back development were doubts over its military utility. But now Jimmy Carter faced one of the most testing decisions of his presidency. Should he proceed with development, and risk damage to his peace-loving image and trouble from Europe, or should he follow his conscience and call a halt to the whole thing, at the risk of giving more ammunition to those who were already writing him off as a weak and indecisive president who was afraid of nuclear weapons?

By spring 1978, after several months of agonizing on both sides of the Atlantic, and a good deal of confusion, Schmidt appeared to have persuaded his Social Democrat party that the neutron bomb made sense. But no sooner had Schmidt indicated his readiness to go along with Carter's wishes and formally back the weapon than Carter suddenly pulled the rug out from under him. He abruptly decided to defer production of the neutron bomb, and though he left open the possibility of a resumption dependent on 'the degree to which the Soviet Union shows restraint in its conventional and nuclear arms programmes' it was a fatuous promise. No one was fooled. It was said that Andrew Young had persuaded Carter to change his mind. Whatever happened, he informed his horrified advisers that the price of going ahead was more than he was prepared to pay: 'his administration,' as one of them later wrote, 'would be stamped forever as the administration which introduced bombs that kill people but leave buildings intact.' Suddenly, as one adviser put it,' 'after a year of twisting arms, the American president cried "April Fool".'

It was scarcely an inspiring spectacle, and in Europe confidence in Carter slid even further. Schmidt, of course, was already fuming to his advisers that the president didn't know what he was doing. (Schmidt, however, was a difficult man to please. He was to dislike Reagan, too. Once, asked whom Schmidt would prefer as American president, one of his aides thought for a moment and then said: 'Helmut Schmidt.') Nor did Carter's decision please the defence community, who thought it the worst kind of error that could be made. In their view, Carter had set a precedent: the Soviets had been given a veto over a Nato deployment decision and, from now on, the Kremlin would feel confident of having a powerful say over what weapons could and could not be sent to Europe. The neutron bomb may have been an unnecessary weapon, and of no military value, but Carter's mishandling of it was to have far-reaching and damaging consequences.

Throughout the neutron bomb affair, the Europeans had kept up the pressure for deploying new intermediate-range weapons on the continent.

The SS20 was now being deployed at the rate of one a week, which strengthened their hand, and Carter was now uniquely vulnerable.

He knew that if he failed to respond firmly to the new Nato initiative he would invite further scorn. The image of him as a weak president would be reinforced; he had to *prove* that he was an effective leader of the Alliance. If he wanted to secure European support for his Salt Two treaty, then reaching fruition, he would be well advised to heed their security concerns. So by the autumn of 1978, knowing the conclusions of the High Level Group, and informed by his advisers that he could no longer ignore the problem, Carter was reluctantly persuaded of the need to deploy new 'intermediate-range' missiles in Europe. But having made up his mind he was determined that there should be no hitch.

The pressure for the missiles, as his advisers were keenly aware, was coming from left-of-centre governments (principally Schmidt's and, in Britain, James Callaghan's). The knowledge that these two men faced fierce opposition from substantial sections of their respective parties had worried Washington from the beginning. Had the two leaders correctly gauged the amount of political fallout there would be? Would they be able to handle the inevitable rallies, the Soviet agitprop, the threats, the blandishments, the diplomatic blackmail?

With all this in mind, Carter sent his national security adviser, Zbigniew Brzezinski, to Europe in October 1978 to assess the position: Brzezinski came away satisfied that Callaghan and Schmidt would be able to handle their opposition. In January 1979 Carter brought matters to a head. At what the world was told, ninety-five per cent truthfully, was an 'economic' summit on the French Caribbean island of Guadeloupe, Carter, Callaghan, Schmidt and Giscard d'Estaing, the French president, met in a small, open-sided beach hut, fringed by palm trees, bathed in sunshine and within earshot of the Pacific surf. The most sensitive topic on the agenda, however, was not economic but nuclear: the four men, and their closest advisers, assembled to discuss the plan for new missiles in Europe.

Carter's own attitude now was not in doubt. His conversion on the road to this nuclear Damascus may have owed less to strategic logic than to guilt at his mishandling of the neutron bomb affair, but he was now anxious to show resolve. Europe might have launched the project, but with the phantom vessels of the multilateral force still haunting Washington, America must now set the course. The deployment programme, said Carter, must go ahead, and as speedily as possible, though an effort should simultaneously be made to tackle the SS20s via arms control. Carter got less than ringing endorsement from all sides – the tetchy, heavy-smoking German chancellor was now beginning to worry about his left wing, and Callaghan too, though he believed the West should be resolute if the Soviets would not budge, stressed the need for new talks. The strongest line came from Giscard, who was solidly behind Carter. France, of course, had no intention of taking any of the new missiles – since 1966, the only nuclear weapons on French soil had been French – but at the same time Giscard, like his predecessor, de Gaulle, knew that the stronger Nato was, the safer France would be too. So it fell to the French, who have never shirked telling their allies to do things they themselves have no intention of doing, to point out that there was little chance of the Soviets agreeing to reduce their SS20 force while the West had nothing to bargain with. Eventually Carter carried the day. And after the summit, officials in both Washington and European capitals had the sense that a Rubicon had been crossed. There was no going back.

What remained to be settled were the details: how many missiles, and of what types – and how to deal with the general wish for 'an arms control solution'. Much of the analytic work on numbers and types had already been done. Washington and the High Level Group had considered several weapons options: a new medium-range ballistic missile codenamed Long Bow, an update of the American F111 fighter bomber then (and now) stationed in Britain, the F111H, the Pershing Two missile and cruise missiles in all three varieties – ground-, air- and sea-launched. Long Bow quickly fell by the wayside (it was only at the feasibility study stage). So, because of general worries about aircraft vulnerability, did the F111H. That left Pershing Two and one of the three kinds of cruise missile.

Pershing Two was an easy choice. There were already 108 Pershing 1A missiles in place in West Germany and replacing these with a similar *type* of weapon seemed to make more political sense than introducing a device no one had ever heard of. In fact, the new Pershing was to be considerably more formidable than the old. It would be moved into the same trio of homes – at Neckarsulm, Schwabisch-Gmund and Neu-Ulm, near the city of Stuttgart in Baden-Württemberg – where the Pershing Ones had been held in operational readiness by the US army's 56th Field Artillery Brigade. And the Pershing Two would be made by the same company – Martin Marietta, of Orlando, Florida. But there the resemblance ended. Where the Pershing 1A, with its maximum range of 460 miles, could carry its up-to-490-kiloton warheads no further than Hungary, Poland, East Germany or Czechoslovakia, with little expectation of hitting anything but sprawling vulnerable targets when it got there, the P2, travelling at 5,000 mph, with its RADAG (radar area terminal guidance) system would be *theoretically* capable of placing its less-than-20-kiloton payload within 25 yards of its chosen destination. Its 1,000-mile range put a huge swathe of Soviet territory west of Moscow at risk, and satisfied the condition that Russia itself should become vulnerable to European-based weapons. (Martin Marietta had initially planned a range more akin to the 1A's, but, they assured the Pentagon, the extra distance could be achieved by simply adding a third 'stage' to the rocket.)

The P2, while (except with a very light payload) unable to hit Moscow, would be able to threaten all of the key Warsaw Pact military nerve centres (and the military command and control facilities just west of Moscow) within its range. Carried on individual Transporter Erector Launchers, the missiles would be able to travel on road or across country and would be capable, because of the Automatic Reference System built into the navigation equipment, of firing not just from pre-surveyed sites but from any convenient spot. Equally, the last-minute course correction capacity, based on radar-comparison of the target area with a computer-stored radar map of the known surroundings, would make the P1 hard to deceive by camouflage.*

But its 1,000-mile range, while adequate for a weapon to be stationed near the front line in West Germany, ruled out the Pershing as an option for other European countries. Schmidt had made it clear that Germany would only take new weapons if other countries on the continent (i.e. not just Britain) shared the burden, and the risks. And cruise missiles seemed the answer to this requirement. They had a range almost twice that of the Pershing Two, and their hedge-hopping flight path, it was believed, would constitute a nightmare for Soviet air defences (one Pentagon estimate suggested Moscow might have to spend $50 billion to guard against cruise). Above all, cruise missiles were *comparatively* cheap.

The question was: should these missiles be ground- or sea-launched? At one point Schmidt pressed for the sea-launched variety: he argued that they would be less vulnerable to attack by the Soviets and that they would not cause as much political trouble as the ground-launched version. He was probably right. But the White House would have none of it: if Schmidt wanted sea-launched missiles, they countered, then what was wrong with the Poseidon missiles already allocated to the Alliance? Had Schmidt been content with these, there would have been no need for the new plan in the first place. Besides, ground-launched cruise would be easier to 'verify' in any future arms control agreement; they would be less costly to install; and the whole logic of the deployment plan called for European countries to take the new weapons on to their *soil* – to demonstrate visibly the 'coupling' between America and its allies. In the end, Schmidt agreed to

---

* All this high technology was not to prove quite so effective when actually tested. Martin Marietta had to contend with a series of embarrassing flops, with the missile consistently missing its target – often by large distances – almost to the eve of the first deployment. So bad indeed was the new Pershing's test performance that Congress came close, on several occasions, to cancelling the whole programme.

the decision; having done so much to press for it, it would have been hard for him to do otherwise.

Having decided on type – a mixture of Pershings and ground-launched cruise – the Alliance had to fix on a number. The final figure of 572 was a compromise: there had to be enough missiles to ensure first that they could not all be wiped out easily in a pre-emptive strike and second that they could penetrate Soviet air defences. There had to be enough, too, to spread among the five countries who eventually agreed to play host (making the packages too small would have been uneconomic). But there was a danger in having too many: a large force of 'intermediate-range' missiles might, it was feared, give America the chance to wage a 'limited' war from Europe without ever having to use its strategic forces. And that was not the intention at all. The intention was to provide a link between the short-range systems on the battlefield and the last-resort strategic ones in America. From this reasoning came the final tally: 108 Pershing Twos to go to Germany, 464 cruise missiles to be spread, in 'squadrons' of 16, between Belgium (48), Holland (48), Germany (96), Britain (160) and Italy (112).

Finally, there was the matter of arms control, and here again the Alliance agreed a compromise. Nato set up a new committee to handle this (comprising mainly officials from foreign rather than defence ministries), and the committee, which came to be called the 'Special Consultative Group', considered three possibilities. Negotiate first and deploy the weapons, if necessary, later. Deploy first and negotiate later. Or do both at the same time.

The first possibility was quickly discounted. Without a definite weapons decision Congress would be sure to block the necessary funds for cruise and Pershing, and the Soviets, busy deploying SS20s at the rate of one a week, would have no incentive whatsoever to negotiate.

The second possibility was discounted, too. Though regarded as the most sensible one in Washington – after all, if the Europeans wanted the new weapons, they should install them; if they didn't, they shouldn't – it got the thumbs down in Europe. European governments believed that only if there was an arms control component in the package could it win the necessary public support.

Thus was the 'dual track' decision born. Nato would not negotiate *before* deciding to deploy; nor would it deploy before deciding to negotiate. Rather it would declare its decision to modernize while at the same time offering the Soviet Union the chance to bring the whole spectrum of weapons – SS20s, cruise and Pershing – under control through mutual agreement. However implausible the arrangement sounded, it was the only one which could satisfy both America and West Germany. And it was the one which was formally endorsed, on 12 December 1979, at a special meeting of Nato's foreign and defence ministers in Brussels.*

That, however, was only the beginning. Over the coming months and years, the Alliance was to be buffeted by precisely the kind of political trouble which Washington had feared and European politicians had all too blithely dismissed. Academic theories about 'coupling', in conjunction with misplaced alarm about Salt and Carter's political weakness after the debacle of the neutron bomb, had combined to produce a decision which was to do damage to the consensus behind Western defence policy.

As one official remembers it, the moment the British government came face to face with the 'peace' movement was on two pleasant summer days in June 1980. Having announced to a packed House of Commons the prospective sites of Britain's two cruise missile bases (Greenham Common in Berkshire and Molesworth in Cambridgeshire), Francis Pym, the defence secretary, journeyed through the English countryside to both areas a week later to explain to local residents that the new bases would mean no disruption to their lives. But at both of the chosen sites for his meetings – Newbury (near Greenham Common) and Molesworth – he faced not polite questions about the effects of cruise missiles on the local flora and fauna and of an influx of American military on local schools, but barracking crowds of demonstrators who pressed round his chauffeur-driven car and waved placards demanding that cruise missiles be kept out of Britain. Pym, a mild-mannered, conciliatory figure, was shaken by the vehemence of the protests.

It was a foretaste of what was to come. The 'peace' movement, largely dormant since the 1950s and early 1960s, was back. Nato had provided it with a catalyst in the shape of a new and controversial weapons programme. The days were over when nuclear decision making had been of little concern outside official circles – a state which had prevailed throughout the 1970s.

Four months after Pym's visits to Molesworth and Newbury came Britain's first major demonstration: all told, some 50,000 people crowded into Hyde Park on a cold, grey October day to demand that the British government adopt a policy of unilateral disarmament. A year before, CND had barely been able to muster 1,000 at a similar rally.

Over the next three years scenes similar to the one in Hyde Park would become familiar in most European capitals. The pattern was different in each country. The least affected of those earmarked to receive cruise was Italy. The socialist government of Prime Minister Craxi accepted the new

* It should also be pointed out that Nato, at the same time, agreed to pull a more than proportionate number of older battlefield nuclear systems (1,000 in all) *out* of Europe.

missiles with a readiness which surprised and delighted Washington. Clearly there was, in this, an element of national pride – the desire to cut a 'bella figura' in an alliance which sometimes showed signs of revolving purely on a US-UK-German axis. Television commentators and journalists made much of the Soviet threat – depicting, in a famous lewd cartoon by Giorgio Forattini, the disparity in nuclear arsenals by showing Nato as a little boy with little to show for himself beside an immensely virile and rampant Brezhnev – and, in general, there was little significant public protest. Even the Italian Communist party, anxious to distance itself from Moscow, was half-hearted in its opposition.

Elsewhere things were more difficult. In Holland, traditionally the most pacifist of Nato countries, the streets at weekends were soon heaving regularly with demonstrators, and the fragile Christian Democrat government was under threat from no fewer than 400 different pacifist organizations under the leadership of the Interchurch Peace Council and the Communist-led Stop De N-Bom. Having proved the cradle of the new movement (during the neutron bomb affair), its organizers, with a little help from the Soviets, simply diverted the protest to the impending cruise deployment.

Similarly, in Belgium, a powerful amalgam of anti-nuclear religious and political groups influenced the shaky coalition government. As in Holland, the Catholic Church was a central force in the burgeoning movement, and in Antwerp the Catholic peace organization, Pax Christi, ran a clearing house for pacifist propaganda called the International Peace Information Centre.

In both countries the peace movement soon gained political clout – as it did in West Germany, where Helmut Schmidt's SPD party was eventually to turn against the cruise decision (though not until it had lost power). In Britain the Labour party, which had done all but give its formal blessing to cruise, turned even more vehemently against it – having been swept from power in June 1979, it voted overwhelmingly for unilateral disarmament at its conference just over a year later.

Nato's 'dual track' decision was not the sole cause of the new 'peace' movement. The brief, incendiary campaign against the neutron bomb in 1978 had first raised public consciousness of nuclear matters; and the general deterioration of East–West relations which followed the invasion of Afghanistan did not help. But the prospect of cruise and Pershing missiles arriving in the continent revived old fears about living next door to nuclear weapons and the vulnerability which resulted from that. The putative missile bases seemed to the disarmers to beg for Soviet pre-emption and to make more likely the prospect of a 'limited nuclear war', with the Soviets and Americans fighting things out in Europe while, through fear of mutual obliteration, keeping their own homelands intact.

It was an ironic charge, since the whole aim of the plan was quite the opposite. It was intended to let the Russians know that if they attacked they would run the risk of having their homeland hit by American nuclear weapons based in Europe. But the complicated nuclear theology involved in this was lost on (or knowingly distorted by) the disarmers. What the Americans were up to, in the view of the veteran unilateralist E. P. Thompson and his disciples, was sending new weapons into Europe to give them a better chance of fighting with impunity. Cruise missiles, he said, 'place us, with finality, within the game-plan of the Pentagon' (this plan, apparently, being to wipe out Europe and leave America intact).

The Kremlin, of course, lost no opportunity to encourage this kind of nonsense. Brezhnev personally decorated his former ambassador to Holland, Aleksandr Yosipovitch Romanov, for his success at marshalling 'the resistance of the people of the Netherlands' against the neutron bomb, and now other ambassadors, plus Soviet newspapers and officials, rallied to try and repeat that success. The US, said the Soviet ambassador to Paris, was seeking to 'Europeanize' an envisaged nuclear war, and to attain strategic objectives without exposing the United States to the risk of total destruction. 'Washington's design,' intoned *Pravda* in April 1980, 'as the West Europeans must increasingly be realizing, is to remove America itself from the line of fire and allocate to West Europe the role of forward "nuclear opponent" of the USSR and the other Warsaw Pact countries, with all the fatal consequences that entails for the West European Nato countries.'

Nonsense it might be. But as the protest movements expanded, and the Russians stepped up their propaganda, myths about the 'dual track' decision flourished. After President Reagan took office in January 1981, for example, it came to be widely believed that his administration, even though it had not taken office until 14 months after the decision was made, was trying to force the new missiles on Europe. Reagan's tough anti-Soviet rhetoric – with his description of the Russians as 'godless monsters' and of the Soviet Union as 'the focus of evil in the modern world' – was, it is true, scarcely calculated to soothe frayed nerves. But the suggestion that he was responsible for cruise and Pershing was ironic: in fact, the new civilian leaders in the Pentagon were highly sceptical about the 'dual track' decision. Richard Perle, the hawkish assistant secretary for international security affairs, would gladly have cancelled it. But it was felt in Europe, and at the State Department, that it must go ahead. To abandon it would have been tantamount to an expression of no confidence in Nato; worse, it would have looked like caving in under Soviet pressure. Rapidly, the decision had come to assume the status of a litmus test of Nato's resolve: was the Alliance still able to implement difficult decisions, or was it not?

Having agreed to back the decision, the Reagan administration also began negotiations with the Russians to satisfy the European hope for an arms control solution which would avert the need for the new missiles. Predictably, the talks got nowhere. Nothing in the history of arms control suggested that the Russians would be prepared to dismantle expensive new missiles which were already in place for weapons which were not even deployed. Instead, as the Carter administration had feared (and the Reagan people felt the same), the Russians simply used the talks, for the most part, to try to divide the Alliance and whip up public opinion against cruise and Pershing.

In the end, of course, the Russians, and the peace movement, failed. The new missiles began to arrive in Europe, on schedule, at the end of 1983. In the two key countries – West Germany and Britain – rightwing governments had been re-elected in mid-1983, which was fortunate, since the main leftwing parties in both countries were now, as we have seen, opposed to the new missile deployments. But in both countries, too, public opinion polls suggested that the new missiles were not popular. Firm majorities were opposed to them. And a growing number of officials, including some who had been involved with the original decision, were beginning to wonder whether it had been wise. 'If it had come down to a choice between having cruise and Pershing and having no peace movements I think I'd have chosen no peace movements,' one of those who had been involved in the decision confessed to me.

That, surely, was the point. For complicated doctrinal reasons, Nato began to install 572 new missiles in Europe. But it proved quite unable to explain to its publics why it was doing this, or why the missiles mattered so much. And now, in the shape of the peace movements, it faced a threat to the public consensus behind defence in Western Europe which had existed, more or less unbroken, since the war.

What, for all of this trouble, was Nato getting? It was getting, at an estimated cost of seven billion dollars, 108 Pershing Twos and 464 cruise missiles. 'A hell of a price tag,' Richard Perle is reported to have said, 'for a marginal military fix.'

The 108 Pershings – if they worked -- would undoubtedly prove formidable weapons. Accurate and fast-flying, they would be able to strike key military targets and command centres west of Moscow. But stationed near the front line they would also be immediate and obvious targets for Soviet attack. This does not mean that the Soviets would use nuclear weapons, but in the event of a Russian invasion of Europe the Russians would almost certainly be able to find the Pershings and, given the relatively small number of targets, have a good chance of destroying them *conventionally*.

And if the Pershings are vulnerable, then the cruise missiles are even more so. In war, mounted four at a time on 30-foot-long, four-wheeled tractor trailers known as Transporter Erector Launchers, a flight of 16 cruise missiles would be moved in a quartet of TELs, accompanied by two similar-sized launch control centres (one operational, one in reserve). Both launchers and control vehicles would be towed by ten-ton heavy-duty tractors, built in West Germany, capable of climbing hills, fording rivers and moving across country independent of the roads. With each missile flight would travel a miniature army of support troops – one flight commander, four launch officers, 19 maintenance men, 44 soldiers and a doctor – carried in a convoy of 16 armoured trucks. Given sufficient warning, the whole caravan would move to one of a series of pre-surveyed firing points, anything up to 100 miles from the home base. But even though in an emergency – and one launcher in each flight is in a state of Quick Action Alert – it is theoretically possible to have action-readiness within 15 minutes of the missiles being moved from their bunkers, the procedure is very cumbersome and the whole convoy of 22 vehicles would be easily spotted from the air (or by satellite). Cruise missiles, therefore, are extraordinarily vulnerable. They would clearly present for the Soviets a prime and large target, either for conventional or, if there were signs of their being moved, for nuclear attack.

And unlike the Pershing, the cruise is not a good weapon (even *in theory*) for the kind of discriminate, selective strikes which Nato had in mind when it took its 1979 decision. The very difficulties it would pose to enemy radar by flying so low could backfire: if, say, one or more were spotted by the Soviets, how would they know how many had been fired? Obviously they would find out when the warheads started exploding, but given the slow flight time of cruise they might not choose to wait that long. And the fact that cruise missiles would take up to five hours to reach their destination (especially from Britain, from which the Soviet Union is virtually out of range) hardly made them ideal for striking military targets. By the time they arrived the target, even if fixed, might no longer matter.

Moreover, just as the Pershing Two has been plagued by development problems,* so too has cruise. In a report published shortly before its deployment in Europe, the General Accounting Office complained that its 'terrain contour matching' guidance system (Tercom for short) might prove ineffective against a 'wide spectrum of high value targets'. The main worry has been the production of sufficiently reliable radar maps of the terrain over which the missiles might have to fly. The maps, fed into the computers of individual missiles, and theoretically enabling them to identify their

---

* An investigation by ABC News in 1983 suggested that in three out of nine tests conducted over land, the army gave their test missile a better chance of proving accurate by placing radar corner reflectors around the target in order to help the warhead to zero in on it. The ABC News report cast doubt both on the Pershing's test record, and on the realism of the tests themselves.

targets, are derived from satellite photographs, and the problem is that, given the changing seasons, the missile radars may 'see' different images of the ground at different times, depending, for example, on whether the trees have dropped their leaves, or whether there is a covering of snow. According to *Skilnick's Radar Handbook*, a standard reference work, 'radar altimeters used over forests, deep snow and deep ice can give erroneous readings. In fact aircraft have flown into the Greenland icecap while their radar altimeters were still registering their altitude just above sea level.' The Soviet Union has many forests, and the Siberian steppes, over which cruise would have to fly, are covered with snow for much of the year.

Cruise missiles, then, promised precious little military advantage. But by the time of their first arrival, millions more people in Europe were worrying about nuclear matters, and about Nato strategy, than had been in 1979. And the peace movements – the most visible expression of this – had, in the view of Michael Howard, the Regius Professor of History at Oxford, sent 'a signal both to Moscow and to the United States not simply that the peoples of Western Europe are not prepared to defend themselves with nuclear weapons, but that they are not prepared to defend themselves at all: a signal that could create a quite terrifying degree of instability by presenting the leaders of the Soviet Union with options that hitherto have been firmly closed to them.'

And while the peace movements have failed in their immediate aim – to stop deployment – they have managed, arguably, to gain more political influence than they ever achieved in the 1950s. In both West Germany and Britain the major opposition turned against cruise. (In West Germany, to be sure, the position of the Social Democrats remains somewhat ambivalent, but the British Labour party is now more firmly committed to unilateralism than at any previous time in its history.) In America's closest ally, then, and in the Alliance's front-line country, the consensus behind Nato's nuclear posture has at the very least been weakened and become more subject to the vagaries of electoral politics than it was before. It remains to be seen how durable this change will be.

The Alliance was unlucky. It had to implement its decision in changed circumstances from those in which it had been conceived (though it must be said that by mid-1979, if not sooner, there were already plenty of signs that détente was crumbling). Nevertheless the decision itself scarcely seemed worth all the trouble. If the allies were so anxious for renewed evidence of the US commitment, then they would have done better simply to update, quietly and without fuss, the nuclear-capable aircraft stationed in Britain rather than to go through the song and dance of the 'dual track' decision, with its implicit invitation to the Soviets to meddle in the affairs of Europe, stir up trouble and try to gainsay a weapons decision which was none of their business.

What the cruise and Pershing decision made plain was the kind of thinking which drives so many Nato decisions. To quote Michael Howard again:

> The belief of some strategic analysts that the Russians can only be deterred from attacking us by the installation of precisely matching systems – 'ground launched missiles must be matched by ground launched missiles' – is politically naive to the point of absurdity. The United States is 'coupled' to Europe, not by one system rather than another but by a vast web of military installations and personnel, to say nothing of the innumerable economic, social and financial links that tie us together into a single coherent system. To satisfy these pedantic analysts, who require still further guarantees, the Americans, whose patience seems inexhaustible, have already allocated Nato a submarine-based force of immense destructive power.
>
> If all this is insufficient to deter the Soviet Union from a course that they are in any case likely to contemplate only in the direst of extremities, what difference will be made by the installation of Pershings and Cruise missiles, particularly if these remain under sole American control?

'Coupling', in short, depends ultimately as much on leadership, will and faith as it does on weapons. The credibility of guarantees in any alliance, especially this one, is a political problem: nothing will force the Americans to come to Europe's assistance. And the imposition of meretricious technical solutions is more often an illustration of weakness than of strength.

PART THREE

The Search for a Way Out

'O Hercules, the valour of men is at an end.'
The Spartan king Archidamus, on seeing a
dart fired by a machine brought from Sicily,
c. 55 BC

Star Wars: the Dream

Not least of the drawbacks of the plan to deploy new cruise and Pershing missiles in Western Europe was that for four years or more, from December 1979 at least until December 1983, it distracted Nato from the task of real importance: improving conventional forces. As Alliance politicians and officials wrestled with the problems of impending deployment, other issues were overshadowed.

Distractions like that caused by cruise and Pershing have become endemic in an alliance unwilling – perhaps unable – to face up to its most serious weakness. Even before the first missiles were installed in the bunkers of Greenham Common, Nato was beginning to grapple with another all-consuming initiative, this time one on a scale which promised to make cruise and Pershing look like a sideshow. If the 'dual track' decision of December 1979 constituted just one more attempt to bolster up flexible response, the so-called 'Strategic Defence Initiative' launched by President Reagan in March 1983 envisaged nothing less than a transformation of the whole basis of the Alliance. What Reagan wanted to do was eliminate, once and for all, the threat of nuclear war.

'Let me share with you a vision of the future which offers hope ...' he said in his often quoted televised speech of 23 March 1983. 'What if free people could live secure in the knowledge that their security did not rest upon the threat of instant retaliation to deter a Soviet attack? That we could intercept and destroy strategic ballistic missiles before they reached our own soil or that of our allies? ... I call upon the scientific community in our country, those who gave us nuclear weapons, to turn their great talents now to the cause of mankind and world peace: to give us the means of rendering these nuclear weapons impotent and obsolete.'

The 'Strategic Defence Initiative', or SDI, quickly became the subject of heated debate. Ardently backed by some, excoriated by others, it featured in a flood of newspaper articles, television programmes, scientific treatises and official documents. Its futuristic new technologies of death rays and orbiting battle stations and breathtakingly sophisticated computers gave graphic artists a field day and brought a world hitherto familiar only through science fiction into countless living rooms. Experts debated the minutiae of the plan in exquisite detail, arguing passionately over how many battle stations might be required to cope with the Soviet nuclear threat and how many megajoules of power might be developed in a race to develop space-based defences. Meanwhile, the tantalizing vision Reagan had conjured'up – of a world free from the terrifying destructive power of nuclear weapons – caught the imagination of millions of people not just in America but throughout the West. After all, who could not be *for* a strategy which rescued mankind from the shadow of nuclear holocaust which has lain over it for forty years? Who would not agree with Reagan that it is 'better to save lives than to avenge them'?

Unfortunately, the president's vision was as flawed as many of the arguments used to support it. As far into the future as we are capable of seeing, and probably forever, there will be no effective 'Star Wars' defence against nuclear weapons. The world will continue to be held hostage to the threat of a holocaust. And the pretence that it might be otherwise is a dangerous, even reckless one, for it builds up hopes which can never be fulfilled. At best, Star Wars could provide, at mind-boggling cost, a half-effective defence which might conceivably boost deterence but which would be more likely to do the opposite.

Star Wars, in short, is the latest and most extreme embodiment of the boundless faith in high technology which has characterized Western defence since the war. As popularly unveiled, it is the technological fix to end all technological fixes. It is based on a dream of achieving perfect defence, a defence *without risk*. It threatens to suck away vast resources from less glamorous, less dramatic but more feasible projects – from *usable* weapons – and to provide a bonanza of undreamt-of proportions for the defence industry. It threatens to spark a new and intensive round of the arms race, in all kinds of weapons, exotic and otherwise, for the Russians do not see Star Wars as defensive, and never will. And it threatens to kill arms control. All in all, it is likely, if pursued, to lead to a vastly more unstable world than the one we currently inhabit. Instead of being offered the 'nuclear-free' future that Ronald Reagan fondly imagines, our children or our children's children are likely to find themselves living amidst greater danger than we do.

Star Wars is the quintessence of the New Maginot Line.

When Ronald Reagan arrived in the White House he pretended to no great expertise in nuclear matters. The arcane details of mirving, throw-weight and fallout were beyond his ken, and seemingly beyond his interest. By his own admission he had been president for two and a half years before he realized that the majority of Soviet nuclear weapons are based on land. (Once he shocked a group of top congressional leaders who had come to discuss the MX by saying: we've got to worry about the land-based missiles and not the submarine missiles, because they're not nuclear. The silence was leaden.) But for all his lack of knowledge, Reagan came to office bearing one stout conviction: the notion of Mutually Assured Destruction, he felt, was as mad as the acronym it gave rise to. It was like two men pointing cocked pistols at each other's heads.

Underlying President Reagan's conviction was a deeply moral view of the world. 'He is a child of the 1920s,' as one European ambassador put it. 'He still believes America is the shining city on the hill.' On several occasions, both before and after he became president, Reagan was reported as saying he believed literally in scriptural forecasts of a climactic war between the forces of light and darkness – the Old Testament prophecies of Armageddon, predicted as likely to follow after the Beast and the Antichrist have appeared and gathered together the heathen nations. (There will be a period of Tribulations, the prophecy suggests, and then there will be a world war between the heathen hordes and Christ's army, paving the way eventually, after Armageddon, for the return of Christ for a thousand-year reign on earth.)

In 1985, James R. Mills, a California state legislator, wrote in *San Diego* magazine about a conversation he had had with Reagan at a dinner fourteen years earlier. Reagan was then governor of California. Just before tucking into a flaming desert of cherries jubilee, according to Mills, the governor brought up the subject of Armageddon.

With firelit intensity he said, 'In the 38th chapter of Ezekiel, it says that the land of Israel will come under attack by the armies of the ungodly nations, and it says Libya will be among them. Do you understand the significance of that? Libya has now gone Communist, and that's a sign the day of Armageddon isn't far off.

'... Ezekiel says that fire and brimstone will be rained upon the enemies of God's people. That must mean that they'll be destroyed by nuclear weapons. They exist now, and they never did in the past ...

'Ezekiel tells us that Gog, the nation that will lead all of the other powers of darkness against Israel, will come out of the north. Biblical scholars have been saying for generations that Gog must be Russia ... It didn't seem to make sense before the Russian revolution, when Russia was a Christian country. Now it does, now that Russia has set itself against God. Now it fits the description of Gog perfectly.'

Mills pointed out, he says, that according to Ezekiel, Ethiopia would also be among the 'evil powers', and that at the time it was not Communist. (But soon afterwards, as he says in his article, that changed when King Haile Selassie was deposed, presumably reinforcing the Christian fundamentalist world-view.)

There have been various efforts, following Reagan's Star Wars speech, to reconstruct how it came about, but what must always be borne in mind is Reagan's own view of the world, his profound belief that it was, and is, intolerable for America and other Christian nations to be eternally vulnerable to the whims of an 'evil empire'. To Reagan, American technology is the West's natural and God-given ally against an intolerable threat.

When he was governor of California, Reagan apparently discussed his dissatisfaction with traditional deterrence theory with some of the rich and influential West Coast conservatives who shaped and financed his political rise. This group, sometimes called his 'kitchen cabinet', included in its number Joseph Coors, the brewing magnate from Colorado, and the late Justin Dart, the industrial multi-millionaire who liked to describe himself as a 'big issues guy'. ('I'm interested in the national economy and our defence ability, not all these crappy little issues like equal rights or abortion,' he once told an interviewer.)

Once Reagan was in the White House, there was no shortage of people ready and eager to press upon his advisers what they saw as the urgent need to develop defences. Among the major lobbyists were two retired military men, air force General George Keegan and army Lieutenant General Daniel Graham. Graham, a small, energetic man with a shock of white hair, was an especially ardent enthusiast. Head of a pressure group called High Frontier, founded by the Heritage Foundation, the conservative thinktank, he had lobbied hard against the 1972 anti-ballistic missile (ABM) treaty which drastically constrained the deployment of ground-based defences and outlawed the testing and deployment of space weapons. Graham had travelled all over America and Europe, accompanied by films and slides, extolling the virtues of strategic defence. He had even written a book on the subject, in which he held out the possibility of America rendering itself safe and performing a 'technological end run on the Soviets' through a Star Wars effort. 'The kind of superiority we should seek,' Graham explained in a 1980 interview, 'is technological superiority – that is, to have some of our military capabilities in an area where the Soviets, with inadequate technology, cannot challenge us ... If we challenge them in a technical way – such as with a space-borne defence system – and make them face an entirely different military equation, we can quickly restore the balance.'

More influential than either Keegan or Graham, however, was Edward Teller, the hawkish physicist who had worked with Robert Oppenheimer on the Manhattan Project to develop the atomic bomb and later became known as 'the father of the hydrogen bomb', the atom bomb's younger and vastly more powerful cousin. Teller, also a long-standing opponent of the ABM treaty, was, at 75, a passionate Star Wars enthusiast. On 14 September 1982, and apparently on three other occasions, he obtained audiences in the White House with President Reagan. His contributions may not have been decisive, but in Reagan, for the first time, he had a president disposed to be sympathetic. For years, strategic defence had been a political orphan. Although research into its potential had proceeded, in a haphazard way, it had been funded by Congress largely as a 'hedge' against any possible breakthrough the Russians might make rather than because of any serious intent to deploy. With the signing of the ABM treaty in 1972, the superpowers had formally renounced space-based defences, opting to base their security – explicitly in the American case, and effectively in the Russian case – on the notion of 'mutually assured destruction'. An attempt by either side to build defences, it had been felt, would do no more than intensify the arms race. Those, like Teller, Graham and Keegan, who argued that MAD *was* mad were a lonely and largely ignored minority.

Just as the military men anxious for Britain to develop the tank in the early years of World War One needed a political champion, so did the star warriors. The tank got Winston Churchill. And, after the presidential election of 1980, Star Wars got Ronald Reagan.

According to George Keyworth II, Reagan's scientific adviser until mid-1985, and a protégé of Teller's, there were three 'primary motivations' which caused the president to launch the Star Wars initiative:

Those motivations were, first the inherent unacceptability – or immorality, if you will – of mutual assured destruction as the guarantor of the world's future; second, the lack of options for future presidents to maintain a secure offensive deterrent; and third, the utter failure of the mechanisms of arms control, as practised over decades, to halt the build-up of enormous stockpiles of nuclear weapons.

If we are to accept Keyworth (and in offering a post hoc explanation he makes the president's position sound more carefully thought-out than the evidence suggests), what Reagan feared was that the massive Soviet build-up of the 1970s, persisting into the 1980s, was threatening strategic stability. With nuclear delivery systems getting more accurate, the spectre of a crippling pre-emptive strike was going to grow. The future brought with it the possibility, in Keyworth's words, 'that many, many thousands of highly accurate nuclear warheads could suddenly rain down on our own retaliatory forces'. Put another way (in the words of a second official), the balance between the superpowers of 'second-strike' or 'retaliatory' forces – clumsy, inaccurate, able only to hit 'soft' targets, i.e. cities – was being replaced by a balance of 'first-strike' forces – precise, accurate and able to strike 'hard' targets, i.e. missile silos and command centres. This, it was thought, was putting both sides on a 'hair trigger' in which the incentive, in a crisis, would be to strike first.

It was, of course, an old fear. The risk of either side making a pre-emptive strike has always been exaggerated: the imperfections of technology, now and in the foreseeable future, mean that to launch a first strike would be a terrible, probably lethal gamble. But, in some quarters, the fear remained potent, and the failure of the Reagan administration to find a 'survivable' basing mode for the MX missile (indeed its difficulties in getting any funding at all for the MX) had spurred the effort to find a new solution to the problem of vulnerability.

Reagan feared that without strategic defence the West might prove increasingly unable to cope with the menacing Soviet build-up. Like all presidents, he had come, once in office, to appreciate the awesome responsibility of having a finger on the nuclear button. But unlike most presidents, Reagan – a moralist who tended to see the world in black and white, and an optimist with a boundless faith in Yankee ingenuity – felt that there had to be a better way.

In late 1982 and early 1983, the political advantages to be gained from a new departure came to intrigue a small group of Reagan's advisers, and especially Robert McFarlane, then the president's deputy national security adviser. With fears of nuclear war rising in America as well as in Europe, sparked by the prospect of new missile deployments (MX, Trident, cruise and Pershing) – and helped along, incidentally, by some of the president's own early rhetoric – the nuclear freeze movement was gaining ground in Congress and America's influential Catholic bishops appeared to be on the point of issuing a militantly anti-nuclear pastoral letter. The arms reduction talks in Geneva were stalled; the Russian missile build-up was proceeding apace. The idea of a bold new initiative, designed to undercut the peace movement, seize the moral high ground, and challenge the Russians to change their ways, had undoubted appeal. The opportunity seemed tailor-made for a president with Reagan's remarkable communicative skills, and it should be said that for *this* purpose – as a 'rhetorical' tool – Star Wars has had a certain success.

The clinching factor was the attitude of the Joint Chiefs of Staff, and above all of the chief of naval operations, Admiral James Watkins. A devout Roman Catholic, Watkins had long shared Reagan's doubts about 'mutually assured destruction'; indeed, according to Pentagon sources, he had more than once caused alarm there by talking as if he believed nuclear deterrence to be morally dubious, and perhaps in the long term unsustainable. (He even developed a habit of inserting remarks to this effect into his speeches, though on the insistence of officials these were always excised before the speeches were given, since they ran quite contrary to and threatened to undermine existing Nato strategy.)

In February 1983, according to the *Philadelphia Inquirer*, the then chairman of the Joint Chiefs of Staff, General John Vessey, faced a dilemma:

> He and Reagan got on so well that the President had recently instituted monthly meetings with the Joint Chiefs. Now the problem was, Vessey couldn't decide what to talk about. He called the chiefs to his office on a Saturday morning.
>
> 'We decided we didn't want to just tell him readiness was up and so forth,' a participant recalled ... 'We wanted to bring the President something new, different and exciting.'

Admiral Watkins came up with a solution. Over the last few months he had talked several times to Edward Teller. He proposed that the time had come for a more serious look at the new technologies which might make it possible to defend against a Soviet ICBM attack.

By now, things were moving swiftly. McFarlane, increasingly struck by the political possibilities of such a new initiative, talked at length to Watkins. And on 11 February 1983, the Joint Chiefs attended a meeting in the elegant Roosevelt Room of the White House, opposite the Oval Office. Watkins made a powerful presentation suggesting that the president throw his weight behind a major research effort. According to one well-placed White House correspondent: 'McFarlane interjected: Are you saying that over time this could lead to deployable systems? Exactly, Watkins replied. McFarlane then polled the other four military leaders around the table. None dissented.' (There is some doubt about the extent of the Chiefs' enthusiasm, however. It is fair to say that none of them, with the possible exception of Watkins, believed that the strategic defence initiative would achieve quite the prominence it did. In the context of a rising defence budget, it was seen more as an 'extra' than as a high priority. No one wanted to sacrifice funds needed for conventional or strategic programmes.)

Watkins had helped provide Reagan with the ammunition he wanted. Collectively, the president and a handful of aides, as a report on NBC television later put it, were 'dazzled' by the new technologies they had heard about, 'lasers, particle beams and other exotic weapons – in their view, America's natural ally against the Soviet military threat'.

Yet it was to be another six weeks before the seminal speech was made.

William Clark, the national security adviser, and his deputy, McFarlane, limited discussions on the forthcoming initiative to a very small group: running it through the usual interagency process, and involving the departments of defence and state, they knew would be a recipe for delays, objections and probably unfavourable leaks. Keyworth, though a true believer, was himself excluded from the detailed planning until about a week before the speech. So was George Shultz, the secretary of state. (Indeed, Shultz had not even attended the crucial meeting on Star Wars on 11 February: there had been a violent snowstorn in the morning, and he had been unable to get to the White House from the State Department. The Joint Chiefs of Staff had been brought from the Pentagon by helicopter. The meeting became known inevitably as 'the snow job'.) Over the belated objections of the secretary of state, and without consulting any of the experts in the State or Defense Departments who handled the day-to-day business of arms control and nuclear policy, Reagan and a handful of advisers made one of the most momentous decisions of his presidency. Not even Caspar Weinberger, the defence secretary, was fully in the know. At a Nuclear Planning Group meeting only two days before the speech neither he nor his key lieutenant, Richard Perle, were able to tell their Nato colleagues anything. (Poor Weinberger, in fact, had to start ringing them up to pass on the news the moment he got back to Washington.) And even Edward Teller had no idea what was coming until, on the day of the speech, he was invited to the White House with other scientists and national security experts to hear a preview of the speech and be told: 'Edward, you're going to like it.'

The speech thus came as an almost total surprise to official Washington, to allies and to the Kremlin alike. Virtually no briefings had been prepared to explain what the president had in mind, or where he thought the abrupt change of emphasis might lead, and the ensuing confusion was considerable. 'Don't worry, gentlemen, it's just another of the president's fireball speeches,' Alexander Haig, the former secretary of state, jokingly told his colleagues on the presidential commission set up to examine America's strategic forces on the day after the bombshell. But it soon became clear that it was much, much more than that.

Immediately after the speech, national security decision directive 6-83 mandated an examination of the available and potential technology. Three investigation teams were set up. One, under James C. Fletcher, former administrator with NASA, the National Aeronautics and Space Agency, looked into nuts and bolts. The second, under Fred Hoffman, who runs a consultancy called Pan Heuristics, reported on policy implications. The third, an interagency team led by a Pentagon official called Frank Miller, was charged with pulling together the results of the first two. The conclusion of the Fletcher panel was, essentially, that 'a robust, multi-tiered ballistic

missile defence system' could 'eventually be made to work'. Although
hedged about with qualifications, the tone of the top-secret report for the
president was upbeat. According to Pentagon sources, it urged that 'a
vigorous research and development programme be pursued. This,' it
continued, 'would permit informed decision on whether to initiate, in the
early 1990s, an engineering validation phase leading to a deployed defensive
capability after the year 2000.'*

The Hoffman report was also upbeat. 'They made the same mistake we
made with mirvs,' one official, a sceptic about Star Wars, told me. 'They
looked at it mainly from the blue [i.e. the Western] side, and asked, what
good can it do for *us*? They didn't look properly at what would happen
if the Soviets did it too.'

The efforts of Fletcher and Hoffman were pulled together by the
interagency team led by Frank Miller. Their report, much more cautious
than Hoffman's, nevertheless urged that work on Star Wars should go
ahead, and that a very thorough assessment should be made of the risks
and benefits. The three studies led, first, to the president's national security
directive number 119, seeking funding for a 'strategic defence initiative';
second, to a recommendation for a five-year technology development plan,
to run between 1985 and 1989. Finally a special office was set up and a
key appointment made. Lt. Gen. James Abrahamson, an air force man
and former director of the space shuttle programme, was brought in to
head the project.

So the ground was laid. What had hitherto been a collection of low-key
and rather haphazard research efforts into the potential of defensive
weapons had suddenly been transformed into a very high-profile and
ambitious programme. Star Wars, once a futuristic dream embraced by a
handful of boffins and true believers, had become serious business. So
what were the implications? Were Reagan and his advisers right to be
dazzled by the new technologies? What, if anything, could be achieved?

A little over a year after Reagan's Star Wars speech, the Pentagon staged
a remarkable demonstration over the Pacific. Shortly before six o'clock
(local time), on a June morning, a Minuteman 1 intercontinental ballistic
missile blasted off from a complex of launch pads on the test range at
Vandenberg air force base in southern California. As the missile soared
upwards, out of the earth's atmosphere, it released a single dummy nuclear
warhead. The target: Kwajalein Atoll, 4,800 miles away in the middle of
the Pacific. It was the kind of test firing which, to the Pentagon over the
last twenty years, had become virtually routine.

---

* Actually, the Fletcher panel ended up almost evenly divided about the feasibility of
strategic defence: the optimistic view prevailed, but not as forthrightly as the more committed
members wished.

What happened next, however, was anything but routine. Twenty minutes after the launch, another rocket (also a Minuteman) lifted off from Kwajalein Atoll itself. The aim of the second missile was to find, intercept and destroy the dummy warhead as it streaked through space at 11,000 mph. The nose cone of this interceptor rocket was a minor miracle of engineering. The crucial part of a project called 'Homing Overlay Experiment' (HOE), it contained within its squat cylindrical shape eight infrared telescopes, a laser gyroscope, a computer and 56 thruster rockets. A hundred miles above the ocean, thanks to all this technology, the miniature homing vehicle made split-second adjustments to its course, its telescope-sensors feeding information to the on-board computer which in turn passed it to the propulsion system. Then, a web of high-tension aluminium spokes, wound tightly round its body in a series of spirals like a closed umbrella, sprang open as the vehicle closed with the dummy warhead. Fifteen feet in diameter, this whirling umbrella was designed to catch the warhead in case of a near miss. In the event it was not needed. The HOE vehicle scored a bull's-eye. A hundred miles above the Pacific, two tiny objects, each barely a yard long and eighteen inches across, met head-on at a combined speed of 22,000 miles per hour and shattered into a cloud of metal dust which quickly burnt itself out in the earth's upper atmosphere.

It was a staggering technical triumph. Back in the Pentagon, the top brass could not conceal their delight. 'It was an absolutely tremendous success,' declared Major General Elvin R. Heiberg II, who headed the army programme responsible for the project. For the first time, the Americans had proved they could 'hit a bullet with a bullet' in outer space. Whatever else, the demonstration revealed that technology had made possible something which would not have been possible ten years earlier.

But as a multitude of critics were quick to point out, shooting down one warhead with one interceptor, in one carefully staged test, scarcely provided grounds for believing that an impregnable missile shield would ever become possible. As one Pentagon official put it to me at the time: 'Anyone who believes that must be on hallucinatory drugs of some kind.' Even if it becomes possible to mass-produce a miniature homing vehicle – which would have to be a hundredth the size of the HOE vehicle – and make it work as well as the test model, the difference would be between keeping out one drop of water and keeping out a storm. In a full-scale Soviet missile assault on the United States hundreds of missiles would release 9,000 or perhaps, by the 1990s, 20,000 warheads, mixed with tens of thousands of decoys – a huge multitude of tiny objects rushing through space. A mere handful of warheads getting through would be enough to destroy America's major cities; even the penetration of one Hiroshima-sized bomb would mean the deaths of hundreds of thousands of people (and most Soviet warheads are much bigger than the bomb that destroyed Hiroshima). Preventing, say, 90 per cent of the Russian warheads from getting through would require a technological feat of quite astonishing proportions, but it would still permit 900 or more warheads to find their targets.

The hypothetical journey of a Soviet intercontinental ballistic missile from lift-off from a silo in Siberia to detonation of the warheads over American civilian or military targets takes approximately 30 minutes. This period can be divided into four distinct phases:

1 *Boost*, which lasts about five minutes, during which the rocket rises out of its silo and up through the earth's atmosphere.
2 *Post-boost*, also lasting about five minutes. The bulky sections (or stages) of the rocket which powered it into space fall away, and the front end, or bus, detaches itself and disgorges up to ten (and, maybe, if the current arms limitation agreements break down, up to 20) independently targeted warheads, plus dozens of decoys and 'penetration aids', such as aluminium foil balloons.
3 *Midcourse*, the longest phase, lasting ten to fifteen minutes during which warheads and decoys travel halfway round the earth through the emptiness of space towards their destination.
4 *Terminal*, the final few minutes as the warheads and penetration aids re-enter the earth's atmosphere; at this point atmospheric drag slows down the warheads, while the searing heat of re-entry causes most of the penetration aids to burn up.

To the would-be defender, each of these phases poses special opportunities – and special problems. The arithmetic of Star Wars varies, depending on who you listen to, but anything like a 'robust' defence will have to be 'multi-tiered'; that is, it will have to entail an effort to strike the attacker in at least three and possibly all four phases of flight. Thus if 80 per cent of ascending missiles can be downed in the boost phase, 80 per cent of the remainder in post-boost, 80 per cent of surviving warheads in midcourse, and 80 per cent of those that make it through the first three tiers in terminal, then the cumulative effect will be that virtually no warheads will get through.

Almost everyone – proponents of SDI and critics alike – agrees that the key to a successful defence lies in 'boost phase kill'. Unless America can 'thin out' hundreds of Soviet missiles in the first few minutes after launch, it has no realistic hope of stopping a massive attack: the problems facing the 'midcourse' and 'terminal' defences – identifying, tracking and striking thousands of tiny individual warheads hurtling through space – will be insuperable. Boost phase kill, on the other hand, offers two advantages. First, all the warheads and decoys carried by a rocket are destroyed *before* they are released into space (like destroying a beehive before it releases a swarm of bees), and second, rising rockets are readily identifiable targets. They are large, and they blast out flames and hot gases, so that any heat-sensing device can spot them (in the words of the anti-Star Wars Union of Concerned Scientists, the flaming afterburn stands out 'like a firefly in a darkened room'). The problems of boost phase kill, however, start with those inexorably posed by geography and the laws of motion. There are *at most* four minutes in which to strike – and probably considerably less, since both America and Russia are becoming capable of developing rockets with a boost phase of only *50 seconds*. And no purely ground-based system could get near enough to do the job without encroaching on Soviet territory. So the US will have to rely on hardware in space, and this presents tricky problems.

In the post-boost and midcourse phases, when the initial stages of the rocket have fallen away, the 'advantages' the defender has are time – twenty minutes or so in which to strike – and the fact that individual warheads are likely to remain on a particular path because, as the SDI director, General Abrahamson, puts it, 'they have to go after specific targets and, thus, because of natural law, don't have the luxury of evasive action'. But the problems, by then, have multiplied. Now hundreds of relatively large targets have been replaced by thousands, or tens, even hundreds of thousands of relatively tiny ones – nuclear and fake-nuclear bullets – hurtling through space. Either they *all* have to be targeted, or the intercepting weapons have to be clever enough to discriminate between real warheads and phoney ones, a task whose magnitude can be imagined.

In the terminal phase, as they enter the earth's atmosphere, most of the decoys frizzle up in the heat or get separated from the warheads by a process known as 'atmospheric sorting' (they are lighter, so fall slower). Meanwhile, the warheads themselves have slowed to about two miles a second and can be shot at with ground-based weapons – guided missiles, artillery, etc. But the warheads by now are also dangerously close, and if primed to explode when hit could still cause terrible destruction even if struck 20 miles above their targets. Besides, since it would be impossible to predict which warheads would get through the outer defences, it would also be impossible to predict which targets should have terminal defences: *every* city, *every* military base and *every* missile field would have to be guarded. In the kind of missile shield envisaged by President Reagan, therefore, terminal defences make little sense.

None of the technologies currently under scrutiny looks likely to be able to do even a fraction of what would be needed to make a full-scale defence conceivable. The Pentagon's own director of research and engineering under Reagan, Richard DeLauer, has described the prospects for success as dependent on breakthroughs in an array of key technologies, each 'equivalent to or greater than the Manhattan Project'.

Kinetic Energy Weapons

The bull's-eye in space scored by the Pentagon on 11 June 1984 was achieved under a project codenamed Homing Overlay. Run by the US army, it long predated Reagan's initiative (it had been conceived in 1978), and was deliberately designed within the constraints of the ABM treaty (which allows for experimental development and testing, so long as it is carried out using recognizable missile ranges).

The 'homing overlay vehicle' which destroyed the dummy warhead did so by *kinetic energy*; that is, by sheer force of impact. Kinetic energy weapons, in the words of Dr Gerold Yonas, SDI's chief scientist, are 'smart rocks' (and they don't have to be that hard: on Yonas's desk is a three-inch-thick sheet of steel with a hole in it made by a plastic pellet fired at 800 mph).

Kinetic energy weapons do exist, which is more than can be said for most of the hardware being contemplated for Star Wars. But they have a number of drawbacks, the most serious of which is their speed. Compared with laser beams, which travel at the speed of light, they are disappointingly slow. They may get faster – those powered by chemical propellants may eventually, if the optimists are to be believed, achieve speeds of more than eight kilometres per second, and those powered by electricity speeds in excess of 25 kilometres per second (an electro-magnetic rail gun, for example, which works like a slingshot powered by electric currents, is being tested at the University of Texas) – but they will always be thousands of times slower than lasers and they will never be fast enough to hit Soviet boosters from Western territory.

This means that the only hope of using them for boost phase kill is to have them mounted on satellites. The satellites will contain rockets in 'pods', and these rockets will be armed with 'miniature homing vehicles'. Theoretically, if so mounted, they will be able to strike ICBMs at the top of their boost phase or in the post-boost phase. But the infrared telescopes on which kinetic energy weapons depend do not work well in the atmosphere, and their effectiveness would be dramatically reduced if the Soviets shortened the boost phase of their missiles so that they burnt out about 80 kilometres above the earth (instead of the present 300–400 kilometres). Also, as the Union of Concerned Scientists have pointed out, the Soviets may eventually be able to design missiles without 'buses' (the warheads and decoys spinning off the instant the rocket burns out), thus making it very hard for kinetic energy weapons to strike in the post-boost phase.

But the most serious headache posed by kinetic energy weapons is that, because of their slowness, and their restricted range, they will have to be mounted on satellites *in low orbit*.

Such satellites will only be over their 'target areas' for about five out of the 94 minutes or so it takes them to orbit the earth. For that reason, and because each satellite will only be able to hold a limited number of interceptors, a veritable galaxy of satellites will be required to ensure that the targets are always covered. Precisely how many has been the subject of fierce dispute, but inevitably, at this stage, the calculations have a back-of-the-envelope quality: they depend on all kinds of assumptions, such as the speed with which weapons can be re-aimed.* But most scientists believe the number will run into hundreds, if not thousands. Just lifting all that weight into orbit will be enormously expensive ($6 million a ton at current prices), not to mention the expense of the satellites themselves (perhaps up to $500 million apiece – the price of two destroyers) or the problems of protecting them against Soviet attack.

Not surprisingly, then, many star warriors, including one of the project's leading lights, George Keyworth, are sceptical about the potential of kinetic energy weapons as boost phase killers. (Apart from anything else, Keyworth points out, satellites firing kinetic energy weapons might not be able to re-aim and fire again quickly enough if they missed with their first shots.)

Keyworth, however, does believe that kinetic energy weapons could be used in the midcourse phase. The homing vehicle which brought down the warhead over the Pacific in June 1984 did so (in effect) in 'late midcourse', and, certainly, kinetic energy weapons could be fired, as happened then, from ground-launched missiles, or from satellites. But the problem would be sheer numbers. To distinguish between real warheads and decoys the 'smart rocks' would have to be 'intellectual giants', as one analyst put it,

---

*The most optimistic estimate of the number of satellites I have come across is 100, each holding 150 interceptors. This was supplied by Zbigniew Brzezinski, Jimmy Carter's national security adviser, Robert Jastrow, a physicist and Star Wars enthusiast, and Max Kampelman, a Washington lawyer subsequently appointed head of the US delegation to the Geneva arms control talks. They suggested in an article in the *New York Times* Sunday magazine that such a 'boost phase defence' could be in place by the early 1990s, that it would be 'sufficient to counter a mass Soviet attack from all their 1,400 (land-based) silos' (submarines are left out, so is any possible expansion of land-based forces), and that it could be accommodated easily within a $45 billion price tag. Many experts find this wildly optimistic and believe that to keep enough kinetic energy weapons within range of Soviet launch sites at all times the US would need many more satellites and perhaps as many as 20,000 interceptors.

and if they were unable to distinguish the difference they would have to go after everything – warheads, chaff, decoys, aluminium balloons, the lot. Since one would have to anticipate a high failure rate, the number of weapons needed to do this would be simply staggering.

Lasers

Military planners have dreamt of laser weapons since the 1950s, when scientists first learnt the trick of producing amplified beams of light. Unlike ordinary light, a helter-skelter mixture of light waves of different frequencies, scattering in every direction, laser beams consist of light waves of identical frequency, marching in perfect step with each other, and finely focused, diffusing little over great distances. (They travel, of course, at the speed of light – 186,000 miles per second.) By the time Reagan unveiled his Star Wars initiative lasers were already being widely used in medicine, industry, and in the military (for rangefinding, guiding bombs and missiles and, increasingly, as high-speed, short-range weapons: in May 1983, the US air force destroyed five air-launched Sidewinder AIM9-L missiles fired in rapid succession with a 10.6 micron carbon diode laser mounted in a large jet transport). But the use to which the star warriors wish to put them is altogether more demanding: what they have in mind are laser beams which can be focused over thousands of miles of space while still remaining powerful enough to burn holes in the skins of Russian missiles.

The most basic and 'mature' form of laser currently in use is the chemical laser, powered by the violent chemical reaction of hydrogen and fluorine. But scientists have reason to be dubious about the potential of chemical lasers.

First, they consist of long 'wavelengths' of light. This makes it hard to focus them with lethal energy across vast distances. A chemical laser beam might have to spend up to seven seconds' 'dwell time' on a missile's skin in order to burn a hole in it, and the problems of keeping the beam focused on precisely the same spot during that time – while the missile rises, say, twenty miles – can be imagined. To be effective, chemical lasers would require immensely complicated and delicate optical systems for aiming their beams.

Another problem would be power. Pumping a chemical laser through the emptiness of space would require a considerable quantity of fuel. The generating equipment would have to be in space, mounted on a fleet of satellites in low orbit. As with kinetic energy platforms, the number required is a matter of fierce debate among scientists – estimates range from one or two hundred all the way up to 1,600 (which is probably over-pessimistic) – but the satellites would have to be huge, weighing a hundred tons or more, and getting them into space (let alone defending them) would pose momentous problems.* Many scientists involved in Star Wars therefore discount chemical lasers. They believe the problems will never be overcome.

More promising, though also fraught with snags, is the technology of excimer and free-electron lasers, both of which emit their energy in shorter wavelengths, or pulses. Capable of concentrating greater energy over greater distances than their long-wavelength cousins, they would in theory require much less 'dwell time' – only a second or so (though this is still not good enough, says General Abrahamson: he believes that lasers will have to be able to do their job in 'perhaps one tenth of a second' to be effective, a tall order indeed). The star warriors are excited about the potential of free electron lasers. In an interview with me in September 1985, George Keyworth singled them out as an area of rapid advance. What had merely been a 'good idea' when SDI was launched had become, thanks to work at top-secret laboratories like Lawrence Livermore in California and Los Alamos in New Mexico, 'one of the most promising areas of technology, a front contender'. The key breakthrough, said Keyworth, had been finding a more efficient way of turning raw electrical power into laser energy.

The hope, then, is that free electron laser weapons will eventually be able to flash lethal rays over tens of thousands of miles. Where would such weapons be based? One answer is 22,000 miles up in space. Satellites there would be in 'geostationary orbit', moving at the same speed as the earth's rotation and therefore hovering always above the same spot on the earth's surface. This removes the need for vast numbers of satellites, but aiming and firing at Soviet rockets from such an enormous distance will not be easy. The accuracy required will be of the order of one in 350 million, according to the conservative British scientist, Professor R. V. Jones, who says it will be comparable 'with having to check in advance that the sights of a rifle are aligned so accurately with the barrel that the

---

*The Union of Concerned Scientists began by estimating the figure at 2,400. One of the SDI scientists, Gregory Canavan, did some calculations of his own, revealing flaws in the UCS figure. But his own calculations have also been challenged. So have those of a paper written at Lawrence Livermore laboratory, suggesting that only 90 satellites would be needed. This, says the British scientist, Professor R. V. Jones, contains 'some fantastic assumptions: the laser satellites would be in six orbits at 300 kilometres altitude; against the simultaneous launch of 1,400 Russian ICBMs, no more than eight satellites could be engaged, and four of them would be expected to destroy some 1,200 missiles, or 300 per satellite, each satellite killing 10 ICBMs per second!'

aiming error would be no more than one bullet diameter at a range of 1,000 miles, without having a chance to fire a trial shot and with the rifle more than 20,000 miles away in space'. And even if a trial shot *could* be fired – against a 'friendly target' (i.e. a missile rising from an *American* silo) – the aiming problem would still be horrendous. Not only that: free electron lasers would require even greater supplies of power than chemical ones, and their generators might prove so bulky as to rule out any hope of hoisting them into space. Thus neither Keyworth nor his mentor, Edward Teller, appears overly enthusiastic about the idea of laser battle stations in space. They 'won't fit the bill', says Teller. 'They must be deployed in great numbers at terrible cost, and could be destroyed in advance of an attack.'

There is an alternative solution: putting the lasers themselves on the ground and bouncing them off mirrors in space. Since lasers do not work well in the atmosphere – its different layers distort them and cause them to shimmer, just as the stars, observed from the earth, appear to twinkle – the battle stations will have to be on mountaintops. That way, the beams fired upwards will only have to cope with the thin upper layers of the atmosphere. But if the Soviets are unsporting enough to attack in bad weather, the defence will be in trouble, since laser beams cannot effectively penetrate clouds. And whether the laser beams are bounced off mirrors in geostationary orbit down to 'battle' mirrors in lower orbit which in turn 'aim' them at the Russian rockets or their nuclear cargo, or whether the beams are leapfrogged across a whole series of battle mirrors in low orbit, the mirrors will have to be gigantic, so cheap that they can be deployed in large numbers, and almost unimaginably perfect. They will have to be able to prevent a phenomenon known as 'spherical spreading' (the beam from a laser, like the beam from a flashlight, tends to widen out with distance), and they will have to be tremendously robust to withstand and redirect the powerful beams fired at them. The mirrors, perhaps 45 to 90 feet in diameter, may be too large to be hoisted into space in one piece, and might have to be assembled in orbit. (The star warriors are counting on breakthroughs in the technology of 'adaptive optics' – the ability to build very thin and flexible mirrors which can change their shape. But at the time of writing the largest example of adaptive optics is a mirror 10 inches in diameter, and what is envisaged would require something two or three orders of magnitude larger.)

All in all, the deployment of a mirror-based defence would be a fantastically elaborate and precise operation, and not surprisingly many scientists dismiss it as expensive and impractical. But if Star Wars is to work, the fantastic will become commonplace. Consider the most controversial, and to some, the most plausible, form of directed energy weapon: the x-ray laser. Potentially the most deadly member of the laser family, it will require no 'dwell time' whatsoever and be capable of explosively vaporizing a missile's skin in a fraction of a second. It would not need to be as carefully aimed as chemical, excimer or free-electron lasers: its 'beam' could be thirty yards or more in diameter.

Edward Teller and his disciples like to put it about that systems like the x-ray laser are the ones that contain real promise. Chemical lasers and the like are more, of a sideshow, discussed in public precisely because their potential is limited. It is a convenient argument, but not wholly convincing, because for Reagan, with his dream of non-nuclear defences, the x-ray laser has one drawback: it derives its colossal power not from chemicals or electricity, but from a *nuclear explosion*. Partly for this reason, its development has always been shrouded in secrecy. In February 1981 *Aviation Week and Space Technology* reported that the Lawrence Livermore laboratory in California had tested an x-ray laser pumped by a bomb (as part of a top-secret programme called Dauphin). The administration subsequently acknowledged the testing programme (which takes place under the desert in Nevada) but it remains highly classified. However, the basic principles of the Dauphin (now renamed Excalibur, after the magical sword which King Arthur pulled from the stone) are clear. The x-ray laser is a nuclear bomb surrounded by a parallel bundle of very thin metallic rods. These rods are gimballed so that they can be aimed at individual enemy missiles. In theory, when the bomb explodes it causes temperatures found in nature only in the interior of stars, floods the rods with radiation and fires them an instant before the whole device is consumed by the nuclear fireball.

X-ray lasers would have to be fired from space, and Congress is unlikely ever to welcome the idea of keeping, say, 1,400 nuclear bombs circling permanently round the earth in low orbit (even if the treaties which forbid the deployment of nuclear weapons in space were revoked). So how would the x-ray laser work? 'You obviously have to get your weapons up *after* the enemy has launched his first salvo, not *before*,' says one Livermore scientist. 'I'm not saying how this would work, but you might do it by sending up your weapon on a missile of your own' (my italics).

Thus the x-ray laser would be a 'pop-up' defence. And coordinating a 'pop-up' defence would not be child's play. Seconds after the warning of a Soviet missile attack, America would have to launch its own defensive missiles, carrying the x-ray laser bombs in their nose cones. The defensive missiles would have to rise fast enough and high enough to fire off and explode their x-ray bombs at the exact moment when the Russian missiles reached the top of their boost phase, or conceivably had entered their post-boost phase. (X-ray lasers do not work in the atmosphere.) To have any chance of accomplishing this, submarines would have to be used, and they would have to be stationed perilously close to the Soviet coastline –

probably in the Arabian Sea just south of Pakistan (about the closest they could get to the major Soviet missile silos strung out along the trans-Siberian railway). Flashing instructions to submarines in the first moments of nuclear war would be very difficult, assuming of course that the submarines had not already been found and sunk. Even that does not do justice to the problem. Submarines take around half an hour to fire off all their missiles, but they give away their position the instant they fire their first salvo. It is likely that, if not found and sunk before they began firing, they would be found and sunk before they had finished. What is more, the submarines would have to be specially built, because the Pentagon would not wish to risk its existing ballistic missile submarine fleet, which forms the backbone of the US nuclear deterrent.

Finally, even were everything to work perfectly, it would take about three minutes to get the rockets carrying the pop-up laser into position to fire. Since the rockets under attack would be ending their boost phase after (at most) *four* minutes, this could pose quite a task. For the three minutes it would take to get the pop-up laser in place do *not* include the time it would take to process and verify information from early warning satellites about the Soviet attack (and currently that takes two minutes), nor do they include the time it would take to get authorization to fire what would be a nuclear weapon into space ... Unless it is assumed that both these things could happen *instantly* then the West would be wasting billions on a weapon which could not possibly work. In sum, the whole operation would call for a command and control system well beyond anything which has so far seemed possible. The x-ray laser would be a 'single-shot' device; if it missed, there would be no second chance. And finally, the Russians would almost certainly find it much easier to build missiles which burn out after 50 seconds than the Americans would to build pop-up lasers.

Particle Beam Weapons

In addition to lasers, there is one other type of directed energy weapon whose potential is being examined by the star warriors. Instead of flashing a beam of light at its target, this would project a stream of atoms or subatomic particles which would penetrate deep into the structure of the target – i.e. missile or warhead – causing implosions, and destroying its innards and other essential components. The effect would be like that of a lightning bolt, which indeed a 'particle beam' closely resembles. The attraction of such a weapon would be its lethality (no worries over 'dwell time': destruction would be instant), but the drawbacks would be considerable.

Particle beams, like x-ray lasers, are quite ineffective in the atmosphere, so their usefulness, provided the generating equipment could be got into space, would be for post-boost and midcourse kill (the attacking rockets would be immune from attack during the crucial boost phase). But even if that was judged to be worth the effort there would remain the problem of getting the generating equipment into orbit. Particle beams require colossal amounts of energy and a single particle beam battle station might have to weigh as much as 500 tons. Finally, particle beams travel more slowly than lasers. To make them reach over half the speed of light you might need even bigger battle stations.

(There is one special type of particle beam which can operate in the atmosphere. Built into a remote hillside at Lawrence Livermore is a tunnel-like laboratory being used for tests of a particle beam weapon which might eventually be adapted so that it can ram its subatomic particles up through the atmosphere, the ultimate aim being to destroy incoming warheads in the 'terminal phase'. The problem at the moment, says William Barletta, a particle beam expert at the lab, is stopping the particle beams from 'kinking' in the atmosphere like garden hoses. With the help of Livermore's Advanced Test Accelerator, he believes this may eventually be solved.)

The technologies available to the star warriors are undoubtedly dazzling. Some may even be ready for systems level development by the 1990s. But a cursory glance, as the one above, suggests that the problems of making them effective are legion. Still, let us concede for the moment that at some stage it may be possible to design lasers, particle beam accelerators and of kinetic energy weapons which are able to burn through the skins of, fry the innards of or destroy by impact existing ballistic missiles. For as yet we have scarcely touched on the *real* problems. The fact is that Star Wars would depend not so much on whether individual gadgets would work, but on whether a system could be created which *as a whole* could function reliably, cope with Soviet countermeasures *and* do both these things while leaving America on the right side of bankruptcy. The evidence suggests that in an even vaguely Utopian form (the provision of a semi-effective defence of 'soft targets', i.e. people) it will be possible to do none of these things.

When interviewed about Star Wars, SDI's rather engaging director, General Abrahamson, likes to point out that 'the long pole of the tent is not the weapons ... it is the infrastructure [and] the command-and-control system'. This would seem sensible enough. At least as much money is being (and will be) spent on this 'battle management' side of Star Wars as on the weapons themselves. After all, before you think about knocking missiles out of the sky you have to consider all sorts of other things: tracking them from the moment they take off, tracking the 'bus' and then the warheads once the boosters have fallen away (much harder, because there is no bright plume of fire to act as a beacon, and warheads are comparatively tiny), sorting warheads from decoys, coordinating your tracking satellites with your weapons-firing devices, enabling each of your weapons to fire at precisely the right moment and at precisely the right target, monitoring what is destroyed and what is not so that you don't waste valuable shots on shattered warheads, and creating a system of command and control which would be resilient and complex enough to cope with this fantastic operation ...

Difficulties proliferate in every corner of the project and the task of 'managing' a defence against hundreds of missiles is far beyond anything the human brain is capable of. Only computers will be able to absorb and process the billions of bits of information quickly enough to provide any realistic chance of success, and the computers themselves will have to be breathtakingly sophisticated, far more so than anything likely to be available in the 1980s. 'The computers would require ten million lines of error-free code,' says Richard Garwin, a top ICBM scientist (and an opponent of Star Wars). 'I don't know anyone who knows that that is possible.'* Certainly no human being could design the software programme for a 'battle management' Star Wars computer: that would have to be done with the aid of computers too. (A typical programmer can produce about 3,000 lines of documented debugged code per year. Producing 10 million lines of code, therefore, might take 1,000 programmers three years or 300 programmers ten years. But these 1,000 – or 300 – programmers would have to work as closely together as a well trained orchestra for an extraordinarily long time, a feat of human cooperation without parallel in human history.) And supposing you *could* design the software, how on earth could you check it for errors? According to General Abrahamson, you would have to put it through 'debugging runs' – perhaps as many as fifty million. But even then there would be no guarantee that it would work properly. Redundancy, of course, might be built in as a hedge against failure: Keyworth, for example, is fond of pointing out that the AT & T telephone system breaks down seldom and contains ten million lines of code. But the AT & T telephone system was developed over many years, with a lot of trial and error, and no one is proposing to bet the security of the Western world on it.

The only way of *guaranteeing* that the system would work in a crisis would be to test it under the actual conditions in which you intended to use it. This, however, would involve starting the Third and probably last World War. So you would simply have to hope that the computer would

* The launch sequence for America's Space Shuttle, by comparison, requires a modest 10,000 lines.

function perfectly in conditions far more strenuous than it would ever have encountered in tests or 'debugging runs'.

Thus *any* Star Wars system – supposing that the technological problems could be solved, and the vast amounts of money found – would be an enormous gamble. We have already noted that most modern weapons work less well in practice than they do in theory, but whereas conventional weapons can be tested in conditions roughly approximating to war, and even nuclear missiles can be tested sufficiently to ensure that enough would get through to cause horrendous damage, the delicate architecture of Star Wars would be another matter. Not until it was too late would anyone know whether it would work or not. Yet despite this, the search for a means of creating an 'autonomous' Star Wars system is proceeding apace.

In October 1983, seven months after President Reagan's speech, the Pentagon announced the launch of a five-year, $600 million research project called the Strategic Computing Programme. It does not fall under the aegis of General Abrahamson and his staff, though they will be the prime beneficiaries if the project is successful. Instead, the programme is being run by the Pentagon's Defense Advanced Research Projects Agency (DARPA), and DARPA has described its goal in a little-known report entitled *Strategic Computing, New-Generation Computing Technology: A Strategic Plan for Its Development and Application to Critical Problems in Defense*. If DARPA ever achieves this goal, noted one Washington computer expert, 'future historians might rank this remarkable document with Albert Einstein's 1939 letter to President Roosevelt recommending development of the atomic bomb'. The goal is nothing less than the creation of computers capable of exhibiting 'artificial intelligence':

> Instead of fielding simple guided missiles or remotely piloted vehicles, we might launch completely autonomous land, sea and air vehicles capable of complex, far-ranging reconnaissance and attack missions ... In contrast with previous computers, the new generation will exhibit human-like, 'intelligent' capabilities for planning and reasoning ... Using this new technology, machines will perform complex tasks with little human intervention, or even with complete autonomy ... Our leaders will employ intelligent computers as active assistants in the management of complex enterprises.

Among the gizmos listed for study in this astonishing report are, for the army, 'an unmanned robot tank' which would be able to fight the Russians all on its own, and for the air force, a 'pilot's associate' – a silicon co-pilot which would be able to assist the human being in the pilot's seat to operate the electronic warfare equipment of complex modern aircraft. But the biggest and most dramatic role the new so-called fifth generation computers might be called upon to perform, of course, would be to assist Star Wars. And the envisaged Star Wars computers would not only have to cope with a huge amount of data very, very fast, they would have to *function automatically*. Not just the processing of data but the decision to fire would be made by computer. There would be no time for human beings to be involved, let alone for anyone to telephone the president.

Those who are pushing SDI have more or less accepted this. 'It seems clear,' concluded the panel of scientists which looked into the nuts and bolts of Star Wars after the president's speech, '... that some degree of automation in the decision to commit weapons is inevitable if a ballistic missile system is to be at all credible.' In April 1984, George Keyworth was asked by Democratic Senator Paul Tsongas, in a hearing of the Senate Foreign Relations Committee, who would make the decision to activate Star Wars. 'We don't know,' replied the president's scientific adviser. 'By the year 1990, it may be done automatically.' Would the system be 'switched on' all the time? Not necessarily. In separate testimony to the House Appropriations Committee, General Abrahamson indicated that when the situation was calm

... many of the automatic features would be shut down and turned off. But were a crisis to build, the President would make those decisions ahead of time, and he would probably tell the Russians, 'Okay, now I am activating an important part of our system', which means that it is automatic. Hopefully, that would begin to reduce the crisis.

Hopefully, we will never find out, for some believe that 'activating' the system would have precisely the opposite effect. Indeed, as computer expert Jonathan Jacky has observed, the testimony underlines just how vulnerable the idea of computer control is:

Keyworth's and Abrahamson's suggestions that the system would be activated only during crises strongly imply that even they do not believe that the system could be made very reliable: if we leave it turned off most of the time, we might reduce the chance of an accident. But many analysts have observed that *a crisis is exactly the worst time to delegate control to an unstable system*. The chances that there will be some incident that triggers a false alert are probably greater then, and the consequences of responding to a false alert could be much worse [my italics].

One of the most complicated computer networks currently in use resides in NORAD, the North American Air Defense Command. The air force technicians at NORAD, whose headquarters are buried deep in the granite heart of Cheyenne Mountain, at the edge of the Rockies, would be the first to know if a Soviet missile attack were launched on America. The consoles which would register blips showing Soviet missiles rising out of their silos are linked to computers which are in turn linked to a worldwide early warning network of tremendous sophistication.

In November 1979, a training tape containing a simulation of a Soviet attack was somehow played through NORAD's 'live' warning system, creating a false alert. The error was quickly spotted, and there was no more than a brief panic. Next year, in June 1980, a 46-cent computer chip in a microcomputer failed, again leading to the transmission of an erroneous message that the US was under attack. About 100 B52 bombers were readied for take-off, as was the president's emergency plane, the 'National Alternative Airborne Command Post', nicknamed 'Kneecap'. As in 1979, the fault was swiftly identified and the readied aircraft were 'stood down'. On both these occasions, however, the world was relatively calm: it simply did not seem likely that the Russians were preparing to launch a 'bolt from the blue'. And at NORAD there is time to make checks, there are human beings 'in the loop', and there have been enough false alarms to instil considerable caution about total reliance on microchips or software – no one, as has been said often enough, 'wants to go to war on the basis of a computer'.

But what if a computer failure at NORAD were to occur during a crisis? The former Pentagon adviser Paul Bracken, who has done a detailed study of the command and control of nuclear forces, points out that it would then be much easier for things to get out of hand. Everyone would be jumpy, the Soviets would see the B52s being readied for take-off, and might respond by scrambling their own bomber forces. Even if the computer failure were detected, a series of 'corresponding alerts' might begin in a kind of hi tech age version of the mobilization/counter-mobilization process which led up to World War One ...

With luck, this will never happen. But given the complexity of Star Wars the likelihood of a computer error would be much greater were the system to be built. Computer errors, as we have noted, would of course occur while the system was operating, causing all kinds of failures. After all, many of the most serious problems in modern conventional weapons are caused by 'bugs' in the software. Take the ill-fated Divad Gun. Most of the basic hardware components – the chassis, the radar, the gun and so on – worked well enough *separately*, but Ford Aerospace could never solve the software problems involved in making them work smoothly together. (It was this which on one celebrated occasion caused the gun to take aim at a latrine fan rather than its designated target.) The Star Wars computers would be thousands if not millions of times more complicated than the computers used in Divad, and unlike the Divad's they could never be properly tested. Unless the star warriors find a way of repealing Murphy's law – the one which holds that if something *can* go wrong it will – computers, like everything else built by human beings, will always be capable of breaking down, and the more complicated they are the more likely it is to happen. Thus one could never have confidence in a Star Wars computer, and the notion that SDI would have to be fully automatic is perhaps the most troubling aspect of the whole project. 'No one who knows about missile defence systems would put the survivability of such systems in the hands of computers,' says Richard Garwin. 'It's like a whole bunch of sparking switches in a gasoline-filled room. The least error in that computer system would launch a nuclear war.'

Even if that is an exaggeration (and, to be fair, many analysts believe it is), and even if the worst that could result from a malfunction of the system would be some bangs and flashes in space and a harmless waste of Star Wars ammunition, the danger of entrusting Western security to a computer-controlled system would still be considerable.

'An accident is not really the problem,' one of those involved in SDI research told me. 'Your lasers might burn a few holes in the Siberian snow, but who cares if that happens? And kinetic energy weapons, if they were fired, would burn out on re-entry, like meteors. They would become ash, molecules distributed in the air, long before they hit the ground. Remember, none of these weapons are weapons of mass destruction.'

This particular scientist, who started out hopeful about the potential of SDI, and has since become more pessimistic, made it clear as we talked that he has no objection, in principle, to 'militarizing space': 'Why not take war to the heavens? It's the best place for it.' Yet despite this, and despite the fact that he worries little about 'accidents', 'taking the control of mighty weapons out of the hands of politicians' would constitute a grave risk. The system, because of worries about its reliability, and because the Russians would presumably wish to be allowed to send missiles into space during peacetime (on tests and space missions), would have to be switched off most of the time. The problem therefore would come during a crisis: Moscow, after all, does not believe that the American Star Wars programme is defensive in nature. It believes that the US is intent on building defences so that it can be free to launch a pre-emptive strike with impunity. And an American announcement that SDI had been 'turned on' might cause the Russians to fear that they were about to be struck. They might then say: 'We'd better go first, while we can.' The decision to switch on could actually trigger a nuclear strike. Leaving the system unarmed and only arming it in a time of crisis could thus give the Russians a wrong signal that the US was preparing for a pre-emptive strike and was arming its defence system to soak up the counter-attack from submarine-launched missiles.

So much for the initial problems. We have seen that *any* system America might build, supposing that the technological difficulties could be overcome and the vast amounts of money found, would be an enormous gamble, and a dangerous one. We have, as yet, scarcely glanced at what the Russians might do. For during the years it took for America to build a defensive system, Russia would almost certainly be working flat-out to render it useless. Let us glance at the countermeasures the Kremlin could take – many of them, unlike Star Wars itself, easily achievable through existing, not futuristic, technology.

'If you start to build Star Wars, we will be obliged to build new nuclear weapons, and more of them, which can penetrate your defensive shield,' says Soviet spokesman Georgi Arbatov. That, of course, would be the simplest thing the Russians could do. According to US intelligence, they already have 'extra' missiles at many of their missile sites enabling them to reload individual silos once an initial salvo has been fired (1,000 is one estimate). They could add to these, deploy new silos, increase the size of their ballistic submarine fleet, and generally bolster an already swollen arsenal by doubling or trebling their current total of 8,000 warheads. They could add countless decoys. 'Any defensive system,' Richard DeLauer, the under-secretary of defence for research and engineering, has said, 'can be overcome by proliferation and decoys, decoys, decoys, decoys.' The Russians could also protect their missiles by giving them specially coated skins which would be hard for lasers to penetrate, or by making their boosters revolve, which would prevent lasers requiring 'dwell time' from accomplishing their task. Lowell Wood, a burly, bearded Livermore scientist, and flamboyant Star Wars advocate, anticipates that this would pose no real problems: the defence, he says, would be using 'a submachine gun against a ballet dancer'. But whereas this might conceivably be true against the nuclear-pumped x-ray laser it would certainly not be true against chemical or excimer lasers.

Another improvement in missilery would be harder to counter: making the boost phase shorter by creating powerful 'fast burn' rockets which would rise swiftly out of the earth's atmosphere. These would give the defence not four minutes but as little as fifty seconds in which to strike before the release of the 'bus'. They could also design rockets which would not require a bus, but which would release their warheads and decoys the instant boost phase was over.

All this, of course, would take time and money, but then so will Star

Wars: only the staunchest optimists believe anything like an effective defence can be in place before the end of the century. And the countermeasures would almost certainly cost far less than the system itself.

One of the more thoughtful critics of Star Wars is James Schlesinger, a tough former defence secretary who is in a good position to assess the issue. In the 1960s Schlesinger worked for the Rand Corporation, the air force thinktank based in Santa Monica, California, and in the early 1970s he moved to the White House to take a job in the 'bureau of the budget'. In both these roles he became closely involved in the 'defences' debate, at the time when the issue first came to the fore in American politics. It was an experience which taught him to be cautious.

In a speech on 25 October 1984, Schlesinger reminded his audience of the cost calculations made in the 1960s. Then, he said, it had been judged that it would take five times as much money to erect a defence as it would to 'neutralize' it. By the 1980s, he conceded, that ratio might have modestly improved, but even that was doubtful. 'It is suggested that the ratio is now in the order of three to one. But that judgement primarily rests upon a single change: the belief that we can intercept Soviet missiles during the boost phase prior to separation of the re-entry vehicles [warheads]. Nonetheless, it is clear that the ratio is still strongly weighted against defence and will remain so ...'

We have already noted that the Soviets could take a number of relatively cheap measures to protect their missiles during the boost phase. Yet Star Wars advocates believe (contrary to Schlesinger) that in the end the defence-offence spending ratio will not be five to one or three to one, but *one to one*, or (preferably) better, and tilted in favour of the defence. That indeed is the critical assumption behind the whole initiative. If it is more expensive to build defences than it is to counter them then there is clearly no point in doing it. You are in a position where your opponent can force you, year after year, to spend more than he does just to maintain the status quo. And as we look at the sheer range of countermeasures available, the whole fanciful arithmetic of Star Wars begins to look more and more dubious.

Earlier in this book we examined the application of 'emerging technology' to the Central Front in Europe – smart weapons linked to super-sophisticated sensors and computers which might some day revolutionize conventional defence. ET would be a 'sequential' system, and 'sequential' systems, as we observed, rarely work in war. There is too much that can go wrong. All sorts of things have to happen in perfect sequence, and the whole system falters if you can disrupt just one element.

Star Wars would be the ultimate sequential system. However much 'redundancy' you tried to build in, in terms of numbers of satellites, numbers of battle stations, etc., you would still require a whole chain of things to happen perfectly to prevent devastating results. The Russians could use conventional weapons to go after ground-based terminals (during the conventional war which would probably precede nuclear war), or they could use sabotage. Teams of 'Spetznaz', Soviet special forces, who would infiltrate allied countries before or during an attack, would clearly make Star Wars installations a high-priority target. Command and communications links would be vulnerable to bombing, blinding, jamming and 'spoofing' – i.e. enemy attempts to break into the system and control it by transmitting on the same frequency – and the enemy would have a choice of different kinds of communications links to disrupt: satellite to satellite, satellite to ground, etc. Besides, communications blackouts could be created over wide areas by the simple expedient of exploding nuclear weapons high in the atmosphere.

Nuclear weapons themselves, indeed, would pose the single greatest headache to a defence. Exploding a mere handful in space – and no conceivable system could prevent that – would cause havoc to the fragile mechanisms of Star Wars. Take just one scenario, offered by a Livermore scientist. The Russians could 'send a series of missiles strung out single file, each missile fused to detonate if it sensed that some defensive weapon was about to destroy it. The resulting fireballs would serve the attackers as blinds, through which successive missiles could penetrate closer to the target. By using enough missiles, the enemy could be certain of finally reaching the target.'

But what of the satellites themselves? Boost phase kill would require, if not a galaxy of orbiting battle stations, then certainly an array of pre-positioned mirrors, communications and sensor platforms ready, at any instant, to begin flashing information to each other and back to earth about an impending Soviet attack. And supposing most of your weapons could be popped up into space just before use – a staggering supposition – then you would have placed even greater strains on command, control and communications links, not to mention the problems you would have protecting launch submarines in hostile waters just off the Soviet coastline. But even then a good deal of hardware would have to be pre-positioned in space – communications satellites, surveillance satellites and the like – and protecting even *these* against nuclear weapons would be well nigh impossible. The x-ray laser which entrances Edward Teller, for example, might prove far more useful in *countering* a defensive system than in aiding it: if able to attack fast-moving rockets it would *certainly* be able, in the hands of the Soviets, to attack satellites and battle stations moving on a well defined course through space ... And in space, as on land, any development pioneered by the US will eventually be imitated by the USSR.

(A small number of nuclear explosions would be sufficient to cause havoc to a space-based defence: the Russians could create these by using a very small number of missiles, each armed with one warhead specially hardened against laser beams.)

But there would be no need for weapons as powerful as nuclear bombs to knock out defensive satellites. They would present large and vulnerable targets. One possible kinetic energy weapon under study is the electro-magnetic rail gun. This would use a burst of electric current to fire General Abrahamson's 'smart rocks' (homing vehicles) along a rail and out across space to their targets. The snag is that such a rail gun might have to be 150 metres long with a bulky power generator at one end, and protecting this – the equivalent, as one sceptic put it, of 'an aircraft carrier in space' – would be a nightmare. The same problem would apply to other forms of battle station.

Scientists involved in Star Wars are well aware of the 'vulnerability problem'. At research labs like Los Alamos in New Mexico and Lawrence Livermore in the dusty heartland of California, they are exploring ways of providing SDI weapons with armour. 'Some of the biggest challenges we face,' acknowledges Dr Gerold Yonas, 'are making weapons not only lethal but survivable – survivable in the sense that boost phase weapons will orbit over the Soviet Union and thus be subject to attack.' One study done by Livermore suggests that the protection of battle stations in space might call for shielding by a million tons of protective material. But that raises another problem. The battle stations would be heavy enough without any protection, weighing perhaps 150 tons apiece: adding huge amounts of shielding would make them even heavier, and hoisting such weight into space would be phenomenally expensive. (At the moment it cost $3,000 to send just one *pound* of material into orbit on the Space Shuttle.) Officials have even suggested, somewhat fancifully, that it might be easier and cheaper to mine the vast amounts of shielding material required from the asteroids or the moon rather than trying to lift it from earth.

The coordinators of the SDI project in Washington remain confident that the problems can be solved. The price of shipping material to space may fall, they say (to, say, $300 a pound). Bullet-proof vests, after all, have become steadily lighter, and lightweight armour, probably made from carbon fabrics, may be invented for space-based weapons. Besides, satellites do not need to be protected by armour alone: they can be made so that they can dodge and weave when attacked, or armed so that they can automatically open fire at objects which get too close. But such measures may resemble Lowell Wood's ballet dancer faced with a submachine-gun. The central dilemma for the star warriors is that most of the hardware being dreamt up would be much easier to use against satellites and space-based battle stations than against missiles and warheads.

A determined opponent would have a host of available options. Innocent-looking commercial satellites could in fact disguise space mines, which, when a conflict threatened, would close in on defending satellites and explode (likely to be especially effective against hardware in high, geosynchronous orbit). Both Russia and America are developing anti-satellite weapons, and anti-satellite weapons have obvious anti-Star Wars potential. The existing Russian ASAT is pretty crude: a small ground-launched rocket, first tested in the 1960s, it has to orbit the globe twice before being in a position to strike its target (and even then, by all accounts, it is likely to miss). But America is developing a more sophisticated ASAT – a 'half orbit' system to be fired from a F15 fighter – and by the time America has even begun to think about Star Wars deployment the Russians are likely to have followed suit and to have developed an ASAT with at least as good a chance of proving successful as the systems it would seek to destroy. Indeed Russian ASATs, and space mines, and killer satellites, might not need to be super-sophisticated. Mirrors stationed in geosynchronous orbit to deflect laser beams down towards Russian missiles, for example, would have to be almost indescribably perfect. (During peacetime, these mirrors might be protected by special shutters, but at some point if war threatened they would have to be unshuttered, and then they would become vulnerable.) The slightest blemish, or warp, or crack would render them useless, and a satellite which exploded nearby, scattering a substance as innocuous as sand, would transform their delicate architecture into orbiting debris.

Thus in the game of counter- and counter-countermeasures which Star Wars would assuredly spark, the likelihood is that *offence* would continue to enjoy a huge advantage over *defence*. And that is putting it mildly. The difference between the two, as *Newsweek* has graphically put it, is 'the difference between building a machine gun and building a computer-controlled defensive-weapons system that would protect soldiers by locating, tracking and destroying enemy machine-gun bullets in the chaos of an all-out battle'. Nuclear weapons have to do *so little* – they are so crude, so imprecise, so unimaginably destructive – that only a few have to get through, and land roughly near a centre of population, to cause unspeakable damage. (The bombs themselves are also surprisingly cheap – in America, about a million dollars apiece, less than the price of an advanced anti-aircraft missile like the Phoenix.) By contrast, Star Wars would have to be extraordinarily fragile and complex, and – to give any credence at all to President Reagan's vision – it would have to do *so much*. It is easier, as has often been observed, to break a fine watch than to mend one.

Faced with such scepticism, the star warriors have a stock response. 'Many ... scientists said a few years ago that we couldn't reach the moon;

and many scientists said that you couldn't possibly put a missile in one continent and hit a target in another continent; and many scientists have said a great many things that have proven to be wrong once the work has been done,' says Caspar Weinberger. All of which is true. But the moon, as others were quick to point out, does not shoot back. Unlike the Russians, it has neither the desire nor the capacity to devise endless ways of stopping the Apollo programme. There is no one on the moon prepared to invest billions of roubles, and years of time, to stop space vehicles from landing. Besides, as the Union of Concerned Scientists have pointed out, it is simply not true to say that science can achieve everything:

> The laws of thermodynamics tell us that one cannot build a perpetual motion machine, and the principle of relativity implies that it would be futile to try to design spaceships that move faster than the speed of light.

Professor R. V. Jones makes a similar point in his own report on Star Wars, published in 1985, when he comments that 'American technological enthusiasm has not always been well founded'. Recalling his own experience of working with the Americans on an attempt to develop a method of submarine detection relying on 'infra-red reconnaissance of the ocean surface', he points out that the British always had doubts about the project, while the Americans were always 'confident and enthusiastic'. In the end, British doubts were vindicated. Jones goes on to warn of the danger of succumbing to the 'emotional appeal' of Star Wars: 'We need to remember the words Louis Pasteur said that he would like to see inscribed on the threshold of all the temples of science: "The greatest derangement of the human mind is to believe in something because one wishes it to be so." Or, in the words of Crow's Law: "Do not think what you want to think until you know what you ought to know." '

Nonetheless, it may be true that there is nothing in the law of physics which makes Star Wars an impossible concept. Just as some of the weapons we examined earlier might work well enough on a dust-free battlefield with the enemy not fighting back, so Star Wars might succeed – eventually – just – in a limited way – if the Russians made no changes whatsoever in their current forces and opted to carry on forever more with what they have now, forswearing any new developments. I am not suggesting they will do this. But if they did – even if they took *no* countermeasures, and American scientists managed to crack all the problems and American engineers managed to construct a flawless system – the West would *still* face devastation in a war. It would be in a similar position, as one SDI analyst puts it, to 'the foolish householder who padlocks his front door and stands guarding it with a shotgun while leaving his back door open'.

Star Wars envisages a defence against ballistic missiles. The whole space-based array would be useless against bombers and cruise missiles, which fly relatively low and would be immune from an attack launched out of the heavens. Indeed, in the 1960s, once the Soviets opted to deliver the bulk of their nuclear bombs aboard intercontinental missiles, America let its once proficient air defence system slip: now, in a war, it would have trouble coping with Soviet bombers (it has a hard enough time detecting and tackling drug-running aircraft). And though America led the way in the development of small, slow-flying and relatively cheap cruise missiles, Russia has stolidly followed in its footsteps. In fact, cruise missiles (especially the sea-launched variety) may ultimately bestow more advantages on the Russians than on the West. The Russians have more submarines available for conversion into cruise missile platforms than the Americans; in addition, the best targets for slow-flying cruise missiles are coastal ones, and America has many more of these than Russia does. So Star Wars raises the prospect of (say) 20 or 30 cruise-missile-carrying submarines converging on the American coast in time of war, ready and able (unless sunk) to rain nuclear devastation on the continent. (The argument that cruise missiles are less dangerous than ballistic ones because they fly slower is at best dubious: they are – theoretically – very accurate, they are small and hard to detect and, once a new generation arrives, complete with Stealth counter-radar technology, they will no longer even be 'slow': besides, launched from submarines just off the American coast, they will scarcely have far to fly to many high-value targets.)

James Schlesinger estimates that if the US goes ahead with Star Wars it will have to spend a minimum of $50 billion a year on an accompanying effort to strengthen air defences against the cruise and bomber threat. Even if it did that, it would still be vulnerable to the 'clandestine delivery' of nuclear weapons – suitcase bombs and the like, perhaps 'wired up' so that they can be detonated by remote control. (In Europe, as we will see, the problems are worse: to take one slightly absurd example, the Russians could even send dogs armed with small bombs across the border into West Germany.)

The upshot of all this is that a Star Wars defence could never work without Soviet cooperation. Not only would the Russians have to agree dramatically to constrain their offensive forces, but they would have to agree to work towards a world in which both sides' defences were given the best possible opportunity to work.

The Reagan administration, of course, had hopes that it might persuade the Russians to share in just such an effort. The president called on them to help create a 'nuclear-free' world. He even suggested that America would be prepared to share the fruits of its Star Wars research, in the hope of helping bring this about. But his hope defied common sense. In the first place, the chances of a future American president agreeing to pass over highly sensitive technological secrets are slim to the point of being absurd. Throughout the 'arms race' America has prized its technological lead and considered it the basis of its strength; the aim has been to stay one step ahead of the Russians and force them to spend money and effort catching up. American ingenuity has compensated for Russian numbers. True, the limits of this philosophy have been explored in this book, but is there really any likelihood of a future American president suddenly deciding to go to the lengths of free collaboration with the country once described by Reagan as 'the focus of evil in the modern world'?

To bestow upon the USSR the USA's most sensitive and secret information would be construed as unbelievably foolhardly, even treasonous: most technologies have more than one application, and a breakthrough which might help the Russians build Star Wars might also help them to develop countermeasures against it, or – worse – to develop new offensive weapons. (The lasers and particle beam weapons currently being contemplated for use against missiles may also, eventually, prove all too usable against people.) What guarantee would there be that the Russians would only use the secrets they were given for defensive purposes? The answer is that there would be none. The relationship between America and Russia is an antagonistic one: each has a diametrically opposed view of the world; neither trusts the other; if they did, there would be no need for huge conventional armies in Europe, for enormous arsenals of nuclear weapons – or for Star Wars. So to suggest that one side will start helping the other is ludicrous.

The same goes, without doubt, for the kind of all-embracing arms control regime which would be necessary to give Star Wars a chance. The chances of the Russians accepting such a regime are slim. There are some, like the American Sovietologist David Rivkin, who argue that they might. The Russians have never been greatly enamoured of nuclear weapons, says Rivkin. And whereas they may once have hankered after a theory of nuclear victory, they have appeared to become, in the early 1980s, more and more dubious about the idea of nuclear 'war fighting'. Add to that the fact that Moscow has always been interested in the concept of 'damage limitation' – in case nuclear war should occur – and you might have the circumstances in which the Kremlin would be prepared to join America in a 'build-down' of offensive forces and a build-up of defensive ones. Moscow's willingness to pursue such a course, indeed, might be enhanced by the knowledge that in a 'Star Wars world' the Soviets would be free, at last, to exploit their conventional superiority over the West (one reason, of course, why many feel the West would be foolish even to attempt it). But achieving the kind of arms control which this vision implies, as Rivkin acknowledges, would require not just a demonstration that Star Wars can work – and highly effectively – but an extraordinarily subtle blend of diplomacy, defence build-up and public relations – a blend which someone like the nineteenth-century Austrian statesman, Count Metternich, might have been capable of but which Nato most certainly is not. And even were the West to design such an arms control strategy, I believe the Russians, whatever the arguments to the contrary, are unlikely to stake all on what would be at best an uncertain and monumentally expensive gamble. From the first, they have seen SDI not as defensive but as *offensive*: viewed from their perspective, it is part of an American defence programme which includes a whole new generation of nuclear weapons, ranging from the D5 missiles to be based in Trident submarines, to 760 prospective sea-launched cruise missiles, 3,000 air-launched cruise missiles, the B1 bomber and the MX.

Instead of arms control, the prospect is of an all-out race in offensive, defensive and 'defence suppression' systems. Consider past experience. The discovery by American intelligence in the 1960s that the Russians were constructing an anti-ballistic missile system round Moscow proved a crucial factor in triggering Washington's decision to 'mirv' its missiles. Enabling each missile to deliver a set of warheads rather than just one greatly increased the chances of the 'offence' being able to defeat the 'defence'. 'Are the Soviets likely to be any less "offensive conservative" than we were then?' asks James Schlesinger.

> Given the Soviet Union's political ambitions, or its neurosis, or its quest for world domination, or its Marxist Leninist creed (depending upon whose eyes one is looking through), how likely is it that in the event of an American deployment of substantial strategic defence, the Soviets would agree to a constraint on offensive capabilities?

And knowing that the Russians would be working flat-out on developing countermeasures to defeat Star Wars, the Americans, of course, would be obliged to do the same. Indeed they already are. In addition to the strategic programmes I have mentioned, the air force is planning the 'Stealth' bomber, intended to be virtually undetectable by Soviet radar, and the Defense Advanced Research Projects Agency is working on a cruise missile with the same attributes: it will use exotic fuels and high performance engines which will enable it (if all goes as planned) to fly at more than three times the speed of sound. What Star Wars system could possibly cope with that?

Meanwhile, the Advanced Strategic Missile Systems programme, centred on Norton air force base in California, is busy examining ways of ensuring that American *ballistic* missiles never meet the kind of fate the star warriors want to provide for Russian ones. The programme is secret, and small beer compared with Star Wars itself (it received only around $1 million in 1985), but more funds are planned, and the ideas being contemplated suggest what might be in store. Most of the research, it seems, is into advanced 'penetration aids' and decoys which would confuse defences and make it harder for them to identify actual warheads. The penetration aids include chaff (clouds of tiny pieces of metal) and, according to the *New York Times*, 'light-reflecting aerosols that confuse enemy sensors; decoys that present enemy defences with a baffling multiplicity of targets; and "defence suppression systems" that home in on enemy radars and destroy them to clear the way for nuclear missiles.' One sophisticated decoy, being developed by a research lab, is apparently capable of reading the signals from enemy radar or infrared sensors and instantaneously devising a counter-signal to fool the defenders into thinking the decoy is a real warhead. Another research project involves the creation of a new agile re-entry vehicle for future American missiles which would be able to zigzag its way through space. Meanwhile, according to the Pentagon, another part of the Advanced Strategic Missile Systems programme is studying ways of protecting missiles in the 'boost phase' of their flight by, for example, disguising the exhaust plumes they emit when lifting off. 'You can always beat the other guy's defences if you know what he's got coming at you,' Major Larry Skapin, an air force missile engineer who represents the programme in the Pentagon, told the *New York Times* in 1985.

The Russians, undoubtedly, have their own version of the Advanced Strategic Missile Systems programme. But stopping the Americans even from *fielding* an SDI system would not prove difficult, if they chose to do so. The weapons involved, after all, would have to orbit over the Soviet Union, and it would take years to get them aloft (a Shuttle launch every two days for five years, in one estimate). There is also the possibility that space-based weapons powerful enough to strike rockets just after they had risen out of their silos might be powerful enough to strike targets on the ground – a point raised by Mikhail Gorbachev, the Soviet premier, at the Geneva summit in November 1985. Neither superpower would be likely to welcome any kind of battle station orbiting above its soil if there was even the slightest chance that this might be able at a moment's notice to incinerate centres of population or key military sites. (I will return to this.)

'Suppose the Russians decided to dispute our right to fly weapons over their territory,' said one man involved in SDI research, 'and whatever we put up they promptly shot down, just as they shot down the U2 and the Korean airliner? What could we do about it?' (At the moment, as this source points out, there are no actual weapons above Russia, only reconnaissance and spy satellites.) An alternative scenario has the Russians sending space mines into orbit close beside pieces of American hardware, immediately they are sent up. America, presumably, would seek to declare an 'exclusion zone' in space of say 100 kilometres in diameter around each orbiting battle station or mirror. But this would be like declaring huge exclusion zones around ships at sea: the chances are that the Russians would simply refuse to heed it.

12

Star Wars: the Reality

Research projects, like wars, are sometimes easier to start than to stop. With the full weight of a presidential commitment behind it, Star Wars had soon gained considerable momentum. When first unveiled in March 1983 it might have engendered a good deal of incredulity and not a little mirth; as one former high-level defence official put it to me: 'People giggled.' Two years later people weren't giggling any more. President Reagan appeared to have talked himself into an almost transcendental faith, believing, as one senior Republican put it, that Star Wars was 'the Second Coming'. The passions the subject evoked on all sides were striking, and the fierce denunciations of opponents seemed only to stir the star warriors into ever more determined, more grandiose expressions of support. The critics were dismissed as nay-sayers or Luddites or worse. It was implied, in some quarters, that their disloyalty to the cause made them anti-American, even pro-Soviet, and that their support of 'mutually assured destruction' made them immoral.

That Star Wars should have such impact was scarcely surprising. It had been launched by an extraordinarily popular president, and one who, in November 1984, was re-elected by an overwhelming majority. It encouraged a generalized longing, felt by millions of people, for escape from the nuclear 'box' (not the least significant of those who have 'come out' for Star Wars is the writer Jonathan Schell, who concluded in his pessimistic book *The Fate of the Earth* that man would have to 'reinvent politics' if he was to escape the nuclear dilemma – a prescription no less apocalyptic, and fantastic, than the president's). The wish to *believe* reflected itself in the opinion polls (though interestingly, the polls also showed that people harboured doubts about its feasibility, and polls on a subject like this are of limited value: so much depends on the way the questions are asked).*

Meanwhile, huge sums of money were at stake. The initial Star Wars programme envisaged spending $26 billion in the first five years, and despite some trimming by Congress, by late 1985 a billion dollars' worth of contracts had been allocated to universities, research outfits and defence contractors. To the scientists involved it was an immediate and irresistible – perhaps the ultimate – challenge. 'Is it any wonder that scientists have fallen in love with nuclear defence?' asked *Newsweek* in 1985:

> Here are fantastic, cataclysmic energies – megavolts and terrawatts and gigajoules, rending the air in microsecond bursts; here is a chance to build the kind of lasers they can only dream about in other fields. Here is a chance to help break the world's precarious dependence on the balance of terror, a chance for nuclear physics to do something for humanity in compensation for inventing the hydrogen bomb. Here is the greatest technological challenge in the world today, out of which may come the next generation of Nobel Prize winners and which may, in its very immensity, solve that most elusive of scientific quests, the search for lifetime funding. To almost everyone else, including Ronald Reagan, Star Wars is an abstraction – a promise of a distant millennium when nuclear weapons will no longer exist, a piece on the global chessboard, a budget line. To scientists, it is as real as lightning.

Not the least of the reasons why it is real to scientists is that it means jobs: at a time when the demand for new types of nuclear warhead is ebbing and when the challenges of nuclear technology have dimmed, SDI offers a promising new field of endeavour and one likely to offer employment at laboratories like Lawrence Livermore and Los Alamos for years to come. (Not all scientists with opportunities to participate in SDI have been beguiled, however: most of the physics professors at the University of Illinois signed a statement saying that SDI was technically dubious and not worth investigating. They refused to accept funding from

---

* A February 1985 poll which asked: 'Do you want the United States to defend Americans against Soviet missiles?' found 90 per cent of its respondents saying 'Yes'; other pollsters who asked questions got similar responses. But a *Washington Post*-ABC News poll in August 1985 made its respondents think rather harder: 'Supporters say such weapons could guarantee protection of the United States from nuclear attack and are worth whatever they cost. Opponents say such weapons will not work, will increase the arms race, and that the research will cost many billions of dollars. How about you: would you say you approve or disapprove of plans to develop such space-based weapons?' Here, 41 per cent of respondents said they approved, while a majority – 53 per cent – said they disapproved.

the SDI organization. And one of the computer world's most respected authorities on large-scale computer programming, Professor David Parnas, had second thoughts in July 1984. Hired to sit on an advisory panel into 'computing in support of battle management', at $1,000 a day, Parnas quit saying he thought it would never be possible to construct a sufficiently reliable computer system to enable SDI to work.)

SDI was becoming real enough, too, to defence contractors. Here was the prospect not just of megavolts and gigajoules but of billions and billions of dollars' worth of business, a bonanza beyond their wildest dreams. No wonder, then, that hundreds of firms wanted to become involved in the research: if experience was anything to go by, research eventually would lead to development, and development to producing hardware. There had to be fortunes to be made from Star Wars.

From across the Atlantic, European governments watched developments with mounting alarm. During Reagan's first term most of those involved in nuclear matters had not taken Star Wars very seriously. They seemed to see it, in so far as they saw it at all, as another American craze which would have to run its course and then, with luck, would simply go away. Only when Reagan was re-elected by a landslide did it become clear that it wasn't going to. And if allied governments were slow to cotton on to the implications of Star Wars, their 'state of mind' when they did, as John Newhouse observed in the *New Yorker*, became what might fairly be described as 'obsessive'.

European officials had many and varied reasons for being unhappy about Star Wars. Their unhappiness was rooted, first, in temperament. Historically less inclined to believe in bold, sweeping initiatives than their American counterparts, they were more disposed to be pessimistic about this one. Whereas Star Wars appealed to something deep in the American psyche, the dream of mastering space, the last frontier (not for nothing is Washington's most popular tourist attraction its impressive Air and Space Museum), Europe was collectively less dazzled. As one scholar of US-European relations put it: 'The Americans are a problem solving people. They still believe that there is a solution to every problem. The Europeans tend to believe that solutions just create new problems.'

More specifically, Europeans had a host of different factors to worry about – geographic, strategic and political as well as technical. They were confused about the real *aim* of Star Wars and troubled by the rhetoric. When officials visited Washington on 'fact-finding trips', which they did quite often, they came back dissatisfied and, it seemed, with precious few facts. The whole project, viewed from European capitals, had not been thought through. The 'technological bandwagon', as one British official put it, seemed 'in danger of running away down the hill, leaving the horses behind'.

Though the Americans protested that the Star Wars umbrella would extend over Europe as well as America, Europe – from almost every perspective – seemed to end up worse, not better off. For one thing, while erecting a defence over America seems fantastic, erecting one over Europe seems even more so. Faced with a growing array of medium- and short-range Soviet missiles, the Europeans would have not half an hour to stop them, but five or ten minutes. (Space-based systems could be fairly effective against SS20s, which have a steep trajectory and travel relatively slowly, but special anti-tactical ballistic missile systems – based on the ground – would be required to provide any hope of stopping SS21s, SS22s and SS23s.) But beyond the technical arguments which troubled European officials were a host of others: political, strategic and financial. If the Americans spent vast fortunes on Star Wars then they would have less money with which to defend Europe, or anywhere else. Would that not increase the pressure for the withdrawal of American troops from the Central Front? And what about 'doctrine'? Flexible response, as we have seen, envisages Nato being able to make small, limited nuclear attacks on the enemy if it begins to lose a conventional war. Would not a half-effective Star Wars system, while unable to cope with larger attacks, be able to cope with small, discriminatory ones? And would not Star Wars, by making nuclear war harder, make conventional and chemical war easier to risk, and thus more likely to happen?

The Americans, it seemed, were bent on fundamentally changing Nato strategy. The last time that had happened, with the shift in the 1960s to flexible response, it had taken eight years and almost torn the Alliance apart in the process. Yet here were the Americans, in the wake of a presidential speech about which no one had been consulted, and with no serious debate beforehand, proposing to change the strategy *unilaterally*, and much more dramatically than ever before, with no one having the least idea whether the replacement was going to work or not. Meanwhile, the strategic environment was likely to get more dangerous, the arms race was going to be jacked up another notch, and arms control was quite possibly going to be dealt a lethal blow. Despite a certain amount of misty-eyed public optimism about a brave new world of defences (some of it construed as fairly cynical), with the Russians coming round to recognize that nuclear weapons would be less effective and therefore deciding there was less point in building them, the principal casualty looked like being the anti-ballistic missile treaty – in the view of many, one of the most solid monuments on the arms control landscape. ('The keystone in the still shaky arch of security,' as the British foreign secretary, Sir Geoffrey Howe, has called it.) Meanwhile, Washington, like Trollope's Septimus Harding, seemed to be suffering 'persistent bouts of morality', and in this case of a rather dangerous kind. The constant suggestion that mutually assured destruction was somehow wrong presupposed that there was a better way; most European officials and politicians felt that there was not.

In some of this, to be sure, there was an element of carping. Flexible response, as we have seen, is scarcely a satisfactory doctrine: the notion of going nuclear first to check a losing conventional war has long seemed somewhat incredible. The Europeans themselves have come up with few constructive ideas for an alternative: and, arguably, the installation of cruise and Pershing, by stirring up concern about nuclear weapons, has increased the pressures for change. Resisting the need to improve their own conventional forces, the Europeans had helped create the conditions which prompted Reagan's radical step.

But in suggesting that Star Wars would solve nothing they had history – and common sense – on their side. The European leaders, as one American opposed to Star Wars put it, feared that the emperor had no clothes. Faced with peace movements which lost no opportunity to denounce nuclear weapons, they could find little comfort in the rhetoric used to defend Star Wars. Politicians like Mrs Thatcher in the UK and Helmut Kohl in West Germany had to live with opposition parties only too happy to exploit the idea that nuclear deterrence was immoral (precisely the implication of SDI). The peace movement which backed those parties had, after all, believed that all along. (In Britain, for example, as one official pointed out, those who believed in unilateral disarmament vastly outnumbered those who believed in SDI. 'You still see plenty of Volvos with CND stickers on them,' commented the official in spring 1985, 'but the faith in Star Wars is still confined virtually to the far right.') The Europeans, having been assured throughout 1981 and 1982 that they must take new cruise and Pershing missiles on their soil, were now being told that these were immoral and soon to become obsolete. So the moral tone in the Reagan administration's rhetoric was likely, in the end, to do much more harm than good. (And not just in Europe. As James Schlesinger put it: '... the justification for strategic defence should never be based on assertions regarding the immorality of deterrence. For the balance of our days the security of the Western world will continue to rest on deterrence. Those were – and are – reckless words.')

The British, and the French, had special worries about Star Wars. At the core of both nations' forces were small, 'independent' nuclear deterrents, and these – far more than the vast arsenals of America and Russia – seemed likely to be threatened by a half-effective Star Wars system. France's 'mini triad' of nuclear forces – its 18 single-warheaded missiles on the Plateau d'Albion, its four nuclear submarines each armed with 16 missiles, and its Mirage bombers – and Britain's four Polaris boats, each carrying 16 missiles, constituted weapons of last resort. They existed simply to *deter direct nuclear attacks on the soil of France and Britain*. Though neither country could destroy Russia, each could 'tear off an arm', in de Gaulle's phrase, and cause enough damage and loss of life to make an attack seem a foolhardy act.

Naturally, therefore, both France and Britain prize their 'minimum deterrents'. France, with its explicitly Gaullist policy, may shelter willy-nilly under the American strategic umbrella but prefers to put its faith in its own. ('However large may be the glass offered to us, we prefer to drink from our own, while touching glasses round about,' said de Gaulle.) And Britain, which in wartime would be Nato's 'unsinkable aircraft carrier' and a prime target, believes that an independent deterrent provides valuable extra insurance. In 1983, when Reagan launched Star Wars, both Britain and France were modernizing their independent deterrents, Britain by buying the sophisticated American Trident system at around $10 billion – a hefty price tag for a small country. Not surprisingly, Star Wars evoked little enthusiasm in Whitehall or on the Quai d'Orsay. Here is what was foreseen:

America, at colossal expense, builds a half-adequate Star Wars system; Russia, spurred on by this, does the same. Each superpower, because it possesses a vast arsenal, is still able to threaten unimaginable destruction to the other. But for Britain and France's deterrents the change is dramatic: they have been rendered impotent. Not possessing the luxury of being able to overwhelm a defence with sheer numbers they know that, if war comes, Russia's half-adequate Star Wars may be just good enough to cope with their small forces. Thus the money spent on these forces would turn out to be a waste; worse, the central pillar of both French and British defence would have collapsed. They would end up depending more and more heavily on America at a time when such dependence would probably be more and more ill-advised, and when the world, because of Star Wars, would seem much more dangerous.

On 22 December 1984, Britain's prime minister, Mrs Margaret Thatcher, visited Ronald Reagan at Camp David. Mrs Thatcher was closer to the president than any other European leader, and a warm admirer. The feeling was reciprocal. (Once, at an economic summit in Versailles, the prime minister rang the president between sessions on a matter she regarded as being of great importance. Reagan listened to the unquenchable flow for a few seconds, then held the telephone away from his ear and said to an aide: 'Isn't she wonderful?') During the arms talks over intermediate nuclear weapons (cruise, Pershing and the SS20), she had helped persuade the president to moderate the US negotiating position. Now once again, she sought to use her influence. For an hour and a half she made the case against Star Wars.

She covered a lot of ground. She discussed arms control, and the danger to the ABM treaty, which she had read in its entirety, and, as a former chemist, she went through the technical arguments in detail, dwelling at length on possible Russian countermeasures such as 'revolving boosters', bombs in suitcases, etc. Above all, she stressed the dangers of continuing to say that nuclear deterrence was immoral and that nuclear weapons could be rendered obsolete. It was, by all accounts, an impressive performance. And at that stage, as the *New Yorker* later observed, Mrs Thatcher became 'probably the only person' who 'told Reagan to his face what is wrong with Star Wars – from a European point of view, at least'. Secretary of State George Shultz and National Security Adviser Robert McFarlane tried to answer her points. So did Reagan himself. He talked at one stage about the awfulness of having a finger on the nuclear button, and produced a letter from Dwight Eisenhower written at Camp David making a similar point. But it was Mrs Thatcher who did most of the talking.

The British Foreign Office had been quicker than most European foreign ministries in grasping the implications of Star Wars. (When a team of US officials visited key capitals early in 1984 to try and dispel 'myths' about Star Wars they reported back to Washington that Britain was the most hostile.) And by the time Mrs Thatcher met Reagan – just after his massive election victory – European concern was growing. Only two weeks earlier, Mikhail Gorbachev, the prospective Soviet leader, had visited London, and impressed Mrs Thatcher as a man she felt the West could 'do business with'. But Mrs Thatcher and her advisers had been struck by the vehemence of Gorbachev's attacks on Star Wars and left in little doubt that if America pressed ahead, Russia would respond and do its best to undercut American defences. Having just endured heavy political fallout over the deployment of cruise and Pershing missiles, neither the British prime minister nor any of her European counterparts wanted a return to the state of high tension with the Eastern bloc which Star Wars seemed to portend.

The upshot of the Camp David meeting was a four-point agreement, signed by both Mrs Thatcher and Reagan. The four points were, in brief, that the West was seeking balance with Russia, not superiority over it; that Star Wars was a research programme (with deployment being subject to negotiation, taking into account existing agreements); that the purpose of the exercise was to enhance and not to undermine deterrence; and that the aim in arms control negotiations should be to seek lower levels of offensive forces.

The four points did, at least, stake out a 'European' position on Star Wars. But in Washington, as most European officials knew, their significance was strictly limited: they did not affect the programme one iota. Equally, when Paul Nitze, the president's special adviser on arms control, made a speech in March 1985 which seemingly echoed the cautionary outlook of Camp David, the Europeans were scarcely reassured. Nitze suggested that any Star Wars system would have to be 'cost-effective' – meaning that it would have to cost less to deploy than to counter – and 'survivable'. European governments, for reasons we have looked at, thought there was no chance of its ever being either. They suspected, moreover, despite Nitze's speech, that SDI was fast becoming *more* than a research programme and that it might end up getting deployed whether it was cost-effective and survivable or not.*

In Reagan's inner circle, as European officials knew, the issue had become like 'a badge of loyalty': you criticized it at your peril. Even defence consultants who did studies for the Pentagon knew that if they voiced sceptical views in public their business might be curtailed. 'The White House is in a "them and us" mode on this,' said one. 'You're either for Star Wars or you're against it. They talk about research but in reality they mean commitment.'

As for whether Star Wars could ever be cost-effective, or survivable, 'they answer the questions with assertions that it can be done,' said this source, two years into the programme. 'They offer no *evidence* to back it up.' On 31 October 1985, Caspar Weinberger, the defence secretary, told the Senate Foreign Relations Committee that he could not conceive 'of strategic defense being more costly than the constant need to modernize and strengthen as each side makes a move to which the other side has to make a response.' Asked if he would change his mind if Star Wars *were* to prove more costly, he said: 'No ... I would not, because I would think the additional cost in protecting people's lives, in protecting this nation, would be far worth anything that it would cost.'

In the White House, and in the makeshift offices occupied by SDI's coordinators a few blocks away in downtown Washington, the mood remained one of buoyant, almost nonchalant confidence. 'I now feel entirely confident we can do it,' George Keyworth told me in September 1985. 'What we need time for is to find the optimum way of doing it.' With excusable hyperbole, one scientist in Washington, who takes a different view, described to me his feelings about the most committed star warriors:

They are blinded by technological optimism. They believe that all they have to do is configure the right pieces of metal into the right

* Almost a year earlier, Frank Miller, the Pentagon official who had chaired the initial inter-agency study on SDI, foreshadowed Nitze's speech in testimony to Congress. Addressing the House Committee on Foreign Affairs on 26 July 1984, Miller said: 'If at some point in the future, the end of this decade, the beginning of the next, the administration decided to come to the Congress to ask you to fund full-scale development and beginning deployment, that administration would have to convince you, as well as itself, that such a system would be effective; that it would be cost-effective; and that it would be survivable ...'

shape and they have achieved their goal ... They think that
international politics is subject to an engineering solution. It's as if
the 1960s and 1970s never happened, as if these people are living in
a time warp, or on another planet ... Star Wars is the defence
equivalent of floating cities, or railway lines under the Atlantic ...

Many scientists involved in SDI research, to be fair, were uneasy about
all the hype. They were disturbed by the showy tests and, in some cases,
by what appeared to be manipulative, self-serving use of 'classified
information'. They feared that the pressure for results might jeopardize
their reputations, and perhaps the chance of the programme yielding
anything at all. In an interview with the *New York Times*, Dr Roger L.
Hagengruber, director of systems studies at the Sandia National Laboratory
in Albuquerque, New Mexico, talked of the general desire to 'have very
early demonstrations, to show lethality', adding that such tests could be
'contrived'. 'These demonstrations have the potential to be what we call
strap-down chicken tests, where you strap the chicken down, blow it apart
with a shotgun and say shotguns kill chickens. But that's quite different
from trying to kill a chicken in a dense forest while it's running away from
you.'

One clear example of this (though Dr Hagengruber did not specifically
cite it) was the September 1985 test of a chemical laser. The target was
the second stage of an old Titan missile, and when it was struck it exploded,
spectacularly. The missile, however, was stationary and on the ground. It
was also held firmly in place by wires so tightly strung, apparently, that
it was sure to come apart when struck by the laser beam.

Rather more serious was evidence which emerged in November 1985
about Edward Teller's pet project, the nuclear-pumped x-ray laser. Despite
its mentor's enthusiasm, it appeared that all was not as well with the
programme as Teller likes to imply: in one underground test in Nevada,
a key 'focusing element' had proved defective, and there were doubts, too,
about the effectiveness of earlier tests. A group of scientists, angry about
the way in which the x-ray laser programme was being discussed, risked
jail sentences by leaking details of the problems to the magazine *Science*.

The question of how to handle Star Wars posed delicate problems for
European leaders. The French, predictably, were the most openly hostile.
Chancellor Helmut Kohl of West Germany, torn between his own doubts
and West Germany's traditional closeness to France on the one hand, and
his loyalty to Reagan on the other, shrank from being publicly critical of
Star Wars. And Mrs Thatcher, intent on preserving her 'special relationship'
with Reagan, judged it best to make her criticisms privately. (It was Mrs
Thatcher, indeed, who became the first European leader to agree in
principle to her country's participation in the Star Wars research

programme. The decision was made more from realism than rhapsody. The British clearly recognized that research was unstoppable with Reagan in the White House, and judged that if Britain did not participate it might miss out in the development of all kinds of 'cutting edge' technologies, some of which might have a lucrative commercial spinoff, and that some of the best and brightest British scientists might be lured across the Atlantic to work on the project in America. Another British motive was the belief that it might prove easier to exert influence from *within*, rather than from without – especially in the light of the Camp David accords.)

In European foreign and defence ministries, there were fewer reservations about criticizing Star Wars. The then British defence secretary, Michael Heseltine, was a leading sceptic. (He had first-hand experience, as one official put it 'of how military-industrial complexes work'.) And on 15 March 1985, Sir Geoffrey Howe, Britain's foreign secretary, made Star Wars the subject of a major address to the Royal United Services Institute in London.

Howe's speech was carefully phrased. He talked of the dangers of ignoring the Russian Star Wars effort (which we will also examine), and he raised many of the major problems posed by SDI – financial, strategic and technical. Might not the money be better spent elsewhere? What would be the consequences for the Alliance?

> In terms of Nato's policy of forward defence and flexible response, would we lose on the swings whatever might be gained on the roundabouts?
>
> The attractions of moving towards a more defensive strategy for the prevention of war are as apparent as are the risks. It would be wrong to rule out the possibility on the grounds that the questions it raises are too difficult.
>
> But the fact that there are no easy answers, that the risks may outweigh the benefits, that science may not be able to provide a safer solution to the nuclear dilemma of the past forty years – all these points underline the importance of proceeding with the utmost deliberation.

The danger of Star Wars, Sir Geoffrey suggested, might be that we would end up by creating 'a Maginot Line in space'. (The French foreign minister, Claude Cheysson, had used a similar phrase a few months earlier.)

Sir Geoffrey's speech occasioned a prompt and savage reaction. It was attacked by the American assistant secretary of defence, Richard Perle, who happened to be in London at the time. And it was the subject of a lengthy leading article in *The Times* which came close to accusing the mild-mannered Sir Geoffrey of 'appeasement'. The piece showed, all too clearly, how much passion Star Wars had stirred up. But for all the heat, there was not much light. *The Times'* leader writer, defiantly hopeful as he was, had no more idea than anyone else whether Star Wars would eventually work, or in what form.

That, of course, was the heart of the matter. What exactly *was* Star Wars? Or rather, what, after two years, had it become? The Europeans suspected that if $26 billion was spent on 'research' something would come out of it, and most insiders in Washington agreed with them. 'You can't spend all that money without something coming out the other end,' as one put it. What would the programme eventually yield? If Reagan's initial vision was fantasy, and most officials suspected that it was, then what was left? What did those involved in the programme *really want*?

The answer to this was not at all clear. Basically, there appeared to be two schools of thought. The first – the one espoused by the president – was that the defences he envisaged would lead the West away from its precarious dependence on nuclear deterrence into the promised land of 'mutually assured survival'. The second, more realistic view held that this was fantasy, at least for the foreseeable future, and that the real aim of SDI must not be to *replace* deterrence but to *boost* it, or as worst-case analysts would say, *restore* it. Those who believed this argued that a less than perfect shield would do, since the principal aim of the system would be to complicate Soviet plans of attack and deny the Kremlin the option of mounting a full-blooded 'first strike' against American missile silos in the expectation that it might be successful.

The three advisory panels which reported to President Reagan on SDI's feasibility in 1983 provided an early preview of the division between the 'get rid of deterrence' and the 'boost deterrence' camps. Essentially, the Fletcher panel, which concentrated on the nuts and bolts, came out for 'mutually assured survival', concluding (albeit after much disagreement amongst its scientists) that 'a robust, multi-tiered ballistic missile defence system' could eventually be made to work. The report stressed, however, that such a system would require cooperation from the Russians – and that its construction would have to be accompanied by reductions in the offensive arsenals of both sides.

The Hoffman panel, by contrast, in its report on policy implications, laid more emphasis on the short-term aim of boosting deterrence. One small scenario it drew involved a Russian conventional attack on Europe in which to prevent Nato from reinforcing its troops the Kremlin authorized a small nuclear strike on a handful of major ports (say five) on both sides of the Atlantic. Might not Russia now feel it could risk such a step without fear of drastic retaliation? the panel asked. If America had a defence in place, however, the Russians would not simply be able to drop five bombs on five ports: they might have to drop 20 or more to be sure of striking their targets. They would consequently have to worry that launching such a large salvo would be much more likely to provoke retaliation.

But the principal concern of the 'boost deterrence' school was a broader one. As we have seen, there is, in America's strategic community, a growing anxiety about the vulnerability of America's land-based missiles, and the danger of pre-emptive strike posed by the Russian missile force, in particular the 5,000 warheads on the huge SS18 and SS19 missiles. In the mid-1980s, having failed, after enormous effort, to find a 'secure basing mode' for the MX, the problem (if there was a problem) loomed as large as ever. And what attracted some people to Star Wars was the notion that an imperfect defence might help solve it: after all, faced even with *limited* defences, the Russians would be less confident about the chances of launching a successful pre-emptive strike.

The simplest, fastest and most modest way of achieving such a defence, of course, would be to do it by erecting ground-based defences round missile sites and other vital military installations. More down to earth, literally, than anything envisaged under the Star Wars programme, this might indeed prove feasible. The kinetic energy homing vehicle which shattered a dummy warhead in space over the Pacific in June 1984 had shown that modern weapons could – if made properly – destroy warheads. And missile silos, unlike cities, are small targets: there would not be the need to cover a huge area. Your aim would simply be to stop one or perhaps two warheads exploding *on the ground* at the silos you chose to defend; if the warheads went off when they were hit, high above the earth, it would not matter. There would be no need to perform the series of scientific and military miracles required to effect 'boost phase kill'. There would not even be a need to defend *all* of your missiles. Since your aim would be to make clear to the Soviets that a first strike could not possibly work, you would simply have to protect a proportion of them, enough to enable you to launch a devastating and accurate retaliatory strike. Besides, even if the defences did not work perfectly, it wouldn't matter. The Soviets would have to take them into account; they would no longer be confident of being able to execute a first strike; nuclear deterrence, in the view of 'missile defence' proponents, would not be replaced, it would be *enhanced*. This limited defence might, of course, incorporate some space-based elements, too. But the most cost-effective 'architecture' would almost certainly involve keeping most of the hardware on the ground.

The notion of boosting deterrence at least has this to commend it: it is more plausible than the notion of rendering nuclear weapons obsolete. Unfortunately, however, it poses a number of problems, both political and strategic.

Take, first, the strategic problem. If America put up a limited defence on its own, and Russia did nothing, then deterrence would certainly be boosted (at least for the West). But the assumption, of course, would have to be that if America constructed any kind of a defence, the Russians would match it. And the uncomfortable truth is that if that happened – and both sides created equal but imperfect defences – then deterrence would probably not be strengthened, but weakened.

The reason for this is complicated, but it has been set out, with mathematical precision, by a retired air force general named Glenn Kent. As a critic of Star Wars, Kent's credentials are hard to question, even, perhaps especially, among conservatives. Unlike many who have attacked the programme, such as the Union of Concerned Scientists, he is a strong supporter of President Reagan and, in principle, a defender of his military build-up. An adviser to successive defence secretaries during the 1960s and 1970s, he belongs to that curious clan characterized by Fred Kaplan as 'the wizards of Armageddon', the systems analysts whose calculations form the basis for America's war plans. Paul Nitze, Reagan's special adviser on arms control and a founder member of the conservative pressure group the Committee on the Present Danger, calls him, simply, 'one of the best mathematicians I have ever met'.

Retired from the Pentagon by the time Reagan unveiled Star Wars, Kent, an engaging man with silver hair and a southern drawl, developed his position on Star Wars for the Rand Corporation. The case he makes is more sophisticated than most criticisms of the programme, and is primarily strategic rather than technical. Deterrence, he points out, is measured by the number of warheads which could be delivered to Soviet targets *after* America has endured a Soviet pre-emptive strike. And it is by this measure that America loses out – dramatically – if both sides develop roughly equivalent defences, the reason being the different structure of American and Russian nuclear forces, and in particular Russia's substantial lead in land-based missiles.

The easiest way to illustrate Kent's calculations is with an example. Were the Russians to launch their SS18 and SS19 heavy missiles (a total of 5,000 warheads) in a pre-emptive strike, they could *theoretically* destroy America's entire land-based missile force, based, as it is, in only 1,000 silos. But at the moment, in a world without defences, America would be able to fire back 3,000 surviving submarine-based warheads (a plausible figure, given the number of submarines likely to be 'on station').

Now let us assume that both superpowers have half-adequate defences, each able to destroy 3,000 of the other side's warheads. Russia's pre-emptive strike becomes less devastating than it was, but given the sheer number of warheads involved, there is still the *theoretical* possibility that it could knock out most American land-based missiles. America's retaliatory blow, however, has been rendered almost impotent. The 3,000 warheads it was relying on to fire back a crushing counterstrike on Russia are soaked up by Russian defences.

Kent plots his calculations on a graph, and they show that for a long time, while both sides are deploying space-based defences, America will be at a grave disadvantage, and that the disadvantage will only disappear when (or rather if) both sides get into a position of having developed extremely robust and effective defences. Until that moment, however – a moment which might never come – Kent's arithmetic suggests that America will have to *deploy its defences at twice the rate of Russia just to maintain an effective deterrent*. He points out, therefore, that if America is going to get into a Star Wars race with Russia it will have to run that race twice as fast as the Russians do, and run it to the end. Will Congress, he asks, in an age of fiscal restraint when the prime worry will be cutting the huge federal deficit, really be prepared to do this? Or does the US risk ending up with the worst of all possible worlds, in which both sides 'break out' of the ABM treaty and the Russians end up deploying a massive Star Wars defence while America does not?

Those who argue that Star Wars will boost deterrence, therefore, rest their argument on a shaky foundation. They claim that limited defences will complicate Soviet plans of attack and create more 'uncertainty' for Soviet planners. But as Kent demonstrates, limited defences will also complicate America's plans to retaliate. And what could be more 'uncertain' for Soviet planners than the idea of a first strike in current circumstances? I argue in this book that fears of 'vulnerability' are desperately overblown and that even if the Soviets *could* make the kind of precisely coordinated surgical strike against land-based missiles which everyone fears, the US would be able to wreak terrible havoc in retaliation by using its sea-based weapons and bombers.

But the idea of defending American missile silos falters for another reason. Those most intimately involved with Star Wars know that 'selling' a defence of missiles is not easy. It does not have much of a constituency amongst the right, who want a full-blown system, nor amongst the left, who think it unnecessary. The complex argument that SDI may boost deterrence and thus in the end save lives is one which previous experience has shown likely to leave the American public cold (even if the argument were plausible). And consider, finally, the practical difficulties of actually constructing a ground-based defence and winning political support for planting interceptor rockets round missile fields, with all the complex of radars and command posts which they would demand. As one insider put it: 'There just aren't enough trucks in Washington to take all the environmental impact statements you'd get up to Capitol Hill.'

Thus the Catch 22 of Star Wars is that what seems politically possible – i.e. a defence of cities – is practically impossible, while what seems practically possible – i.e. a ground-based defence of some missile silos – is both likely to leave America worse off *and* politically impossible. Reagan himself stressed on several occasions that an attempt to defend weapons might prove 'destabilizing'. He did so in his initial speech in 1983, and again in a speech to the National Space Club on 29 March 1985, when he said that Star Wars 'is not, and should never be misconstrued as, just another method of protecting missile silos'.

In the light of this, the administration was bound to sound confused. As James Schlesinger observed, Reagan's initial speech:

held out to American citizens the unqualified hope that they need not forever live with the nuclear threat over their heads. Through the vigour of American technology, some day – even if not until the 21st century – our cities would once again be safe from nuclear attack, as they have been for most of the nation's history. In that lay the political appeal of the speech – and we should understand that its appeal is fundamentally political – for invulnerability to nuclear assault is what the American public believes is going to be achieved.*

Thus officials, whatever their reservations about space-based defence, knew that they had to emphasize this to keep the programme going. Otherwise Star Wars might simply cease to be. A British official, asked what happened when he asked 'hard questions', captured the flavour:

The answer is always 'We don't have the answers now.' ... They say the purpose of the research is to find the answers. 'Well, wouldn't the money be better spent on projects of a less uncertain nature?' we ask. There is usually no response to that. Sometimes they say that what may come out of all this is defence of hard targets [missile silos]. But when we say: 'If it's hard targets you want to defend, why do it in space, where it won't work and where the systems will be vulnerable? Why not do it on the ground, where it might work?',

---

*If further evidence of this was needed, it came in an advertising campaign mounted by the pro-Star Wars lobby in the run-up to the superpower summit in November 1985. One rather preposterous advert featured a cartoon drawing of stick people, a dog, a house and a sun. A little girl says in a cute voice: 'I asked my daddy what this "Star Wars" stuff is all about ... He said that right now we can't protect ourselves from nuclear weapons, and that's why the president wants to build a peace shield.' The stick people and the sun frown as big red missiles come booming at them; but happily a dome-like arc is drawn over the scene just in time and the missiles bounce off harmlessly. 'It would stop missiles in outer space so they couldn't hit our house,' continues the voice, 'then nobody could win a war ...' The arc becomes a rainbow and the people and the sun smile. The house unfurls an American flag. 'My daddy's smart.'

they say: 'We won't get the money unless we do it in space.' It's all circular. No one other than the president has made a clear statement, but no one among the Americans whom Europeans talk to thinks his concept is anything other than nonsense and fantasy.

That may be a little harsh. But certainly those who advised President Reagan before his initial speech do not appear to have thought through the implications of what they were proposing. In the circumstances, it was hardly surprising that even those disposed to be sympathetic to Star Wars sometimes ended up adding to the confusion. A case in point was an editorial in the usually level-headed *Economist* on 3 August 1985. The magazine carried on its cover a picture of a devastated Hiroshima in 1945, with the caption: 'The case for Star Wars'. (It could equally well have labelled the picture 'The case for CND', or shown a picture of London or Paris, fully restored and at peace for forty years, under the headline 'The case for deterrence'.) The editorial began, strikingly, like this:

> The time is, let us say, 1925. The French army possesses a force of about 8,000 tanks, impervious to machine-guns and ordinary artillery and unstoppable by other tanks, which can crunch its way through to Berlin within 24 hours. The German army has about 8,000 tanks of its own which can do the same to Paris. The conventional wisdom of 1925, nodding sagely, says that this will prevent another Great War because both sides know that if they march for the other's capital they will lose their own: it is the safety of deterrence. Enter an inventor, claiming that he thinks he knows how to make an anti-tank weapon which can stop at least a fair proportion of these hitherto unstoppable monsters. Is he told to forget it?

Assuming that no one could answer 'Yes', the *Economist* proceeded to the point:

> On next Tuesday's 40th anniversary of the dropping of the atomic bomb on Hiroshima, a world which has long believed that the only defence against nuclear mass slaughter is to threaten nuclear mass counter-slaughter should be contemplating the nuclear equivalent of that parable of the tanks.

Certainly it should, yet not in the manner the *Economist*'s leader writer was suggesting. Soon after 1925 the French *did* believe they had come up with a weapon which could 'stop at least a fair proportion of these hitherto unstoppable monsters'. It was called the Maginot Line. Only it ended up stopping precious little. Had France decided to stick with its force of

'8,000 tanks' it might well have wound up defeating the Germans, not losing to them, as it did. Besides, as the *Economist*'s own front cover graphically illustrated, there is a world of difference between tanks and nuclear weapons. Nuclear deterrence works precisely because nuclear weapons *can* inflict such ghastly destruction: if the French had had 8,000 nuclear weapons rather than tanks, Hitler would have had to be very mad indeed to have attacked them.

On one count, at least, there was agreement between Washington and the European allies. Whatever the doubts about Star Wars – what Caspar Weinberger, the defence secretary, called Reagan's 'inspiring vision' – no one doubted the need for *research*. This belief, of course, was enshrined in the Reagan–Thatcher Camp David accords. And it was easy to see why.

From the beginning, the Russians had attacked Star Wars noisily, self-righteously and at every available opportunity. But for all the moral outrage they expressed, they were scarcely innocents in the field. They themselves were busy exploring potential defensive weapons too – indeed, as one US official put it, America was in some respects the 'Johnny-come-lately' in the business.

Let us glance back a moment. The Russians, like the Americans, began working on anti-missile defences in the late 1940s, and in the 1960s they constructed an actual system round Moscow. It was, to be sure, a crude affair, and unlikely to stop much. But it was enough to spur Washington to launch an ABM programme of its own (and also to ensure that Washington pressed ahead with the development of multi-warhead missiles – mirvs). Eventually, as we have observed, both sides decided to forswear proper defences by signing the ABM treaty in 1972, which outlawed the testing or deployment of weapons in space. The Russians, fearing America's vaunted edge in high technology, showed themselves anxious to avoid an additional arms race in anti-missile systems, while Washington, for its part, had been at best half-hearted about ABM development. There was little support for ABMs in Congress, where they were seen as likely to cost vast sums and prove ultimately futile. A leakproof system did not look remotely feasible, and although the ABM treaty *did* allow the construction of two ABM systems per side (later reduced to one), Washington chose not to make use of this concession. So while the Kremlin preserved their Galosh network round Moscow, the Americans were quick to mothball one they had planned to deploy at a missile field in Grand Forks, North Dakota. Basically, the ABM treaty codified one of the central truths of the nuclear age, however perverse it might seem: that attempting to defend yourself would lead only to an intensified arms race and make the world more unstable for both sides.

Security, as Winston Churchill had put it in the 1950s, would be 'the twin brother of annihilation, and safety the sturdy child of terror'.

Despite this, the Russians have never quite accepted the notion of a defence-free world. They have espoused, instead, a policy of 'damage limitation'. Their civil defence effort has always been on a grander scale than America's; they have ploughed more money into hardening missile silos and command centres – and into anti-aircraft defences. In some estimates, they have spent, during the 1970s and early 1980s, as much on defence as they have on offence.

In doing this they have taken full advantage of their licence under the ABM treaty to modernize their Galosh system round Moscow, deploying, in the early 1980s, two new kinds of anti-missile missile, the SH-04, designed to hit warheads in space, and the SH-08, designed for striking warheads which have re-entered the earth's atmosphere and are on their way down to their targets in the 're-entry phase'. In the early 1980s, too, the Russians have been developing a new 'high-performance' surface-to-air missile, the SA-12 (codenamed 'Gladiator' by Nato), supposedly for use against aircraft but capable of striking targets at a height of more than 100,000 ft. In 1983 and 1984 the SA-12 was tested on several occasions against a 'target vehicle' sent into space by a tactical missile. Pentagon officials accepted the tests as legal under the terms of the ABM treaty but pointed out that the SA-12 could eventually be capable of intercepting incoming warheads, especially if armed with a nuclear warhead itself.

In addition to this, the Russians have constructed six large, 'phased-array' radars which could, the Pentagon believe, form the basis for a nationwide ABM system. One of these has been built just outside the village of Abalakovo, near Krasnoyarsk, in the heart of Siberia. A large building, about 100 yards long and 22 storeys high, it touched off a flap in Washington when it was discovered, already half complete, by US intelligence in 1983. The Krasnoyarsk area had not been subject to intensive satellite surveillance because no one had expected the Russians to build there. Under the conditions of the ABM treaty, phased-array radars are supposed to be built only on the perimeter of each superpower, not inland; on the perimeter, they can perform the vital role of providing warning of a nuclear attack; inland, they can theoretically also be used to 'service' an ABM system (by passing on precise information about incoming missiles to battle management radars which would in turn be linked to anti-missile rockets).

The arguments about Krasnoyarsk are complex. The Russians may have built their radar where they did, not so much to service an ABM system as because it was difficult to build it elsewhere: the north-eastern border of Russia, beyond Krasnoyarsk, is impossibly marshy in summer and frozen solid above the permafrost in winter. There are no proper roads or railway lines. Clearly, the Kremlin wanted to plug a gap in the 'early warning' coverage offered by its existing five radars, and Krasnoyarsk did this, enabling them to monitor the flight path which American submarine-launched missiles would take if fired from the Pacific at the Soviet SS18 and SS19 missile fields to the south. But the fact is that Krasnoyarsk constitutes a violation of the ABM treaty. And by building it, the Russians have strengthened the hands of those advocating Star Wars and, to an extent, complicated the task of those opposing it.

But only to an extent. Many defence and Soviet analysts find far-fetched the notion that Russia is preparing to 'break out' of the ABM treaty and construct, with great speed, an effective defence against American missiles. Most of what they have done is entirely consistent with the ABM treaty, and though Krasnoyarsk is an exception, there are even doubts about this. The main dissent from the US interpretation comes from Britain. The Russians claim that their Abalakovo radar is primarily designed for tracking objects in space, a function permitted by the treaty. The British government has argued that it will be impossible to tell whether the Russian claim is true or not until the radar is switched on and becomes fully operational. Because of its 'special relationship' with America, Britain is in a strong position to judge (it has access to much of the intelligence data on the radar), and Downing Street's attitude has irritated, even amazed Washington. 'I am dumbfounded by the British attitude to this,' one US offcial told me. 'It seems to me they've been bending over backwards to justify the Soviet position. It's uncharacteristic.'

Perhaps. But what underlay the British case was a relatively benign assessment of the *military* importance of the new Soviet radar. While Pentagon officials worried that it could have been built to play a key role in an ABM system, this was widely disputed, and not just in London. A report by British intelligence analysts to the Cabinet's Joint Intelligence Committee in January 1985 (first revealed by the American magazine, *National Journal*) concluded that Abalakovo was 'unlikely' to be able to serve as an ABM radar. Interestingly, the British report drew on a secret CIA assessment, completed in 1984, which came to a similar view.

A number of experts, including some administration officials, have confirmed this assessment. They say that the radar's face is not set at an optimal angle for ABM battle management; that there are no interceptor missiles or associated radars near the site (of the kind necessary in an ABM system); and that it will operate at the wrong frequency for a battle management radar. (They can tell from the way the transmitters are spaced out.) Finally, Abalakovo has not been specially 'hardened' and presents a large and extremely vulnerable target – one likely to be 'taken out' quite easily at the beginning of a war. The best guess, say these experts, is that it is an early warning radar in the wrong place, built inland because of the difficulties of construction on the Siberian border. (The Russians, in various unofficial forums, have themselves attempted to indicate that this is precisely what it is.)

Thus, while Washington are clearly right that the radar constitutes a violation of the treaty, it scarcely appears to present a grave threat. The same, according to many analysts, is true of other aspects of the Soviet strategic defence programme. Though the Russians are certainly modernizing their ABM system round Moscow, the new types of interceptor – SH-04s and SH-08s – are both nuclear-tipped, which would cause problems if they were ever used, since the first to explode would probably blind the tracking radars; the radars themselves, colourfully códenamed (by Nato) Pawn Shop and Flat Twin, are also relatively old-fashioned (Pawn Shop operates entirely mechanically; Flat Twin, slightly more advanced, is half mechanical, half electronic). The technology, in short, is on a par with what the Americans were exploring in the late 1960s when they planned, but subsequently abandoned, construction of their anti-missile system in North Dakota. The fear among some in the administration is that the Russians are secretly building and stockpiling a large number of these components for their new system (codenamed ABM-X-3), so that they can use them, eventually, to defend not just Moscow but the rest of the country too. There is no evidence to support this. The building work on ABM-X-3 appears to be leisurely, and is not expected to be complete until 1987. And at the research and testing site of Shary Sagan in south central Asia and other major Soviet facilities, there is apparently no sign of the kind of frenetic activity which might be consistent with a massive production effort.

Despite this, the Reagan administration's rhetoric about the Soviet defence programme became increasingly alarmist. 'When you look at what the Soviets are doing in both strategic offence and defence,' said the president in October 1985, 'you realize that our SDI research programme is crucial to maintain the military balance and protect the liberty and freedom of the West.'

In the same month, Caspar Weinberger went even further. The Russians, he charged in a speech in Philadelphia, had abandoned 'the notion of deterrence through agreed mutual vulnerability' and were racing ahead with their own anti-missile defence programme.

Yet the Defense Intelligence Agency, the most hard-line of the American intelligence agencies – initially set up because the CIA was considered insufficiently alarmist about the Soviet threat – has estimated in declassified testimony that it would take the Russians 'up to ten years' to 'break out' of the ABM treaty (in which time, of course, America could do the same). And a study done for the Joint Chiefs of Staff in 1985, drawing on DIA material, assumed, apparently, that while in ten years America might be able to field a reasonably effective space-based anti-missile shield, Russia would by then be capable only of a relatively crude ground-based defence.

Testimony by the Pentagon's Research and Engineering Department backed this up. In surveying 20 areas of high technology, it identified the Americans as behind the Russians in none, equal to them in five and ahead in 15 (even though in some of these it suggested the gap was closing). Some officials dispute the report, pointing out that the Russians are ahead in some areas of laser and particle beam research, but even if that is true, and if the Russians have developed a capacity to blind American satellites with laser beams, few believe that they are anywhere near achieving sufficiently powerful lasers to shoot down missiles. Besides, in the most crucial area of all – computers – the Pentagon suggested that the American lead was actually increasing. (The Russians are still struggling to master 'third generation' computers, whereas the Americans have already mastered the fourth generation, able to transact 100 million instructions per second and, as we have seen, are working on a fifth generation.) Lieutenant General James Abrahamson, SDI's director, states that: 'In the key technologies needed for a broader defence, such as data processing and computer software, we are far, far ahead.'

The Pentagon's rhetoric about the Soviet anti-missile effort reminded some defence experts of the alarm over the alleged 'missile gap' between Russia and America in the early 1960s (there was a gap – in America's favour). These experts accept that the Russians take defence very seriously (after all, as one analyst put it, they have tried to protect their national capital: America, though it could have opted to do so, did not). They accept, too, that the Russians have spent a lot of money on air defence, civil defence and the like (though a survey among thousands of Russian émigrés in America conducted during the years of the Reagan administration found the evidence of a massive Russian civil defence effort very flimsy). What many experts did not accept was that the Russians were about to break out of the ABM treaty, or that Moscow believed it could construct anything resembling an effective defensive system.

Weinberger's argument that the Russians have abandoned deterrence, therefore, appears to be stretching a point. Arguably, in fact, the Russians have taken certain steps since the late 1970s which *reduce* their incentive to build a full-blown defence. They have developed two types of land-based mobile missile, the SS24 and the SS25, and though the SS25 constitutes a breach of the Salt Two treaty which permits the building of only *one* new missile per side, the decision to 'go mobile' is one which, in principle, many analysts welcome. (It will make Russia's land-based force less vulnerable, thus reducing the temptation for the Kremlin to 'use it or lose it'.) And the Abalakovo radar, for all the controversy it has created, is stabilizing in the sense that it completes the early warning coverage of what might, in a crisis, be a very nervous Kremlin.

Then there is the evidence of Soviet military doctrine. In the 1960s and early 1970s, as we have noted, a number of prominent military men in Russia made statements suggesting that a nuclear war might be winnable. Such statements are not heard nowadays. Since around 1977, Russian political leaders'and some Russian generals too have stressed that nuclear war would .lead to catastrophe for both sides – and, significantly, there have been no statements to the contrary. The Russians may not have a word for deterrence, and they may not call the balance of terror 'mutually assured destruction', but they nevertheless appear to accept the concept. Besides, if what the Pentagon fears is a Russian break-out from the ABM treaty then Reagan's Star Wars initiative, far from encouraging Soviet restraint, is likely to have the opposite effect.

In June 1985, for example, a prominent Soviet analyst, with ties to Gorbachev, told an assembled group of Washington's defence and Soviet specialists that the key to stability was each side's capacity to deliver a crushing retaliatory blow against the other. Against this background, he said, SDI marked a qualitative change. But SDI wasn't going to work, he went on. It was a non-starter technically. Consequently, therefore, there must be *another* aim behind the initiative. The official proceeded to spell out the common Soviet view that because of the contradictions SDI *must* be designed for offensive purposes, in order to give America a first strike capability over Russia. We have worst-case planners, too, he said. We also have to be pessimistic. The implication – that Moscow would react to the American programme, and react strongly – was clear enough.

Some in Washington, indeed, were concerned that Reagan's Star Wars plan might give the Russians an excuse and an incentive to effect the very 'break-out' from the ABM treaty which everyone feared. In a Senate Armed Services Committee hearing in March 1984, a year after Reagan's speech, Sam Nunn, the Democrats' leading defence expert, raised this question with Richard Perle, the administration's deputy under-secretary for international security policy. 'I am ... concerned,' said Nunn, 'that the Soviets may feel they have been given help, public opinion-wise, because the President made such a pitch publicly about what we were going to do in the whole ABM area and how that was such a wonderful thing for world peace. It seems to me they have been given a carte blanche propaganda tool they can use very much to go along with an ABM break-out [i.e. a sudden decision to flout the treaty and go flat-out to erect a defence]. I don't think the President intended to do that. I am not suggesting that.' But that, clearly, was the danger. 'All they have to do is quote back how these ballistic missiles defences are wonderful for peace and make the world safe and abolish offensive weapons and all that business ...' Perle elected to address the question off the record, but many in Washington shared precisely the fear which Nunn expressed.

What, then, were Reagan's critics recommending?

First, that quiet, low-key research, such as that which had been proceeding before Star Wars arrived, was important and should continue: it provided a 'hedge' against possible Soviet breakthroughs and might even one day, far off into the next millennium, yield the kind of technology which *would* make population defence thinkable. (The Star Wars initiative, on the other hand, with the political heat it generated, seemed calculated only to raise false hopes and to spur the Russians on to greater efforts.)

Second, the critics believed that the key to preventing an unconstrained and horrifically expensive space race lay in arms control. In order to succeed, an arms control deal, like previous deals, would have to be modest, and though precisely what could happen in negotiations is beyond the scope of this book, the shape of such a deal is apparent as I write: it would involve both sides accepting that research must go on, a cast-iron commitment to the ABM treaty (with considerable tightening of its language and with the Reagan administration agreeing, perhaps indefinitely, to renounce testing and deployment of space-based systems), and cuts – perhaps quite substantial cuts – in the offensive forces of both sides. Conceivably, both sides could also agree to modify the ABM treaty to allow more extensive deployment of ground-based defences for protecting missile silos (if this were done as part of an arms control agreement it might win the political support in America it would otherwise lack, though, as I have suggested, it might not be sensible). But, perhaps most crucially of all, a new treaty would outlaw or dramatically constrain testing of anti-satellite weapons, or ASATs.

ASATs, of course, are already with us. The Russians have a fully tested system and the Americans, at the time of writing, are beginning to test one. The prospect of large-scale ASAT deployment, however, still lies in the future: it is in neither side's interest for it to happen. If it *does* happen the West will suffer the most. From Nato's point of view, indeed, it is hard to imagine a more nonsensical weapon than one capable of destroying satellites.

Satellites play many critical roles. In a crisis, for example, reconnaissance satellites would be vital to provide early warning of a possible nuclear attack. If one side was able to blind the other by knocking out its reconnaissance satellites the dangers would be intense: the side which had been blinded might suspect it was about to be attacked and, in the circumstances, decide to get its blow in first. Blinding your adversary in the nuclear age, as E. P. Velikhov, the vice president of the Soviet Academy of Sciences, puts it, would be 'tantamount to repeating the biblical story of Samson. The blinded adversary will let the skies fall on his head and on the enemy's head, too, of course.'

Those in the Pentagon who dislike the idea of an ASAT ban rest their case on two arguments. First, they say, an ASAT ban would be impossible. The Russians have already deployed a system: it is small, and could be easily hidden in holes in the ground. There would be no chance of the West's being able adequately to verify that the ban was being observed.

But the Russian ASAT is a very crude device. It weighs two tons and has to be propelled into space by a huge, liquid-fuelled, SS9 booster rocket. It is so crude that it has little chance of success unless it is fired from the ground when the designated target is immediately overhead, which means that its firing crew may have to wait up to 24 hours for the turn of the earth to bring it into the right position. Then, once this blunderbuss is launched, it cannot make a direct ascent but has to do at least one and probably two orbits of the earth before it is ready to blow up its target with a warhead which explodes in a hail of shrapnel. This process may take up to three hours, and after that time the odds are still high that the Russian ASAT will miss: in 20 tests between the 1960s and mid-1985, almost half have been failures. (The new American ASAT, by contrast, is much more sophisticated: launched by an F15 jet fighter at a height of about 18 miles, it can speed towards its target, boosted by a two-stage solid-fuelled rocket, at 500 miles a minute, much faster than its Russian counterpart, and it can *theoretically* reach that target in only half an orbit.)

The argument that a ban is impossible because of the existing Russian ASAT is nonsense. In the first place, if forbidden to carry out further testing, the Russians would soon lose any vestige of confidence they may currently have in their system. At the same time, some relatively modest changes in American satellites could make them unassailable unless the Americans developed something new: these changes would involve building better-protected satellites, making them more agile, so that they could take evasive action if threatened, and, in some cases, sending them into higher orbit (much of which is being done anyway). Given this, the Russians would derive no benefit at all from secretly storing their current ASAT weapons in holes in the ground.

The second argument that can be heard in defence of ASATs is more complicated. It goes like this. Nato is an alliance divided by water: in a war on the Central Front it would depend on being able to bring vital reinforcements and supplies across to Europe *by sea*. The Soviets, however, would be able to use their ocean reconnaissance satellites called RORSATs to track allied shipping and make it possible for submarines, and perhaps bombers too, to wreak havoc. To protect its convoys, therefore, the West has no option but to develop ASATs so that if a war breaks out it can destroy the Soviet RORSATs.

This argument is as untenable as the first one. For one thing, the US navy believes it is already able to interfere heavily with RORSATs (by jamming and other electronic means). Even if the navy exaggerates its capacity (as some believe it does), the West is overall much more dependent on satellites than the East, whatever the danger posed by RORSATs. The Warsaw Pact, for example, can depend on land lines for communications; Nato cannot.* And for intelligence reconnaissance and surveillance, too, the West depends on satellites to a much greater extent than the Warsaw Pact.

There remains only one argument left to justify ASATs, and it is an argument not much aired in public. The argument is that Star Wars will not be possible if ASATs are banned. Under the ABM treaty, it is permissible to proceed with ASAT testing, and this loophole, the Pentagon hopes, will enable it to test some of the technology which will eventually be vital for SDI. Many SDI weapons, indeed, will have to perform a very similar role to ASATs, only, as well as satellites, they will have to be able to shoot down missiles too. So by agreeing to an ASAT ban the Pentagon would be agreeing to radical constraints on the Star Wars programme. It does not wish to do that. Thus the Reagan administration's certification to Congress that it was negotiating in good faith to ban ASATs in arms control could be compared, as Republican Senator Charles Mathias put it, to the game played by Alice in *Through the Looking Glass*, in which she tried to believe 'as many as six impossible things before breakfast'.

The arms control deal I have suggested would scarcely represent a dramatic breakthrough. Smallish cuts in missile arsenals, a recommitment to the ABM treaty (a way would have to be found of solving the problem of Krasnoyarsk), and a ban on ASAT tests would scarcely amount to the 'inspired vision' of SDI. But in a profoundly complicated and divided world, it is probably the best that can be hoped for. An ASAT deal, in particular, might avert a race in especially silly and destabilizing weapons. (Arguably, too, the West should seek a ban on ATBMs – anti-*tactical* ballistic missiles. These are systems potentially capable of shooting down medium- and short-range ballistic missiles – systems like the Soviet SA12, which, though ostensibly an anti-aircraft weapon, has been tested in an ATBM role. The West has nothing comparable to the SA12, and a ban on ATBMs would close a major loophole in the ABM treaty.)

---

* The present generation of Soviet ASATs cannot threaten communications satellites, since these are in geosynchronous orbit, and beyond its range. But future generations undoubtedly will.

The irony of Star Wars, of course, is that by launching it, and by scaring the Soviets, Ronald Reagan may have put himself in a better position to achieve such a deal than any previous administration. 'I don't think this genie should ever have been let out of the bottle,' remarked one very senior American official to a friend in early 1985, 'but now that it has I'm going to make them pay to stuff it back in again.' And as John Newhouse, who worked for the Arms Control and Disarmament Agency during the Carter administration, observed, the Soviets might be prepared to pay:

> Their internal problems are a litany of woes; their empire in Eastern
> Europe is trembling on its foundations; and they are caught up in
> an unending race with the United States – a faster horse – round the
> weapons-technology track.

At the time of writing, however, the prospect of such a deal does not look likely. True, the opposition to SDI is likely to grow. There are signs that the chiefs of staff, who rashly endorsed the project in 1983, are beginning to have second thoughts: as pressures on the defence budget grow they will face hard choices, and SDI is unlikely to seem a priority to their various services (though the chief of naval operations, Admiral Watkins, remains personally devoted). And to be sure, defence projects *have* been cancelled in the past: take the embryonic ABM system of the late 1960s, or America's once extensive air defence network, or the Divad Gun. A wise investor does not pour 'good money after bad', say the optimists, and sooner or later the American government, which is strongly influenced by economic forces, will have to drop Star Wars whether it does a deal or not – better, then, to do a deal while the currency is still worth something.

Whatever happens, though, Ronald Reagan will never persuade the Russians to accept not just disarmament but Star Wars too. As a *Washington Post* columnist put it, asking them to 'accept an entirely new and staggeringly expensive competition to build defensive weapons' together with 'the elimination of a large fraction of their offensive weapons' is like telling them 'there's about to be a famine, so please throw out all the canned food in your basement'. It just won't happen. Arms control and Star Wars will not be able to coexist, and if Star Wars does not die then arms control surely will. Not only will the prospect of all future agreement evaporate, but so will existing ones (such as the ABM treaty), as both sides engage in an out-and-out race in defensive and offensive arms.

The trouble is, however, that despite the talk of arms control there are a significant number of people in Washington who would welcome precisely that. Ronald Reagan may believe that both Star Wars and arms control are achievable, but they do not. They believe that arms control, as practised to date, has been a one-way street, both pointless and dangerous, and they would gladly be rid of it. The Kremlin, they argue, has consistently fared better at the bargaining table than the White House: unfettered by public opinion, as democratic governments are, it has been able to play a tougher hand and to lull America into a false sense of security, while, unnoticed by the public, the military balance has tilted dangerously in favour of the East. Not only that: the Soviets have not even respected the agreements they have signed. They have brazenly cheated (as in the case of the Krasnoyarsk radar).

Those who doubt the value of existing agreements say that what they are after is 'real' arms control, but the kind of agreements they envisage are now, and will always be, beyond the bounds of the possible. What these people believe, then, is that America will have to resign itself to an arms race, and that it had therefore better try to win it.

Star Wars, from this perspective, makes sense. The US would almost certainly *lose* a purely offensive arms race; the Soviets would be able to deploy more new missiles, and deploy them faster (as they have done, indeed, for years). Take MX: initial plans to deploy 200 under Carter had shrunk by 1985 to 50 in vulnerable silos. And some Pentagon officials wonder gloomily whether America will *ever* be able to win support for another land-based missile after MX.

But in an arms race involving both offensive *and* defensive weapons (say the hard-liners) America would have some advantages. First, the Russians would be forced to divert rivers of roubles from potentially lethal missiles into relatively harmless defensive systems (a bonus for America); second, the Soviets would be competing with America in an area where America would indisputably be strongest – at the leading edge of technology. What's more, says this school of thought, the Russians would never be able to keep building their offensive forces, *and* develop countermeasures to America's Star Wars programme, *and* build their own Star Wars at the same time – they simply would not be able to afford it.

Under this logic, therefore, the hard-liners not only do not care whether arms control collapses: they want it to. They want to make the American Star Wars programme unstoppable by the time Reagan leaves office in 1989 and, to this end, they believe that if the Soviets start working flat-out on space systems, and flagrantly 'break out' of the ABM treaty, then this will help their cause. Congressmen will see what is happening and realize that America has no alternative but to follow suit, and they will cough up the funds accordingly. Otherwise, as one insider put it, they will be faced with a 'technological Pearl Harbor' – a world in which Russia has a defensive shield and America does not (we will return to this in a moment). What the hard-liners want, then, is an out-and-out offence-defence race. They believe that the US may eventually emerge on top: the

Soviet economy, already perilously strained, will be unable to stand the competition. America will have restored its 'lost security' not through arms control but through its own technological efforts. ('The days when we were the only bully on the block with a big stick have gone,' as one SDI researcher puts it. 'Some of the advocates of SDI believe that if we can take Russia's stick away and go back to being the only bully on the block then we'll be all right again.') Russia, finally, will collapse, bankrupt, on to the 'ash heap of history'. That vision, it seems to me, is the real driving force behind Star Wars.

On 31 July 1984, the official Soviet newspaper, *Pravda*, ran a piece under the headline 'Dangerous Illusions in Washington'. The article was not about Star Wars, but about cruise missiles, which the newspaper attacked as follows. The United States, it said, 'once sought to outdistance the Soviet Union in ballistic missiles, and that did not work ... It tried with independently targetable multiple re-entry vehicles, MIRVs, and again that did not work. It won't work this time either.' For all the piece's bluster and self-righteousness, *Pravda* had a point. America invented mirvs, but the Soviets soon caught up, and because they began with bigger missiles (and less public opinion problems) deployed more of them than America. Similarly, America devised cruise missiles as a system which it would take the Soviets years and billions of roubles to match. But two months after the *Pravda* article appeared, the first Soviet cruise missile deployments, on submarines and bombers, were announced. In the long run, as we have seen, this development will probably turn out to be against Western interests, too. The *Pravda* article did not mention Star Wars, but the implication was clear: if the US did it they would do it too. (Indeed, many believe that Russia will only ever become *capable* of building Star Wars if America pioneers the ground first: just as Moscow made the crucial breakthrough in mirv technology by acquiring vital components from the West, so they would probably have to acquire crucial pieces of Star Wars technology from America in order to construct defences.)*

If the US and the Soviets do begin a flat-out arms race in defensive and offensive weapons, there is no guarantee that the US will 'win' it, even if it had anything to gain by so doing. It is not just the Russians who would have to find enormous sums of money. The only certainty is that the race itself would be extraordinarily dangerous. On this we can call in the

---

* When the Russians first attempted mirving, in the 1960s, they ran into all kinds of snags because they lacked the precision tools necessary to manufacture key components of a mirv guidance system (specifically, the requisite ball bearings). Their problems were resolved at the beginning of the 1970s when they acquired 100 Centaline machines from the United States. The sale was approved over the objections of the Pentagon.

testimony of Caspar Weinberger, who calls Star Wars 'an inspired vision'. 'It takes very little imagination to realize what a vastly more dangerous world this would be if they [the Soviets] attained this ability to destroy our missiles, and we did not have a similar capability,' he said on one occasion. And on another: 'If the Soviets get strategic defence and we don't, it would be very much like the world in which the Soviets had a nuclear weapon and we did not.'

If Russia gets Star Wars and America does not, in other words, then America will be at a desperate disadvantage. It will know that Russia can attack it with impunity (or relative impunity). But what happens if America gets Star Wars first? Would not the world suddenly become 'vastly more dangerous' for the Russians? Would they not suddenly realize that America had the potential to strike *them* with relative impunity? There are some who say that the Russians could not possibly believe that, on the grounds that the West are the 'white hats' and not aggressive, but this is naive in the extreme. *Whichever* side lost a Star Wars race would feel desperately insecure, and almost certainly put its offensive forces on a hair trigger. And the fact that whichever side 'won' would probably end up with a less than effective system does not change the argument. As Richard Garwin points out, even a dud strategic defence could threaten stability. 'Think of a plastic gun used in a robbery. Thieves armed with nothing more have been shot and killed.'

The truth about a Star Wars race is that the *winning* side – the side which got Star Wars first – would have acquired, in the eyes of the *losing* side, a 'first strike capability' much more real than any which could come from offensive missiles alone. For the sake of argument, let us assume that America wins the space race. As seen from the Kremlin, America would now be in a position to land a crushing nuclear blow, knocking out many Russian missiles, while at the same time being protected against the inevitably 'ragged' retaliatory strike which Russia would then be capable of sending back. Would the Russians allow this to happen? They would know that they might come off better if they struck first: that way, using *all their missiles*, they would have a good chance of overwhelming America's defence with sheer numbers – it might seem preferable to being destroyed and unable to mount a proper retaliatory strike. So Star Wars could, contrary to the wishes of its advocates, make both sides not less but much more jumpy than they are now.

The situation, as one prominent defence analyst puts it, can be expressed in medieval terms. Imagine two knights, each of whom possesses only a sword, he says: that is the situation we are in now. Each can strike the other, but he knows that if he does he will be struck back. But suppose one of the knights obtains a shield. Then he knows that he can strike the other with impunity – and catch the return blow on his shield. That is

what the world would be like if one side got Star Wars and the other
didn't. The analogy can be carried further: if both sides got swords and
shields then each would strive to find another weapon – say, a mace – in
order to be able to disarm *both* the other's sword *and* his shield ... An
SDI race, in other words, would be dangerous throughout: in an atmosphere
of distrust, with no arms control, and each side fearful that the other
might achieve a workable defence first, there would be frequent temptations
for small-scale attacks on satellites or even pre-emptive strikes. The race
would be one which neither side could afford to lose, and each side might
simply decide to shoot down any weapon put into orbit above its territory.
Only with extraordinary cooperation between the superpowers would Star
Wars make sense, and the irony of the project is that those who advocate
it most strongly are those least disposed to believe in the likelihood of
such cooperation. Besides, such a perfect relationship as here envisaged
would surely obviate the need for Star Wars.

And even were both sides to reach the promised land of fully deployed
defences, neither's would be perfect, and both would be dependent on
what one scientist described as 'paranoid computers' – computers which
would be primed to react to the slightest sign of a possible attack, whether
it be a genuine threat or an accidental one (such as a stray satellite moving
too close to a sensitive platform). These computers could interact in
frightening ways, and it is not beyond the bounds of possibility, as we saw
earlier, that they could actually cause a nuclear war.

Finally, it is worth returning to the matter of cost. No one has a clue
as to what this might be. Estimates range the whole way up to a trillion
dollars. It could of course be higher (especially if improved air defences
to deal with cruise missiles, etc, are added in). Most defence projects, as
we have seen, end up costing far more than anyone anticipates, and for
something as vast and teeming with unknown engineering problems as
Star Wars (it would be the biggest enterprise ever undertaken in the history
of mankind) this would be truer than ever.

In the early 1970s, when James Schlesinger served in the White House
budget office, one of his responsibilities was to review the US army's plans
for the construction of the 'Safeguard' defensive system then being
contemplated for protecting American missile fields. 'The Safeguard
system,' he says, 'turned out to be the only weapon system development
in my experience in which staggering overruns were already revealed *prior*
to the inception of work.'

What would be the consequences of expending billions in a vast and
probably futile and unnecessary attempt to bolster deterrence? There would
be a shortage of funds for other things. Money spent on Star Wars is
money *not* spent on something else, and either the defence budget would
have to expand dramatically – an unlikely event given America's ballooning

budget deficit – or the Pentagon would have to change its priorities. Let us glance back again to what happened when Safeguard was on the drawing board:

The fiscal 1971 budget, first submitted by the Pentagon, proposed a reduction of seven army divisions and a substantial Europeanization of European defence. Of course, the Army did have the honour of developing the Safeguard system. But it also seemed embarked on the path to eating itself out of house and home – at the cost of its conventional capabilities.

If Star Wars ever goes ahead, this problem will recur – on an infinitely grander scale. The sums poured into constructing the fantastic gadgetry of Star Wars would be money which, if properly applied, could make a huge difference to America's conventional forces, perhaps the difference, in a war, between whether or not nuclear weapons had to be used.

No wonder, then, that Sir Geoffrey Howe should worry in his speech to the Royal United Services Institute about the effect of Star Wars 'on all the other elements of our defences, on which Western security will continue in large part to depend'. All the evidence suggests that pursuing the chimera of a space-based defence (unless the Russians make it impossible not to do so) would be a disastrous course. It would be disastrous not because it is based on an ignoble vision – it is not – nor because scientists are incapable of devising gadgets to shoot down missiles – that, some day, may be possible – and not because 'live Americans' are not better than 'dead Russians' (to use the false choice often put), but because, considered in terms of what it would have to achieve, it *would not work*. It is not a project worth betting the future of the Western world on. Its legacy would be utterly different from Reagan's vision of what it might be, and almost entirely bad. It would cripple arms control, and it would place a great and perhaps intolerable strain on the Western Alliance – an alliance which, as we will see in the next chapter, will have problems enough to overcome in the years ahead without the burden of Star Wars.

13

The Future of Nato

In late 1981, during the superpower talks about Euromissiles in Geneva, Yuli Kvitsinsky, the chief Soviet negotiator, told Paul Nitze, his American counterpart, the following story:

A bear was travelling by train when he noticed, hopping along in the corridor outside his compartment, a rabbit. The rabbit seemed nervous, so the bear asked: 'What's the matter, rabbit?' 'I think the inspector is coming,' said the rabbit, 'and I don't have a ticket.' 'Never mind,' said the bear. 'Come in here next to me and I'll protect you.' The rabbit hesitated, but decided he had better do as he was bid. He hopped on the seat next to the bear. Moments later, they heard the inspector coming down the corridor. 'What am I going to do?' said the rabbit anxiously. 'Don't worry,' said the bear. 'I will hold you out of the carriage window by your ears, so the inspector won't be able to see you. Then, when he's gone, you can come back in again.' The rabbit looked rather dubious about this but felt he had no option but to agree. So the bear picked him up by the ears

(and at this point Kvitsinsky clenched his right fist)

and dangled him out of the window. When the inspector came in, the bear showed him his ticket. But the inspector was suspicious. 'What have you got in that hand outside the window?' he asked. 'Oh ... nothing,' said the bear.

And Kvitsinsky suddenly unclenched his fist and held up an empty hand ...

The story was offered to Nitze with no explanation or moral, and Nitze accepted it in the same spirit. It was conceivable, however, that Kvitsinsky had a moral in mind: allies don't matter, he was saying, great powers should abandon them when it seems necessary to do so. Certainly such a moral would have been appropriate, because the Soviets, at the time – during the run-up to the cruise and Pershing deployments in Europe – were attempting both to persuade the Americans to renege on their commitment to deploy (to make the bear drop the rabbit), and to persuade the Europeans that the Americans were not negotiating seriously.

Trying to drive a wedge between America and its allies, of course, has been a long-term preoccupation of Soviet foreign policy, and the impending deployment of cruise missiles provided an opportunity to practise it. The problem, for the West, is that the Alliance is becoming more and more vulnerable to attempts to divide it. Differences between Europe and America are greater now than they have ever been, on a whole variety of issues, and many analysts forecast that things will get worse. The old conventional wisdom, that Nato is forever facing crises and forever weathering them – German rearmament, Suez, France leaving the military structure, the Vietnam War, MLF, INF, and so on – is gradually being replaced by another: that Nato is bound eventually to collapse, and unless dramatic changes are made may do so by the end of the century. An increasing number of people on both sides of the Atlantic are questioning whether it should be preserved, or whether the time has come to tear up the North Atlantic Treaty, send the Supreme Allied Commander back to Washington and pension off the Secretary General.

On the face of it, it would not be altogether surprising if the Alliance was due for a shake-up. If, in the beginning, it was an arrangement whereby the United States provided most of the effective defence of the West while Europe, to everyone's advantage, got on with rebuilding its political and economic institutions, then clearly things have changed.

The idea of being hitched to Europe, in an alliance lasting 40 years, would have been anathema to America's founding fathers. 'Europe has a set of primary interests,' declared George Washington, the first president, as he left office, 'which to us have none, or a very remote relation ... It must be unwise in us to implicate ourselves, by artificial ties, in the ordinary vicissitudes of her politics, or the ordinary combination and collision of her friendships and enmities.'

The current of isolationism runs strongly through American history. In both world wars the US hesitated before becoming involved, and after 1945 many influential figures resisted the notion of an Atlantic alliance on the grounds that America stood to gain little, that it didn't need Europe and that, in the last resort, a Russian takeover of the continent would not matter much. Why not retreat behind the atomic bomb and two oceans and construct a Fortress America? Even President Truman, in the act of sending troops to Europe, made it clear that he found inconceivable the

possibility of a *permanent* American military presence there. In the end
Europe would be strong enough to make the arrangement unnecessary.
'Eventual European unity and European self-defence were corollaries of
the North Atlantic Treaty. It is doubtful whether the US Senate would
have approved of the treaty if it had not been for these two presuppositions,'
observed the historian Theodore Draper in a 1982 article in *Encounter*.

Yet the arrangement persisted, and it did so without Europe moving
towards unity or self-defence, and despite some fundamental changes. In
the first place, the Soviet Union, a 'European' power when the Alliance
began, armed only with conventional weapons, steadily expanded its
influence abroad and built up a nuclear arsenal to rival America's. The
nuclear umbrella which America extended confidently over the Atlantic
came to look less watertight to those it sheltered and more like a lightning
rod to its bearer. Meanwhile, coinciding with Russia's rise to nuclear parity
were profound developments both in America and in Europe.

The changes are familiar enough: America's political centre of gravity
has moved gradually west, and become less Eurocentric. The people who
shaped America's postwar foreign policy were, for the most part, members
of the 'old East Coast establishment' – bankers, lawyers and industrialists
whose views had been shaped in New York and, above all, in Wall Street.
Their understanding of Europe was based on frequent contact with its
institutions and travel to its cities, and their belief that the economic health
of America was intimately bound up with the health of Europe, and that
America would be perilously exposed if the European continent went
Communist, translated into the firm conviction that the forward defence
of America began on the Elbe.

There are still many, in the State Department and the Pentagon, who
hold this transatlantic view. But the influence of the old East Coast
establishment in American politics has declined. As the old smokestack
industries of the north and east have faltered, so new industries, many of
them based round high technology, have sprung up in the west and south.
According to the nationwide census, four million people decamped from
the so-called 'frostbelt' to the 'sunbelt' in the 1970s alone, and the shift
has been reflected in Congress: New York State had 47 representatives in
1946, now it has 34; California had 25 representatives in 1946 and now
has 45. Inevitably, as America's centre of gravity has moved westwards,
Europe has come to seem less important, both culturally, with most of
America's new immigrants coming from Mexico, Central America and
Asia, and economically, with the discovery of new and expanding markets
in the vast Pacific basin. California, after all, is almost twice as far from
Europe as New York is. 'Economically Europe is a good trading partner
for the US,' wrote an international businessman who wants Nato dissolved:

But Japan is a bigger trading partner than any country in Europe and soon will overwhelm Europe in this role. Southeast Asia has some of the fastest developing economies in the world and has more people than all of Western Europe. Then there is East Asia, so vast in its potential as to stagger the imagination. There is also the Pacific rim of South America and beyond that South Asia and Africa wait ... Indeed, when we measure the near-optimized markets of Europe and its 250 million persons against the near-unoptimized 1.5 billion to 2 billion people of the Pacific basin alone, Europe seems a puny affair.

In the pages of the *Wall Street Journal* and elsewhere – once bastions of transatlanticism – such sentiments have become familiar. They are not yet typical, but they may become so. The economic interdependence of Europe and America is no longer as strong as it was. The Atlantic, as Sir Oliver Wright, the British ambassador to Washington, pointed out in a speech in Massachusetts in 1982, has 'grown wider'.

While America has changed, so too has Europe. It is no longer the battered, impoverished continent it was in 1949, when Nato was founded. Theoretically at least, it is capable, now, of defending itself: it has about the same gross national product as the US and it generates more international trade. In some respects it has become an 'economic superpower' in its own right.

But as Europe has got back on its feet, so, as in America, has a new generation come to the fore, a generation more sceptical about military power, more unwilling or unable to understand its role in keeping the peace, less concerned about Russia and less sympathetic towards America. It is a generation which remembers dimly, if at all, the Stalin purges or the building of the Berlin Wall. As one British analyst has noted: 'America does not connote to them the Marshall Plan and the Berlin Airlift, or even John Kennedy, but rather Vietnam and Watergate.'

The starkest evidence of this anti-Americanism is in the European left, and especially in the modern-day peace movement, much stronger and better organized than its 1950s predecessor. To the anti-nuclear left, the overwhelming desire is to be rid of America, and it seems to be this, as much as a fear of nuclear weapons, which lies at the heart of unilateralism. For as Theodore Draper put it in his admirable essay: 'The campaign to get nuclear weapons out of Europe is at the same time a campaign to get the United States out of Europe.'

This campaign reached new heights in the wake of the cruise decision: the nuclear weapons being objected to, of course, were American ones, under the control of a president whom the protesters did not trust. Their fate was in his hands, and in their view the risks of such dependence now greatly outweighed its benefits. Sometimes, indeed, America seemed even *worse* than the Russians. 'The United States seems to me the more dangerous and provocative,' wrote E. P. Thompson in the *New Statesman* in 1981, 'and its general military and diplomatic strategies, which press around the Soviet Union with menacing bases ... It is in Washington, rather than Moscow, that scenarios are dreamed up for "theatre" wars ...'

But where such hyperbole is the hallmark of the anti-nuclear leaders, distrust in American policy has grown in European capitals, too. European governments have become more ready to criticize, and less passive. On the whole, they distrusted Carter as weak and indecisive, but found Reagan's confrontationalist attitude to Russia equally if not more upsetting. Differences of perspective showed up in successive rows – over Poland, Grenada, the building of the Siberian gas pipeline, the handling of international terrorism – as well as in festering disagreements about US policy towards Central America or the Middle East. Though there have always been rows, European leaders, responding to grass-roots pressure, have become less willing to accept US leadership of the Alliance than they once were. Where the leftwing West German politician Egon Bahr may talk, rather absurdly, about the US treating Europe as a protectorate, Helmut Kohl, the West German leader, is making a similar point about the changed relationship, though more politely, when he characterizes the transatlantic relationship as 'friendship and partnership, but not dependency'. Or, as Ambassador Wright said in his Massachusetts speech: 'The change in the power relationship between Europe and America has meant that Europe considers its view of the Soviet Union as valid as America's view and as equally worthy of consideration and discussion.'

At the heart of the changed relationship, of course, is money, and the vexed question of 'burden sharing'. Given its own (relative) rise in wealth, and America's (relative) decline, is Europe doing enough for its own defence? With the surge in American defence spending of the early 1980s has come a parallel surge of resentment against Europe for not paying its way. While the US was increasing its defence budget by around 7 per cent a year, the pledge by the allies to increase theirs by 3 per cent a year was, as one US official put it, 'more honoured in the breach than in the observance'. 'I thought we cut a deal,' one congressman told me, 'but you guys haven't stuck to it.' The American build-up, as he and other politicians were quick to point out, entailed sacrifice: more guns equalled less butter, or at least less help for the poor, and it was not just the American right that complained. Senator Sam Nunn, the clever Georgian Democrat who was chairman of the Senate Armed Services Committee under Carter, consistently gave it as his view that unless Europe got its act together the security commitment might have to be rethought. 'The American poor and working class,' he told a private breakfast on Capitol Hill in 1982, 'are becoming increasingly fed up at having to pay for the defence of the European rich and middle class.'

Administration officials voiced similar emotions. 'We've gutted our social programmes. You have not,' said one State Department man. William Brock, then US trade representative, echoed his sentiments: 'Forty per cent of American workers have had their pay frozen or have actually taken pay cuts. Europeans have made no such adjustments. They're just going their merry way.'

In this atmosphere, the spectacle of regular European anti-nuclear marches did not help. The peace movement seemed, to some US politicians and officials, to exemplify a deeper malaise in Europe ('Protestant angst', Richard Perle called it). The 'rivers of appeasement', it was thought, ran deep. Not only were European governments conspicuously reluctant to pay their share for the common defence, they were seen as failing, at the same time, to mollify the 'cry babies ' (as one White House man-labelled them) who criticized and in an important way *undermined* the defence America was trying to supply. *Not only, it seemed, did Europe not want to be defended by America, but large segments of it did not want to be defended at all.* The sight, on American TV screens, of protesters milling about US bases and shouting abuse at American soldiers hardly enhanced support for the Alliance; apart from anything else the behaviour appeared unfriendly and rude. When London Weekend sent a film crew to a town in the heart of 'middle America', Parma in Ohio, they came back, unsurprisingly, with shots of residents saying they were 'hurt' by Europe's attitude, fed up with its criticism, and convinced, in the words of one businessman, that 'European countries [should] take control of their own destiny'.

This kind of sentiment was reflected in Mansfield-type stirrings in Congress. Former Senator Mike Mansfield of Montana introduced a series of amendments in the early 1970s calling for large-scale troop withdrawals from the Central Front. The amendments always failed, though not always by a large margin, but there are plenty of people in the Congress of the 1980s prepared to pick up this banner. In 1982, the Republican whip in the Senate, Ted Stephens of Alaska, called for a re-examination of America's 'commitment to Europe'; he and Senator Larry Pressler had been dismayed by the 'hostile attitudes' to the US military they discovered on a trip to West Germany. More tangibly, both House and Senate have cut back the funding for some fairly routine European items (such as a Pentagon request for $6 billion towards providing pre-positioned equipment on the Central Front for two extra American divisions intended to reinforce the troops there in time of war). And in 1984 the staunchly pro-Nato Sam

Nunn introduced an amendment which, if passed, would have led to a phased withdrawal of 90,000 US troops from Europe by the end of the 1980s unless Europe took certain steps to boost its own defence. Nunn's salvo was intended as a warning shot across Europe's bow (it was even questionable whether he wanted it to pass), but it illustrated how the irritation with Europe in the Senate was not limited to one party or the other but was becoming more and more widespread. 'Uncle Sam,' as one Midwest senator put it, 'just can't do it all any more.'

The 'case against Europe' was often exaggerated. Uncle Sam was not doing it all, or anything like it. As their ambassadors in Washington were frequently pointing out, European nations would supply 85 per cent of the ground forces and 80 per cent of the aircraft at the outset of a war on the Central Front (though the arrival of American reinforcements would radically change that ratio). But disagreements between West and West have grown steadily more difficult to resolve, and the prospect of Nato falling, or drifting apart, is no longer unthinkable.

The unhappiness on both sides of the Atlantic feeds on itself, symbiotically. The American deficit is like a cancer: its effects, hidden at first, are liable to become more visible, and as it takes its toll the American defence budget will come under more and more strain. As that happens, the cries to reduce the 'European' share will intensify.

The precise size of that share is hard to measure, but a fair estimate is about 30 per cent. The Pentagon, in 1984, counted the 'incremental operating costs' of stationing US forces in Europe at about $2 billion, the total cost of European-deployed forces and early reinforcements at $90 billion and the total cost of *all* forces which might be committed to a European war at about $177 billion. Some analysts use even higher figures. They point out that most equipment currently being designed and built for US forces (such as the M1 tank and the Bradley) is designed with Europe in mind, and that the whole *thrust* of American army and air force procurement is Europe-orientated. One analyst, Earl Ravenal, writing in the magazine *Foreign Affairs*, estimated in 1985 that on current trends (and allowing for inflation), 'Europe will cost the United States $2.2 trillion' over the next ten years. To Ravenal, and others, this is too much. 'Americans,' he says, 'are faced with an increasingly demarcated choice: the salvation of Europe, or their own solvency and safety.'

I do not believe Americans are faced with any such choice. But let us consider, first, the consequences of Nato falling apart, or being finally dissolved. Would either Europe or America benefit from such a move?

Those in the US who advocate the disbanding of the Alliance believe that both America and Europe are now better placed to look after their respective security interests separately rather than together. They believe that, if forced to do so, Europeans would overcome their differences and unite to form a common defence pact solid enough to stand up to the Russians. Equally, they believe that America, free from the tiresome burden of defending Europe, would be freer to pursue its own national interests than it is now. There is no evidence that either of these propositions is based on anything other than wishful thinking.

Take Europe first. Faced with the military strength of the Soviet Union – a strength which the West as a whole finds it tough to match – Europe would have to exact a colossal sacrifice from its people to have any hope of mounting a credible defence of its own. The whole structure of post-war European defence has been built round its alliance with America: to start again, and fashion a new and more ambitious pact, would require a superhuman effort, one which would probably be beyond Europe's economic and political reach. Without being able to count on American troops, or American reinforcements, it would have to develop not just massive conventional forces of its own, but a credible nuclear component. (The idea that the US could still plausibly threaten retaliation for a nuclear attack on Europe once the Alliance had been dissolved, and American troops removed, is fantasy.)

The beginnings of a European nuclear deterrent exist, of course, in the shape of the independent forces of Britain and France. But these are small, and suited principally to protecting the two countries which possess them. Would West Germany ever believe they would be used on its behalf? West German politicians are nervous enough about the American guarantee. They would be much more uncertain about a Franco-British one.

For Europe, the likeliest outcome of a dissolved Nato would not be the development of a robust, unified defence but a gradual, confused slide into neutralism. Britain, indeed, far from remaining a nuclear power in its own right, might actually lead the way. The British Labour party, which has long flirted with unilateralism, is now wedded to it. If it wins an election it is committed to removing all nuclear weapons from British soil. The independent deterrent would go, without even the pretence of trying to negotiate it away, and though that in itself would scarcely cripple the Alliance, *all* other nuclear weapons in Britain would have to be scrapped or removed as well, and all American bases closed down. In the current climate, of course, this would be precisely the kind of action which might trigger the end of Nato – a goal which Labour says it does not want but which its policy suggests it does. (Judging from policy documents it appears to hope that having disarmed itself, Britain would be able to continue to shelter willy-nilly under the American umbrella, a strategy characterized by one State Department official as 'Nato without the risk'.)

If Labour followed its policy, however, it could cause the already simmering discontent in Washington to reach boiling point, and the pressure to withdraw American troops, the main military pillar of the Alliance, could prove unstoppable. That in turn would leave West Germany, the country in the front line, considerably more exposed, and many believe that West Germany would gradually seek a greater 'accommodation' with the East, and be followed in the process by the other smaller nations of central Europe.

West Germany might choose an alternative course: it might develop its own nuclear arsenal. In doing so, however, it would take a perilous step, and one which would horrify the European left (who fiercely opposed German rearmament in the 1950s). Since World War Two there has been a taboo on the German possession of nuclear weapons, and the Russians, with memories still vivid of the suffering they endured at German hands during that war (20 million dead), have always made plain that they would regard such a move as intolerably provocative. Nevertheless, with West Germany polarized and demoralized, there would be bitter dispute between those who, in effect, wished to move towards nuclear arms and those who wished to move towards Moscow's arms: in the circumstances, the Kremlin might find irresistible the temptation to interfere. Berlin, in particular, would suddenly be intensely vulnerable.

A neutral Europe, of course, would not worry the peace movements. They would welcome the removal of American troops and nuclear weapons. They believe that in a Europe left to its own devices, tensions would subside and the chances of war, especially nuclear war, would be less. They might be right. But they rest their case on a total faith in Soviet good intentions. They believe that the Kremlin would not attempt to exert pressure on Europe, either peacefully (by, say, interfering in the political process of other countries) or by the use of force, and that even if it did Europe would find ways of resisting. The experience of Afghanistan, Vietnam and Algeria, Anthony Wedgwood Benn has observed, 'may prove' that 'a determined people is the best guarantee against permanent domination from outside'. This is no doubt of great comfort to the Afghans, the Vietnamese and the Algerians, and it may even reassure Mr Benn.

But Europe would be plunging into neutralism at a time when Moscow faces terrible, perhaps intractable problems and when it might feel more and more tempted to use the one element which makes it a superpower: its military strength. A neutral Europe, therefore, would scarcely guarantee a more stable world. If Nato collapsed, the chances of a miscalculation by the Russians would be greater, and of a war between the superpowers just as great. And Europe, even if not directly involved, would probably be devastated by such a war (both sides regarding the continent as a prize they could ill afford to lose). The peace movements would prefer to be red rather than dead. They might end up both.

But those in America who advocate the withdrawal of US troops are just as wrong-headed. They believe that an America cut loose from Western Europe – 'Prometheus Unbound', as one commentator put it – would be freer to act unilaterally and follow its own national interests. In fact, there is no evidence that America would become any more decisive, ruthless or comfortable than before with the use of military force. Those who argue that their country would be tougher and less inhibited without the Europeans often seem to be clutching at a pretext for America not taking actions it would be unlikely to take in any case. Besides, it is hardly in America's 'national interest' to allow the Soviet Union to intimidate and perhaps take over the European continent: were that to happen, America would be far more vulnerable than it is now.

An America without allies, of course, is precisely what the Russians would like to see. 'We must divide the West,' said Nikita Khrushchev in a 1961 speech, 'not unite it by crude attacks on capitalism.' Yuri Andropov, when general secretary of the Soviet Communist party, told an audience in Karelia (Soviet-occupied Finland):

> The Soviet Union's European policy remains unchanged ... Our position is clear. Europe must become a continent of peace and good-neighbourly cooperation. Here, in Karelia, we have to emphasize the significance of the Soviet Union's good-neighbourly cooperation with Finland. Soviet-Finnish relations today ... represent the very kind of détente which makes for a more lasting peace ...

A weaker America and a Finlandized Europe: both, clearly, would suit Russia in its bid to achieve what Russian theoreticians have referred to as the 'Era of Global Democratic Peace'. The Russians will continue to exploit differences within the West, and though many of their propaganda campaigns have been strikingly crude, and arguably counter-productive, they are likely to get more and more help.

Not for nothing, for example, has SDI, the 'Strategic Defence Initiative', been rechristened, jokingly, the 'Soviet Dream Item' by European diplomats. At heart, it is isolationist. Consider the words of the eminent star warrior Edward Teller, in a speech given in March 1983. 'We need to be in a situation,' he said, 'where no matter how other conflicts come out, we can at least be safe at home, without allies.' Or, as Britain's Professor Lawrence Freedman has put it, from another perspective:

> Should the Americans succeed in creating this protection for themselves, it's unlikely that it would be as successful with regard to its allies and thus [America] will become in a way isolated from its allies, protected by its own fortress, and no longer as interested or

sensitive to their interests. Indeed if the Americans do succeed in eliminating offensive nuclear weapons, in removing nuclear weapons from the security equation, then that removes from the Europeans one of the basic stabilizing factors of the last four decades that has helped keep the peace in Europe.

It is to be hoped that a potentially dangerous row over Star Wars can be averted. Politicians on both sides of the Atlantic must hold on to the conviction that world stability cannot possibly be improved by the fragmentation of the West and that Nato, despite all its problems, is worth preserving. 'There is only one thing worse than fighting with allies,' said Winston Churchill, 'and that is fighting without them.' Or, as an American diplomat put it to me: 'Whichever way you look at it, the West would be worse off without Nato than it is with it.'

14

Conclusion

It is easier to identify Nato's problems than it is to prescribe solutions, for it is in the nature of defence that you may not know whether you have got it right until it is too late. As Dame Rebecca West once suggested, military planning before a war seems an exact science, like astronomy, while afterwards it seems more like astrology.

There are, however, two facts which need to be borne in mind in contemplating the future of Western defence. The first is that the pressure to 'get it right' is greater now than it has been in the past: if there is another world war, it will almost certainly be fought much faster, and be settled more swiftly, than any previous conflict. (It has been estimated that the first twelve hours of artillery fire in a war on the Central Front would use up more ammunition than the whole of the Battle of El Alamein.) There will be no time to gear up industrial production, to redesign hardware, to make elaborate changes in tactics.

The second inescapable fact is that Western defence ministries are going to become increasingly hard up. If defence budgets continue to rise they will not, in real terms, rise very much. America's build-up in the early 1980s has been financed by huge federal deficits, deficits which threaten to burden the country for at least a generation and which mean that from now on defence will get a smaller slice of the cake.* (Indeed, the Reagan defence build-up, ironically, has ensured that there will not be another such build-up in the near future, and it may mean that there will be *less* money available for defence in the late 1980s than there might have been had the build-up been more modest in the first place.) In Western Europe, where America's allies are facing growing domestic problems (declining industries, rising unemployment, etc.), there will be no extra money for defence either. Budgets may keep pace with inflation, but they are unlikely

---

*The Gramm-Rudman bill, passed by Congress in late 1985, which seeks to achieve a balanced budget by 1992, seems certain to have a dramatic effect on defence.

to do more than that. So whatever Nato does, it will not be able to tap into any vast new resources. No amount of blood-curdling rhetoric about the Soviet threat will change this. Besides, trying to do too much, as we saw in the last chapter, will end Nato. The Alliance will simply fall apart under the strain.

Yet modern weapons are getting more expensive at a dizzying rate; every year we can buy fewer planes, fewer ships and fewer tanks. The cost of hardware is rising much faster than defence budgets are likely to. Congressman Denny Smith estimates that each new generation of weaponry costs between two and five times as much as the previous one. So if we are not to have a constantly dwindling defence establishment the money will have to go further. We will have to gain more 'output' for less 'input'.

In both America and Europe, therefore, there is urgent need for change in the way we think about defence. The hope has been that a numerically superior enemy can be defeated by harnessing the latest in high technology, that we will be able to fight a 'sanitized' war in which our weapons will be able to stop the enemy, as often as not, before he has even crossed the horizon and had a chance to fire back. As David Evans, a lieutenant colonel in the US marine corps, wrote in the *New York Times* in October 1984, there are two assumptions behind this 'video-game vision' of defence:

> First, the enemy will accommodate us by charging blindly into the teeth of this technology; secondly, he will continue to do so in the face of unacceptable losses. In short, a predictable foe destroyed by arms that always work perfectly.

The Soviets, as we have seen, are unlikely to oblige us by charging blindly into the teeth of Western technology, and the weapons are unlikely to work perfectly. Instead, weapons designers, seeking to squeeze an extra 5 per cent capability out of a given system by cramming in the latest gadgetry, often add an extra 30 per cent, or more, to the cost. And many of the enormously expensive weapons they produce are chronically unreliable and ill-conceived. Watching the process, one is reminded of the British peer who was given to exclaiming: 'My God, why can't they let it alone?' Like the Sorcerer's Apprentice, the Pentagon knows how to start the magic, but not how to stop it.

It is in America, as we have seen, that this hi-tech bias is most deeply rooted. In part, it is a cultural phenomenon, an outgrowth both of American utopianism and of the 'pioneering spirit'. The history of American society is a history of frontiers being broken and new ones being sought. It started with wagon trains moving west, but increasingly the tools of discovery have become hi-tech tools and the heroes have become the wizards of hi tech – the astronauts in the space programme, the doctors who can produce man-made hearts, even clever computer salesmen like Stephen Jobs, the founder of Apple. The danger is that technology, instead of being simply a useful tool to help us do things, is becoming the be-all and end-all. The ultimate view of technology is one which holds that it can manufacture worldwide peace for ever and ever, amen. Thus, a White House aide was quoted as saying at a 'pep' session on Star Wars on the eve of the 1985 superpower summit that the programme was marvellously assertive policy, like the Republican party itself. 'It asserts the fundamental morality of peace through strength,' said the aide, 'and the fundamental morality of peace through technology.' It takes something like the Space Shuttle disaster in January 1986 to remind us that there are limits.

In the defence establishment, the hi-tech bias is bolstered by enormously powerful institutional forces. It is in everyone's interests to press ahead to 'the next generation'. The effectiveness of individual service chiefs tends to be measured more and more by their ability to win money out of Congress rather than by any potential ability to win wars. The temptation to exaggerate requirements, and to exaggerate the threat, is ever present. The first responsibility of defence contractors is to their shareholders, rather than to the national interest, and when they turn out weapons ill-suited to any battlefield they 'salve their conscience', as the Pentagon's inspector general, Joseph Sherick, has put it, by saying: 'Well, we'll never have a war, and we won't use that, and if we do, we'll always fire 10 of them anyway.' Meanwhile, Congress meddles insistently in the military. Some 24 congressional committees and 40 subcommittees oversee the Pentagon, which, according to the *Washington Post*, fields more than a half-million telephone inquiries from Capitol Hill every year. But its collective urge is to 'micro-manage' rather than to reform. In the end, for individual congressmen, short-term, parochial interests almost invariably triumph over broader strategic ones.

I confess that in the light of this, and in the light of similar pressures in Europe, I see little prospect of dramatic changes in the way Nato organizes its defences and procures its weapons. The forces which pervert or prevent rational planning are too strong to permit fundamental change. To that extent, this is a pessimistic book. I have no magic cure-all to propose, no bold new strategy to propound, certainly no new technological gimmick to offer. I write principally on the assumption that the most necessary requirement, if there are to be even small changes, is a well informed and concerned public, for only through this can the chances be increased of bringing to power better informed and more concerned politicians – politicians aware of the need to extract better value for money. (I am conscious, however, that as weapons get steadily more and more complicated, and the strategies used to justify them more and more abstruse, the difficulties for laymen in making sensible judgements about defence become ever greater.)

With all that in mind, I will offer one or two basic and perhaps rather obvious thoughts about the future. There are few ideas of reform which Nato has *not* toyed with at some stage or other, and I can scarcely claim that the suggestions I make are original. In some cases, they simply involve doing more of things that are being done already. In no cases are they grotesquely expensive or especially glamorous. Nothing, indeed, could be more literally down-to-earth than the first.

1 *Creating More Obstacles on the Central Front*

'What is the object of defence?' asks the great Prussian strategist, Carl von Clausewitz, at the beginning of book six of *On War*. And he answers: 'Preservation. It is easier to hold ground than take it. It follows that defence is easier than attack, assuming both sides have equal means ...'

In central Europe both sides do not have 'equal means'. But one of the West's advantages is that it *owns the land* which would be under attack. The Russians, as we saw in chapter 6, would attempt to smash through Nato's defensive line at weak points, and as fast as possible. One way of making this harder for them to do is better preparation of the terrain close to the border. As the historian John Keegan has put it, the best way of rendering the Central Front impenetrable is 'to take a pick and shovel to it'.

A system of barriers, or obstacles, does not need to be as elaborate as France's Maginot Line – far from it. It does not even need to involve constructing extensive minefields and barbed wire fences (at least in peacetime). Much could be done to slow an armoured thrust through the creation of 'natural' obstacles – planting trees or hedgerows across principal corridors of attack, for example. Tanks cannot knock down trees; they would have to be cleared, a difficult and time-consuming process and, in war, a dangerous one. Other possibilities include constructing more man-made lakes close to the inner German border; building 'steps' into canals to render them impassable to tanks; arranging for the flooding of low-lying areas by canals and rivers in time of war; and building more dykes alongside roads that run parallel to the border. Tanks have difficulty getting past even three-foot walls. Such walls are not unattractive, they run alongside countless country lanes all over Europe, and yet building more of them would put difficult obstacles in the way of invading forces bent on moving fast.

Now a certain amount of so-called 'terrain enhancement', it is true, has already been carried out. And much of West Germany already presents formidable obstacles to a would-be invader. 'The most important man-made peacetime obstacles to the movement of enemy forces exist already,' says John Tillson, a Pentagon analyst. 'These are the cities and towns in the defensive zone.' But more natural obstacles would not go amiss, and Nato could – and should – create more artificial obstacles, too: trenches, anti-tank positions and the like. It could and should prepare more of the 12,000 bridges in the defensive zone for demolition in time of war. Tillson estimates the total cost of 'prechambering' half of these bridges for explosives and preparing an equal number of roads and other features for demolition at about $900 million, and a 'landscaping programme' at about the same amount – the cost, altogether, of two armoured divisions. Obviously these prechambered bridges and roads would not be packed with explosives until war began, and would not be blown until the Russians were close by.

Finally, Nato could take advantage of a liquid explosive called nitromethane. Nitromethane, like many inflammable chemicals, burns only gently if it is set alight in the open air. If, however, it is compressed and then blown up with a two-pound explosive charge it can do considerable damage. What its advocates propose is the laying of lengths of plastic pipe across critical 'axes of advance' on the Central Front, quite close to the border. The pipe, six inches in diameter, would lie seven feet underground, low enough to ensure that, once down, it would not interfere with farmers ploughing the soil or sowing crops. It might be laid in 300-metre sections. All that would be visible, at various roadsides, would be the end of the pipe, protruding above ground and covered with a cap and a pressure valve.

In a crisis, diesel tankers, probably owned by civilian companies, would be filled with nitromethane at military storage sites. The chemical would then be poured into the plastic pipes, and explosive charges would be set. If the crisis abated, the fluid would be pumped back out and restored to its original tanks. If not, it would be triggered, probably by reserve soldiers watching from observation posts near the pipes. The resulting explosions would create ditches about 10 yards wide and 20 ft deep, quite impassable by tanks.

Action like this would cause chaos to the fine timetable of a Warsaw Pact invasion, and hours of delay. Engineering units would have to be called up to erect bridges over the ditches, or fill them in, and in the meantime they – and the tanks waiting to cross – would be vulnerable to Nato fire. It is hard to imagine a more effective way of disrupting an attack. 'If Nato wants a proper conventional defence of the Central Front, it has to prepare the ground better,' one Pentagon man, who has spent years studying Soviet tactics, told me. 'The fact that we are not doing this tells me we're not serious.' (Israel, by contrast, which *is* serious, relied heavily on fortifications and barriers to defend itself against much larger Syrian forces in the 1973 Middle East war.)

The West German government, always reluctant to take the kind of steps which might signify a permanent division between itself and East Germany, is not enthusiastic about barriers (though some West German generals are more sympathetic). But the separation of the two Germanys is a fact of life. And the argument sometimes made that barriers are offensive, and would give Nato a better position from which to launch an attack, is far-fetched. They are considerably less 'offensive' than futuristic deep-strike weapons which might be fired at Soviet back-up forces, and they are no more offensive than maintaining large standing armies in Germany, as Nato does at present. Besides, they would require relatively little land (less than 0.01 per cent of West German soil, in one plan), and they would be simple and cheap. A persuasive case can be made that the West Germans, in exchange for the continued American commitment to their defence, should be prepared to make the relatively modest sacrifice which a better system of barriers would entail.

There is another problem with barriers, of course, quite apart from the political one. They generate little enthusiasm among procurement executives, for the commonplace reason that planting hedges and laying plastic pipes scarcely constitute exciting projects at the cutting edge of technology. They have none of the allure of supersonic fighters, or nuclear-powered aircraft carriers – in short, as one Pentagon official put it, 'they're not sexy ... The military planners have turned the defence programme over to the high technology guys and the big corporations and they're going to rue the day.'

2 *Operational Alternatives to Gadgetry*

The ill-fated Divad anti-aircraft gun having finally met its demise, the US army has now turned its attention to finding a successor. And it is a fair bet that a whole new series of horror stories will soon come to be written about a gold-plated 'son of Divad'. I am told that new army specifications call for an anti-aircraft gun which will be able to strike Soviet helicopters not four kilometres away, but six, and strike them as they 'pop up' from behind hills. By the time this book comes out the defence industry will be hard at work examining ways in which this might be achieved.

Instead of seeking such a sophisticated follow-on to Divad, however, why does the army not contemplate an operational solution? One possibility, suggested to me by a former US army officer, would involve arming small units of infantry with much shorter range anti-aircraft weapons, and planning to deploy these close to the front line – out in front of the main body of tanks and infantry – so that they would be able to strike down helicopters *before* they posed a major threat to US forces.

This is just one instance where more thought about tactics, and less about technology, would benefit America and the alliance in general. There are all kinds of others, as I suggested earlier in this book: moving the emphasis, in air power, away from 'deep strike' towards 'close air support', and, at sea, from aircraft carriers towards smaller vessels, land-based aircraft and submarines, are two of the more obvious alternatives put forward.

In the same vein, Nato would do well to think more carefully about how it might use what the military like to call 'civilian assets' during a war. One example: ocean-going tankers and cargo vessels, as the Falklands war illustrated, can be adapted to provide alternative launch platforms for vertical take-off jets and helicopters. This, during a war at sea, would enable Nato to disperse some of its jets and helicopters more widely for reconnaissance, close air defence, etc., and that would make a lot of sense. (Aircraft carriers, after all, are extraordinarily expensive and concentrated targets.) Nato might even work out an arrangement with assorted shipowners and operators by which, in exchange for a contribution to costs, new vessels are equipped, or older ones adapted, to carry appropriate launch platforms and other facilities which could be used in a war.

3 *Better Use of Manpower*

With Nato likely to face more and more problems maintaining fully manned, well trained armed forces in the late 1980s and 1990s, the importance of reserves has come to loom steadily larger. Already, the West Germans are capable of mobilizing a million men in under a month, and other continental European countries can also call on large forces of trained reserves. Many defence experts see properly equipped and trained reserves as the key to a stronger Nato defence, and have developed elaborate plans for their use.

There are others better qualified than I to assess these plans, but there is clearly a strong argument for allowing reserves to train with equipment as good as that used by regulars (a lesson which the Americans seem to have learnt rather more thoroughly than the Europeans). The question of how and where reserves should be deployed is more controversial. Some argue that the most effective role they could play would be close to the front line, freeing regular, more heavily armoured divisions to provide greater 'defence in depth'. This, however, would require an extraordinarily well trained and highly motivated reserve force and while West German reserves might measure up those of other Nato nations probably would

not. Wherever deployed, though, reserve forces would provide valuable
extra manpower in any war on the Central Front.

For though Nato obviously needs tanks – to regain ground which has
been lost and, if necessary, to make counter-attacks – defending infantry
armed with TOW missiles, or their European equivalents, can go a long
way towards offsetting the disparity in tank numbers between the Warsaw
Pact and Nato which so exercises military planners. (The TOW, to digress
for a moment, is a relatively effective weapon. Critics argue that operating
it entails considerable risk for the soldiers involved, which may be true,
but it is hard to find any effective weapon which can be operated without
danger – and those who argue that Nato should cease trying to build
weapons which seek to remove all risk, as I do, can scarcely have it both
ways by arguing, on the other hand, that weapons like TOW are silly
because they involve risk.* Besides, the TOW is not as risky as has
sometimes been suggested. The idea that, to fire it, soldiers will have to
stand up, exposed, on the battlefield, for ten seconds or so, is stretching
a point. TOW missiles travel 1,000 metres every three or four seconds,
and soldiers firing at tanks are unlikely to be further away than 1,000
metres. Moreover, they are likely to be in some sort of cover – amongst
trees, for example – rather than standing in the middle of open terrain.
Finally, the cost effectiveness of TOW – priced at about $7,000, it can
destroy a Soviet tank worth half a million dollars – is a strong argument
in its favour.)

More emphasis on reserves, and on the potential of dismounted infantry,
might facilitate the kind of tactical changes which would give Nato greater
'defence in depth'. Some of these tactical changes are already in train. The
US army, as we have seen, has developed a new doctrine, laying more
emphasis on manoeuvre, less on fighting wars of attrition. And the four
Nato armies responsible for the 200-kilometre northern sector of the
Central Front, to take one other example, have been organized into a
more efficient and more 'integrated' fighting unit.

The moving spirit in these changes was a British general, Sir Nigel
Bagnall, who commanded Nato's Northern Army Group in the early
1980s. What he did, essentially, was to form a new 'back-up' force for his
four armies. This force, comprising the so-called 'operational reserves' (as
distinct from the *national* reserves, i.e. part-time soldiers, that we have just
examined), is three times the size of the old one (which was composed of
separate units from each of the four army corps of the Northern Army
Group: the Dutch, the West Germans, the British and the Belgians). And
the new force, heavily equipped with tanks, would enable the Northern

---

*The 'fire and discard' Viper, which I described in chapter 2, is a different matter: it
simply was not a very effective weapon.

Army Group to provide more defence in depth, to mount counter-attacks on Soviet forces and even, if it seemed necessary, to thrust into East Germany itself.

Bagnall's changes have had to be carefully wrought: the West German government are understandably sensitive about any retreat from forward defence. But German generals, in particular the German chief of staff, General Hans-Henning von Sandrart, have quietly helped implement the new concept of operations and each of the defence ministries has given its approval. Furthermore, General von Sandrart, writing in Nato's *Sixteen Nations*, has warned against an 'over-literal interpretation' of forward defence; like others in the German military, he appears to recognize the growing need for a more fluid deployment of forces on the Central Front.

It is from changes like these – from the better use of existing manpower and resources, rather than from any acquisition of shiny new hardware – that Nato will benefit most.

In this context, recent developments in France clearly benefit Nato. After 1965, when it left the military structure of the Alliance, France sought to have the best of both worlds. Through Gaullism, it avoided the political problems of belonging to Nato – and having American nuclear weapons on its soil – while at the same time being defended *in spite of itself*. For as Theodore Draper has observed, France 'is in the peculiar position of needing the Alliance in order to benefit from staying out of it'. It knows that despite possessing its own nuclear weapons it would be perilously vulnerable if Nato ever collapsed or became too weak. (Would the French *really* go nuclear to stop a Soviet conventional attack? It seems unlikely.) Thus François Mitterrand, having savaged the Alliance in his autobiography as an empty shell based on 'the fiction of American intervention in Europe in time of war', has taken a very different tone since becoming president of France, and France under Mitterrand has become steadily more worried about the weakness of the Alliance and, above all, of its northern neighbour, West Germany.

The consequence has been that French military policy in the early 1980s has evolved in a more European direction. The French have reorganized and strengthened their conventional forces. They have created a new 47,000-man 'force d'action rapide', designed to operate beyond France's borders, and have exercised this with the West Germans. If a war occurred, the best guess, now, is that French forces would move into West Germany to assist the common defence, and this, for Nato, is obviously welcome.*

*It makes sense from France's perspective, too. Just as, before World War Two, the French attempted to construct a purely national defence (ignoring allies), and ended up being badly beaten, so the Gaullist approach would avail them little in a crisis. Alistair Horne commented in *To Lose a Battle*: 'There are moments when one feels that – like the Bourbons, only worse – France has learned nothing and forgotten everything.'

4 *Injecting More Sense into Procurement*

The spate of stories about gold-plated ashtrays, coffee makers and lavatory seats may be an illustration of the law developed by C. Northcote Parkinson – that the importance of an item is inversely proportionate to the attention given to it. In one sense, however, the attention given to such trivial examples of Pentagon profligacy has served a purpose. It has helped trigger a growing restiveness about the inadequacies of the US procurement system – a restiveness which now embraces politicians of many different political hues.

Gone are the days, indeed, when critics of US procurement can be dismissed as 'liberals' whose real aim is to cut the defence budget. In the vanguard of those now calling for sweeping reforms are Senator Barry Goldwater, the staunchly anti-Soviet chairman of the Senate Armed Services Committee, and other leading conservatives. This is a natural enough development. Conservatives, after all, have traditionally abhorred waste. (One might add here that conservatives have also, traditionally, had a very strong grasp on the limits of the possible and been inclined to distrust soaring grandiose visions such as that offered by the star warriors.) Public attacks on the Pentagon's procurement system are increasingly coming from the Pentagon itself. Take David Evans:

> Speaking for myself, I think that exaggerated force requirements, inappropriate technology and high costs are symptomatic of a runaway system. A forty-five per cent real increase in defence spending over the past four years has been necessary just to keep the force from shrinking. The former Army Chief of Staff, Gen. Edward C. Meyer, was on target when he said: 'Either we are going to spend ourselves into extinction, or we have to come up with alternative strategies and new ways to allocate resources.'

So what should be done? The loosely knit coalition of 'military reformers' in Congress, in government and in assorted thinktanks have many and varying ideas. While everyone agrees there is a problem, and that it is getting worse, no one can quite agree on what needs to be done. There is a long list of prescriptions, some of them sensible, some not so sensible, and some of them quite unworkable.

Still, there are certain measures which could do nothing but good. One is firing a large number of the 54,000 bureaucrats who do the Pentagon's shopping. (A good place to start might be with those who break the law. Most critics of the Pentagon accept that the laws governing procurement practices are adequate; it is just that they are inadequately enforced.)

A second measure which makes sense would entail subjecting the Pentagon's modern creations to vastly more realistic tests than the farcical 'success-oriented' variety they tend to go through now. The situation at the moment, as one senator has put it, is 'like having a student grade his own final exams'. Under pressure from Congress, the Pentagon *has* created an office of 'operational test and evaluation', intended to be independent of the people responsible for weapons development. But at the time of writing this is very small, with a staff of 17 and a budget of under $12 million, and scarcely up to the task of monitoring the 140 new weapons currently in the pipeline. Similarly, a new 'Joint Live Fire Test Program' has been instituted to test the survivability of American planes and combat vehicles by firing live ammunition at them. But when the army, after 'intense negotiations', agreed to allow its Bradley Fighting Vehicle to be tested under this programme in December 1985 – with results which predictably suggested, according to one of the officials involved, that the atmosphere inside the vehicle became 'simply intolerable' after each hit due to ammunition fires or the triggering of the automatic fire extinguisher – the army immediately disputed the verdict, contending that the Bradley had met its requirements and that only minor modifications were necessary to make it more resistant to attack.

The army's reaction illustrates the problem. The services dislike intensely the notion of independent testing because it threatens to jeopardize support for programmes in which they may have invested years of effort and millions, if not billions, of dollars. (The navy flatly refuses to let its ships ever be subjected to the 'Joint Live Fire Test Program'). Yet without making full-scale independent testing compulsory for every weapons system, the endless procession to the battlefield of fragile and over-complicated hardware will continue.

A third reform, often proposed, is blocking off the 'revolving door' between Pentagon and industry and disrupting what is currently a highly incestuous partnership. I recognize that this is a difficult issue: clearly the Pentagon can benefit from hiring some industrialists – they are familiar with the tricks contractors can play, for one thing – and clearly the defence industry can benefit from hiring some people who understand the Pentagon's needs. Finding a way of slowing down this two-way traffic is nevertheless desirable, and possible, though, as with other changes, it will require considerably more vigilance from the top, and a greater readiness to enforce the law.

A more obvious reform would involve strengthening, and making more independent, the Joint Chiefs of Staff, and in particular the chairman. At the moment each of the chiefs, except the chairman, is totally beholden to his service. The chairman himself has no real powers, and military procurement is thus dominated by the individual services, who dream up strategies which help them justify the weapons they want (rather than the other way round) and push tenaciously for their 'share' of the budget with scarcely even a nod in the direction of overall planning. Each service concocts grossly over-ambitious lists of what it wants and, in the end, through a process of haggling and compromise, the chiefs reach agreement on what each can have. The idea that *real* choices are made (giving up, say, a wing of F15s for an army division) is a joke. There is a glaring need for a more centralized system, and for a more powerful and more independent Joint Chiefs of Staff organization – one less beholden to the individual services.* A revamped JCS might be made up, not of the heads of each service, as now, but of other, specially selected senior military officers, and it might be headed by a chairman with considerably strengthened powers.

The defence industry, meanwhile, would clearly benefit from a dose of what Senator Grassley calls 'creeping capitalism'. In the present climate, there is too little of the free enterprise on which America prides itself, and many big defence contractors – monopoly suppliers to the Pentagon of particular pieces of equipment – are handed a licence to waste money. They face no competition, and all too frequently have no incentive to cut costs or improve quality. Unless that changes, the US defence industry will continue to produce weapons which are grotesquely overpriced, over-elaborate and, all too often, ineffective.

The argument that Europe should build a stronger defence industry of its own, and become less dependent on American weapons, is a compelling one. In part through increased cooperation on defence projects it has already moved in this direction. In the 1970s, for example, the US sold Europe about nine times as much equipment as it bought in return. Now that ratio has dropped sharply. In 1984, for example, the 14 European nations in Nato agreed to buy $3.81 billion in defence goods from the US, while at the same time arranging sales to the US which totalled $1.19 billion, yielding a US advantage in the transatlantic arms trade of three to one, well below the 1970s average. Such a trend may not altogether please America, which although it has long borne the brunt of financing Nato, has also enjoyed the profits which come from its large surplus in the arms trade with Europe. But as the *Wall Street Journal* has pointed out, 'Extravagance and fraud in the US defence industry haven't placed American arms contractors in the best position to complain about administration support for a more competitive European arms industry',

---

* This indeed was one of the major recommendations of an exhaustive congressional study on 'defence organization' produced for the Senate Armed Services Committee in October 1985.

and on the whole America can only welcome increased signs of cooperation and independence in Europe.

Such cooperation could be dramatically increased, as I have argued, given more readiness to compromise on the part of national defence establishments. In the late 1960s Britain faced a golden opportunity to collaborate with the Dutch in the building of a new frigate. The collaboration, strongly backed by the then British defence minister, Denis Healey, would have suited both countries admirably. Each was saddled with frigates whose hulls were wearing out; both countries shared a long naval tradition; there even appeared to be a natural division of labour (Britain to concentrate on ship design and propulsion, Holland on electronics). The Dutch, however, had one stipulation. The new frigate must be short enough to fit into their docks at Den Helder. The Royal Navy proceeded to design a warship which failed to meet this stipulation, and the collaboration fell apart. The result was that Britain built the Type 22, a heavily gold-plated vessel with an aluminium superstructure and elaborate missile systems of dubious effectiveness, at a cost of £130 million. The Dutch, by contrast, built a smaller, simpler frigate which cost approximately half that and which has enjoyed considerable success on the export market.

Two other British examples illustrate the best and worst of European procurement.

Consider, first, Britain's determination to preserve its own torpedo industry (it is the only European country which refuses to buy torpedoes from the Americans). In the late 1970s, faced with a choice between buying the lightweight Mark 44 torpedo, to be modified under a 'near term improvement programme' known as NEARTIP, for around £250 million, and the possibility of developing its own new lightweight torpedo (Stingray), the UK government opted for the latter. The result: a programme whose cost spiralled upwards to about one billion pounds. Admittedly, the British Stingray is ultra-sophisticated – a true guided weapon which can be fired from a submarine or dropped from an aircraft and then home in, automatically, on its target – but it has cost Britain four times as much as buying American would have done: the money saved from buying American, indeed, might have allowed the navy to purchase three or four new frigates.

A rather more encouraging project – indeed an object lesson for Nato procurement bureaucracies – was Britain's Hawk. The Hawk is a training aircraft (though some countries have bought it with a rather more ambitious role in mind). It is a light and simple aeroplane, and easy to fly. It was designed in the mid-1970s and when it went into production the RAF offered British Aerospace handsome bonuses if they could beat standards which were set for its maintainability. Faced with the incentives, British

Aerospace did precisely that, and through clever, economical design created parts which would last longer and be easier to change than on most aircraft. The result was that Hawk has enjoyed enormously successful export sales. It is one of Nato's minor success stories, an illustration of what can be achieved through businesslike procurement.

It is not beyond Nato's wit, or means, to develop a more robust conventional defence, and to do so without hefty increases in spending. Such a defence would not have to be impregnable, it would simply have to appear solid enough to deny the Soviets a quick victory, the only kind of victory they would contemplate trying to achieve. Any extension of the period for which Nato could hold out before coming under pressure to 'go nuclear' would work to the West's advantage. It would allow more time for reinforcements to arrive, more time for negotiations, more time for cooler heads to prevail. It would postpone the moment when the West might be tempted to take a fateful decision and enter a room, in the words of one British general, 'which no one's ever been in before'. And though modern conventional weapons – those that work – can wreak terrible havoc (a modern shell can split into a million fragments, a thousand times as many as its World War One equivalent), they would not, if used, risk destroying the globe. Nuclear weapons would.

Existing Nato strategy, which envisages the first use of nuclear weapons, is not very plausible. It seems to many a bluff which, though useful for deterring war, would not be very helpful if war actually occurred. (Richard Betts, a senior defence analyst at the Brookings Institution in Washington, has called it a 'great white lie' – white because it is told for the best of intentions, but a lie nonetheless.) There is, of course, the danger that the Russians themselves, in a war in Europe, could decide to go nuclear first, thus forcing Nato to respond. But as we in the West can imagine the consequences of nuclear escalation, it follows that the Soviet leaders can, too. The point is that the *onus* of going first would have been switched to *them*. They, not Nato, would have to take the agonizing decision to start a nuclear war.

There remains the problem of what the West should do about its existing nuclear arsenal. The short answer is that it does not need to do a great deal. Nuclear deterrence, I have argued in this book, is considerably more robust than it is often assumed to be – either by the peace movements or by American conservatives. It would matter little if several years went by without the West deploying any new nuclear weapons. We would not be one whit less secure. Having said that, there is clearly a case for *some* modernization, both for political and strategic reasons: all weapons, whether tanks or nuclear delivery systems, wear out sooner or later and, in the end, need to be replaced. The trouble with the nuclear freeze movement is that it would freeze everything, good or bad, necessary or unnecessary.

The guiding principle for Nato should be sufficiency – by which I mean maintaining, as a deterrent to an attack on Western Europe, a relatively small arsenal of battlefield weapons, and enough strategic weapons to be sure of being able to mount a devastating retaliatory strike on the Soviet Union, even after enduring a first strike. What Nato does not need is a vast redundancy of such weapons: this is both pointless and a waste of money. Equally pointless, and potentially dangerous, is the deployment of new 'destabilizing' weapons which might threaten the nuclear stalemate and lead one side or the other to entertain the notion that it might get away with a pre-emptive strike.

Experts disagree as to what 'sufficiency' means, but one thing it does not mean is matching the Soviets system for system. The Soviet build-up, of course, is excessive. 'They feel they don't just need a belt and braces, but a piece of string as well,' as one British official put it to me. Viewed from Moscow, Russia is a land ringed by enemies, forced to consider not just America but the independent deterrents of Britain and France and a growing threat from the Chinese. Russia's paranoia is probably increased by Nato's implicit threat of nuclear first use, which they are determined to demonstrate would be a foolhardy act. It is bolstered too by a 'production line mentality' – a tendency to crank out systems which appear to be effective in great numbers.

But the fact that Moscow overproduces nuclear weapons does not mean that the West needs to follow suit. The SS20 is a good example. At the time of writing there are 441 of these missiles in place, two thirds of them trained on Western Europe. Doubtless the Soviets fear that some SS20s might not work, and that others might be destroyed by conventional weapons before they could be used. But so huge a deployment still makes little sense. There is no reason why the Alliance should allow itself to be intimidated. If the Soviets choose to invest millions of roubles in weapons which can make the rubble bounce, that is their privilege. It does not require the West to waste millions of dollars in response.

To an extent, the idea of sufficiency is already catching on. When, after initial Western deployments of cruise and Pershing missiles, the Soviets began deploying an array of new short-range weapons 'in retaliation' (SS21s, SS22s and SS23s), Nato conspicuously declined to react. And when, also 'in retaliation', the Russians announced that they were going to deploy more nuclear-armed submarines close to the American coastline, President Reagan sensibly said that he would not be losing any sleep over this. Both Soviet gestures were pointless and likely to yield no military advantage. Nato has committed itself to pulling out a total of 2,400 nuclear weapons from the Central Front, and America, since the early 1960s, has eliminated 8,000 warheads from its strategic arsenal and roughly halved the 'payload', or destructive capability, of that arsenal.

At the same time, however, America's current strategic programme is unnecessarily ambitious. Does America *really* need – in addition to its Star Wars programme – not just new Trident submarines but MX, the B1, Midgetman, Stealth, several new cruise missile programmes and the array of new warheads which are being developed? Surely not. Budgetary pressures will certainly ensure that many of these programmes are scaled back, but the cuts will probably be as irrational as the build-up. One way of making the process more rational might be for the White House to create a standing commission on nuclear forces similar to the Scowcroft Commission which was formed in 1982 to advise the president on strategic matters after the MX missile got into trouble in Congress. The Scowcroft Commission was temporary; a permanent, bipartisan commission along the same lines, however, might make nuclear weapons procurement less subject to the vagaries of presidential politics and inter-service rivalry, and help defuse unfounded scares like the 'missile gap' and the 'window of vulnerability'. In general, indeed, the whole nuclear issue could benefit from nothing more than what William Kaufman, the veteran defence expert, calls 'a dose of benign neglect'.

The kind of nuclear programme which would emerge from a more rational assessment of the threat, and of Nato requirements, would be considerably less ambitious than the existing one. It would not include MX, but it might include the B1. The B1 is a versatile weapon, able to perform a conventional as well as a nuclear role and, though complicated and expensive, has the distinction of coming off the production line at roughly the anticipated cost and, amazingly, slightly ahead of schedule. There is an argument for pursuing Stealth technology, but not for installing it in yet another bomber; if it works, it will surely be adequate to apply it simply to air-launched cruise missiles, making them (and thus the B1) better able to penetrate Soviet air defences. Given the worries over the vulnerability of land-based missiles, the Midgetman programme, too, may be worth preserving. But the most important piece of nuclear modernization, by far, is the Trident programme. Some strategists argue, and I accept, that America would have done better to stick with its original, less accurate 'C4' version of the actual missile system rather than pressing on to develop the more accurate, more sophisticated 'D5'. (Apart from anything else, this would have caused fewer headaches in Britain, which needs to modernize its existing Polaris deterrent and which has followed America down the D5 track – in the interests of 'commonality' – even though C4 would have been perfectly adequate for British needs.) It is true, too, that the Trident submarines being built reflect the standard US navy disease of 'giantism': a larger force of smaller submarines would probably have made more sense than the small force of huge ones currently taking shape. But the sea has become, and is likely to remain, the best place for nuclear weapons, especially for the West, which is far ahead of Russia in submarine technology. And to that extent it surely makes sense for America to concentrate most on the sea-based leg of its nuclear 'triad'.

No doubt some day we will have to confront the spectacle of 'submarine vulnerability', just as we have confronted 'ICBM vulnerability', and equally there is no doubt that when we do its dangers will be exaggerated. Both sides, even now, are working flat-out to make the sea 'transparent' – even though it is in neither's interests to be successful – the Americans mainly through the development of listening devices, the Russians by concentrating more on 'non-acoustic' methods of detection. Already, alarmist reports have circulated in the Pentagon about Russian developments in the field of synthetic aperture radar. Moscow hopes that this, based on nuclear-powered satellites, may eventually enable it to identify American submarines from their 'internal waves' (i.e. their wakes). But American ballistic submarines are very quiet, can travel very deep, and when moving slowly send to the surface only the faintest 'internal waves'. It is likely to be at least another generation or two before the Russians make the kind of breakthroughs necessary to track them.

In the endeavour to preserve nuclear stability, arms control is clearly important. But its contribution is likely to be modest. The notion that the superpowers' arsenals will ever be negotiated down to very low levels and perhaps eventually to nothing is fantasy (with or without Star Wars). Nothing in history, either before or since World War Two, suggests it to be even a remote possibility. Holding out the hope that it might happen is dangerous: it raises expectations which can never be satisfied and it places an intolerable burden on the whole arms control pro-cess.

Thus neither Salt One, nor its unratified successor, Salt Two, has done much to slow down the arms race. They have not enabled defence establishments to become smaller; they have not noticeably reduced the risks of war; they have done nothing to limit the likelihood of appalling casualties if war occurred – in short, they have done little towards furthering the kind of goals which were laid out by arms control experts like Thomas Schelling and Bernard Brodie in the 1950s.

This is not surprising. America and Russia see the world very differently, and a host of factors – geographical, political and military – make equitable agreements hard to arrive at. What looks fair to the West usually looks unfair to the East, and vice versa. (How do you take into account America's technological edge, for example, or Russia's imposing air defence network, or the fact that Russia is ringed with enemies, or that America is separated from its allies by an ocean?) Arms control negotiators are invariably striving to obtain a political and military advantage for their own side, and it sometimes seems, in the words of Helmut Sonnenfeldt, that 'what is negotiable is not significant and what is significant is not negotiable.' Even some of the more far-reaching agreements which *have* been reached – banning nuclear weapons on the seabed, or on the North Pole, or on the moon, for example – outlaw things which neither side much wants to do anyway.

Nevertheless arms control has, arguably, lent a measure of 'predictability' to the arms race and the very process of talking, over the last 20 years, has made dangerous misunderstandings between the two sides – about particular programmes, about strategic intent – less likely than they might otherwise have been. Moreover, arms control answers a political need in the West. There may be a grain of truth in the jibe that it is 'conducted for the amusement of the allies', but people in America, as well as in Western Europe, would be less inclined to keep supporting high defence budgets if it was jettisoned. And though the Soviets undoubtedly have a case to answer over violations of existing agreements, the charges are often overdone. Overall, the Soviet compliance record has been good, and their more questionable behaviour may stem, in part, from the general deterioration of East-West relations during the late 1970s and early 1980s: treated as a pariah by Washington, and as the 'evil empire', their incentive to 'play by the rules' radically diminished.

Thus, 'we may not be able to design a whole new city but we can at least try and mend the potholes in the road', as one expert put it. It is worth, for instance, continuing the attempt to agree 'confidence-building measures' – improvements in the Moscow-Washington hot line, exchanges of information over military manoeuvres, and other steps intended to prevent crises blowing up through misunderstandings, or getting out of hand if they do occur. In nuclear negotiations the main focus of Western efforts should be less on balancing numbers than on channelling and restraining developments in technology. Balancing numbers is very hard, as we have noted, and it tends to encourage both sides to hang on to old, unnecessary weapons as 'bargaining chips' (America's Titan missiles; the Russian SS4s and SS5s), and even to deploy new ones for the same purpose (America's MX). Even if the vision being discussed in Geneva as I write – a 50 per cent reduction in the strategic arsenals of the superpowers – were to become reality it would have more symbolic than military value. Both sides would still be able to make the rubble bounce several times over. Indeed, if both sides had very small arsenals the dangers might be greater than they are now: if you have a large arsenal, the difficulties the other side has in imagining a way of destroying it in one fell swoop are correspondingly large.

So what can arms controllers do about the march of new technology? Clearly they cannot halt it, even if this were a desirable end. As the Washington defence analyst Barry Blechman has written:

> Technological change can no more be stopped – or 'frozen' – than knowledge of how to design and manufacture nuclear weapons can be banished from the minds of men and women.... It is unrealistic and counter-productive to assume that national leaders will agree to cease applying the products of new technologies for the enhancement of the security (or the power) of their nations. If anything, we should assume that the evolution of weapon technologies will accelerate in the future, in keeping with the general trend in the rate of technological change.

But proposals for a blanket ban on new technology – such as that implicit in the 'nuclear freeze' movement – are probably not desirable anyway. Some future developments may benefit the West, just as some past ones have: photo-reconnaissance satellites, which have given us a much clearer picture of the size and character of Soviet forces; 'permissive action links' and other nuclear safety mechanisms which have greatly reduced the risks of nuclear war happening by accident.

Many developments in technology, however, are potentially destabilizing and more likely to cause both sides headaches than to enhance anyone's security. It is too late to ban 'mirving', one such development, or cruise missiles, another. But we are not too late, at the time of writing, to ban, or drastically restrict, the testing of anti-satellite weapons. ASATs must be candidates for the prize of 'most destabilizing weapons ever devised', and will cause terrible problems for both sides, perhaps especially for the West, if they are allowed to proliferate and to be developed into effective satellite killers. The arguments for a ban on testing of both existing and new systems are overwhelming, and a ban on the testing and deployment of ATBMs would also make considerable sense.

So, I believe, would a complete ban on the testing of nuclear weapons. In 1963, after Kennedy and Khrushchev 'stared into the abyss' during the Cuban missile crisis, the superpowers agreed a Limited Test Ban Treaty which forbade the testing of nuclear devices in the atmosphere. Two subsequent agreements, in 1974 and 1976, have sought to limit underground tests to no more than 150 kilotons, though these have never been ratified by the US Senate.

There are various arguments made *against* a test ban. One is that through testing both superpowers have been able to develop smaller, less destructive warheads. A second is that such a ban could never be verified. A third, advanced by the Pentagon, is that the West needs to keep testing in order to ensure that its weapons work properly. A fourth is that America is behind Russia in the nuclear arms race and needs to test so that it can develop new weapons and catch up. Finally, the British and French are dubious about a comprehensive test ban in part because, unlike America, they have small nuclear arsenals and are unable to envisage 'swamping' Russian defences around Moscow with a large quantity of warheads. They say that they have to rely instead on refining their arsenals to be sure that enough weapons would penetrate in a crisis.

I find these arguments unpersuasive. Why do both sides need to go on developing smaller, more accurate warheads? It is precisely such developments which have encouraged the fantasies about fighting and prevailing in limited nuclear wars. Verification is certainly a problem, but developments in seismology have made it possible to monitor and identify even small nuclear explosions, and America would be fully justified in arguing not only for an adequate number of seismological stations on the soil of both superpowers but also for 'on-site inspections' to insure against cheating. (American officials say that they need a better understanding of the geology of the Russian test site at Plesetsk for effective monitoring of tests.) But the Russians have already indicated that they might go along with this. Why not challenge them and see?

A test ban would make it far harder for both sides to develop new and destabilizing weapons. It would also make it harder for them to feel confident about existing ones, which in turn would reduce concerns about a 'first strike'. For a first strike means that all your weapons have to work perfectly. Deterrence does not require anything so demanding. You simply have to know that *enough* of your weapons will work to make possible a devastating *retaliatory* strike, and since the superpowers now possess about 25,000 nuclear weapons apiece they would remain utterly confident of this, even after a comprehensive test ban. The Reagan administration suggests that a major reason why billions of dollars need to be spent on Star Wars is to 'complicate' Soviet plans of attack and make a first strike seem implausible. But a comprehensive test ban could achieve the same result at vastly lower cost and bring all kinds of benefits in its wake. It could, in effect, close the 'window of vulnerability' (in the eyes of those who believe it exists) – a window which Washington has kept fretting about ever since President Reagan entered the White House but has done nothing whatsoever to 'close'. A test ban, finally, could play an important role in reducing one of the greatest dangers of our age: that of nuclear proliferation. Third World countries, watching the superpowers continue to expand their arsenals and to test new weapons at the same time as they preach the virtues of non-proliferation, are understandably less than impressed. A comprehensive test ban, however, signed by both America and the Soviet Union, would give both the right to enforce it. (Under such circumstances, for example, were Libya's Colonel Gadafy to obtain a nuclear weapons facility, the United States would be fully justified in attacking and destroying it. The Soviets would have no choice but to accept such an outcome.)

As we have seen, however, there are a great many careers tied up in the nuclear weapons business, and the institutional pressures against a test ban are strong. Nevertheless, the case for ratifying the two existing treaties, and then for pursuing negotiations aimed, eventually, at ending testing altogether is strong. In the long run, it would undoubtedly save money, since it would slow down the process by which both sides keep making additions to their arsenals. A ban on nuclear testing, indeed, could be followed by a ban, or a drastic restriction, on the number of missile tests which could be carried out by each side.

In addition to striving for a ban on ASATs and nuclear testing, the West should also – as I argued in chapters 11 and 12 – adopt a much more cautious attitude to Star Wars.* The likelihood is that if the current enthusiasm for space-based defence is allowed to proceed unchecked the world will end up a considerably more dangerous place. It is clearly in the interests of both sides to redraft the ABM treaty where necessary – taking account of recent developments in technology – and, at least for the foreseeable future, to agree to stick to its provisions. I would argue that it makes sense to do this even if it is impossible at the same time to obtain deep cuts in the nuclear arsenals of both sides. Otherwise we may end up in the world envisaged by George Kennan:

> The technological realities of this competition are constantly changing from month to month and from year to year. Are we to flee like haunted creatures from one defensive device to another, each more costly and humiliating than the one before, cowering underground one day, breaking up our cities the next, attempting to surround ourselves with elaborate shields on the third, concerned only to prolong the length of our lives while sacrificing all the values for which it might be worth while to live at all?

Even that vision, unfortunately, scarcely captures what the world might

---

*It is worth noting, incidentally, that one reason for the Pentagon's reluctance to pursue a nuclear test ban is the belief that nuclear technology may play an important part in a space-based defence. The x-ray laser being contemplated for boost phase defence will require an intense and protracted series of underground tests, and these tests have already begun.

be like if both sides enter into an untrammelled Star Wars race. In chapter 9 I described Star Wars as the quintessence of the New Maginot Line, the ultimate technological fix. But France's Maginot Line was static, and conspicuously defensive. It was bad for France, because it absorbed too much money and lulled the French into a false sense of security, but it constituted no casus belli. (Arguably, in fact, it was in Germany's interest that it should be built.) A Maginot Line in space, however, would be in no country's interest; it would be a defence that would decrease every country's security: not only would it cause desperate instabilities as it was being constructed, and probably once it was complete, but it would also, almost certainly, have an offensive capability.

Why this should be is, really, blindingly obvious. Weapons in space, whether satellites in low orbit armed with kinetic energy interceptors or 'directed energy' devices, would almost certainly be able to destroy ground targets. They would have to be powerful enough to destroy missiles soon after lift-off, which means that they would probably be powerful enough, at the very least, to destroy 'soft targets' on the ground. According to Robert English, a Pentagon policy analyst between 1982 and 1985, two separate studies – one by a private defence research firm, the other by a science laboratory – 'have concluded that space-based lasers could incinerate flammable targets and set numerous fires on the enemy's home soil'. Such laser devices, whether based on satellites or bounced off mirrors from ground stations, might be able to destroy everything from early warning radars to communications centres. They might, in fact, be able to do so more easily than striking rocket boosters rising quickly out of Soviet silos. (The targets would be fixed; there would be none of the tracking or discrimination problems.) And though, initially, space-based weaponry would probably be unable to destroy intercontinental ballistic missiles in their silos, or other 'hard' targets, that possibility, too, might eventually open up. And at that point, as English wrote in the *New Republic* in February 1986, the situation could become hazardous in the extreme:

The 'surgical' precision of such weapons would make the temptation of a first strike much harder to resist. Even more disconcerting is the extraordinary speed with which space-based weapons could attack. To date, none of the numerous advances in strategic weaponry over the past 20 years have been able to make a first strike credible. No matter how overwhelming one's advantages in megatonnage or accuracy, no attacker could ever escape devastation as long as the enemy had enough time to launch his missiles in retaliation. However, space-based weapons might reduce a half hour of warning to a mere two or three minutes. Of course, the side that felt threatened by such a system might well be compelled to shift from a 'launch-under-attack' or 'launch-on-warning' posture to one of 'launch-under-crisis' for fear of losing the bulk of its retaliatory force before it even knew it was being attacked. A more hair-trigger world is hard to imagine.

Neither the peace movement nor the radical right are likely to be much impressed by the arguments I have made in this book. Their fantasies are curiously similar. The peace movement believes in the complete abolition of nuclear weapons. But nuclear weapons will never be abolished. A 'nuclear-free world' could never be verified: the knowledge of how to make the weapons is freely available and will remain so. And even if the superpowers pulled off the miracle of scrapping their arsenals, it would make a conventional or chemical war seem more possible and mean that the world had become vulnerable to any tinpot dictator sufficiently power-hungry or wicked or unscrupulous to decide to build them and threaten their use. We cannot 'abolish war', or 'reinvent politics', or do any of the other Utopian things which the disarmers would have us do.

But it is not only the peace movement which dreams romantic dreams. The star warriors want to abolish nuclear weapons too – through the wonder of modern technology. While CND, and the Greens, express the Luddite wish to get back to a lost world where nuclear weapons do not exist any more, the radical right entertains notions which have just as little relevance to the real world. Common sense is often in short supply in debates on defence.

The truth is that the West is going to have to learn to live with less security than it might want. This is difficult, especially for America, which is sheltered by two oceans and, for most of its history, has been effectively invulnerable. But in the nuclear age there is no such thing as absolute security, and by striving to attain it we risk ending up worse off than we are at present. In the words of Frederick the Great: 'He who strives for absolute security often ends up with no security at all.'

Those who advocate a no-holds-barred arms race with the Russians court just such a fate. They say that arms control is a snare and a delusion and that the West's only way forward is to keep upping the ante, developing more and more sophisticated strategic weapons until the Russians, exhausted and bankrupt, finally give up. We are richer and smarter than they are, the argument goes: we can win. But the Russians will not give up. And if they do find themselves facing bankruptcy, what then? Will they give up quietly, abandon their empire, surrender? Or will they in desperation decide that they have no choice but to go to war? In any case, an unbridled arms race would probably bankrupt the West as surely as it would cripple the East. Even if it did not, it would leave our economies so damaged as to make it seem questionable whether the effort had been worth it. If you destroy your economy, after all, you have destroyed the very fabric of the society you are seeking to defend.

Even the argument that intensive military research yields all kinds of benefits for the civilian economy holds less water now than it once did. There have undoubtedly been important spinoffs from developments pioneered by the defence industry – computers, jet engines, even graphite tennis rackets – but many argue that military technology has now become so exotic that there will be far fewer such spinoffs in the future. Some, indeed, argue that the emphasis on the military applications of science is weakening America's ability to compete with Japan in other areas of technology. Jerome Wiesner, a former president of MIT who served as science adviser to presidents Eisenhower and Kennedy, believes that there is a danger, if current trends continue, of America becoming a 'totally military culture'.

Achieving real security for the West is more than a matter of simply inventing more and more sophisticated weapons. The real challenge for the rest of this century and after will be managing the East-West conflict in such a way as to minimize the chances of disaster. The idea shared by the peace movements and the radical right – that it all comes down to weapons – is silly. As Michael Howard pointed out in *The Times* in January 1984:

> We must look deeper for the things that really matter ... Can the Soviet Union continue to control its East European empire? Will that control remain, indefinitely, and be politically acceptable to the West? Can the Germans, East and West, incrementally develop a relationship which will not call in question the entire postwar settlement of the Continent? Will the nations of western Europe be reduced to ungovernability by the social discontent arising from their economic problems and thus once more constitute an attractive target for Soviet penetration? And most important of all, will the United States continue to regard western Europe as a region so vital to its own security that it will persist, in spite of all the frustrations and humiliations involved, in maintaining so complex an alliance?
>
> Factors such as these will determine whether the balance is stable or not; not SS20s, Pershing 2s or numbers of Soviet tanks. If the underlying political structure remains stable it will not be disturbed by weapons imbalances, or be at the mercy of crises, accidents and misperceptions. If it is not, then peace cannot be preserved either by anxiously matching weapon for weapon or by dramatic gestures of one-sided disarmament.

These are wise words. The Russians constitute, in the end, as much a political as a military problem. We must lean as heavily on diplomacy as we do on technology. When Russia's veteran former foreign minister, Andrei Gromyko, met President Reagan in September 1984, he talked about the 'push of technology' and according to one account 'repeatedly wondered aloud whether the great powers would be able to control arms or whether arms would take control of them'. One might argue that Gromyko, during his 30-year tenure in the Soviet foreign ministry, contributed little to the business of 'controlling arms'. But like President Eisenhower in his valedictory warning about the powers of the 'military industrial complex', he was expressing a very real danger. We must be careful lest the technocrats take us over completely, and lest technology becomes an influence which dwarfs all others in the shaping of foreign policy. We have already progressed some way down that road, and Star Wars threatens to take us considerably further. My prescription for Western defence – a gradual, incremental improvement in conventional forces, less reliance on nuclear weapons and a greater emphasis on diplomacy – is not a very exciting one, but it is, I believe, more realistic than the goal of the star warriors. It is also less risky. The danger to be faced is that an attempt to rely too heavily on technology could lead to more than just mutual bankruptcy. It could lead, in Winston Churchill's graphic phrase, to a return of the Stone Age 'on the gleaming wings of science'.

NOTES AND SOURCES

I have not attributed a number of personal interviews. Books referred to, and others drawn on, appear in the Bibliography. The following abbreviations have been used: *DT, Daily Telegraph*; *FT, Financial Times*; *IISS*, International Institute for Strategic Studies in London; *LA Times, Los Angeles Times*; *NYT, New York Times*; *ST, Sunday Times*; *WP, Washington Post*; *WSJ, Wall Street Journal*.

Introduction

page

1 'He was not': Guizot, *History of France*, p. 551.

2 'planted against': Duffy, *Siege Warfare*, p. 9.

first use of breech loading rifle and artillery: Prof. Michael Howard cites both these examples in 'The Forgotten Dimensions of Strategy' in Towle (ed.), *Estimating Foreign Military Power*, p. 264. But he adds: 'This [technological] superiority was far from decisive: the Franco-Prussian War in particular was won, like the American Civil War, by superior logistical capability based upon a firm popular commitment.'

3 'trying to offset': Steven Canby, 'The Alliance and Europe: Part IV, Military Doctrine and Technology' (Adelphi Paper no. 109, IISS, winter 1974–5.)

5 'they could not': Kaufman, *McNamara Strategy*, p. 104.

footnote: Robert Reich, 'High Tech, a Subsidiary of Pentagon Inc.', *NYT*, 29 May 85.

6 'nearly enough': Fred Hiatt and Rick Atkinson, 'Is the Trillion-Dollar Buildup Exacting a Hidden Cost?', *WP*, 1 Dec. 85.

Chapter 1

11 taking threat seriously: see, for example, Robert Neild, *How to Make up your Mind About the Bomb*, p. 9ff.

12   'Relaxation of tensions': remarks by Secretary General Brezhnev at 25th
      Congress of the Communist Party of the Soviet Union, Foreign Broadcast
      Information Service, FBIS–SOV–76–38., 28 Feb. 76.

      'your first thought': CBS Television, 'The Defense of the United States', 14
      June 1981.

14   'When the Russians get': quoted in John Barry, 'A Week in Politics Special',
      Channel 4 Television, 30 March 84.

18   'has never attempted': United States Military Posture for FY 1976, statement
      by Chairman of the Joint Chiefs of Staff, Gen. George Brown, USAF, p.
      70.

      'In this': Dr Malcolm Currie, Programme of Research, Development, Test
      and Evaluation, FY 1976 (statement submitted to the US Senate Armed
      Services Committee), 7 March 75, pp. 1–2. Both Currie's and Brown's
      remarks are also quoted in *New Weapons Technologies* by Richard Burt
      (Adelphi Paper no. 126, IISS, summer 1976).

      'rests on': *NYT*, 21 Sept. 80.

      'Technology ... is': text of speech appears in *Current Policy*, no. 220,
      published by the State Department under the title 'Essentials of Security:
      Arms and More', 18 Sept. 80.

19   *Titanic* story: see, for example, William Kaufman, *The Defense Budget*
      (Washington, DC: Brookings Institution, 1983), p. 99.

      'Be reassured': Horne, *To Lose a Battle*, p. 104 (Penguin edition).

20   'Rapidly, the Maginot': ibid., p. 63.

Chapter 2

22   'silly transaction': Bill Keller, '3 Navy Officers Relieved of Duty in Ashtray
      Case', *NYT*, 31 May 85.

23   'Whenever in the old days': Wavell, *Generals and Generalship*, p. 3.

      'hardly reassuring'; George Wilson, 'Army Gun Said to Be Vulnerable to
      Cold', *WP*, 6 March 85.

      'Unless the army': ibid.

24   'Pretty soon': Gregg Easterbrook, 'Divad', *Atlantic Monthly*, Oct. 82, p. 31.

26   Divad test in early 82: ibid., p. 37.

27   'In a flir-to-flir duel': ibid., p. 31

28   'jammed so frequently': 'Sergeant York Musters Out', *Newsweek*, 9 Sept. 85.

      'Knocking out a tank': Bill Keller, 'Demise of the Sgt. York Gun: Model
      Weapon Turns to Dud', *NYT*, 28 Nov. 85.

      'Soviet pilots': ibid.

29 'The programme': 20/20, ABC Television, 13 Dec. 84.

'I would say': ibid.

'like testing': Gregg Easterbrook, 'Why the Divad Wouldn't Die', *Washington Monthly*, Nov. 84.

32 'To demonstrate' et seq.: 20/20, ABC Television, 13 Dec. 84.

33 'died of embarrassment': *NYT*, 28 Nov. 85.

34 'enemy outnumbers you by two to one' argument: see Lanchester, *Aircraft in Warfare*.

35 'What we're dealing': John J. Fialka, 'Embattled Weapon', *WSJ*, 17 Feb. 82.

36 'If it gets': ibid.

'powder keg': Gary Hart, 'Our Soldiers' Lives Depend on Reform of Way We Buy Arms', *Newsday*, Feb. 85.

'The Bradley is': 'The Winds of Reform', *Time*, 7 March 83.

37 'Unfortunately, while': Luttwak, *The Pentagon and the Art of War*, p. 226.

38 defenders of the M1: see ibid., p. 223.

39 'The overwhelming evidence': George W. S. Kuhn, 'Ending Defense Stagnation' in Holwill (ed.), *Agenda '83*, p. 99.

'The competition': Richard Barnard, 'US Comes Through Gut-Wrenching Tank Games in Third Place', *Defense Week*, 29 June 81, vol. 2, no. 31.

40 Rasor study: Dina Rasor, 'Fighting with Failures', *Reason*, April 82.

problem with Mark II system: study by Franklin C. Spinney, quoted in Kuhn, op. cit., p. 89.

41 'In the early 1970s': quoted in ibid., p. 92.

'The Army's': ibid.

43 'there isn't any': George Dvorchak, 'Getting It on in the All-Aspect Arena', *Tactical Analysis Bulletin*, 25 July 79.

44 Murray on Amraam: 'AMRAAM: "An Expensive Bird" of Limited Use?', *National Journal*, 24 July 82.

45 'When you're up': CBS, 'The Defense of the United States', 17 June 81.

'In massed fighting': Dvorchak, op. cit.

46 footnote: Rick Atkinson and Fred Hiatt, 'To Prepare for War, We Need a Revolution', *WP*, 15 Dec. 85.

47 'in the year': Rone Tempest et al., 'Servants and Masters', *LA Times*, 10 July 83.

F16: best account of its development in Fallows, *National Defense*, chapter 4.

'the greatest' quoted in Kaldor, *Baroque Arsenal*, p. 189.

48   price of German Tornado: Roger Boyes, 'The Tornado rattles Bonn's defence planners', *FT*, 21 Aug. 80.

'critical ... targets': letter from Air Chief Marshal Sir Denis Smallwood, *DT*, 22 April 77.

49   effectiveness of helicopters: see Gregg Easterbrook, 'All Aboard Air Oblivion', *The Atlantic*, Sept. 81.

50   'The 60 per cent': Morton Mintz, 'Fiasco in Weaponsland', *WP*, 25 July 82.

'If the question': ibid.

'don't like the gun': ibid.

51   attacked telephone poles: CBS, 'The Defense of the United States,' 17 June 81.

'Clearly it didn't': Morton Mintz, 'Air Force's Maverick Missile: Troubled but Inevitable', *WP*, 23 Feb. 82.

'It's like': ibid.

52   'What you get': Mintz, 'Maverick: Pressing for Production', *WP*, 25 Feb. 82.

53   'I'd have': Frank Greve, 'Dream Weapon a Nightmare', *Philadelphia Inquirer*, 2 May 82.

54   tendency ... to explode: Walter Pincus, 'Army Kills Controversial Anti-Tank Arm', *WP*, 30 Sept. 83.

'swamp of ... waste': William Greider, 'The Education of David Stockman', *The Atlantic*, Dec. 81.

'You want something': 'Where to Cut Defense', *Newsweek*, 20 Dec. 82.

'its accuracy': George C. Wilson, 'Pentagon Makes 1.6 Billion [dollar] Bet on Shell', *WP*, 11 April 83.

55   'Thus ... it will': ibid.

Investigation by ABC: 'Another Gold-Plated Fiasco', 20/20, ABC Television, 13 Feb. 86.

56   'including two steerable': Bill Sweetman, 'Unmanned Air Vehicles Make a Comeback', *International Defense Review*, vol. 18, no. 11, 85.

'The airframe': ibid.

57   Hellfire: Walter Pincus, 'Cheaper Addition to Laser System Growing in Expense', *WP*, 7 Sept. 83.

58   'Indeed ... those': Anthony Farrar-Hockley, 'The Scope and Direction of

New Conventional Weapons Technology (2)' (Adelphi Paper no. 144, IISS, spring 1978).

Chapter 3

59   'We can spend': Senator Roger Jepsen, quoted in 'Arming for the '80s', *Time*, 27 July 81.

army 'hollow' etc: see Richard Halloran, 'Pentagon Taking Renewed Pride in its Personnel', *NYT*, 16 May 85.

60   'America's ... computer edge': Thomas H. Etzold, *Defense or Delusion? America's Military in the 1980s*, p. 102.

61   'dune buggy': Dennis Farney, 'High-Tech Soldiers: Army Division Tests Unconventional Gear To Increase Mobility', *WSJ*, 26 June 85.

'... its tactics': ibid.

62   'one of the few': CBS Television, 'The Defense of the United States', 16 June 81.

'You are left': ibid.

63   exclusion of JDA: 'Defense Organization: The Need for Change', Staff Report to the Committee on Armed Services, US Senate (Washington: US Government Printing Office, 1985), p. 368.

'The JDA's': Michael Duffy, 'Grenada: Rampant Confusion', *Military Logistics Forum*, July–Aug. 85 p. 23; see also committee report cited above, p. 368.

64   'continues to purchase': committee report, p. 365.

'For example, the Army': ibid.

'We blew them': Luttwak, *The Pentagon and the Art of War*, p. 19.

Chapter 4

67   'I've been trying': Michael Kramer, '$1.5 Trillion For Defense? How to Understand Reagan's Big Buildup', *New York*, 22 June 81.

'without doubt': Jon Connell, 'Man Behind the US Navy Build up', *ST*, 11 Sept. 83.

'would lead': ibid.

68   'I take an oath': ibid.

69   '... the mighty whale': Luttwak, *The Pentagon and the Art of War*, p. 221.

'very much in harmony': Bill Keller, 'The Navy's Brash Leader', *NYT Magazine*, 15 Dec. 85.

'I have yet': *ST*, 11 Sept. 83.

70   'Even if Lehman': interview with the author, but also see Komer, *Maritime Strategy or Coalition Defense?*

      'the likelihood fallacy': Komer, *Maritime Strategy*, p. 69.

      'What is really': ibid., p. 59.

71   carriers never 'sunk': Etzold, *Defense or Delusion?*, p. 101.

      'The modern Aegis': editorial, *NYT*, 2 April 84.

      'the centrepiece': see, for example, Fred Kaplan, 'Navy Defense System Criticized', *Boston Globe*, 7 Feb. 84.

72   'were not as low-flying': Charles H. Mohr, 'Republican Charges Ship Missile System Fails', *NYT*, 7 Feb. 84.

      'operational requirements': *NYT*, 2 April 84.

      'a serious mismatch': ibid.

      'The consequent imbalance': Kuhn, 'Ending Defense Stagnation', in Holwill (ed.), *Agenda '83*, p. 73.

73   crew had 'dwindled': *NYT Magazine*, 15 Dec. 85.

      'Give the navy': Komer, *Maritime Strategy*, p. 73.

74   'In rejecting': Kuhn, in Holwill (ed.), *Agenda '83*, pp. 96–7.

75   'because conventional': ibid., p. 97.

Chapter 5

76   'nothing so inefficient': Rone Tempest, et al., 'Servants or Masters?', *LA Times*, 10 July 83.

      General Dynamics saga: best account in extensive series of articles in *St. Louis Post-Dispatch* (e.g. 17 March, 31 March, and 22 May 85).

77   Extent of abuses: 'Fraud Probes Target 45 Defense Contractors, Panel Told': *Washington Times*, 25 April 85.

78   'a log floating': 'Defense Inc.', Rick Atkinson and Fred Hiatt, *WP*, 20 May 85.

      'if all': David Martin, news report, CBS Television Network, 5 Feb. 85.

79   whistle: detailed report in *WP*, 20 May 85.

      Council on Economic Priorities study: see Adams, *Iron Triangle*.

      cost of HARM: Hiatt and Atkinson, 'Defense Inc.', 19 May 85.

      'the surgical removal': ibid.

80   'They've got': ibid.

81   'If we told': Fox, *Arming America*, p. 138.

      'Everyone's missed': 'Defense Inc.', *WP*, 19 May 85.

82   'The lesson': editorial, 'Dogfight of the Decade', *NYT*, 23 April 85.

'to get something': 'Defense Inc.', *WP*, 19 May 85.

Tax study: see Robert S. McIntyre, 'Disarm the Deficit: End Corporate Tax Dodges', *WP*, 24 March 85.

83   'It's like': 'Defense Inc.', *WP*, 31 May 85.

'Anything that succeeds': 'Defense Inc.', *WP*, 20 May 85.

navy study: 'Defense Inc.', *WP*, 1 April 85.

84   poll: Peter Grier, 'Support Fades for Bigger Arms Budgets', *Christian Science Monitor*, 15 May 85.

85   PAC money doubles: 'Servants or Masters?', *LA Times*, 10 July 81.

'a public works': ibid.

86   'Joe, they've built': Steven V. Roberts, 'Political Aims of Lawmakers Bring Military Budget Rises', *NYT*, 17 May 85.

87   Record argument: see, for example, Jeffrey Record, 'Ground the F18 Programme', *NYT*, 2 Nov. 81.

contractors double 'government ... offices': *LA Times*, 10 July 81.

'We know': CBS, 'Defense of the United States', 17 June 81.

'I speak': Fox, *Arming America*, pp. 128–9.

88   'target list': Excerpts from Congressional Contact Tally Computer Log obtained by The Project on Military Procurement, Washington. Released, 14 June 82.

89   Ptarmigan: see Jon Connell and Sarah Hogg, 'Defence: Last of the Overspenders?', *ST*, 31 Jan. 82.

90   Duplication Survey: see Robert Kleiman, 'Europe Acts to Interlock Arms', *NYT*, 25 March 86. Also see, for further examples, Klepsch Report, *Two-Way Street*, p. 88.

'Without Nimrod': James Adams and John Witherow, 'The Scandal of Nimrod as Cost Soars Past £1.5 billion', *ST*, 28 July 85.

'to refuel': *NYT*, 25 March 86.

91   shortages: see James Adams, 'Can Carrington Revive Nato?', *ST*, 24 June 84.

'If the cee cubed eye': ibid.

92   request to 'go nuclear': ibid.

93   team of US engineers: Capt. J. W. Kehoe and K. S. Brower, 'U.S. and Soviet Weapon System Design Practises', limited-circulation paper, Oct. 81.

'rough casting': ibid., p. 34.

boxer losing shorts: Suvorov, *The Liberators*, pp. 62–75.

'The total number': Kehoe and Brower, p. 34.

94   'Comrades, make it simple': quoted in ibid., p. 1.

'There's a sort': CBS, 'The Defense of the United States', 17 June 81.

95   'The worry': ibid.

'The Soviet': interview with author. For full exposition see Cockburn, *The Threat*.

'We believe': Isby, *Weapons and Tactics of the Soviet Army*, p. 104.

96   'By ignoring': report by Franklin C. Spinney, 'Defense Facts of Life', 5 Dec. 80, p. 128. Originally a limited-circulation paper, later published as a book: see Bibliography

'Technology proved indecisive': Jeffrey Record, *WP*, 29 Jan. 84.

97   Skipper: 'Defense Inc.', *WP*, 21 May 85.

'They used': ibid.

Chapter 6

98   Soviet plan of attack: John Barry, 'A Week in Politics Special', Channel 4 Television, 30 March 84.

99   'brought us': Phil Stanford, 'The Automated Battlefield', *NYT Magazine*, 23 Feb. 75.

100 Interview with Tegnelia appeared in *Military Technology*, 1981. Quoted in Michael R. Gordon, 'Highly Touted Assault Breaker Weapon Caught Up in Internal Pentagon Debate', *National Journal*, 22 Oct. 83, pp. 2152ff.

101 account of Assault Breaker tests: Michael R. Gordon, ' "E.T." Weapons to Beef up Nato Forces Raise Technical and Political Doubts', *National Journal*, 19 Feb. 83, p. 364.

102 'If you attach': ibid., p. 367.

paper on Assault Breaker: Steven L. Canby, 'The Conventional Defense of Europe: The Operational Limits of Emerging Technology', Working Paper No. 55 delivered to the Wilson Center, 29 May 84.

103 'Operational Manoeuvre Group': C. N. Donnelly, 'The Soviet Operational Manoeuvre Group, a new challenge for Nato', *International Defense Review*, vol. 15, no. 9, 1982.

104 'are not going': Barry 'A Week in Politics Special', Channel 4 Television 30 March 84.

105 'one shot one kill': Richard Burt, 'New Weapons Technologies: Debate and Directions' (Adelphi Paper no. 126, IISS, summer 1976), p. 15.

Part Two

107 'Everything about': Brodie, *The Absolute Weapon*, p. 46.

Chapter 7

109 'moment of ... truth': Kaplan, *Wizards of Armageddon*, p. 298.

Khrushchev speech: ibid., p. 292.

110 'with high confidence': ibid., p. 299.

'the low tens': ibid., p. 301.

'If ever': ibid.

111 'In long conversations': Robert S. McNamara, 'The Military Role of Nuclear Weapons: Perceptions and Misperceptions', *Foreign Affairs*, autumn 83.

113 '(The) resourcefulness': John Foster Dulles, 'Challenge and Response in United States Policy', *Foreign Affairs*, Oct. 57.

'If seventy divisions': Osgood, *Nato*, p. 109.

114 Carte Blanche: ibid., p. 126.

'In Europe': ibid., p. 125.

'more rather than less': ibid., p. 107.

118 'the balancing act': Legge, *Theater Nuclear Weapons*, Rand Report R29644FF, April 83, p. 19.

120 'it would be': Field Marshal Lord Carver, 'Nuclear Weapons in Europe', Council for Arms Control Second Annual Lecture, 9 Nov. 83.

warfighting: see, for example, Colin S. Gray and Keith Payne, 'Victory is Possible', *Foreign Policy* 39, summer 80.

122 The area between ...: in the ensuing discussion I have drawn on an unpublished draft paper by Paul Bracken.

'Were Nato': ibid.

123 problem of stopping war: see Desmond Ball, 'Can Nuclear War Be Controlled?' (Adelphi Paper no. 169, IISS, autumn 1981). Also Bracken, *Command and Control of Nuclear Forces*.

125 'islands of force': Bracken, p. 232.

'If there is': ibid., p. 231.

Chapter 8

127 'two scorpions': Robert Oppenheimer, 'Atomic Weapons and American Policy', *Foreign Affairs*, July 53.

'American forces': Richard Burt, 'US Stresses Limited Nuclear War in Sharp Shift on Military Strategy', *International Herald Tribune*, 7 Aug. 80.

128 'prevail and be able': Richard Halloran, 'Pentagon Draws Up First Strategy for Fighting a Long Nuclear War', *NYT*, 30 May 82.

'Combat operations': Douglass and Hoeber, *Soviet Strategy for Nuclear War*, pp. 22–3.

'There is': ibid., p. 7.

'It is': quoted in 'Soviet Military Power: Questions and Answers', *The Defense Monitor*, vol. 1, no. 1, 82.

129 accept 'a ... balance': quoted in Theodore Draper, 'How Not to Think about Nuclear War', *New York Review of Books*, 15 July 82.

'Some of': Wieseltier, *Nuclear War, Nuclear Peace*, p. 36.

130 'gave us': George C. Wilson, 'The Missile Gap the MX Can't Close', *WP*, 14 Dec. 80

131 'It's our ... feeling': Fred Kaplan, 'Would US Missiles Hit or Miss?', *Nuclear Times*, April 83.

132 'We had': editorial, 'Ornery Missiles', *NYT*, 8 Dec. 84.

'purple plague': Kaplan, *Nuclear Times*, April 83.

133 'Guaranteeing to launch': *NYT*, 8 Dec. 84.

135 'It has never': R. Jeffrey Smith, 'An Upheaval in US Strategic Thought', *Science*, 2 April 82.

'it does not': ibid.

'A far more': ibid.

136 'The Soviets': ibid.

139 'the trees chase': 'The MX System: Boon or Boondoggle?', *Newsweek*, 26 May 80.

142 'If only': quoted in, for example, Elizabeth Drew, 'A Political Journal', *New Yorker*, 9 May 83.

143 '... to the degree': *Science*, 2 April 82.

'to a certain extent': ibid.

144 'What in the name': quoted in ibid.

'There is': McGeorge Bundy, 'To Cap the Volcano', *Foreign Affairs*, Oct. 69.

145 pressure of flexible response: see, for example, Gregory Treverton, 'Nuclear Weapons in Europe' (Adelphi Paper no. 168, IISS, summer 1981).

Chapter 9

147 'better than evens': John Barry, 'The Nuclear Double Talk Tearing Nato Apart', first of three articles, *Times*, 17 Aug. 81.

149 the 'spectre': Barnet, *The Alliance*, p. 373.

152 'Perhaps the most': 'A Headache for Arms Control', *FT*, 15 Feb. 77.

155 Schmidt's IISS speech: to IISS, 28 Oct. 77.

Chapter 10

160 'the symbol': Barnet, *The Alliance*, p. 376.

161 'his administration': Brzezinski, *Power and Principle*, p. 304.

168 'place us': Thompson and Smith (ed.), *Protest and Survive*, p. 43.

'the resistance': US Arms Control and Disarmament Agency booklet, *Soviet Propaganda Campaign against Nato*, Oct. 83, p. 16.

'Washington's design': ibid.

170 GAO report on cruise: see Fred Kaplan, 'Much Ado about Wonder Weapons', *Boston Globe*, 22 Nov. 81.

footnote: ABC News investigation, Peter Lance, 1 and 2 Aug. 84.

171 'a signal': Professor Michael Howard, letter to *Times*, 3 Nov. 81.

172 'The belief': ibid.

The following additional sources have been drawn upon in chapters 9 and 10:

John Barry, series in *The Times*, 31 May–2 June 1983; 'Revealed: the Truth about Labour and Cruise', *ST*, 6 Feb. 83.

'The Elephant and the Monorail', Channel 4 Television Week in Politics Special, 11 Dec. 83.

Lynn E. Davis, 'US INF Policy', paper prepared for meeting of Danish Commission for Security and Disarmament Affairs on 'Nuclear Modernization in Europe' in Ebeltoft, Denmark, 27–28 April 83.

David C. Elliot, 'Decision at Brussels: The Politics of Nuclear Forces', Discussion Paper no. 97 for California Seminar on International Security and Foreign Policy, Aug. 81.

James A. Thomson, 'The LRTNF Decision: Evolution of U.S. Theatre Nuclear Policy, 1975–9', *International Affairs*, April 84.

Second Interim Report on Nuclear Weapons in Europe prepared by the North Atlantic Assembly's Special Committee on Nuclear Weapons in Europe for the Committee on Foreign Relations, United States Senate, Jan. 83.

Part Three

Chapter 11

175 President Reagan's speech (excerpted): *Survival*, vol. 25, no. 3, May–June 1983.

177 submarine-based missiles not nuclear: *Newsweek* (Election Extra), Nov.– Dec. 1984.

'with firelit intensity': James R. Mills, 'A 1971 Conversation with Ronald Reagan', *San Diego Magazine*, Aug. 85.

178 'technological end run': Graham, *High Frontier*, p. 3.

'The kind of superiority': Frank Greve, 'Out of the Blue: How "Star Wars" Was Proposed', *Philadelphia Inquirer*, 17 Nov. 85.

179 'primary motivations' speech: Dr G. A. Keyworth II, to the Fifty Club of Cleveland, 6 May 85.

180 McFarlane's role: see, for example, Lawrence I. Barrett, 'How Reagan Became a Believer', *Time*, 11 March 1985.

181 'He and Reagan got on': *Philadelphia Inquirer*, 17 Nov. 85.

'McFarlane interjected': *Time*, 11 March 85.

president 'dazzled': report by Marvin Kalb, 'The Real "Star Wars" – Defense in Space', NBC Television, 8 Sept. 84.

182 'Edward ... like it': ibid.

'Don't worry, gentlemen': Elizabeth Drew, 'A Political Journal', *New Yorker*, 9 May 83, p. 49.

183 Pentagon demonstration: see, for example, Jon Connell and Peter Wilsher, 'Collision Course', *ST*, 17 June 84.

186 'firefly in a darkened room': Union of Concerned Scientists (UCS), *Fallacy of Star Wars*, p. 56.

'they have to go': Edgar Ulsamer, 'The Battle for SDI', *Air Force Magazine*, Feb. 85, p. 49.

DeLauer testimony: US Congress, House Subcommittees on Research and Development and Investigations, Hearing on H.R. 3073, People Protection Act, 98th Congress, 1st session, 10 Nov. 83.

187 missiles without 'buses': see, for example, UCS, op. cit.

188 number of satellites required: see Zbigniew Brzezinski, Robert Jastrow, Max M. Kampelman, 'Defense in Space is Not "Star Wars"', *NYT Magazine*, 27 Jan. 85. See also Professor R. V. Jones, 'New Light on Star Wars', Policy Study no. 71 (London: Centre for Policy Studies, 1985)

189 destruction of Sidewinders: see Jones, op. cit. p. 11.

190 'perhaps one tenth of a second': *Air Force Magazine*, Feb. 85, p. 52.

Jones on laser accuracy: op. cit., p. 12

footnote: for dispute between UCS, Canavan, etc., see, for example, *Newsweek*, 17 June 85, p. 37, and Jones, op. cit., p. 18.

191 'They must be deployed': Edward Teller, letter published in *Commentary*, vol. 79, no. 3, March 1985.

192 Dauphin programme: Malcolm W. Browne, 'Stopping Missiles with Energy Beams', *Discover*, June 1983, p. 30–1.

'You ... have to get': ibid., p. 31.

194 'the long pole': 'Star Warriors', *Newsweek*, 17 June 85.

196 'future historians': Jonathan Jacky, 'The "Star Wars" Defense Won't Compute', *The Atlantic*, June 1980, p. 20.

'Instead of fielding': ibid.

197 quotes from panel of scientists and Keyworth: ibid., pp. 21–2.

'... many of the': ibid., p. 22.

'Keyworth's ... suggestions': ibid.

198 Bracken study: Bracken, *Command and Control of Nuclear Forces*.

199 'No one who knows': *Newsweek*, 17 June 85.

200 'If you start': interview with Erik Amfitheatrof in 'Upsetting a Delicate Balance', *Time*, 11 March 85.

estimate of 'extra' missiles: Stephen M. Meyer of MIT, quoted in Charles Mohr, 'What Moscow Might Do in Replying to Star Wars', *NYT*, 6 March 85.

'Any defensive system': testimony to US Congress cited for p. 186.

'a submachine gun': *Newsweek*, 17 June 85.

201 'It is suggested': James Schlesinger, speech to National Security Issues Symposium, 25 Oct. 84, published in *International Security*, summer 85.

202 'send a series': Browne, op. cit., p. 32. For possible countermeasures also see, for example: Richard L. Garwin and Kurt Gottfried, 'Even Half Way Is Wrong', *NYT*, 12 Feb. 85.

203 'Some of the biggest': William J. Broad, '"Star Wars" Research Forges Ahead', *NYT*, 5 Feb. 85.

204 'the difference': *Newsweek*, 17 June 1985.

'Many ... scientists': 'The Real Star Wars', NBC, 8 Sept. 84.

205 'The laws': UCS, op. cit., p. 50.

'American ... enthusiasm': Jones, op. cit., p. 24.

'We need': ibid., p. 25.

208   'Are the Soviets': Schlesinger, speech, 25 Oct. 84, cited at p. 201.

209   'light reflecting aerosols': Bill Keller, 'Air Force Seeking More Wily Missile', *NYT*, 11 Feb. 85. Also see Keller, 'Defense Department Seeks More Money for Secret Weapons, Analyst Says', *NYT*, 12 Feb. 85.

      'You can always beat': ibid.

Chapter 12

212   'Is it any wonder': *Newsweek*, 17 June 85.

213   'computing in support': Charles Mohr, 'Scientist Quits Antimissile Panel, Saying Task Is Impossible', *NYT*, 12 July 85.

213   'state of mind': John Newhouse, 'The Diplomatic Round', *New Yorker*, 22 July 85.

214   'the keystone': speech by the Rt. Hon. Sir Geoffrey Howe, reported in *The Times*, 16 March 85.

215   'the justification': Schlesinger, speech cited at p. 201.

216   'However large': *New Yorker*, 22 July 85.

217   'probably the only person': ibid.

218   'of strategic defense': quoted in Leslie H. Gelb, ' "Star Wars" Advances: The Plan vs. the Reality', *NYT*, 15 Dec. 85.

      footnote: testimony by Frank Miller, Hearings before the Subcommittee on International Security and Scientific Affairs, of the Committee on Foreign Affairs, House of Representatives. 10 Nov. 83, 10 April, 2 May and 26 July 84.

219   'early demonstrations': William J. Broad, 'Science Showmanship: A Deep "Star Wars" Rift', *NYT*, 16 Dec. 85.

      Leak on x-ray laser: R. Jeffrey Smith, 'Experts Cast Doubt on X-ray Laser', *Science*, 8 Nov. 85.

220   'In terms of': Howe, speech cited at p. 214.

      Times leader: 'Howe's UDI from SDI', *Times* 18 March 85.

221   boosting deterrence: see, for example, Fred S. Hoffman, 'The SDI in US Nuclear Strategy', Senate testimony reprinted in *International Security*, summer 1985 (vol. 10, no. 1).

224   run it to the end: see David Ignatius, 'In Star Wars Debate, Tactical Issues Nearly Get Lost in the Shuffle', *WSJ*, 15 Oct. 85.

225   'protecting missile silos': quoted in ibid.

      'held out to American citizens': Schlesinger, speech cited at p. 201.

      'The answer is': *New Yorker*, 22 July 85.

footnote: Lloyd Grove, 'The "Star Wars" Soft Sell', *WP*, 4 Nov. 85.

226   'The time is': 'The Case for Star Wars', *Economist*, 3 Aug. 85.

229   British report: Michael R. Gordon, 'CIA Is Sceptical that New Soviet Radar is Part of an ABM Defense System', *National Journal*, 3 Sept. 85.

230   'When you look at': Gerald M. Boyd, 'Reagan Sees Soviet "Deception" on Arms', *NYT*, 13 Oct. 85.

       Weinberger speech: Caspar Weinberger, to the Philadelphia World Affairs Council, 3 Oct. 85.

231   Pentagon testimony: The FY 1986 DOD Programme for Research, Development and Acquisition, 7 March 85.

       'In the key technologies': R. Jeffrey Smith, 'Star Wars Chief Takes Aim at Critics', *Science*, 10 Aug. 84.

232   'I am ... concerned': Part 7 of fiscal 1985 DOD authorization hearings by the Senate Armed Services Committee, 15 March 84.

235   'six impossible things': Hedrick Smith, 'U.S. Strategy of Toughness. A Counter to the Russians', *NYT*, 23 Aug. 85.

236   'I don't think': 'Star Wars: Will Space Battle Stations Work?' *ST*, 24 Feb. 85.

       'Their internal problems': John Newhouse, 'The Diplomatic Round', *New Yorker*, 31 Dec. 84.

       'accept an entirely new': Robert Kaiser, 'A Disarming Lack of Candor', *WP*, 10 March 85.

239   'It takes very little': ibid.

240   'The Safeguard system': Schlesinger, speech cited at p. 201.

241   'the fiscal 1971 budget': ibid.

       'on all the other': Howe, speech cited at p. 214.

Chapter 13

242   'A bear': story appears in John Barry, 'Geneva Behind Closed Doors', *Times*, 31 May 83. Also in John Wallach, 'Walk in the Woods', *The Washingtonian*, Jan. 84.

243   'Europe has': quoted in 'Nato's Death Is Now Thinkable'. *International Herald Tribune*, 14–15 Nov. 81.

244   'Eventual European unity': Theodore Draper, 'The Dilemma of the West: A Transatlantic Parting of the Ways?', *Encounter*, March 82.

       'Economically Europe': Ronald E. Nairn, 'Should the US Pull Out of Nato?', *WSJ*, 15 Dec. 81.

245   'grown wider': Sir Oliver Wright, British Ambassador to the US, 'The Atlantic Grows Wider', speech to the Fletcher School of Law and Diplomacy, Tufts University, Hereford, Mass. 21 April 83.

'America does not connote': Stephen F. Szabo, 'The Successor Generation in Europe', *Public Opinion*, vol. 6, no. 1, Feb.–March 83.

'The campaign': Draper, *Encounter*, March 82.

246   'The United States': quoted in Alun Chalfont, 'The Great Unilateralist Illusion', *Encounter*, April 1983.

'friendship and partnership': Draper, *Encounter*.

'The change': Wright, speech cited p. 245.

247   London Weekend film: 'The NATO Alliance: Still Europe's Best Hope?', *Weekend World*, London Weekend Television, 8 April 84.

dismay of Stephens and Pressler: see, for example, 'Scowls across the Atlantic', *Economist*, 7 Jan. 84.

248   European share: see, for example, Timothy Garton Ash, 'Goddam Nato and Goddam Tories', *Spectator*, 10 Aug. 85.

'Europe will cost': Earl C. Ravenal, 'Europe Without America: The Erosion of Nato', *Foreign Affairs*, summer 85.

250   'may prove': *Encounter*, March 82.

251   'Prometheus Unbound': *Spectator*, 10 Aug. 85.

'We must divide': quoted in Phillip A. Petersen and John G. Hines, 'Military Power in Soviet Strategy Against Nato', *RUSI Journal*, Dec. 83.

'The Soviet Union's': ibid.

'Era of ... Peace': ibid.

'Soviet Dream Item': Professor Michael Howard, 'Is Arms Control Really Necessary?' Council for Arms Control Fourth Annual Lecture, 8 Oct. 85.

'We need to be': 'The Old Lion Still Roars', *Time*, 4 April 83.

'Should the Americans': Weekend World, 'The Arms Talks: What Chance of Success?', London Weekend Television, 10 March 85.

Chapter 14

253   planning like astronomy: quoted in Towle (ed.), *Estimating Foreign Military Power*, p. 30.

254   'video-game vision': David Evans, 'A Runaway Pentagon', *NYT*, 3 Oct. 84.

255   'salve their conscience': Rick Atkinson and Fred Hiatt, 'To Prepare for War, We Need a Revolution', *WP*, 15 Dec. 85.

24 Congressional committees: ibid.

256   'What is': Clausewitz, *On War*, p. 357.

'take a pick': quoted in Pascall, *Trillion Dollar Budget*, p. 78.

257 'The most important': John C. F. Tillson IV, 'The Forward Defense of Europe', *Military Review*, May 81.

'prechambering': estimate in ibid.

260 change in Northern Army Group: see, for example, David Fairhall, 'Nato Clears the Way for a Non-Nuclear Defence', *Manchester Guardian Weekly*, 23 June 85.

261 'over-literal interpretation': Lieutenant General Hans-Henning von Sandrart, 'Forward Defence – Mobility and the Use of Barriers', *Nato's Sixteen Nations*, Jan. 85.

France needs Nato: Draper, 'The Dilemma of the West', *Encounter*, March 82.

'the fiction': quoted in ibid.

footnote: 'There are moments': Horne, *To Lose a Battle*, p. 71.

262 'Speaking for myself': David Evans, *NYT*, 3 Oct. 84.

263 'like having': Michael R. Gordon, 'Billion-Dollar "Failures" May Slip Through Pentagon Weapons Testing Net', *National Journal*, 24 July 82.

'intense negotiations': Michael Gordon, 'Army Disputed on Tests of Weapon', *NYT*, 26 Jan. 86.

'simply intolerable': 'The Folly of Untested Weapons,' Editorial, *NYT*, 7 Feb. 86.

264 'Extravagance and fraud': Gary Putka, 'Arms-Trade Balance With Nato Nations Turns Against the US', *WSJ*, 8 Nov. 85.

266 'great white lie': Richard K. Betts, 'Compound Deterrence versus No First Use: What's Wrong Is What's Right', *Orbis*, winter 85, vol. 28, no. 4.

271 'Technological change': Dr Barry M. Blechman, 'New Technology, Stability and the Arms Control Deadlock', in Mellenthin et al. (ed.), *Nato Under Attack*.

273 'The technological realities': Kennan, *Russia, the Atom and the West*.

274 'have concluded': Robert English, 'Why Star Wars is Offensive', *The New Republic*, 24 Feb. 86.

'The "surgical" precision': ibid.

276 'We must look deeper': Professor Michael Howard, 'Peace: the Vital Factors', *Times*, 13 Jan. 84.

277 'push of technology': Newhouse, *New Yorker*, 31 Dec. 84.

Select bibliography

Adams, Gordon *The Iron Triangle: The Politics of Defense Contracting* (New York: Council on Economic Priorities, 1981)

Barnet, Richard J. *Real Security: Restoring American Power in a Dangerous Decade* (New York: Simon & Schuster, 1981)
  The Alliance: America-Europe-Japan, Makers of the Postwar World (New York: Simon & Schuster, 1983)

Betts, Richard K. *Cruise Missiles: Technology, Strategy, Politics* (Washington DC: Brookings Institution, 1981)
  Surprise Attack (Washington DC: Brookings Institution, 1982)

Bracken, Paul *The Command and Control of Nuclear Forces* (New Haven and London: Yale University Press, 1983)

Brodie, Bernard *The Absolute Weapon* (New York: Harcourt, Brace & Company, 1946)

Brzezinski, Zbigniew K. *Power and Principle: Memoirs of the National Security Adviser, 1977–1981* (New York: Farrar, Straus and Giroux, 1983)

Calder, Nigel *Nuclear Nightmares, an Investigation into Possible Wars* (London: British Broadcasting Corporation, 1979)

Clausewitz, Carl von *On War*, edited and translated by Michael Howard and Peter Paret (Princeton, New Jersey: Princeton University Press, 1976)

Cockburn, Andrew *The Threat: Inside the Soviet Military Machine* (New York: Random House, 1983)

Coker, Christopher *US Military Power in the 1980s* (London and Basingstoke: Macmillan, 1983)

Deitchman, Seymour J. *New Technology and Military Power: General Purpose Military Forces for the 1980s and Beyond* (Boulder, Colorado: Westview Press, 1979)

Department of Defence *Soviet Military Power 1985* (Washington DC: US Government Printing Office, 1985)

Douglass Jr, Joseph D. and Hoeber, Amoretta M. *Soviet Strategy for Nuclear War* (Stanford: Stanford University Press, 1979)

Duffy, Christopher *Siege Warfare: The Fortress in the Early Modern World, 1494–1660* (London and Henley: Routledge & Kegan Paul, 1979)

ESECS (Report of the European Security Study) *Strengthening Conventional Deterrence in Europe* (London and Basingstoke: Macmillan, 1983)

Etzold, Thomas H. *Defense or Delusion? America's Military in the 1980s* (New York: Harper & Row, 1982)

Fallows, James *National Defense* (New York: Random House, 1981)

Fox, J. Ronald *Arming America* (Cambridge, Mass.: Harvard University Press, 1974)

Freedman, Lawrence *The Evolution of Nuclear Strategy* (London and Basingstoke: Macmillan, 1981)

(ed.) *The Troubled Alliance: Atlantic Relations in the 1980s* (London: Heinemann, 1983)

Gansler, Jacques S. *The Defense Industry* (Cambridge, Mass.: MIT Press, 1980)

Graham, Daniel O. *High Frontier: A New National Strategy* (Washington DC: Heritage Foundation, 1982)

Guizot, M. *The History of France from the Earliest Times to the Year 1789* (London: Sampson Low, Marston, Low & Searle, 1873)

Holst, Johan J. and Nerlich, Uwe (ed.) *Beyond Nuclear Deterrence: New Aims, New Arms* (New York: Crane, Russak & Company Inc., 1977)

Holwill, Richard N. (ed.) *A Mandate for Leadership Report: Agenda '83* (Washington DC: Heritage Foundation, 1983)

Horne, Alistair *To Lose a Battle: France 1940* (London and Basingstoke: Macmillan, 1969; Harmondsworth: Penguin, 1979)

Isby, David C. *Weapons and Tactics of the Soviet Army* (London: Jane's Publishing, 1981)

Kaldor, Mary *The Baroque Arsenal* (New York: Hill and Wang, 1981)

Kaplan, Fred *The Wizards of Armageddon* (New York: Simon & Schuster, 1983)

Karas, Thomas *The New High Ground: Strategies and Weapons of Space-Age War* (New York: Simon & Schuster, 1983)

Kaufman, William *The McNamara Strategy* (New York: Harper & Row, 1964)

Kennan, George F. *Russia, the Atom and the West* (New York: Harper & Brothers, 1958)

The Klepsch Report *Two-Way Street: USA-Europe Arms Procurement* (London: Brassey's, 1979)

Komer, Robert W. *Maritime Strategy or Coalition Defense?* (Cambridge, Mass.: Abt Books, 1984)

Lanchester, F. W. *Aircraft in Warfare: The Dawn of the Fourth Army* (London: Constable, 1916)

Legge, J. Michael *Theater Nuclear Weapons and the NATO Strategy of Flexible Response* (Santa Monica: Rand Corporation, 1983)

Lunn, Simon *Burden-sharing in NATO* (London: Routledge & Kegan Paul, 1983)

Luttwak, Edward N. *The Pentagon and the Art of War* (New York: Simon & Schuster, 1984)

Mearsheimer, John J. *Conventional Deterrence* (Ithaca and London: Cornell University Press, 1983)

Mellenthin, F. W. and Stalli, R. H. with Subik, E. (ed.) *Nato Under Attack* (Duke University Press, 1984)

Neild, Robert *How to Make up Your Mind about the Bomb* (London: André Deutsch, 1981)

Osgood, Robert Endicott *NATO: The Entangling Alliance* (Chicago: University of Chicago Press, 1962)

Pascall, Glenn *The Trillion Dollar Budget: How to Stop the Bankrupting of America* (Seattle and London: University of Washington Press, 1985)

Pearton, Morris *The Knowledgeable State: Diplomacy, War and Technology since 1830* (London: Burnett Books, 1982)

Pringle, Peter and Arkin, William *SIOP, Nuclear War from the Inside* (London: Sphere Books, 1983)

Rasor, Dina (ed.) *More Bucks, Less Bang: How the Pentagon Buys Ineffective Weapons* (Washington DC: Fund for Constitutional Government, 1983)

Scheer, Robert *With Enough Shovels: Reagan, Bush & Nuclear War* (New York: Random House, 1982)

Schell, Jonathan *The Fate of the Earth* (New York: Alfred A. Knopf, 1982)

Schwartz, David N. *NATO's Nuclear Dilemmas* (Washington DC: Brookings Institution, 1983)

Smith, Dan *The Defence of the Realm in the 1980s* (London: Croom Helm, 1980)

Smith, Gerard *Doubletalk: The Story of SALT I* (New York: Doubleday, 1980)

Spinney, Franklin C. *Defense Facts of Life: the Plans/Reality Mismatch* (Boulder, Colorado: Westview Press, 1985)

Stein, Jonathan B. *From H-Bomb to Star Wars: The Politics of Strategic Decision Making* (Lexington, Massachusetts: Lexington Books, 1984)

Suvorov, Viktor *The Liberators* (London: Hamish Hamilton, 1981)

Talbott, Strobe *Endgame: The Inside Story of SALT II* (New York: Harper & Row, 1979)

Deadly Gambits (New York: Alfred A. Knopf, 1984)

Taylor Jr, William J. *The Future of Conflict* (Washington DC: Centre for Strategic and International Studies, 1983)

Thompson, E. P. and Smith, Dan (ed.) *Protest and Survive* (Harmondsworth, Middlesex: Penguin Books, 1980)

Towle, Philip (ed.) *Estimating Foreign Military Power* (London: Croom Helm Ltd., 1982)

Union of Concerned Scientists (UCS) *The Fallacy of Star Wars* (New York: Vintage Books, Random House, 1984)

Wavell, Gen. Sir Archibald *Generals and Generalship* (New York: Macmillan, 1943)

White, Andrew *Symbols of War: Pershing II and Cruise Missiles in Europe* (London: Merlin Press/European Nuclear Disarmament, 1983)

Wieseltier, Leon *Nuclear War, Nuclear Peace* (New York: Holt, Rinehart and Winston, 1983)

Index